AUSTRIAN ECONOMICS IN DEBATE

The Austrian school has a long history of challenging prevailing orthodoxies in economics and debating with the representatives of competing traditions. This book presents a collection of essays which analyse a number of these discourses in depth. In so doing, they cast new light on the nature of both Austrian and non-Austrian economics, on their differences and similarities, and on the important and continuing role of the Hayekian and other Austrian contributions to economics.

The essays presented here are written by an outstanding team of international specialists in the field. They cover a wide range of topics, including the relationships between the Austrian and Swedish theories of the business cycle, the ongoing debates between Austrians and (post-)Keynesians, Schumpeter's 'Walrasian' stand in the socialist calculation debate and the Austrian roots of neo-institutional economics. The studies stress the unique Austrian contributions to economic methodology and to the theory of entrepreneurship, while revealing unexpected methodological and philosophical similarities between, among others, Hayek and Marx.

This volume demonstrates how the Austrian challenge and the debates it inspires can continue to benefit contemporary developments in micro- and macroeconomic theory, and can offer valuable insights into other, ostensibly conflicting, schools of thought.

The editors: **Willem Keizer** is at the Department of Economics and Econometrics, Free University of Amsterdam. **Bert Tieben** is at the Department of Economics and Econometrics, Free University of Amsterdam and Tinbergen Institute. **Rudy van Zijp** is at the Directorate for Technology Policy, Ministry of Economic Affairs, The Hague, The Netherlands.

ROUTLEDGE STUDIES IN THE HISTORY OF ECONOMICS

AUSTRIAN ECONOMICS IN DEBATE

Edited by Willem Keizer, Bert Tieben and Rudy van Zijp

Routledge
Taylor & Francis Group

LONDON AND NEW YORK

First published 1997
by Routledge
2 Park Square, Milton Park, Abingdon, Oxfordshire OX14 4RN

Simultaneously published in the USA and Canada
by Routledge
711 Third Avenue, New York, NY 10017

First issued in paperback 2015

Routledge is an imprint of the Taylor and Francis Group, an informa business

Typeset in Garamond by Routledge

British Library Cataloguing in Publication Data
A catalogue record for this book is available from the British Library

Library of Congress Cataloguing in Publication Data
Austrian economics in debate / edited by Willem Keizer, Bert Tieben,
and Rudy van Zijp.
p. cm.
Includes bibliographical references and index.
1. Austrian school of economists. I. Keizer, Willem. II. Tieben, Bert,
1967– . III. Zijp, Rudy van, 1961– .
HB98.A972 1997
330.15'7–dc21
96–53668
CIP

ISBN 13: 978-0-415-75689-1 (pbk)
ISBN 13: 978-0-415-14054-6 (hbk)

CONTENTS

CONTENTS

CONTRIBUTORS

William N. Butos is Professor of Economics at Trinity College, Hartford, Connecticut.

Richard M. Ebeling is the Ludwig von Mises Professor of Economics at Hillsdale College, Michigan.

Steve Fleetwood is at the Department of Economics, De Montfort University in Leicester.

Nicolai J. Foss is at the Institute of Industrial Economics and Strategy, Copenhagen Business School.

J. Patrick Gunning is at the Institute of Public Finance, National Chung Hsing University, Taipei.

Willem Keizer is at the Department of Economics and Econometrics, Free University of Amsterdam.

Laurence S. Moss is Professor of Economics at Babson College, Babson Park, Massachusetts.

Bert Tieben is at the Department of Economics and Econometrics, Free University of Amsterdam and Tinbergen Institute.

Emiel F.M. Wubben is at the Department of Strategic Management and Business Environment, Erasmus University, Rotterdam.

Leland B. Yeager is at the Department of Economics in the College of Business, Auburn University, Alabama.

Carlo Zappia is at the Department of Economics, University of Siena, Italy.

Rudy van Zijp is at the Directorate for Technology Policy, Ministry of Economic Affairs, The Hague, The Netherlands.

1

INTRODUCTION

Austrian economics in debate

Bert Tieben and Willem Keizer

Over the past century the Austrian school has played a major role in the development of economic theory. As one of the three founding currents of the so-called 'marginalist revolution' of the 1870s, its major contribution was the introduction of the subjectivist approach into economics. With Streissler (1972) we may doubt whether the Austrian school was particularly 'marginalist' at all, despite the fact that it was Wieser who coined the term 'Grenznutzen', marginal utility. Austrian theory concentrated on the 'Nutzen', not on the 'Grenze'. Its real essence was the subjectivist approach to economics: from its subjective definition of an economic 'good' followed the object of the science, its value theory and all the inferences from that. Austrian economists believe that the introduction of subjectivism was a more radical part of the 'marginalist' revolution than the application of marginal calculation. 'Marginalism' is only a calculating technique borrowed from mathematics and applicable in various sciences, whereas subjectivism forms the core of a specific science of human action. As far as Austrian economists are concerned, the proper name of the revolution that occurred in the 1870s should be the '*subjectivist* revolution'.

The implications of subjectivism are far-reaching and were not fully comprehended at the time, or even today by most economists. If all value depends on 'scarcity' then a subjective factor, the subjective knowledge human beings have of the relationships between objects and their subjective wants, is co-decisive for that object being an economic good and hence for its value. From this subjective approach the doctrine of 'consumer sovereignty' follows: all economic activity is ultimately initiated and determined by the subjective valuations of consumers, including the potential 'consumers' of the services of their own property (all factor owners, including workers). Thus, all of economic life – including entrepreneurship, production and trade – depends on the subjective valuation of objects by human beings and the interpersonal differences in their valuations. Had economic theory after 1870 followed the subjectivist path, a very different theory from that dominant today would have developed.

1

However, the technical brilliance of Walras's demonstration of the functional interdependence and mutual determination of all economic variables in one comprehensive system so impressed the profession that most of the successors of the marginalist–subjectivist revolution followed his path of marginalist calculation in mathematical terms instead of verbal subjectivist terms. Mathematical marginalist calculation necessarily led to equilibrium economics, as the purpose of incremental changes in variables is to establish a point of equality or balance between the counteracting forces involved. Thus, marginalist economics naturally became the study of equilibrium states and the derivation of their marginality conditions. This is what the later 'neoclassical' microeconomics came to be all about. This branch of the marginalist–subjectivist revolution attracted the majority of economists to its specific paradigm through the 'scientific' rigour of its mathematical logic and the inferences which could be derived from that. Thus it succeeded in establishing itself as the ruling 'neoclassical' paradigm by the beginning of the 1930s.

In comparison, the lack of rigour in the argumentation of non-mathematical economics and the imprecision of its inferences estranged most twentieth-century economists from the alternative verbal schools of thought. This held for all the heterodox paradigms in the early twentieth century: the historical, Marxist, institutionalist and Austrian schools. As the main course in the development of the science turned away from them, these alternative paradigms came to appear as so many culs-de-sac when compared with the rapid development of the neoclassical mainstream.

During this process the Austrian school continued to defend and propagate its subjectivist programme by engaging in a number of running debates with the neoclassical, Marxist and historical paradigms. Today the Austrians are primarily known for their radical opposition to the empiricist methodology and mathematical formulation of the neoclassical mainstream and their faith in a free market society. They criticize the lack of realism of modern mathematical economics and aim to bring theory into closer conformity with reality. In their view economic theorizing should start from the recognition that human action is subjectively determined and purposeful. It should also account for the important role which institutional arrangements play in conditioning human action. Their political convictions make them the natural opponents of the Marxist and Keynesian schools of thought. As the primary inheritors of classical liberalism they reject on principle the rational–constructivist ideas propagated by these schools.

This contrary position warrants a critical study of the 'Austrians in Debate'. The chapters in this book study the relationships between the Austrian paradigm and its major contemporary opponents by analysing several of the controversies they were engaged in. They were selected from the contributions to the 1995 Amsterdam conference of the Dutch research group on the history of economic thought, which was devoted to this subject. The overall aim of the conference was to discuss:

- why Austrian economists found (and still find) it necessary to combat differing paradigms;
- what was the role of this critical attitude in establishing and developing Austrian economics as a distinctive current in the history of economic thought; and
- whether possibilities exist for cooperation with other schools of thought in order to put economics on a more realistic track than that pursued by the neoclassical paradigm.

In short, this book looks into the role played by theoretical controversies in the development of the Austrian school and suggests how to build bridges towards competing paradigms, both to ensure the continuing vitality of Austrian thought and to further economic science in general.

THE COMBATIVE REPUTATION OF THE AUSTRIAN SCHOOL

More than any other school in economics the Austrian school has a reputation for being highly critical of economic methodologies, theories and policies not in accordance with its own tenets. Many of the great debates in the history of economic thought over the past century have revolved around 'Austrian' themes or involved economists belonging to this school. Indeed, their persistent critical attitude has earned the Austrians the dubious reputation of being a particularly quarrelsome lot, perpetually feuding with adherents of competing economic schools over issues ranging from abstract methodology to practical government policy.

This reputation for contrariness began with the Austrian school's founding father, Carl Menger. He founded a tradition in economics which differed in outlook, method and contents from the contemporary orthodoxies when he published *Grundsaetze der Volkswirtschaftslehre* (Principles of Economics) in 1871. In spite of the book's salute to Menger's German colleagues in the preface and its dedication to the doyen of the German Historical School, Wilhelm Roscher, Menger radically breaks with the ruling paradigms of his time by rejecting the empiricist methodology of the historical school and the objective theory of value of the British Classical School. Thus he sets both the direction for the future development of a distinctive 'Austrian' economics and the tone for its subsequent discourse with alternative paradigms.

This position set the Austrians apart from other schools of economic thought and led to several major controversies between them. In the history of the school several such debates can be distinguished between:

- Menger and Schmoller over methodology;
- Böhm-Bawerk and the Marxists over the Marxian theory of value;

- Mises/Hayek and various socialists over economic calculation in a socialist society;
- Hayek and Keynes over business cycle theory and government intervention; and
- Hayek and neoclassical economists over methodology and epistemology.

This inconclusive list shows that the Austrians were engaged in many of the theoretical debates characterizing the development of economic theory over the past century.

The first and best-known of these was of course the famous 'Methodenstreit' between Menger and Schmoller, the leader of the younger German Historical School. It raged in the last quarter of the nineteenth century over the latter's rejection of the concept of universal economic laws and their advocacy of an empiricist methodology, while Menger upheld the existence of such absolute laws which can be discovered through deductive reasoning (see Bostaph 1978). In Menger's view economics was an 'exact' science, seeking to explain the events constituting its domain of inquiry as manifestations of 'universal' laws – regularities that are valid for all times and places. Such explanations were self-evident and did not require verification. At the time the debate gave the Austrians the label of a 'theory-only' school, which rejected all attempts to found economics on inductive methods and empirical research. Menger's view on the nature of economic 'laws' set him apart from the co-founders of the marginal approach, Jevons and Walras, because they at least paid lip service to the demands of verificationism. Menger's early anti-empiricism was pursued furthest in Mises' 'a priorism', according to which the fundamental laws of economics are a priori true, as each individual knows them from introspection. Since then the issue of empirical testing in economics has been a bone of contention between the Austrian and the neoclassical schools (Caldwell 1982: 120).

Even more than the Methodenstreit, the 'socialist calculation debate' is responsible for the pugnacious image of the Austrian school and its reputation for persisting in opposition even when the tide of economic theorizing is against it. This debate is probably the longest-running controversy in the history of economic thought, now approaching its eightieth year. Mises and Hayek charged that a socialist economy could not effect a welfare-maximizing allocation of resources because it could not establish rational scarcity prices. Although there was a period of more than three decades (1940–75) in which most economists held their views to be conclusively refuted, both Mises and Hayek persisted in their opposition to the accepted wisdom on this issue.

In the early 1930s Hayek was Keynes's main rival in the field of monetary and trade cycle theory (Hicks 1967: 203). In 1931 he launched a sharp attack on the theoretical content and the methodological underpinnings of Keynes's *Treatise on Money* (see Chapter 5 in this volume). This started a still-continuing debate about the foundations of monetary and trade cycle theory, the ability of the market economy to automatically correct monetary imbalances and on the role of monetary policy. In another sharp controversy of the 1930s Hayek opposed Knight and Kaldor on the nature of capital and the relevance of the so-called 'Ricardo effect'. There are several other examples of controversies on Austrian themes and even of the Austrians quarrelling among themselves, such as when the young Schumpeter disagreed with Böhm-Bawerk on the nature of the rate of interest and the recent divergence between the pupils of Mises and those of Hayek over the true nature of the Austrian paradigm (see Vaughn 1992).

The critical attitude of Austrian economists to contemporary theorizing and their persistence in opposition long after the majority of the profession had concluded that their specific cases were lost gave the Austrian school the reputation of being a quarrelsome dead end in the development of mainstream economics, capable only of carping at the latter from the sidelines of historical relevance. In 1962 the Dutch economist Jan Pen probably voiced the opinion of most of his colleagues when he referred to a 'soured Austrianery' and the 'rancorous character' of the later Austrians (meaning Mises and Hayek), who according to him 'always and everywhere were mistaken in matters of economic policy' (Pen 1962: 244, 246 [translation by the authors]). Such was the common view of the school by the mid-1960s.

COMMON ORIGINS OF THE AUSTRIAN AND OTHER MARGINALIST SCHOOLS

Recent research calls for reconsideration of this standard view of the Austrian school. In the first place, the Methodenstreit created the incorrect impression that Menger's subjective approach was in fundamental conflict with the German tradition in economics. An unfortunate consequence of the Menger–Schmoller controversy was the accentuation of the methodological differences between the schools they represented, thus obscuring their common roots in an older German economic tradition. Streissler has argued that Menger's subjectivism was not as revolutionary as is commonly believed by Anglo-Saxon economists. It was embedded in an older German tradition where both costs and utility were used to explain price formation. In this environment the subjective value theory was perceived only as a shift in emphasis and not as the full-scale rejection of an established tradition, which it was in the Anglo-Saxon context of classical cost-of-production theories (Streissler 1990a: 47). According to Streissler the early Austrians founded their paradigm on the German economic tradition, which included the subjective definition of an economic good, the use of marginalist concepts and a general equilibrium approach of treating commodity and factor prices as instances of the same problem of price determination (Streissler 1990a: 44–9). Unfortunately this development of what Streissler calls a 'proto-neoclassical economics' in Germany itself came to a premature halt when nationalist sentiments and the ideology of the new German Empire favoured the historical school with its rejection of the belief in universal economic laws (Streissler 1990b: 159). Due to the growing influence of Schmoller and his followers the Austrians were isolated as the opponents of the newly dominant Historical paradigm in Central European economics.

Böhm-Bawerk's assault on Marx's labour theory of value in his 'Zum Abschluss des Marxschen Systems' (1896) did not strike his Central European colleagues as being that unusual. In their literature it had been customary to criticize Ricardian labour theories of value (see Engels's comments on this in his preface to Volume II of *Das Kapital*), so that it was only natural that an economist of the subjectivist school should strike a deadly blow at the biggest chink in Marx's armour, the 'transformation' of the labour values of Volume I into the production prices from Volume III.

Furthermore, the Austrian and the neoclassical paradigms were both part of the revolt against classical economics in the 1870s and both strove for a purely theoretical economics based on deductive reasoning, as against the inductive method of the German and English Historical Schools, then also in the ascendant. Both schools have their theoretical origins and a major adversary in common. As a result both the Austrians and the neoclassicists believed for many decades that they belonged to the same broad marginalist stream of thought.

The main difference between Menger and Jevons/Walras was that the latter advocated the mathematical method. They argued that economics deals with quantitative magnitudes and should therefore be treated mathematically (Jevons 1957: 3; Walras 1960: 3). Menger on the other hand considered mathematics of little use in finding the true causes of economic value, which to him lay in subjectivism. It was his 'readiness to take the human mind with all its limitations as his starting point . . . [which] really distinguishes Menger from Jevons and Walras' (Lachmann 1978: 59).

But these differences did not cause any fundamental disagreements between the originators of the marginalist–subjectivist revolution. The correspondence between Walras and Menger, Böhm-Bawerk and Wieser clearly shows that, although their methods differed, they were aware of the novel character of their work and felt they were pursuing a common goal (Walras to Böhm-Bawerk, 1 August 1888, in Jaffé 1965, vol. II: 256; Böhm-Bawerk to Walras, 7 August 1888, *ibid.*: 260; Wieser to Walras, 18 June 1890, *ibid.*: 413). Their main aim was to develop a unified theory of prices and to give economics a sounder theoretical footing, which was lacking in the variegated theories of their classical predecessors. These had perceived commodity and factor prices, national and international values and the laws of distribution as different phenomena, each requiring its own theoretical explanation. This ultimately led Classical economics to a state which Jevons described as 'chaotic' (Jevons 1957: xvi). He tried to clear up this situation by distinguishing between the empirical and the theoretical branches of economics. He was not opposed to the empiricism of the English Historical School as such, but found it belonged to a different branch of economics, that of economic sociology. He regarded his *Theory of Political Economy* as a starting point for establishing the theoretical foundations of economics. Realizing that he could not yet offer a systematic theory of economics itself, he laid down the general principles for a mathematical economic theory.

Jevons's aim to develop a unified and comprehensive body of economic theory was shared by Menger and Walras. Towards the end of the nineteenth century the time was ripe for such a comprehensive theory, for theory per se. In their endeavour to provide this the three marginalist currents had a common cause and a common opponent, the German and English Historical Schools, and empiricism in general. Their efforts to establish a unified theory of all prices based on marginalistic principles brought them closer together, as their fellow economists still had to be won over to the case for 'theory'. The common cause for theoretical economics made the marginalists 'comrades-in-arms' (Kirzner 1990: 246). It is this sense of alliance which is ignored in Jaffé's erroneous contention that the differences between them were more important than anything they had in common (Jaffé 1976: 511). In fact, the sense that they were fighting for a common cause lasted well beyond the point when the Historical School ceased to exist. It led to such a degree of convergence between the marginalists that in 1932 Mises remarked that although

> we usually speak of the Austrian and the Anglo-American schools and the school of Lausanne . . . [the fact is] that these three schools of thought differ only in their mode of expressing the same fundamental idea and that they are divided more by their terminology and by peculiarities of presentation than by the substance of their teachings.
>
> (Mises in Kirzner 1990: 245)

By then most Austrians believed that their ideas had been absorbed into the neoclassical mainstream to such an extent that they felt no reason to maintain a doctrinally distinctive 'Austrian' label (Kirzner 1994: xvii).

In the 1930s this belief would radically change, when they came to realize that their specific research programme differed fundamentally from that of the neoclassical school, by then established as the new mainstream orthodoxy. Debating with the neoclassical economists became for them a major method by means of which they came to discover and articulate their own distinctive approach.

THE GROWING DIVERGENCE BETWEEN THE AUSTRIAN AND THE NEOCLASSICAL SCHOOLS

The Austrian school did not really start to realize and emphasize its distinctiveness as a research programme different from mainstream neoclassicism until the great debates of the 1930s. In 1929 Hayek still saw the equilibrium theory of the Lausanne school as the starting point for *all* economic explanation (Hayek 1933: 42n, 86, 95–6). It builds on 'the fundamental thesis of static theory', which states that prices always keep supply and demand in equilibrium (*ibid.*: 76). In this respect prices are understood as 'expressions of a necessary tendency towards a state of equilibrium' (*ibid.*: 85). However, by 1933 Hayek started to realize that a theory dealing with the complexities of an economy developing in time could not start from these static premises. To explain *how* the price mechanism coordinates the activities of millions of individuals and thereby moves the market in the direction of equilibrium, the theoretical conception of equilibrium itself had to be changed. Equilibrium theory should not start by, *ab initio*, assuming the full coordination of plans. Instead, it should explain how the economy reaches this state. According to this reformulation, 'equilibrium' refers to that situation in which all market participants expect to be able to realize their planned activities. For Hayek and the Austrians the process of coordination, and not the ultimate state of equilibrium, should be the focal point of theoretical research. Consideration of the role that subjective knowledge plays in this process made Hayek aware of the fundamental differences existing between the static nature of the equilibrium theory of the Lausanne school and his own conception of equilibrium as the coordination of economic activities (e.g. Hayek 1937, 1945).

Hayek's growing awareness of this rift coincided, though not accidentally, with important new developments in equilibrium theory. This indicated that the differences between the Austrian and the neoclassical paradigms were more fundamental than those in 'terminology' and 'presentation' alone, which Mises had alluded to in the early 1930s. These developments showed that by formulating equilibrium theory in mathematical terms the neoclassical economists were resorting to a methodology which conflicted with the Austrian approach.

Of course, the objectives of mathematical equilibrium theory had already been formulated earlier by Jevons, Walras and Fisher, but for several reasons it was not until the 1930s that the Austrians realized that a mathematicized economics conflicted with their own approach. One reason was that, in spite of Jevons's and Walras's zeal in advocating the use of mathematics, economics largely remained a verbal science for several decades to come. In Britain economists did not follow Jevons's call to develop their science along mathematical lines. Instead they favoured the approach of Marshall, who had relegated mathematics to the footnotes and appendices of his *Principles of*

Economics (1890). Walras's letters testify to his efforts to convince his colleagues of the benefits of the mathematical method, but in most cases he failed to get a sympathetic hearing. Ingrao and Israel (1990: 170) conclude that by 1910 Walrasian equilibrium analysis was virtually dead. However, in the 1930s more able mathematicians (such as Hicks and Samuelson in the Anglo-Saxon and Wald and Von Neumann in the German-speaking countries) rescued it from oblivion and gave the development of mathematical general equilibrium analysis a powerful new impetus.

Perhaps the cold reception of Walras's ideas explains why Menger never considered the mathematical method a threat to his 'exact' method. Their correspondence shows that Menger saw Walras as an ally in his battle to defend the cause of an 'exact' or 'analytical' method against his German opponents propagating the empirical method (letter of February 1884 in Jaffé 1965, vol. II: 5). Menger defined economics as an exact science aimed at formulating universal economic laws which show the causal connections between economic phenomena (Alter 1990: 105) and in the light of this aim mathematics simply did not appear very important to him. In Menger's opinion mathematics could only be used to describe economic relationships already found by other methods of inquiry. Confined to this role, the mathematical method could never penetrate into the real essence ('das Wesen') of economic phenomena (Jaffé 1965, vol. I: 768; vol. II: 3). The reason why Menger considers mathematics impotent in this regard is that it cannot explain the motives which ultimately determine economic behaviour and therefore the exchange value of commodities (*ibid.*: 4). If the value which people attach to commodities is subjective, then price theory must deal with the needs people seek to satisfy and the degree to which they think that different commodities are able to satisfy those needs. A mathematical formulation of their ratios of exchange will not provide this insight.

In 1932 Hans Mayer elaborated this point. He recognized that by pursuing economics as a branch of mathematics, the neoclassical economists were adopting a methodology alien to the Austrian approach. He argued that a mathematical explanation of price determination cannot explain how economic decisions give rise to prices because it treats all variables as if they exist simultaneously. By describing economic relationships in a system of simultaneous equations, mathematical general equilibrium theory cannot show how a sequence of actions results in price formation. To emphasize this distinction, Mayer distinguishes between the *causal–genetic* mode of explanation of Austrian theory and the *functional* mode of the mathematical equilibrium theories (Mayer 1932: 148). In contrast to the functional explanation, a causal–genetic theory is stated in terms of the ends which people pursue and the means they employ to achieve them (Cowan and Rizzo 1996). Mayer's distinction was a sign of the growing discomfort of Austrian economists with the direction microeconomics was taking in the 1930s. It showed that, in contrast to Mises' earlier statement, not all of the ideas fundamental to the Austrian tradition had been or could be accommodated in the neoclassical paradigm.

More than anything else it was the socialist calculation debate which led Hayek and Mises to realize and articulate the distinctiveness of their ideas (Kirzner 1988). The debate can be divided into three or four different phases, all of which were important for the gradual crystallization of the Austrian paradigm (the following discussion builds on Keizer 1994). The first phase was a controversy between Mises and a number of Central European Marxists over the need for economic calculation and rational prices to achieve a welfare-maximizing allocation of scarce resources. It seems improbable today, but the fact is that this evident truth was by no means commonly known or accepted by many professional economists (let alone laymen) around 1920. This phase of the debate was conclusively won by Mises, who thereby established the importance of scarcity pricing for economic rationality. In the next phases of the debate more theoretically sophisticated socialist economists responded in two ways, employing the concepts from the other two marginalist approaches, the Walrasian and the Marshallian. Some advanced E. Barone's 1908 proof that a Walrasian general equilibrium model, yielding a set of optimal prices, could also be established for a society in which the means of production were owned by the state. If Mises wanted to maintain his critique of socialism, he would have to refute this Walrasian response. He did so by attacking the methodological foundations of general equilibrium theory: its static premises and its abstraction from change and the resultant fundamental uncertainty. General equilibrium only applies to a stationary (Mises' 'evenly-rotating') economy, which is an imaginary and unrealistic construct.

In 1935 Hayek augmented Mises' case with his knowledge-argument, saying that socialist planners can never possess the knowledge required to allocate resources as efficiently as the market system. All human knowledge is subjective and therefore dispersed over millions of individuals. It is often of a tacit nature and can therefore only be manifested in free market prices, which by definition are lacking in a socialist economy. However, a part of his argument created the impression that the Austrians considered the problem facing the socialist planners as merely 'impossible in practice', on account of the complexity of the calculating task to solve a real-life general equilibrium model. This point seemed much weaker than Mises' 'impossible in principle' argument. The socialist answer to Hayek's practicality charge was to circumvent it by means of a decentralized trial-and-error procedure using markets for consumer goods and labour. This 'market socialist' model (first proposed by O. Lange and finalized in 1944 by A.P. Lerner) was based on Marshallian partial equilibrium theory. Hayek and Mises in turn responded to this solution by attacking the methodological and theoretical underpinnings of all neoclassical equilibrium theories, whether Walrasian or Marshallian.

In countering the neoclassical responses to their critiques, Mises and Hayek were driven to articulate their differences with both Walrasian general and Marshallian partial equilibrium theory. In their criticism of the foundations of neoclassical theory they were gradually led to discover and explicate their own distinctive Austrian paradigm. From the viewpoint of the history of economic thought the importance of the socialist calculation debate does not lie in the question of 'who won?', but in the catalytic role it played in the development of the Austrian paradigm and hence in the opening and widening of the rift between it and neoclassical theory.

But the debate did more than that. It made Hayek and Mises aware of the essence of Austrian thought and of the extent to which it differed from the approach taken by neoclassical microeconomics. It now appeared to them that the confluence of all 'marginalist' currents that Mises had believed in earlier was wrong; in fact it had not occurred at all. As a result of this insight Hayek and Mises came to distinguish sharply between their efforts to establish a science aiming at understanding the systemic forces leading the market economy towards the coordination of individual plans and the neoclassical paradigm focusing on the mathematical analysis of equilibrium states. It is the difference between a science of purposeful human action in an institutionally specified environment characterized by fundamental uncertainty and a mathematically formulated 'pure logic of choice' of a Robbinsian maximizer.

ECLIPSE AND RESURGENCE OF THE AUSTRIAN SCHOOL

Unfortunately for Austrian economics, the moment when its leading theorists recognized the distinctiveness and import of their approach coincided with the eclipse of that approach in academic and professional circles. In the 1930s many promising German and Austrian scholars fled the Nazi regime, dissolving the continental fountainhead of the school (Craver 1986). Robbed of its home base, the responsibility for continuing the tradition rested on Mises and Hayek. Most of their fellow Austrians found employment in England and America and adopted the neoclassical approach dominant there. At the London School of Economics Hayek confronted the opposition of Keynes and the Cambridge tradition. Upon his appointment to the Tooke Chair in 1931 he challenged Keynes by writing a highly critical review of his *Treatise on Money* (Hayek 1931b, 1932). It has been argued that Hayek deliberately sought this conflict to establish himself as a leading theorist (Mongiovi 1990). Hayek himself declared that Robbins had invited him to the LSE 'to fight Keynes' (Hayek in Kresge and Wenar 1994: 77).

Even so, Hayek failed to stem the Keynesian tide and by the end of the 1930s Austrian economics had almost disappeared as a separate school of thought. A major handicap in countering the rise of Keynesian economics was the narrow scope of Hayek's monetary thought, which was exclusively concerned with the problems of inflation. Even in the early 1930s he never ceased to point out the dangers of inflation, while the reality of everyday showed that it was deflation which caused the misery of mass unemployment. For all its theoretical flaws Keynes's 'banana parable' (Keynes 1930: 158–60) at least showed how deflation could push an economy into a state of prolonged depression without activating forces to stimulate recovery (Barens 1989).

Hayek's disregard for this reality alienated even his closest allies. In 1971 even Robbins regretted having opposed Keynes on the issue of public spending in the 1930s, calling it 'the greatest mistake of [my] professional career' (Robbins 1971: 153). Furthermore, in this period the demands on economic science were changing rapidly. It seemed that Keynes's eclectic work provided a much richer source for developing empirical, mathematical and policy applications. Hayek had built his monetary theory around a capital theory which treated capital as heterogeneous goods. The complexities of the relationships between the different stages of production made it impossible to formalize the theory, while empirical research was an activity the Austrians were opposed to on principle. In contrast Keynes stressed that economic theory should be built on operational concepts (Keynes 1936: 59; Blaug 1991: 180). This allowed his theory to fill the contemporary need for operationalizing economics as an instrument for economic policy. Another reason for the rapid spread of Keynesian ideas is that the *General Theory* abounded in novel predictions which invited further theoretical refinement and empirical testing (Blaug 1991: 187).

Considering the success of the Keynesian revolution it is remarkable that Hayek never challenged the *General Theory* when it appeared in 1936. In retrospect he suggested that he was discouraged from doing so by Keynes's habit of changing his mind when faced with serious criticism. However, he later admitted that this was only part of the reason for his silence on the book. He even wrote to Keynes that he intended to publish some comments on it (letter of 2 February 1936 in Keynes 1979: 208). That Hayek never involved himself in the debates following the publication of the *General Theory* is possibly explained by the fact that he was so immersed in his own theoretical studies that he did not recognize the potential danger of Keynes's ideas. In the mid-1930s he devoted his intellectual energy to the development of a more satisfactory theory of capital that would answer the severe criticisms of his *Prices and Production* (1931a) (Hayek in Kresge and Wenar 1994: 90–1). When after seven years the outbreak of war forced him to publish the results of this work prematurely (*The Pure Theory of Capital*, 1941), the Keynesian revolution was already well under way. In retrospect it seems that the Keynesian revolution took Hayek and the LSE by surprise (McCormick 1992: 181–2).

The Austrians must have mixed feelings in looking back on the 1930s. On the one hand the controversies of this decade almost led to the disappearance of the school, but on the other hand they made the Austrians realize what the essence of their tradition was. It was their subsequent formulation of this insight which rescued the school from oblivion and inspired its revival in the 1970s.

A key event in this revival was the South Royalton conference in 1974, which gave a group of young economists the opportunity to learn about Austrian economics from academics who had studied directly under its nestors (Vaughn 1994). Several developments made its teachings again stand out as a strong alternative to the prevailing neoclassical and Keynesian orthodoxies. In the 1970s Keynesian macroeconomic policies appeared powerless against the combination of mounting inflation and unemployment rates. In line with the concerns of the monetarists and neoclassicists, the Austrians pointed out the dangers of inflationary policies and stressed the importance of institutions and other structural factors affecting economic performance. Their objections against neoclassical theory concentrated on a methodological issue. In its purest form, neoclassical theory depicts a world of perfect competition, which keeps markets in a state of general equilibrium and simultaneously secures a welfare optimum. This postulated Arcadia stands in stark contrast to the daily reality of a world in disarray. The Austrians wanted to imbue economic theory with a stronger sense of reality, thereby appealing to economists who felt dissatisfied with the unending task of constructing mathematical models of this fictitious world. Curiously, in this respect the Austrians shared the critique of the so-called 'radical economists' of the 1970s to a considerable extent.

The Austrian alternative deals with real markets and real entrepreneurs, who both cause change and uncertainty and adapt to it. The resurgent interest in Austrian premises revived an old tradition in economics which understood equilibrium as a *process* to be understood, rather than as a state to be described in mathematical equations. According to this view equilibrium theory should analyse the inherent forces in a market economy which continuously nudge markets in the direction of equilibrium. As a result of the analytical refinement of the general equilibrium paradigm after World War II, this older approach had been supplanted by an exclusive concern with the mathematical analysis of a system of markets already in equilibrium. This approach leaves the question of how the system reaches this state largely unanswered. Many young economists started to think that Austrian theory could serve as a basis for finding answers to this question, as the market process forms the core of the Austrian paradigm.

BERT TIEBEN AND WILLEM KEIZER

THE FUTURE OF AUSTRIAN ECONOMICS: CONTROVERSY OR COOPERATION?

Contemporary Austrians face the challenge of developing this heritage into a research programme capable of re-establishing itself in the vanguard of economics. This is not an easy task, despite their perception that neoclassical economics is a degenerating (or at least stagnating) research programme (e.g. Boettke 1996; Rizzo 1996). Austrian economists believe that they ask the questions that matter, offer a better understanding of how the market economy works and can generate theories which meet the demand for more realism. New developments in their work increasingly recognize the importance of disequilibrating forces and pay more attention to the prerequisites of equilibrating behaviour. They deal with such thorny issues as the implications of endogenously produced change and the reconciliation of the concepts of equilibrium and unpredictable change (Rizzo 1996: xvii–xxvii). In these fields contemporary Austrian economists are asking stimulating questions which do not fit the neoclassical approach.

Modern Austrians believe that neoclassical economics is unable to reconsider its foundations and evolve a new set of research questions because it continues to use a predominantly mathematical mode of analysis (Boettke 1996). In their opinion current developments in neoclassical analysis concern further theoretical refinements, while ignoring the apparent anomalies in this approach. Over the past decades economics has performed poorly in recognizing, explaining and dealing with several of the most pressing economic problems of our time, such as:

- the persistent inflation in the 1970s
- the surge in structural unemployment in the 1980s
- the rising costs of the Western welfare states
- non-convergence in the developmental paths of industrialized and non-industrialized countries.

In spite of the fact that contemporary surveys of the state of economics often have the word 'crisis' in their title, this poor record has not led to the abandonment of the neoclassical paradigm. One explanation for its continuing appeal is that it has shown considerable flexibility in confronting anomalies. To escape the accusation of ad hoc theorizing, it postulated new assumptions and adjusted its models to account for anomalies, while retaining the core assumptions of equilibrium, stable preferences and constrained optimization. Thus neoclassical theory continues to expand its domain, to the point of invading the research fields of related sciences (see Hirshleifer 1985).

However, the apparent success of neoclassical economics in overcoming its 'crisis' must be qualified. To a considerable extent it consisted of finding novel applications for its standard theories. To adopt a Lakatosian term, the changes took place in the 'belt' of the paradigm, leaving its 'core' untouched. A less charitable reading would call it 'putting old wine in new bottles'. Neoclassical equilibrium theories gave way to new-Keynesian analyses of market failure, and models of perfect competition could be adapted to account for product differentiation. Despite these developments the basic questions asked and the techniques employed to answer them remained essentially the same. The recent surge of interest in the problems of 'imperfect information' and 'imperfect markets' is part of the continuing quest of the neoclassicists to found their macroeconomics on their micro-models of individual optimizing behaviour (van Ees and Garretsen 1990).

These developments serve an important purpose: by extending their analysis to cases involving asymmetric information and market failure, the neoclassical economists strive for greater realism. The economics of imperfect information and market failure are not only interesting theoretical issues, they also express the belief that economics is able to give a more accurate description of real market behaviour by decreasing the level of theoretical abstraction. However, the additional assumptions incorporating such features have the drawback of increasing the complexity of their mathematical treatment. More advanced mathematical techniques are needed to solve these problems and often require the introduction of specific assumptions to obtain a tractable solution. This 'selective realism' (Boettke 1996: 30) has its price in terms of economic relevance. It leads to the introduction of subsidiary assumptions which only serve a mathematical function and have no economic meaning. Given the tension between the demand for both realistic assumptions and formal rigour, the suspicion arises that neoclassical economics is held hostage by its own methods. It is no longer the problems of the real economy which determine the direction of its research. The field of inquiry of mathematical economics is limited to the problems that its methods are technically capable of solving. The analogy that comes to mind is the old joke about the drunk who, on a dark night, searches for his lost key under a lamp post just because 'that is where the light shines'.

These considerations raise some questions about the future of economics in general, and of Austrian economics in particular. If Austrian economics is really the progressive research programme it claims to be, does it have the potential of replacing the stagnating neoclassical paradigm, or will the appeal of mathematical rigour also prove too strong for future generations of economists? Will the role of the Austrian approach remain confined to playing the devil's advocate to a mainstream science which continues to build on neoclassical foundations? The onus lies on the Austrian economists. If their economics is truly an 'extraordinary' science ready to supplant an orthodox economics 'at the point of breakdown' (Dolan 1976: 4), it must prove that it provides a better insight into the functioning of a real-life market economy. In the recent past the neo-Marxist paradigm failed to oust neoclassical orthodoxy because it could not provide a realistic and fruitful body of theory that was convincing to the majority of the profession. It therefore got trapped into repetitive exegeses of 'what Marx really meant'. There is a similar danger facing Austrian economists; of rehashing the theories of their 'classics' instead of breaking new ground on the basis of their distinctive concepts.

The key concept here is the 'scientific persuasiveness' of a body of theory. Whether it is on account of its 'technical lock-in effects' (Boettke 1996: 25) or because it provides a plausible and useful account of many important features of markets (Vaughn 1994: 165) and thus satisfies our demand for operational economic concepts (Bellinger and Bergsten 1990), the fact is that mathematicized neoclassical economics continues to dominate our science. Austrian economists must convince the profession of the actual and potential fruitfulness of their distinctive approach. Speculating on the future of Austrian economics, Boettke and Prychitko (1994: 290) state that it can only survive as a vital tradition by increasing the number of economists doing both theoretical and applied research along Austrian lines.

In the past, the best way for Austrians to gain attention was to criticize the neoclassical approach. In recent years little constructive work along Austrian lines has been published in the major journals, perhaps because of the school's reluctance or inability to formulate its theories in mathematical language. The Austrian papers that were published mostly criticized the lack of realism or the failing methodology of neoclassical analysis, rather than developing their own theories. In this way they provided a useful source of economic 'intuition' for neoclassical economists, making their formalized theories understandable in terms of real-life human action. The neoclassical heuristic that described movements of, or along, supply and demand curves does not show how profit-seeking economic actors actually effect the adjustments which bring about the coordination of their activities. Thus Austrian theory can 'flesh out' the abstract logic of neoclassical theory by supplementing its own distinctive explanation. However, it is clear that to sustain its revival Austrian economics must go beyond its traditional role as gadfly, interpreter or even conscience of the neoclassical mainstream (Vaughn 1994: 167; Boettke 1994, 1996). Its own constructive work must demonstrate its superiority, regardless of which criteria one should apply to measure that.

The exact nature of the relationships between the Austrian paradigm and its competitors is difficult to define. Like the phenomena it addresses, economic theorizing is a process in constant flux. At times a stable pattern may emerge, in which most economists join in executing a research programme they consider 'normal' science, but new concepts will inevitably arise and scientific convictions may shift. A research programme once considered innovating and progressive may stagnate or degenerate in a matter of years. The Austrian tradition experienced such a decline in the 1930s, to reappear as a promising paradigm once again in the 1970s. In considering the road ahead the Austrians must rethink the goals they seek to achieve and, with that, their relationships with competing paradigms. On the one hand Austrian economics is part of the broad marginalist stream, which opposes it to other heterodox schools of thought such as the Historical School, the American institutionalists and the Marxists. On the other hand, in seeking to develop a body of theory which may replace (rather than supplement) the formalistic concepts of neoclassical equilibrium thought, the Austrians may well benefit from Marxist, (neo-)institutionalist or post-Keynesian ideas. They have a common concern with the problems of uncertainty and historical time. In contrast to mainstream economics they try to deal with the consequences of disequilibrium forces and endogenous change. It is not yet decided which strategy the Austrians should follow in the future, whether to cooperate with those with shared concerns or to confront them.

THE AIM AND CONTENTS OF THIS BOOK

By studying the Austrians in debate the essays in this volume may help to define, clarify and develop the relationships between the Austrian paradigm and its major contemporary alternatives. They were presented as papers at the 1995 Amsterdam conference on this subject. Because the essays approach it from different perspectives and cover historical, methodological and theoretical issues, the total picture which emerges from this book is meant to be neither comprehensive nor unidirectional.

The book consists of four parts, the first of which contains the general introduction and the keynote address by Leland Yeager. They introduce the main theme by surveying the development of Austrian economics and its relationship to that of economic theory in general. In his keynote address Leland Yeager observes that mainstream macroeconomics is currently in disarray. This gives Austrian economists the opportunity to draw attention to their distinctive approach and set macroeconomics on a sounder course. Austrian economics has two characteristics that make it well equipped to do so. First, it deals with the coordination problem, thus bridging the current gap between micro- and macroeconomics. Second, Austrian economics is more realistic than the other free-market-oriented schools because it accentuates the complexities of the extended economic order.

The second part adopts a historical perspective and shows that Austrian economists initiated and contributed to many important developments in the history of economic thought. In Chapter 3, Richard Ebeling discusses the relationship between Austrian and Swedish economics during the interwar period. Although both research traditions developed some sort of period analysis, they failed to provide a satisfactory theory of expectations formation and in Ebeling's view it is remarkable that they both neglected Mises' writings on this subject. Ebeling argues that Mises might well have provided

Austrians and Swedes with a better insight into how economic agents come to form their expectations, thus improving the internal consistency of their theoretical systems. The next two chapters provide modern interpretations of particular issues in two famous historical debates and seek to correct some misapprehensions underlying their traditional presentation. In Chapter 4 Willem Keizer addresses the peculiar position of Schumpeter in the socialist calculation debate. He claims that Schumpeter's admiration for mathematical economics in general and for Walrasian general equilibrium theory in particular prevented him from appreciating the specific Austrian arguments of Mises and Hayek and led him to adopt an uncharacteristic (and ultimately wrong) neoclassical stance in the debate. In Chapter 5, Bert Tieben reinterprets another well-known debate and answers the question why Hayek and Keynes were unable to pursue a potentially fruitful discourse on their novel work in the field of the monetary business cycle.

The third part offers reinterpretations of particular aspects of Austrian methodology and its relationship with competing paradigms. In Chapter 6, Steve Fleetwood argues that from a critical–realistic point of view the methodological programmes of Marx and Hayek show some remarkable similarities which could form the basis for an Austrian–Marxist dialogue. In Chapter 7, Laurence Moss examines a major difference between the methodology of the modern neo-Austrians and the approach of the Austrian 'classics'. He regrets that their emphasis on conjectural history leads modern Austrians away from questions which traditionally formed the basis of their thought experiments. The older Austrians used imaginary constructions such as the 'benevolent dictator' to examine the conditions for maintaining an efficient modern economy. Such questions seem to have disappeared from modern Austrian theorizing. Moss argues that, as a result, contemporary Austrian analysis has a much narrower scope, focusing on the evolution of institutions and rules conducive to the market process. In seeking to describe these processes it abandons the traditional thought experiment. Patrick Gunning discusses an example of this modern disregard for the thought experiment in Chapter 8. Adopting Mises' method of imaginary constructions, he seeks to redefine the Austrian theory of entrepreneurship as the science of Distinctly Human Action. He states that by ignoring this method, Kirzner's conception of entrepreneurship is non-subjectivistic and therefore essentially non-Austrian.

The last four chapters examine the prospects for a fruitful cross-fertilization between the Austrian and other contemporary paradigms. In Chapter 9, Emiel Wubben discusses the relationship between Austrian and post-Keynesian economics. While recognizing the important differences between them, he argues that they cover much common ground and may well benefit from closer cooperation. In the same vein it is sometimes asserted that there are important similarities between Hayek and the neoclassical economists. William Butos considers this relationship in

Chapter 10 by examining the compatibility between Hayek and the rational expectations hypothesis. He makes use of Hayek's *Sensory Order* to construct a theory of subjective expectations, but concludes that such a Hayekian theory of expectations differs in significant aspects from the hypothesis of rational expectations. The compatibility thesis must therefore be rejected, as far as this aspect of their business cycle theories is concerned.

In Chapter 11, Nicolai Foss examines another field in which Hayek is often regarded as an important precursor of contemporary theorizing, that of institutional economics. He states that a distinguishing characteristic of the Austrian tradition is its fundamental concern with institutions. Hayek and Mises anticipated modern neo-institutional theory in a number of dimensions, such as their comparative–institutional analysis, their process view of the market and their concern with institutional change. Foss believes that in several of these areas neo-institutionalists may still have something to learn from the Austrians. Finally, by comparing Hayek's concept of personal knowledge with the notion of private information used in modern contract theory, Carlo Zappia demonstrates in Chapter 12 how specific Austrian insights in the functioning of economic institutions may benefit contemporary microeconomic theory. He argues that the idea of personal knowledge can be used to account for the possible permanence of rents in equilibrium, a fact which post-Walrasian microeconomic theories recognize but fail to explain. His analysis reflects a growing awareness that the future development of economic theorizing may be furthered by the cross-fertilization of ideas from competing traditions. In this process an 'Austrian Economics in (continuous) Debate' with other traditions could well act as a fruitful catalyst.

REFERENCES

Alter, M. (1990) *Carl Menger and the Origins of Austrian Economics*, Boulder, CO: Westfield Press.

Barens, I. (1989) 'From the "banana parable" to the principle of effective demand: some reflections on the origin, development and structure of Keynes' *General Theory*', in D.A. Walker (ed.) *Twentieth-Century Economic Thought*, Aldershot: Edward Elgar, 111–32.

Bellinger, W.K. and Bergsten, G.S.(1990) 'The market for economic thought: an Austrian view of neoclassical dominance', *History of Political Economy*, 22 (4): 697–720.

Blaug, M. (1991) 'Second thoughts on the Keynesian revolution', *History of Political Economy*, 23 (2): 171–92.

Boettke, P.J. (1994) 'Alternative paths forward for Austrian economics', in P.J. Boettke (ed.) *The Elgar Companion to Austrian Economics*, Aldershot: Edward Elgar, 3–17.

——(1996) 'What is wrong with neoclassical economics (and what is still wrong with Austrian economics)', in F. Foldvary (ed.) *Beyond Neoclassical Economics*, Aldershot: Edward Elgar, 22–40.

Boettke, P.J. and Prychitko, D.L.(1994) 'The future of Austrian economics', in P.J. Boettke and D.L. Prychitko (eds) *The Market Process*, Aldershot: Edward Elgar, 287–93.

Böhm-Bawerk, E. (1896) 'Zum Abschluss der Marxschen Systems', in H. Meixner and M. Turban (eds) *Die Marx-Kritik der Österreichischen Schule der National-ökonomie*, Giessen: Andreas Aschenbach (1974), 47–132.

Bostaph, S. (1978) 'The methodological debate between Carl Menger and the German Historicists', *Atlantic Economic Journal*, 6 (3): 3–16.

Caldwell, B.J. (1982) *Beyond Positivism: Economic Methodology in the Twentieth Century*, London: Unwin Hyman.

Cowan, R. and Rizzo, M.J. (1996) 'The genetic–causal tradition and modern economic theory', *Kyklos*, 49 (3): 273–317.

Craver, E. (1986) 'The emigration of the Austrian economists', *History of Political Economy*, 18 (1): 1–32.

Dolan, E.G. (1976) 'Austrian economics as extraordinary science', in E.G. Dolan (ed.) *The Foundations of Modern Austrian Economics*, Kansas City, KS: Sheed & Ward, 3–15.

Ees, H. van and Garretsen, H. (1990) 'The right answers to the wrong question? An assessment of the microfoundations debate', *De Economist*, 138 (2): 123–45.

Hayek, F.A. (1931a) *Prices and Production,* 1st edn, London: Routledge & Kegan Paul.

——(1931b) 'Reflections on the Pure Theory of Money of Mr J.M. Keynes (I)', *Economica*, 11 (August): 270–95.

——(1932) 'Reflections on the Pure Theory of Money of Mr J.M. Keynes (II)', *Economica*, 12 (February): 22–44.

——(1933) *Monetary Theory and the Trade Cycle*, New York: Kelley (1975).

——(1935) *Prices and Production*, 2nd edn, London: Routledge & Kegan Paul.

——(1937) 'Economics and Knowledge', *Economica* 4 (n.s.): 33–54.

——(1941) *The Pure Theory of Capital*, London: Routledge & Kegan Paul.

——(1945) 'The use of knowledge in society', *American Economic Review*, 35: 519–30.

Hicks, J.R. (1967) 'The Hayek story', in *Critical Essays in Monetary Theory*, Oxford: Clarendon, 203–15.

Hirshleifer, J. (1985) 'The expanding domain of economics', *American Economic Review*, 75 (6): 53–68.

Ingrao, B. and Israel, G. (1990) *The Invisible Hand*, Cambridge, MA: MIT Press.

Jaffé, W. (ed.) (1965) *Correspondence of Léon Walras and Related Papers*, 3 vols, Amsterdam: North-Holland.

——(1976) 'Menger, Jevons and Walras de-homogenized', *Economic Inquiry*, 14 (December): 511–24.

Jevons, W.S. (1957) *The Theory of Political Economy*, 5th edn, New York: Kelley (1965).

Keizer, W. (1994) 'Hayek's critique of socialism', in J. Birner and R.W. van Zijp (eds) *Hayek, Coordination and Evolution*, London: Routledge, 207–31.

Keynes, J.M. (1930) *A Treatise on Money: I The Pure Theory of Money*, The Collected Writings of John Maynard Keynes, vol. V (1971), D. Moggridge (ed.), London: Macmillan.

——(1936) *The General Theory of Employment, Interest, and Money*, The Collected Writings of John Maynard Keynes, vol. VII (1973), D. Moggridge (ed.), London: Macmillan.

——(1979) *The General Theory and After: A Supplement*, The Collected Writings of John Maynard Keynes, vol. XXIX, D. Moggridge (ed.), London: Macmillan.

Kirzner, I.M. (1988) 'The economic calculation debate: lessons for Austrians', *Review of Austrian Economics*, 2: 1–18.

——(1990) 'Commentary', to S. Boehm, 'The Austrian tradition: Schumpeter and Mises', in K. Hennings and W. Samuels (eds) *Neoclassical Economic Theory, 1870–1930*, Dordrecht: Kluwer, 242–9.

——(1994) 'Introduction', in I.M. Kirzner (ed.) *Classics in Austrian Economics*, vol. II, London: Pickering & Chatto, vii–xx.

Kresge, S. and Wenar, L. (eds) (1994) *Hayek on Hayek: An Autobiographical Dialogue*, London: Routledge.

Lachmann, L. (1978) 'Carl Menger and the incomplete revolution of subjectivism', *Atlantic Economic Journal*, 6 (3): 57–9.

Marx, K. (1867–94) *Das Kapital*, 3 vols, Berlin: Dietz (1973–4).

Mayer, H. (1932) 'Der Erkenntniswert der funktionellen Preistheorien', in H. Mayer (ed.) *Die Wirtschaftstheorie der Gegenwart*, vol. 2, Wien: Springer, 147–239.

McCormick, B.J. (1992) *Hayek and the Keynesian Avalanche*, London: Harvester Wheatsheaf.

Mongiovi, G. (1990) 'Keynes, Hayek and Sraffa: on the origins of chapter 17 of the *General Theory*', *Economie Appliquée*, 43: 131–56.

Pen, J. (1962) 'Verzuurde Oostenrijkerij', in *Het aardige van de economie*, Utrecht: Aula-pockets, Het Spectrum, 241–6.

Rizzo, M.J. (1996) 'Introduction', in G.P. O'Driscoll and M.J. Rizzo, *The Economics of Time and Ignorance*, 2nd edn, London: Routledge.

Robbins, L. (1971) *Autobiography of an Economist*, London: Macmillan.

Streissler, E.W. (1972) 'To what extent was the Austrian school marginalist?', in R.D.C. Black, A.W. Coats and C.D.W. Goodwin (eds) *The Marginal Revolution in Economics*, Durham, NC: Duke University Press, 160–75.

——(1990a) 'The influence of German economics on the work of Menger and Marshall', in B.J. Caldwell (ed.) *Carl Menger and his Legacy in Economics*, Durham, NC: Duke University Press, 31–68.

——(1990b) 'Menger, Böhm-Bawerk and Wieser: the origins of the Austrian school', in K. Hennings and W. Samuels (eds) *Neoclassical Economic Theory, 1870–1930*, Dordrecht: Kluwer, 151–89.

Vaughn, K.I. (1992) 'The problem of order in Austrian economics: Kirzner vs Lachmann', *Review of Political Economy*, 4 (3): 251–74.

——(1994) *Austrian Economics in America: The Migration of a Tradition*, Cambridge: Cambridge University Press.

Walras, L. (1960) 'Économique et Méchanique', *Metroeconomica*, 12 (1): 3–13.

2

AUSTRIAN THEMES IN A RECONSTRUCTED MACROECONOMICS

Leland B. Yeager

DISARRAY AND OPPORTUNITY

It is standard nowadays to notice disarray in macroeconomics and monetary theory. Fundamentalist Keynesianism, as we might call it, dominated textbooks and policy circles for roughly three decades. Experience and theory have now discredited it. The fundamentalists brooded about inadequacy of total spending (or occasionally the reverse), about the propensity to consume out of real income, and about a saving gap that grows with income and wealth, thereby becoming harder to fill with investment spending, especially as real capital formation leaves fewer attractive opportunities for further private investment. Even now, a few economists still cling to this doctrine by default and still recommend expanding 'aggregate demand' to 'stimulate' national and world economies, albeit at the cost in price inflation implied by the equally discredited notion of the Phillips curve.

An alternative school of Keynesian interpretation stems from Robert Clower (1984) and Axel Leijonhufvud (1968, 1981). As history of economic thought it may be questionable, but its substance deserves ample attention. It features such concepts as absence of the (supposed) Walrasian auctioneer, incomplete and costly and imperfect information, false price signals, sluggish price adjustments, quantity changes as well as price adjustments, the duality of people's decisions about particular transactions according as they do or do not meet frustration in accomplishing other desired transactions, and the 'income-constrained process' of infectious recession and recovery.

A quite different group of self-styled Keynesians based at Cambridge University expresses sweeping scepticism about market-oriented economic theory. In the United States, economists associated with the *Journal of Post Keynesian Economics* form still another school.

'Monetarists' or 'monetary-disequilibrium theorists' in the tradition of David Hume, Henry Thornton, Clark Warburton, Milton Friedman, Anna Schwartz, Karl Brunner, and Allan Meltzer continue to be active. Their influence has been eroded, however, by misinterpretations of recent experience and by attention paid to two schools that have distorted and exaggerated certain monetarist tenets. The new classical economists (including Robert Lucas (1987), Thomas Sargent, and Robert Barro) proclaim rational expectations and equilibrium always (in effect, everything is always coordinated, or almost so). Their position gained attention more because of its coherence with theoretical and methodological fashion than because of its empirical substance, now widely recognized as deficient (Howitt 1990: chapter 4).

The real-business-cycle school carries the exaggerations of new classical economics still further. It interprets macroeconomic fluctuations as efficient responses to underlying real changes (as in technology) rather than as consequences of monetary disturbances. (Robert King, Charles Plosser and Edward Prescott have written along this line. Strongin (1988) and Stockman (1988) provide convenient surveys. Gary Hansen and Randall Wright (1992) provide an example of tinkering with this theory to rescue it from recalcitrant observed facts; they would do well to remember about Ptolemy and epicycles. Hansen and Prescott convey the impression, without explicitly saying so, that they are answering 'yes' to the question posed by the title of their 1993 article, 'Did technology shocks cause the 1990–1991 recession?')

Both the new classical and real-business-cycle schools tacitly attribute near perfection to markets, as if their members were congratulating themselves on being 'more free-market-oriented than thou'. (I am reporting my impression of doctrines, not conjecturing about anyone's motives nor saying that exaggeration crowds out scholarly substance. Still, fads do come and go in the academic world.) Self-parodying free marketry has given self-styled New Keynesians an opportunity to look sensible by contrast. They share several key perceptions of reality with the monetarists (examples of the work of this misleadingly named school appear in Mankiw and Romer (1991)). As Axel Leijonhufvud (1986) has noted in a more general context, macroeconomists have been playing musical chairs with doctrinal positions and labels.

This disarray gives Austrian economists, as well as the New Keynesians, an opportunity to gain attention and set the main stream of macroeconomics on a sounder course. Two major characteristics, besides others mentioned below, equip the Austrian school for seizing this opportunity. First, it focuses on the central problem bridging micro- and macroeconomics: the problem of economy-wide coordination (Gerald O'Driscoll (1977) aptly named his doctoral dissertation *Economics as a Coordination Problem*). Second, it is readier than other free-market-oriented schools to face reality as it is, 'warts and all'.

LELAND B. YEAGER

COORDINATION

Robert Clower observed that

> [T]he approaches of the Keynesians, monetarists, and new classical
> economists to monetary theory and macroeconomics will get us exactly
> nowhere because each is founded, one way or another, on the conven-
> tional but empirically fallacious assumption that the coordination of
> economic activities is costless.
>
> (Clower 1984: 272)

As this remark suggests, the key question of money/macro theory is not
'What determines whether aggregate demand for goods and services is
deficient or excessive or just right?' but 'What determines whether the
processes of exchange and coordination in an economy of decentralized
decisionmaking are working smoothly?'

Austrian economists recognize the disaggregated character of economic
activity. They take seriously the profound differences between an advanced
economy of fine-grained division of labour and the nearly self-sufficient
miniature economy of a medieval monastery or manor or of the Swiss family
Robinson on its desert island (see Eucken 1950). Knowledge of wants,
resources, technology, and market opportunities, including knowledge of
temporary and local conditions, is radically decentralized and simply could
not be made available to central planners in anything approaching its
fullness. If knowledge is not to be wasted, production and consumption
activities and decisions about them must be radically decentralized (Hayek
1945). Specialization greatly enhances productivity. People produce their
own particular goods and services to exchange them away, thereby exercising
demand for what other specialists are producing. But what coordinates all
these fragmented activities?

The debates over economic calculation under socialism and capitalism
initiated by Ludwig von Mises and Friedrich Hayek illuminate the scope of
this question (see the literature reviewed in Yeager (1994)). Even the mere
physical meshing of activities portrayed in a self-consistent input–output
table is difficult enough to achieve in the absence of genuine markets and
prices, as Soviet experience testifies. Full coordination is a still more
demanding task. Physical and psychological substitutabilities and comple-
mentarities among goods and services and factors of production in their
various uses in consumption and production must be considered in such a
way that no unit of a productive resource goes to satisfy a less intense final
demand instead of a more intense demand. Market bids and offers for
resources and final goods play a central role in this process, but its very
complexity permits glitches, as history illustrates.

Forces of unbalanced supply and demand tend, to be sure, to press
disequilibrium prices towards their market-clearing levels. What ensures,

24

however, that these coordinating forces operate rapidly enough and that impediments to transactions do not reinforce each other in the meanwhile to a degree that shows up as recession or depression? Because the fundamental insight of Say's Law is correct – supplies of particular goods and services constitute demands for others – the *fundamental* macroeconomic problem cannot be one of deficiency of aggregate demand. However, anything that impairs the processes of market exchange also impairs production. People work and produce only in the expectation of being able to exchange their outputs away, and they will not persist indefinitely (especially not in buying inputs for unsaleable outputs) if their attempted exchanges keep on being frustrated. Goods and services exchange for each other not directly but through the intermediary of money, and monetary disorder can snarl up the process of exchange, so impeding production. Austrian economists are prepared to take this snarl seriously.

These considerations help argue, incidentally, for putting the *micro* semester of a Principles of Economics course before the *macro* semester, even though, perversely, teachers at many colleges follow the opposite sequence. Students can hardly understand disruptions of coordination until they know that a coordination problem exists in the first place and understand how the market process solves it when it is working well.

Coordination requires more than correct prices. In Walrasian models of general equilibrium, the 'auctioneer' not only achieves the whole array of market-clearing prices but also puts trading partners in contact with one another, obviating the costly mutual searches that would otherwise be necessary.[1] In the real world, however, a worker may be unemployed not necessarily because he insists on too high a wage rate but because he and a suitable employer have not yet made contact. Various start-up costs of a new employer–employee relation also enter into the story. In the real world, prices are not the only bearers of signals and incentives about potential transactions. Quantities also perform these functions – quantities of goods, services, factors in accomplished transactions, those in frustrated transactions, and inventory buildups and rundowns. Inventory management, quality verification, advertising, and informational and other such activities bear on whether transactions can go forward to the mutual benefit of the parties. All these activities have 'transactions costs' in an inclusive sense of the term. Many of them impede not only actual transactions but even messages of willingness to buy or sell.

Costs and complexities of reality help explain the value of habits, routines, and long-term business relations, as between supplier and customer, employer and worker, and borrower and financial institution. Not every business relation is continuously open to the price revision that abstract equilibrium theory might seem to recommend. The very concept of different degrees of liquidity of various financial and real assets reflects recognition that price is not the only determinant of whether potential transactions get consummated. If all goods were perfectly liquid, as tacitly assumed in the Walrasian model, then impediments to communication would have been removed. (Howitt (1990), writing partly under the inspiration of Clower and Leijonhufvud, surveys some of the foregoing themes, as does Okun (1981). Howitt, as well as Hall (1991), comments on difficulties of finding trading partners in 'thin' as opposed to 'thick' markets. By analogy, my installing a telephone benefits people who might want to reach me but imposes a congestion cost on people who might want to reach people talking with me.)

Whether a particular transaction can go forward depends on much more than the terms subject to negotiation between the two potential trading partners. Whether a manufacturer and a potential employee could both benefit from their relation depends on more than the wage rate. It depends on prices charged by competitors and suppliers; the terms on which energy, transport, and credit are available; market conditions facing potential customers; inventories of various kinds; and much else besides. Changes which affect such conditions occur all the time. They challenge entrepreneurs to cope with them, perhaps by developing new business opportunities to replace fading ones. In ordinary times, entrepreneurs make myriads of interdependent microeconomic adjustments without palpable macroeconomic disorder.

When major economy-wide disruptions occur, however, it is not surprising that the many necessary interlocking adjustments should stretch out painfully over time. Much besides prices and wages must change, for even a purely monetary shock (whatever exactly that might be) has 'real' consequences. Knowledge must be transmitted and received, risk assessed and allowed for, combinations of factors and products in production and consumption revised, search conducted, trading partners contacted, and new quantities of goods produced and exchanged. Stickiness of prices and wages delays the transmission of appropriate signals and incentives. 'Price stickiness' is therefore a traditional and convenient shorthand term alluding to the myriad obstacles to prompt and painless adjustment. It is important to remember, however, how wide the range of circumstances is for which this term is a shorthand label.

By adopting the fashionable assumption of rational expectations, new classicals and subsequently even the New Keynesians tacitly assumed away central aspects of the economy-wide coordination problem. They replaced a vision of people trying to set prices and quantities and to strike bargains in a world of fragmentary and dispersed information with an unrealistic vision of remarkably well-informed people – informed, to be sure, not of specific future quantities and prices but well informed on average about well-defined probability distributions. To assume rational expectations oversimplifies the problems of coordinating people's beliefs. 'No one makes systematic errors in guessing the values of variables that depend in turn upon others' guesses' (Howitt 1990: 12–13).

'IMPERFECTIONS' OF REALITY

In using their word, I am deliberately defying theorists who judge reality 'imperfect' when compared with textbook chapters on equilibrium under pure and perfect competition and who thereby damn reality for being real. Of course no Walrasian auctioneer is at work achieving ideal outcomes. Of course not all imaginable intertemporal markets and contingent-state markets exist. Of course full coordination is never achieved; and it is approached, to the extent that it is, through the piecemeal, asynchronous gropings of myriad entrepreneurs. Theory relevant to the real world cannot confine itself to equilibrium analysis and comparative statics. Instead of a state of affairs, competition is a process. Except perhaps for organized exchanges for standardized commodities and securities, no impersonal 'market' adjusts prices to changed conditions. *People* change prices, and only after they have perceived *reasons* to do so. Reasons include opportunities offered by changes in technology and notably include the perceived market imbalances and frustrations of transactions at the old prices. Perceptions and responses are not instantaneous. Markets do not clear instantly.

Already in his *Theory of Money and Credit* (1912/1981) Ludwig von Mises had no trouble recognizing such facts of reality. Many prices are deliberately set, obviously in retail trade, and set by trial and error.

> Now this phenomenon is not accidental. It is an inevitable phenome-
> non of the unorganized market. In the unorganized market, the seller
> does not come into contact with all of the buyers, but only with single
> individuals or groups . . . . Consequently the seller fixes a price that in
> his opinion corresponds approximately to what the price ought to be
> (in which it is understandable that he is more likely to aim too high
> than too low), and waits to see what the buyers will do. . . . The sole
> way by which sellers can arrive at reliable knowledge about the valua-
> tions of consumers is the way of trial and error.
>
> (Mises 1912/1981: 186–7)

Institutional forces work to postpone price changes otherwise called for by small or transitory changes in supply and demand (*ibid.*: 134). 'Every change in the market data has its definite effects upon the market. It takes a definite length of time before all these effects are consummated, i.e., before the market is completely adjusted to the new state of affairs' (Mises 1963: 652).

> [C]hanges in the factors which determine the formation of prices do
> not produce all their effects at once. A span of time must elapse before
> all their effects are exhausted. Between the appearance of a new datum

and the perfect adjustment of the market to it some time must
pass. . . . In dealing with the effects of any change in the factors operating on the market, we must never forget that we are dealing with
events taking place in succession, with a series of effects succeeding
one another. We are not in a position to know in advance how much
time will have to elapse.

(ibid.: 246)

Mises recognizes a certain inertia of prices (1981: 133–6). Relatedly, he
recognizes that flexible exchange rates tend to move ahead of their
purchasing-power parities; relatively, prices of many goods and services are
sluggish (Mises 1963: 455–6). (Mitchell (1908/1966: 259–83) observed the
same phenomenon in detail in the US 'greenback' period of 1862–78.) Mises
also observes more of a historical element in the value of money than in the
value of any ordinary good:

[A] historically continuous component is contained in the objective
exchange value of money.

The past value of money is taken over by the present and transformed by it. . . . Prices change slowly because the subjective valuations of human beings change slowly. . . . If rapid and erratic
valuations in prices were usually encountered in the market, the conception of objective exchange value would not have attained the significance that it is actually accorded both by consumer and producer.

In this sense, reference to an inertia of prices is unobjectionable.

(Mises 1912/1981: 133)

It is so far as the money prices of goods are determined by monetary
factors, that a historically continuous component is included in them,
without which their actual level could not be explained.

(ibid.: 135)

Without saying so explicitly, Mises clearly implies that money's role as
unit of account contributes to the stickiness of prices. People are in the habit
of formulating their subjective valuations of goods in terms of the money
unit, and subjective valuations ordinarily do not change suddenly. Even if
relatively objective developments do call for a change in the market value of
any ordinary good or of the money unit itself, people require time to
perceive and react to these changes and to reformulate their valuations of
goods in money (ibid.: 133–5; Mises 1963: 426).

A leading theme of Mises' monetary theory is that money is far from
neutral in its effects on quantities, incomes, and relative prices (1963:
408ff.). Prices do not automatically set themselves in proportion to the total
quantity of money, as a naive interpretation of the quantity-theory equation
might suggest. Some changes occur relatively rapidly, others after long
delays. People's responses to ongoing monetary and price inflation change as

experience accumulates and expectations change accordingly. Mises' discussion of *differential* price changes constitutes emphatic recognition of the stickiness of many prices. This recognition is not a distinctively Keynesian notion, despite careless remarks by textbook authors who neglect the history of economic thought.

Like other Austrian theorists, Mises accepts the concept of general equilibrium – the evenly rotating economy, as he calls it – as a valuable tool of analysis. Using this tool in no way entails a supposition that the

> final prices corresponding to this imaginary conception are . . . identical with the market prices. The activities of the entrepreneurs or of any other actors on the economic scene are not guided by consideration of any such things as equilibrium prices and the evenly rotating economy.
>
> (1963: 329)

Austrians are concerned with process – not merely with functional relations in the mathematical sense but with what actually happens, with who does what and why and how. An interest in process bars exclusive infatuation with the equilibrium state.[2] Austrian economics pays attention to what goes on in disequilibrium. It sees the scope for entrepreneurship afforded by disequilibrium. Recognition of disequilibrium is one aspect of Austrian *realism*. Austrians are willing to see the world as it actually is. They are not sidetracked into supposed 'rigorous' theorizing about imaginary worlds that diverge from reality in crucial respects. Austrians recognize that pure and perfect competition, like equilibrium, are abstractions which do not characterize reality. These imaginary extreme conditions do have a role in theorizing, but economists should recognize when they are inapplicable to reality. In understanding money/macro phenomena and in building bridges between macro- and microeconomics, it is essential to recognize that sellers are generally *not* pure price takers and that they are not already selling all the product or all the labour that they want to sell at the prevailing price. In some contexts it is important to recognize that prices are *set* and not impersonally determined by the interplay of atomistic supply and demand.

The Austrians' concern for factual reality is often overlooked because of their supposed insistence on a purely a priori method. This term, notably as used by Ludwig von Mises, unfortunately does invite misinterpretation. So used, *a priori* suggests an unintended sharp contrast with *empirical*. Mises did not mean that all the important strands of economic theory can be spun out of factually empty logical truisms. He relied, rather, on axioms for which factual evidence is so overwhelming that we can hardly imagine a world to which the axioms did not apply (see Rothbard 1957). Austrians do not – or should not, anyway – confine the honorific term 'empirical' only to propositions dug out by arduous labour and of doubtful general validity after all.

In related respects, Austrians are more realistic than self-congratulating 'empirical' researchers. They open their eyes to what sorts of method have and what sorts have not so far brought important results. They look at the facts bearing on whether or not stable functions exist that quantitatively and dependably describe relations among economic magnitudes and that might be relied on for forecasting. They are at least as ready as other economists to accept the facts that call into question over ambitious, activist, fine-tuning policies, whose success presupposes knowing durable quantitative relations.

MONEY

As already mentioned, severe disturbances might conceivably overwhelm decentralized entrepreneurial efforts to cope with them. In principle, 'real' rather than monetary factors might be the cause. It is instructive to ponder what would happen to gross domestic product if a country's telephone system were somehow to fail for several months (Hall 1991: 23) or, more starkly, if this were to happen to all its electronic communications and data processing. In historical fact, however, it is implausible to blame any such 'real' disturbances for the major recessions and depressions actually experienced. Instead of being readily attributable to changes in capacities to produce output, recessions and depressions exhibit what look like pervasive deficiencies of demand; pervasive difficulties in finding customers and finding jobs. A 'real' theory that assumes continuous market equilibrium is hard put, furthermore, to explain the eventual macroeconomic recoveries.

Even a real disturbance as great as the shift from war to peace in 1945–6 brought hardly a macroeconomic ripple. Perhaps the most plausible examples of real disturbances causing recession have been the two oil-price shocks of the 1970s, and even these had monetary aspects. They not only made old patterns of quantities and relative prices wrong but also shrank real cash balances and reshuffled their ownership. Furthermore, previous money and price inflation helped trigger the oil shocks themselves (and this inflation in turn arguably traced to a built-in bias of the Bretton Woods system).

Ludwig von Mises aptly entitles one of his chapters 'The fallacies of the nonmonetary explanations of the trade cycle' (1963: 580–6, at 554–5). He particularly criticizes what he calls 'the two most popular varieties of these disproportionality doctrines' (*ibid.*: 583): the durable-goods (or echo-effect) doctrine and the acceleration principle. He judges them hard to square with the *general*, economy-wide character of business expansions and contractions (*ibid.*: 585).

The monetary theory of discoordination, on the other hand, can cite ample historical and statistical evidence from a wide range of times and places. It is unnecessary to review this evidence here, but undue neglect warrants a plug in the list of references for Harry Gunnison Brown's (1933) insightful and prescient article in the monetarist tradition. It was written just a few days before Franklin Roosevelt took office at the depths of the Great Depression. In articles of 1989 and 1990, Christina and David Romer review recessions evidently caused by monetary policy in the United States since World War II.

To understand what scope monetary disorder has for doing damage, it helps to recall the immensely valuable services that money renders when it is working even half-way properly. It vastly facilitates the exchange of goods and services for one another. Indirect exchange through money takes place not only among people working in different sectors of the economy, but also over time. Through building up and drawing down cash balances and through credit transactions, people can arrange to receive what other people produce either before or after they deliver their own outputs. This inter-temporal aspect of money facilitates the pooling and mobilization of savings and so promotes real capital formation, which, like specialization, enhances productivity.

Money serves not only as the medium for exchange but also as the unit of account, the unit in which prices are quoted, bookkeeping accomplished, contracts written, debts expressed, subjective evaluations formulated, benefits and costs of activities appraised, prospective and past profits and losses estimated and recorded, and taxes levied. The vital roles of market prices, profits, and losses expressed in money received attention in the debates over socialist economic calculation initiated by Ludwig von Mises. When monetary disturbances require substantial changes in general levels of prices and wages, then, *whether or not* these changes occur promptly, the functions of prices, profits and losses in conveying signals and incentives suffer disruption. One notable glitch is the debt-deflation aspect of depression described by Irving Fisher (1933). More generally, comparable effects occur when price inflation or deflation turns out substantially greater or slighter than people had allowed for in their borrowing and lending and other plans. Previously scheduled debt and interest payments can become disruptively burdensome when debtors and so their creditors suffer disappointments of kinds other than or in addition to price-level or price-trend changes (recent US experience provides dramatic examples).

Money is potentially a 'loose joint', as Hayek has said (Garrison 1984), between decisions to produce and sell things on the one hand and decisions to buy them on the other hand. In accomplishing exchanges, people (and business firms) routinely receive payments into and make payments from *holdings* of money, a fact whose significance Mises well understood in developing his cash-balance approach to monetary theory (Mises 1912/1981). The sizes of cash balances desired are related to the sizes of people's expected inward and outward flows of payments (among other variables). If desired amounts of money exceed or fall short of actual amounts, people try to adjust their holdings by modifying their behaviour on the markets for goods and services and securities. As Mises wrote:

> A shortage of money means a difficulty in disposing of commodities for money. . . . Under the present organization of the market, which leaves a deep gulf between the marketability of money on the one hand and the marketability of other economic goods on the other hand, nothing but money enters into consideration at all as a medium of exchange.
>
> (1912/1981: 157)

Recent theories of the difficulty in making contact with potential trading partners help illuminate the familiar decline of the velocity of money in recessions (see the cited works of Clower, Leijonhufvud and Hall, and particularly Clower 1990: 82). With many desired transactions thwarted, people find themselves, more or less by default, holding more money than usual in relation to their incomes and expenditures. The grim business scene, together with uncertainty and precaution, counts against acting to get rid quickly of cash balances that would otherwise seem excessive.

In some ways, as just implied, an imbalance between the supply and demand of money is self-aggravating. More generally, supply and demand are kept in equilibrium less readily for money than for ordinary goods and services. Because money is the one thing routinely traded on all markets, its supply and demand do not confront each other on a market of its own and cannot be equilibrated with each other through a price adjustment of its own. Equilibrating processes do operate, but only indirectly over time and in a piecemeal manner through trials and errors in adjusting quantities and prices on innumerable specific markets. When an excess demand for money requires widespread cuts in prices and wages, sellers and wage negotiators in many or most of the markets for individual goods and services have reason to delay cuts of their own while waiting for a clearer reading on market conditions and waiting to see what other sellers – competitors, workers, suppliers – will do.

Rapid coping with monetary disequilibrium is difficult because knowledge about tastes, resources, production possibilities, exchange opportunities, money and credit conditions, and conditions in specific markets is scattered across millions of separate minds. Because the market is, among other things, a mechanism for conveying signals and incentives, it would be inconsistent both to recognize these functions yet to suppose (as the rational-expectations theorists nearly do) that transactors *already* have the knowledge that the price system is working to convey. The market process has no quick and easy substitute.

Mises repeatedly emphasized the delayed and nonuniform responses to money-supply changes (1912/1981: 162–3, where he cites observations of David Hume and John Stuart Mill; 1990: chapters 4–6). 'The essence of monetary theory is the cognition that cash-induced changes in the money relation affect the various prices, wage rates, and interest rates neither at the same time nor to the same extent' (1963: 555). Although Mises focuses his critical attention on money and credit expansion and its consequences, he recognizes the damage done to business when a credit expansion ceases (1963: 568): 'Deflation and credit contraction no less than inflation and credit expansion are elements disarranging the smooth course of economic activities' (1963: 567). Mises alludes to the damage done by deflation and credit restriction required by Britain's return to the prewar gold parity of its currency after both the Napoleonic wars and World War I (1963: 568).

THE TIME ELEMENT

Perhaps more so than other schools, Austrian economists grasp the significance of one banal fact: economic plans and activities stretch out over time. This is just one reason why price flexibility cannot keep markets continuously cleared. People cannot do everything at once; they cannot set all prices at the same time and revise all of them equally often. Long-term contracts fix some prices, and principal and interest on debt are in the nature of preset prices. A change in the general level of prices necessarily disrupts previous price relations.

A more general point is that coordination requires intertemporal as well as inter-industry meshing of plans and activities. Roger Garrison (1984) identifies the intersection of the 'market for time' and the 'market for money' as the subject matter of macroeconomics. Money is not the only Hayekian 'loose joint' in a self-equilibrating market system. A merely loose relation also holds between a definite assortment of capital goods and the subsequent demand for the corresponding consumer goods. This looseness permits macromaladies such as 'overinvestment' or 'underinvestment' or 'malinvestment'. Once committed to a certain course, people cannot 'instantaneously and costlessly change that commitment; thus the passage of time and its irreversibility are matters of paramount importance in understanding economic activity' (Laidler 1975: 5).

One link between the macro universals of time and money (so called by Garrison 1984) is that people hold money to cope with Keynes's 'dark forces of time and ignorance'. To the extent that they want to postpone consumption while keeping their options open about the timing and specific types and amounts of their future consumption, people can do so by holding financial claims, notably including money. Keeping options open is possible for individuals but is not possible for the economy as a whole (or is possible only to a lesser extent, through construction of versatile rather than highly specialized capital goods). Private attempts to do the socially impossible – keeping options open – epitomize the intertemporal 'loose joint'.

Fundamentalist Keynesianism worried about the separation of saving decisions from investment decisions. Since both types of decision concern the future, a saving/investment imbalance implies a lack of inter-temporal coordination. The interest rate (or whole array of rates) alone cannot ensure equilibrium between saving and investment, for interest is not the price of those two aggregate flow magnitudes. Instead it is the price of loans, broadly interpreted, or, better phrased, the price of 'waiting' performed through ownership of claims and other assets.

Imbalance between saving and investment implies monetary disequilibrium; yet the interest rate is not the equilibrator, either, of money's supply and demand. To understand the relation between saving, investment, and money, let us focus on the case of oversaving, seen as the pervasive deficiency of demand for currently produced or producible goods and services. As follows from the two-sided character of markets and of both actually accomplished and unsuccessfully attempted transactions, and as Walras's Law states, supply-and-demand imbalance for some things implies imbalance in the opposite direction for other things. (The aggregate value of all excess demand quantities, due account taken of algebraic sign, is identically equal to zero.) In the case considered, excess supply (negative excess demand) for currently produced goods and services implies (positive) excess demand for other things. What might this other thing or things be?

People who are trying to save (instead of fully spending their current incomes on consumption) are by that very token trying to acquire savings, which means real or financial assets. But which assets? If the savers themselves are buying labour and other resources to construct new capital goods, they are not contributing to any deficiency of current total spending. (Hindsight might later reveal the particular mix of capital goods constructed to be inappropriate, but that is a problem different from oversaving.) If, instead, savers are acquiring new stocks or bonds from issuers who use the monetary proceeds (the command over resources released from supplying current consumption) to construct capital goods, again no problem of oversaving arises. If savers are buying already existing physical assets or securities, the question shifts to what their sellers are trying to do with the proceeds. If those asset sellers are using the proceeds for consumption or new capital construction, again no oversaving occurs. If they are trying to shift wealth into other vehicles of saving, the question reappears of what these other vehicles might be: what is the item or items whose excess demand matches the deficiency of demand for currently produced goods and services?

How, furthermore, could the excess demand for this something persist? Consider how an initial or incipient excess demand might work itself out.

1 The quantity of the item might increase, as with automobiles and certain claims on financial–intermediary institutions.

2 Its price might rise or its yield (such as the interest rate paid on it) might fall, as with Old Masters, securities, and claims on financial intermediaries.

3 If its quantity and price are both rigid, frustrated demand for the item might divert itself onto other items, with macroeconomic consequences much the same as if the diverted demand had run in favour of the substitute goods in the first place.

4 For only one thing does none of these responses to excess demand operate and for which some quite different process must operate. That item is money, the actual medium of exchange. (Even nearmoneys can respond in quantity or price or yield.)

Under the current US monetary system, the quantity of money depends on the policy-determined stock of government base money and the circumstances represented in the textbook money-multiplier formula. Of the four supply-and-demand equilibrating mechanisms, number 1, the quantity response, is not free to work 'automatically' (not apart from monetary policy, as existing institutions do not allow the actual quantity to fully accommodate itself to changes in the demand for money at the existing price level). Mechanism 2, the price response, does not work because money lacks a price of its own. Mechanism 3, diversion of demand, does not work because money supply and demand do not confront each other and do not exhibit their imbalance on a specific market from which excess demand might be diverted. (Besides, what would diversion mean for the very medium of exchange itself?) Because money is the medium of exchange, excess demand for it is not clearly apparent. Everyone can obtain as much money as he thinks he can 'afford' to hold under his circumstances by restraining his purchases, if not by his eagerness in selling whatever he has for sale. (A depressed level of income does affect how much money people think they can 'afford'.) Market difficulties appear to pertain to sales of goods and services, not to money.

With none of mechanisms 1, 2, and 3 operating, the market process of re-equilibrating money's supply and demand has to be the roundabout process of adjusting innumerable prices and wages on the individual markets for goods and services. For reasons already noted, prices and wages cannot immediately jump to their new equilibrium level and pattern. Meanwhile, transactions, production, and employment suffer.

The supposed problem of oversaving boils down, then, to monetary disequilibrium. Unsurprisingly, what looks like oversaving – a general deficiency of demand posing an economy-wide impediment to transactions – is connected with the medium of exchange, which is also, in our current system, the medium in which prices are correctly or incorrectly set or adjusted or left unadjusted.

Suitable monetary institutions and policy would avoid macro discoordination of saving and investment and a general excess or deficiency in demand for current output. By themselves, however, they cannot ensure both that a proper share of current income is saved and devoted to capital formation and that resources are properly allocated among capital-construction projects by economic sectors and by degrees of remoteness from final consumption. Nothing can ensure such ideal results – and the very meaning of 'proper' in this context is unclear. People do not have perfect foresight, so some capital-construction projects are bound to turn out, in retrospect, to have been unwise, while others will turn out to have deserved greater emphasis. Furthermore, nothing guarantees that the proper share of income will be saved and invested or, in other words, that 'society' will discount the future at the proper rate. (These are inherently fuzzy concepts anyway; and again, it is pointless to blame reality for being real.)

Still, avoiding monetary disruption means avoiding a major obstacle to the functioning of the price system. Undistorted by monetary influences, the interest rate is free to play its coordinating role, along with other prices. A well-functioning price system allows people to use their own decentralized knowledge and judgments in allocating their resources between current consumption and investment to achieve greater future consumption. Monolithic central decisions that might turn out monstrously wrong are avoided. Entrepreneurs whose judgments turn out consistently sound will tend to acquire greater control over resource allocation than those whose judgments turn out consistently mistaken. Even if the inherited array of capital goods does prove at any time to be what hindsight deems a mistake – as it inevitably will to some extent – market signals and incentives will help promote an efficient use of this array. The bond and stock markets play a role in mobilizing information and in facilitating recombinations of the inherited complex of capital goods. A stable unit of account would aid these market processes and the economic calculation that they presuppose.

INSTITUTIONS

Not all of the foregoing is standard Austrian economics. It does fit in well, however, with several leading traits of the Austrian school: its emphasis on the coordination problem, its forthright perception of messy reality and the scope it leaves for entrepreneurial activities, and its putting money and time at the centre of macroeconomics. One further trait is an Austrian concern for institutions. It contrasts in this respect with the hyper-free-marketry of the new classical and real-business-cycle schools, which have cultivated analysis of abstract models uncontaminated by institutional detail. Austrians practise comparative–institutional analysis, which does not mean comparing the real world unfavourably with the Walrasian vision of general equilibrium. When told that reality is unsatisfactory in this or that respect, Austrians are inclined to ask: 'Unsatisfactory compared to what?' Like members of the

Public Choice school, Austrians know better than automatically to regard government as superior to private enterprise in accomplishing various tasks.

The aggregate-demand/aggregate-supply analysis still dominating the textbooks almost invites itchy-fingered attempts to fine tune the macro-economy. By contrast, the Austrians' concern with fine-grained specialization and the task of coordination directs attention to the question of what framework of institutions and more or less steady policies – institutionalized policies – can best facilitate the operation of market processes.

The Austrian concern with institutions shows up in the debate over economic calculation under socialism and capitalism and in discussions of monetary standards and monetary reforms. It shows up in the attention that Ludwig von Mises and Friedrich Hayek paid to history in their writings and conversations. Distinguishing sharply between theory and history, they warned against misconceiving economics as numerical aspects of recent (or earlier) economic history. Aware of how important and how changeable institutions are, Austrians are sceptical that a country's economic 'structure' can be pinned down econometrically in functions of stable form and with stable coefficients. As Austrians realize, nothing can fully substitute for the insights that history affords.

A DISAGREEMENT ABOUT BUSINESS CYCLE THEORY

My enthusiasm for Austrian strands of macroeconomics does not extend to the business-cycle theory propounded by Mises and Hayek more than 60 years ago. Austrian economists continue reciting it so widely in speech and print that one hardly knows where to begin or end with citations (see, however, Ebeling (1978) and, for fuller discussion, Yeager (1986: 378–82); Tullock (1988) renders another adverse judgment). Briefly, the theory attributes recession or depression to a preceding excessive expansion of money and credit. Perhaps responding to political pressures for lower interest rates (or resisting real developments tending to raise rates), the monetary authorities begin expanding bank reserves. Cheapened and more abundant credit suggests, falsely, that people have become more willing to save and free resources for investment projects. Firms respond by investing more ambitiously than before, especially in capital goods whose ripening into goods and services for the ultimate consumer will take a relatively long time. This large time element makes demands for higher-order capital goods relatively sensitive to the reduced interest rates.

Actually, the theory continues, resources freed for long-term-oriented investment have not become more abundant. Industries producing higher-order capital goods, lower-order (closer-to-the-consumer) capital goods, and consumer goods compete more intensely for resources. This becomes especially true as workers in the artificially stimulated industries, whose contributions to output of consumer goods are far from fruition, nevertheless

37

try to spend their increased incomes on current consumption. Sooner or later falsified appearances must bow to reality. Shortages or increased prices of resources necessary for completing capital-construction projects will force some of them to be abandoned. A tightening of credit, with loans no longer so easy to get and interest rates no longer so artificially low, may play a part in this return to reality; for money and credit expansion could not doggedly persist without threatening unlimited inflation. Workers are laid off from the abandoned projects and purchases of inputs for them are cancelled; the downturn is under way. Resources already embodied in those projects turn out to be at least partly wasted. In the ensuing depression, unwise projects are liquidated or restructured, and the wasteful misallocation of resources begins being remedied – belatedly and painfully.

Some such scenario appeals to Austrian economists who like to stress that money is not neutral and that its expansion exerts differential effects on individual prices, including interest rates, and on individual economic activities. A theory's appeal on quasi-methodological grounds is not the same thing, however, as evidence supporting it over rival accounts of boom and downturn. Furthermore, the Austrian theory hardly even purports to explain the ensuing recession or depression phase. Depression is a pervasive phenomenon, with customers scarce, output reduced, and jobs lost in most sectors of the economy. Depression can hardly be portrayed as an intersectoral struggle for resources exacerbated by distorted signals in interest rates and other prices. Austrian economists can explain this phase only lamely, mentioning maladjustments being worked out painfully over time – unless they go beyond their own distinctive theory by invoking the monetary factors of 'secondary deflation'.

The Austrian story, though conceivable, is incomplete yet unnecessarily specific. It tells how the injection of new money creates specific price distortions bringing specific responses, but it demonstrates neither their necessity nor their importance for the business downturn, let alone for the depression itself. The theory tacitly assumes an implausible susceptibility of business investors to being repeatedly fooled by policy-induced distortions in interest rates. In contrast, the monetary-disequilibrium story can handle the phenomena of boom and depression with less specific suppositions and with abundant support from theory and from qualitative and statistical history.

Austrians offer little evidence for their cycle theory beyond its supposed plausibility and its coherence with their methodological preferences. To my knowledge, the chief published exception to this statement is Charles Wainhouse's article of 1984. Using US data from 1959 to 1981, Wainhouse finds that expansions of money and credit do occur, do affect interest rates, do appear to affect output of producer goods, and do appear to be followed by temporary shifts in relative prices of goods far from and near to final consumption. He offers no empirical discussion, however, of actual business downturns and the ensuing recessions. He merely finds several facts consistent with Austrian theory.

However, innumerable facts are consistent with almost any theory. Wainhouse (1984) does not find, and as far as I know did not look for, evidence which might discriminate between the Austrian theory and its rivals. His findings are compatible, in particular, with monetary-disequilibrium theory. The specific Austrian scenario is not necessary to understand why demands for capital goods, particularly of higher orders, fluctuate more widely over the business cycle than demands for consumer goods and for investment goods close to final consumption. Monetary-disequilibrium theorists put less stress than the Austrians on shifts in the interest rate and relative prices not because they deny them but because such shifts are less central to their own account of the business cycle. Nor do the monetarists scorn capital theory, which they recognize as vital in dealing with important questions. When accounting for the phenomena of recession and depression, however, monetarists understandably emphasize the centrepiece of their story – a disequilibrium relation between the nominal quantity of money and the general level of prices and wages.

OPPORTUNITIES AND SUGGESTIONS

The current disarray in macroeconomics and the exaggerations of lately fashionable free marketry give Austrian economists an opportunity to earn the attention of the mainstream. In business-cycle theory, their broad time-and-money orientation holds more promise than the specific application of capital and interest theory criticized above, which may have seemed more plausible under certain past historical-institutional conditions than it is in general. Otherwise, Austrian macroeconomics has much in common – and could develop even more in common – with monetarism, with the works of Clower, Leijonhufvud, and Howitt, and even with New Keynesianism. (We should not be afraid of labels, which have been especially misapplied in recent years.)

Austrians have much to say about the absurdity of the undefined fiat US dollar, whose value rests precariously on nothing better than the changeable policies of the Federal Reserve, badgered from all sides with contradictory, changeable, and short-run-oriented advice. They have much to say about how this monetary anomaly abets irresponsible government, reflected in persistent budget deficits. It is unnecessary to identify sound money exclusively with a particular commodity standard of relatively brief historical duration. As Hayek and several younger Austrian economists have shown, several alternative monetary reforms are of great theoretical and practical interest.

Rising Austrian economists may well find dissertation topics in the areas of monetary history, monetary reform, alternative market institutions,[3] property rights, and institutional history. A search for historical episodes of macroeconomic disorder of *non*-monetary origin and character, whether or not any actually turn up, could be instructive. Going beyond preservation and transmission of cherished truths, Austrians can exploit their distinctive insights to help gain new knowledge and sounder public policy.

NOTES

1 Léon Walras did not postulate the auctioneer explicitly (not only can I not find the auctioneer in Walras's writings; I have been reassured on this point in conversation with Donald Walker, perhaps the leading expert on Walras in the United States). This auctioneer, a secretary of the market possessing prodigious informational and calculatory abilities, is an invention of interpreters concerned with making Walras's vision theoretically complete.
2 The Austrians' scorn for the neo-Walrasian brand of general-equilibrium theory is well known. Some Austrians might well focus their scorn better, however, than they habitually do.
3 Peter Howitt recommends studying how real-world institutions function very differently from the centralized Walrasian auction (1990: 51). He says that: 'Further progress will depend upon supplying institutional detail . . . including the inventory-holding, advertising, negotiating, inspection, and even price-quoting services of intermediaries and other market-making institutions of real life' (1990: 19).

REFERENCES

Brown, H.G. (1933) 'Nonsense and sense in dealing with the Depression', *Beta Gamma Sigma Exchange*, Spring: 97–107.
Clower, R.W. (1984) *Money and Markets*, Donald Walker (ed.), New York: Cambridge University Press.
——(1990) 'Keynes's General Theory: a contemporary perspective', *Greek Economic Review*, 12 (Supplement): 73–84.
Ebeling, R.E. (ed.) (1978) *The Austrian Theory of the Trade Cycle and Other Essays*, Washington, DC: Ludwig von Mises Institute. Reprinted 1983. (Reprinted in this booklet are essays by Ludwig von Mises (1936), Gottfried Haberler (1932), Murray N. Rothbard (1969), and Friedrich A. Hayek (1970).)
Eucken, W. (1950) *The Foundations of Economics*, trans. T. W. Hutchison, London: Hodge.
Fisher, I. (1993) 'The debt-deflation theory of great depressions', *Econometrica*, 1: 337–57.
Garrison, R.W. (1984) 'Time and money: the universals of macroeconomic theorizing', *Journal of Macroeconomics*, 6: 197–213.
Hall, R.E. (1991) *Booms and Recessions in a Noisy Economy*, New Haven: Yale University Press.
Hansen, G.D. and Prescott, E.C. (1993) 'Did technology shocks cause the 1990–1991 recession?', *American Economic Review*, 83: 280–6.
Hansen, G.D. and Wright, R. (1992) 'The labor market in real business cycle theory', Federal Reserve Bank of Minneapolis *Quarterly Review*, 16: 2–12.
Hayek, F.A. (1945) 'The use of knowledge in society', *American Economic Review*, 35: 519–30. Reprinted in Hayek, F.A. (1949) *Individualism and Economic Order*, chap. IV, London: Routledge & Kegan Paul.

Howitt, P. (1990) *The Keynesian Recovery and Other Essays*, Ann Arbor: University of Michigan Press.

Laidler, D.E.W. (1975) *Essays on Money and Inflation*, Chicago: University of Chicago Press.

Leijonhufvud, A. (1968) *On Keynesian Economics and the Economics of Keynes*, New York: Oxford University Press.

——(1981) *Information and Coordination*, New York: Oxford University Press.

——(1986) 'Whatever Happened to Keynesian Economics?', paper delivered at a conference on The Legacy of Keynes, Gustavus Adolphus College, Saint Peter, MN, 30 September and 1 October.

Lucas, R.E. Jr (1987) *Models of Business Cycles*, Yrjo Jahnsson Lectures, Oxford and New York: Basil Blackwell.

Mankiw, N.G. and Romer, R. (eds) (1991) *New Keynesian Economics*, 2 vols, Cambridge, MA: MIT Press.

Mises, L. von (1963) *Human Action*, revised edn, New Haven, CT: Yale University Press.

——(1981) *The Theory of Money and Credit*, first published 1912. This edition trans. by H. E. Batson (from 1934 edn), Indianapolis, IN: Liberty Classics.

——(1990) *Money, Method, and the Market Process*, selected by Margit von Mises, edited by Richard M. Ebeling, Auburn, AL and Norwell, MA: Ludwig von Mises Institute and Kluwer Academic Publishers.

Mitchell, W.C. (1966) *Gold, Prices and Wages Under the Greenback Standard* (first published 1908), Berkeley, CA: University of California Press, reprinted New York: Kelley.

O'Driscoll, G.P. Jr (1977) *Economics as a Coordination Problem*, Kansas City, KS: Sheed Andrews & McMeel.

Okun, A.M. (1981) *Prices and Quantities: A Macroeconomic Analysis*, Washington, DC: Brookings.

Romer, C.D. and Romer, D.H. (1989) 'Does monetary policy matter? A new test in the spirit of Friedman and Schwartz', National Bureau of Economic Research *Macroeconomics Annual*, 121–70, 170–83.

——(1990) 'New evidence on the monetary transmission mechanism', *Brookings Papers on Economic Activity*, 1: 149–98, 199–213.

Rothbard, M.N. (1957) 'In defense of "extreme apriorism"', *Southern Economic Journal*, 23: 314–20.

Stockman, A.C. (1988) 'Real business cycle theory: a guide, an evaluation, and new directions', Federal Reserve Bank of Cleveland *Economic Review*, 24 (4): 24–47.

Strongin, S. (1988) 'Real boats rock: monetary policy and real business cycles', Federal Reserve Bank of Chicago *Economic Perspectives*, 12: 21–8.

Tullock, G. (1988) 'Why the Austrians are wrong about depressions', *Review of Austrian Economics*, 2: 73–8.

Wainhouse, C.E. (1984) 'Empirical evidence for Hayek's theory of economic fluctuations', in B. N. Siegel (ed.) *Money in Crisis*, San Francisco, CA: Pacific Institute for Public Policy Research, 37–71.

Yeager, L.B. (1986) 'The significance of monetary disequilibrium', *Cato Journal*, 6: 369–99.

——(1994) 'Mises and Hayek on calculation and knowledge', *Review of Austrian Economics*, 7 (2): 93–109.

3

MONEY, ECONOMIC FLUCTUATIONS, EXPECTATIONS AND PERIOD ANALYSIS

The Austrian and Swedish economists in the interwar period

Richard M. Ebeling

In the mid-1970s, I once asked Fritz Machlup if any of the Swedish economists had ever visited Vienna in the 1920s or 1930s. He thought a moment and said, 'Yes, once Bertil Ohlin came for a visit, with his wife.' I then asked if he remembered anything of Ohlin's visit. Again, Machlup thought a moment, then he smiled and replied, 'His wife wore a very beautiful dress.' That seemed to be all that Fritz Machlup recalled of any Austrian–Swedish contacts in Vienna during the period between the wars.

In fact, the Austrians and the Swedes were closely connected during this period.[1] Indeed, their approaches originated from the same sources. In monetary and business-cycle theory, both schools viewed themselves as building on the contribution of Knut Wicksell, and, in turn, Wicksell built his own theory of money and production on the earlier writings of Eugen von Böhm-Bawerk. In 1911, Wicksell pointed out that even after reading all the critical evaluations of Böhm-Bawerk's theory of capital over the years

> my long-standing admiration for Böhm-Bawerk's achievement has not been diminished thereby . . . [I]t is now possible, so long after its appearance [*The Positive Theory of Capital*], to venture the statement that it is, and will remain, one of the milestones on the road to progress in political economy. It seems difficult to say anything about the general concept of capital or its mode of operation which is not to be found completely elucidated in that excellent and thought-provoking work.
>
> (Wicksell 1911b: 176, 178)

In turn, in the 1914 edition of *Capital and Interest*, Böhm-Bawerk referred complementarily to Wicksell's *Value, Capital and Rent* and his *Lectures on Political Economy* (Böhm-Bawerk 1959: 360, 476).

In 1912, in the preface to the first edition of *The Theory of Money and Credit*, Ludwig von Mises referred to Wicksell as one 'to be counted in the first line of those who developed the new ideas' most promising in the monetary and banking theory, though Mises believed that Wicksell's solutions were not entirely successful. Neither did he consider it an accident that Wicksell's 'work is standing on the foundations laid by Böhm-Bawerk's theory of capital and interest' (Mises 1924: x). Wicksell reviewed Mises' book two years after it was published. He believed that there were several grounds upon which to criticize it, but began the review by saying that 'This is a very studiously written, serious book'. He also pointed out to the reader that Mises 'follows very closely my views regarding the relationship between interest and capital prices' (Wicksell 1914: 197–9).

In the late 1920s and the 1930s, Wicksell's ideas were taken up by both Austrian and Swedish economists. The writings of members of these two schools, while in many ways parallel, were not identical. They asked many of the same questions, though their methods and conclusions were not always the same. In the 1930s they were both interested in understanding the processes and sequences of industrial fluctuations, but in ways that often differed in essentials from what, by the late 1930s and 1940s, came to be known as the Keynesian approach. The Austrian and Swedish approaches often overlapped because, in many of their writings, their starting point was the Austrian, or Böhm-Bawerkian, emphasis on the 'roundaboutness' of production and the time element in that roundabout process. The fact that production takes time leads to the concept of a 'period of production'. 'Waiting' for the period of production to be completed opens up analysis to consideration of the quantities and characteristics of the resources and commodities that are 'tied up' during the duration of the production period.

Once the analysis goes beyond the Crusoe level, questions begin to emerge concerning the degree to which the investment and savings plans of interdependent transactors are consistent with each other during the waiting period. The analytical horizon opens for inquiring as to what the market conditions are for intertemporal plan coordination, what may cause discoordination of intertemporal plans and, if such plans do not match, what the sequential effects and consequences may be of the adjustment process that leads (perhaps) back to a condition of coordinated plans. Thus, what became the distinctive hallmarks in much of the writings of both the Austrian and the Swedish schools during this period were what came to be known as 'period analysis', 'plan analysis' and 'process analysis'.

BÖHM-BAWERK AND KNUT WICKSELL

For Böhm-Bawerk, causality controls all the processes in the world in which man lives. If he is to control or reshape his world to fit his purposes, man must understand the laws of causality and make his actions conform to them. He can then use those laws to serve his own ends. One of the fundamental laws, Böhm-Bawerk argued, was the greater productivity (other things held given) of processes that are more 'roundabout'. Looking at the production process from a technological point of view, every product that comes into existence has its beginning centuries ago.

> The boy who whittles a willow whistle with his pocket knife is, strictly speaking, only continuing an operation begun by the miner who centuries ago dug the first shovelful of earth for the sinking of the mine shaft that was used to bring up the iron for the blade of the boy's pocket knife.
>
> (Böhm-Bawerk 1959)

But to give to each of these long-gone steps in the production process their proper weight, Böhm-Bawerk invents his notion of an 'average period of production'. It is meant to measure the average time interval between the expenditure of the first primary factors of production and the point at which a finished product is valuable for use. The average period of production is Böhm-Bawerk's *backward-looking* estimate of the period of time over which physical inputs have been invested for the production of a finished commodity. The longer the average period of production, the more 'roundabout' the production process (*ibid.*: 3–15, 85–8).

The period of production also has an economic meaning for Böhm-Bawerk, defined by the constraint of available savings. For production there must be capital, but capital has several meanings. In Böhm-Bawerk's schema, capital is defined as intermediary or produced means of production. They come into existence, are maintained, replaced or increased only through the application of the primary means of production: resources and labour. Resources and labour must be shifted from their potential use for immediate satisfaction and be directed, instead, for the making of capital goods. Resources must also be applied for the manufacturing of consumption goods for those whose labour (along with resources and the produced means of production) will be applied during the production period, at the end of which the finished product (resulting from their endeavours) will be available for sale and use. Consequently, part of the savings available for investment is an advance of present goods to workers during the period of production (*ibid.*: 95–101).

In the aggregate, the chosen investment projects which may be undertaken, with their respective periods of production, are limited by the available savings to successfully sustain and maintain them. The amount of savings will depend upon the subjective valuations of the participants in the market concerning prospective gain (in terms of the value of the future greater productive output) relative to the cost of deferring the use of factors of production that could otherwise be utilized in the present for current consumption. The rate of interest emerges from the interaction of people's time preferences (*ibid.*: 290–341). Thus, the rate of interest acts as the 'break' on which of the alternative investment projects are undertaken and therefore on the selected time horizons out of the technologically possible periods of production.

Böhm-Bawerk argues that the plans of market participants are intertemporally coordinated and modified through changes in the interest rate and cost of factors of production used in investment projects containing different production periods. If savings were to increase, the demand for final goods would decrease (or in a growing economy, would not increase to the level that would have been possible if all the additional higher real income had been devoted to consumption). The corresponding decline in the interest rate would increase the present value of investment projects with longer time horizons and this would, in turn, bring about a change in the relative prices for factors of production; their prices would decline in those activities with a shorter time horizon and rise in those with longer time horizons. The allocation of factors of production among projects with alternative production periods is determined by their relative prices, and these reflect their value in alternative investment projects. The profitability of these investment projects and their corresponding periods of production are limited by the interest rate, and this reflects the time preferences of the market agents who evaluate the attractiveness of future goods over present goods (*ibid.*: 112–15).[2]

Wicksell used Böhm-Bawerk's capital theory as a framework for pursuing his own problem of the distinction between 'natural' and 'money' rates of interest. Wicksell argues that in a condition of barter where present goods trade both for each other and for future goods, there would be a tendency for market forces to establish an interest rate that balances the supply and demand for real capital.

> The rate of interest at which the demand for loan capital and the supply of savings exactly agree and which more or less corresponds to the expected yield on the newly created capital, will then be the normal or natural real rate.
>
> (Wicksell 1911a: 193)[3]

If, instead, money (rather than goods directly) is loaned at an equivalent rate of interest, money would then be serving as 'nothing more than a cloak' over a process that could, conceptually, have been carried out just as easily without it (Wicksell 1898: 104; 1911a: 193).

However, the intercession of money into the intertemporal exchange process does make a difference:

> [W]e are concerned with precisely what occurs, in the first place, with the middle link in the final exchange of one good against another,

which is formed by the demand of money for goods and the supply of goods against money.

(Wicksell 1911a: 159)

In the monetary economy, 'Liquid real capital (i.e. goods) are never lent . . . it is money which is lent, and the commodity capital is then sold in exchange for this money.' In Wicksell's view, 'It is not, as is often supposed, merely the form of the matter that is just altered, but its very essence' (Wicksell 1898: xxvi, 135).

Since money is lent, and not real capital, the monetary authority is able to increase the supply of money available for lending and to lower the money interest rate. Anticipated yields or profits on potential investments will now seem greater than before the fall in the money rate, meaning that at the margin production projects will appear attractive to undertake that did not at the previous higher money rate of interest (Wicksell 1898: 89; 1911a: 186). However, not all types of investment are affected equally by the change in the interest rate. Those with longer time horizons will be influenced to a greater degree because of the present value effect (Wicksell 1898: 91–2, 143, 149, 155; 1911a: 195–6). To analyse the consequences from a divergence between the natural and money rates of interest, Wicksell constructs two models.

In Wicksell's first model, the period of production is one year for all firms. At the beginning of the year, entrepreneurs borrow money from capitalists (indirectly through a bank). The borrowed funds are then dispersed to the factors of production as money income, and the money income is used to purchase commodities during the year from commodity dealers (whom Wicksell assumes to be the capitalists). At the end of the year, entrepreneurs sell their finished output to the capitalist dealers for a sum just sufficient to repay the principal and interest on their loans, and the interest payments are assigned to the respective accounts held by the capitalists at the bank (Wicksell 1898: 137–41).[4]

A fall in the money rate of interest, due to a monetary expansion, induces an attempt by entrepreneurs to expand output. Money wages and other factor prices begin to rise as entrepreneurs bid against each other for scarce means of production, with the additional money borrowed at the lower rate.[5] If, as Wicksell assumes, entrepreneurs have expectations that the final goods prices at the end of the period will be the same as at the beginning of the period, factor bidding can only go as far as the fall in the interest rate has increased the anticipated profit margins, and competition among entrepreneurs will, in fact, eliminate those anticipated gains. Entrepreneurial disappointments, however, will be reversed when, at the end of the one-year production period, they are surprised to find that the money prices for their goods are also higher (assuming that money demand for final output rises in proportion to the increase in factor incomes). In the next period, with all factor and final output prices having risen proportionally, and assuming the monetary authorities continue to follow the same policy, entrepreneurs will once again face a situation in which the money rate of interest is below the equilibrium 'natural' rate (with entrepreneurs taking the present prices as their expectations for the coming period). This sets in motion Wicksell's cumulative process (Wicksell 1898: 141–9).[6]

In this one-year production period, all changes are purely nominal effects. However, Wicksell then constructs a second two-year production period model. Now, when the money rate of interest is lowered, the capitalization effect creates a higher profitability for investment products requiring two years for completion instead of one. Resources are drawn into two-year investment projects from one-year production processes. This results in less finished output at the end of the first year and, due to their greater scarcity, consumer prices now rise. Entrepreneurs successfully complete their two-year investment projects, at which point a greater quantity of goods is available on the consumer market.

In this second model, *real* as well as *nominal* changes are set in motion. Based on the lower money rate of interest, entrepreneurs begin two-year investment projects in excess of the planned savings of consumers. The incompatibility between them becomes evident when, at the end of the first year, consumers demand a larger portion of final output than has been provided for. Consumers are 'forced' to save via the higher consumer goods prices, and the entrepreneurs are able to successfully complete their two-year period of production. No mechanism is suggested by Wicksell as to how the disappointed consumer spending plans, which materialized through higher final output prices, could in any way bring about a negative feedback on to entrepreneurial investment decisions. All that Wicksell offers is the possibility that when the two-year investments are finished, consumers may benefit from their forced savings through the availability of a greater quantity of final products at that point in time (Wicksell 1898: 155–6).

LUDWIG VON MISES

Ludwig von Mises' *The Theory of Money and Credit* interweaves several theoretical schemata. His first task is to develop a theory of the value of money that overcomes the 'Austrian circularity' problem. He does this through his 'regression theorem' and, at the same time, he also derives the demand for money in the context of a 'cash balance' approach.[7] Mises' second task is to develop a theory of variations in the value of money, which he does by elaborating a theory of the non-neutrality of money. His third task is to develop a theory of fiduciary media (or money substitutes) on the basis of which he then uses Böhm-Bawerk's capital theory and Wicksell's theory of the natural and money rates of interest to present a theory of the business cycle (Ebeling 1985: 35–59).

For Mises, there is no dichotomy between the structure of relative prices and the general purchasing power of money (or the general 'price level'). In his view, money has no single price on the market. Instead, the value or purchasing power of money is represented by the set or array of exchange ratios between the monetary unit and all the goods against which money trades on the market (Mises 1953: 216).[8] Any change in the structure of relative prices necessarily means a change in the general exchange value, or purchasing power, of the monetary unit – as represented by that array of exchange ratios between the money and market commodities. At the same time, any change in the general value of money involves a change in the structure of relative prices, because it is only through changes in the individual supplies and demands for goods that market participants can demonstrate any changes in their desire to demand or supply money (the interaction and equilibrium between which establishes the value of money).

Mises' theory of the non-neutrality of money is a sequence, or process, analysis. Consistent with his strict adherence to methodological individualism, Mises argues that any change in the conditions of the demand for or supply of money always originates in the circumstances of the individual participants on the market. Their changed circumstances are transmitted to the market through modifications in their respective demands for or supplies of specific goods (Mises 1928: 95–103; 1953: 160–8). Mises' classic examples are of increases in the supply of money:

> The additional quantity of money does not find its way at first into the pockets of all individuals; not every individual of those benefited first gets the same amount and not every individual reacts to the same additional quantity in the same way. Those first benefited – in the case of gold, the owners of the mines, in the case of government paper money, the treasury – now have greater cash holdings and they are now in a position to offer more money on the market for goods and services they wish to buy. The additional amount of money offered for them on the market makes prices and wages go up. But not all the prices and wages rise, and those which do rise do not rise to the same degree . . . Thus, price changes which are the result of the inflation start with some commodities and services only, and are diffused more or less slowly from one group to the others. It takes time till the additional quantity of money has exhausted all its price changing possibilities. But even in the end the different commodities are not affected to the same extent. The process of progressive depreciation has changed the income and the wealth of the different social groups. As long as this depreciation is still going on, as long as the additional quantity of money has not yet exhausted all its possibilities of influencing prices, as long as there are still prices left unchanged at all or not yet changed to the extent that they will be, there are in the community some groups favoured and

some at a disadvantage. Those selling the commodities or services whose prices rise first are in a position to sell at the new higher prices and to buy what they want to buy at the old still unchanged prices. On the other hand, those who sell commodities or services whose prices remain for some time unchanged are selling at the old prices whereas they have to buy at the new higher prices . . . As long as the inflation is in progress, there is a perpetual shift in income and wealth from some social group, to other social groups. When all price consequences of the inflation are consummated, a transfer of wealth between social groups has taken place. The result is that there is in the economic system a new dispersion of wealth and income and in this new social order the wants of individuals are satisfied to different relative degrees, than formerly. Prices in this new order can not simply be a multiple of the previous prices.

(Mises 1940a: 72–3)

Mises' theory of the business cycle is a particular application of this temporal-sequence theory of the non-neutrality of money. Accepting the Böhm-Bawerkian framework, Mises argues that the degree of roundaboutness is determined by the point at which investment profitability at the margin is tending to equality with the prevailing natural interest rate; that is the point at which the periods of production which are undertaken and which are profitable to undertake are sustainable on the basis of the amount of savings available in the economic community. Lowering the money rate of interest below the natural rate acts as the inducement for undertaking longer, more roundabout periods of production. Factors of production, as a consequence, are drawn into these more roundabout projects. However, Mises takes issue with Wicksell at this point. Wicksell presented his thesis under the assumption that, if projects of a two-year duration were to supplant some of the one-year investment projects, the smaller quantity of consumer goods at the end of the first year merely raises their prices, with no change in consumer goods available until the end of the second year. Mises, however, sees a self-reversing set of forces that may come into work.

Consistent with his emphasis on the wealth and income redistributive effects that a monetary expansion tends to generate, Mises argues that, as the lowering of the money interest rate results from an expansion of bank credit, there may be shifts in wealth between social groups, and specifically from those with lower to those with higher saving preferences. This can bring about a situation in which some of the longer roundabout processes may be sustainable, since the redistribution of income and wealth has been in such a direction that some of the additional savings needed to sustain them have been generated through money's non-neutral impacts on members of the society (Mises 1928: 126–7; 1953: 384–8).

But while this may occur to one degree or another, Mises argues that the rise in the factor money incomes during the expansionary process will usually tend to put upward pressure on the price of consumer goods. The increased money demand for final goods and services will now reverse the profitabilities of investment projects, from those with longer periods of production to those with shorter periods of production. The scarcity of the factors of production must mean that if one sector of the economy is to utilize more of them, other sectors will have less factors available for use.[9] The longer, more roundabout investment projects are not all completed (as Wicksell assumed they would be in his two-period model). Rather, the scarcity of resources precludes the satisfying of the demand for present goods (as reflected in the actual savings/consumption ratio of income earners) and the plans of entrepreneurs undertaking these more roundabout projects. This, in Mises' view, is the basis for the emergence of the 'crisis' point of the business cycle (Mises 1928: 118–30; 1953: 396–404). The longer the period during which monetary expansion has continued and the money rate has been kept below the natural rate, the more severe may be the crisis:

> The greater this additional quantity of fiduciary money, the more factors of production have been firmly committed in the form of investments which appeared profitable only because of the artificially reduced interest rate and which prove to be unprofitable now that the interest rate has again been raised. Great losses are sustained as a result of misdirected capital investments. Many new structures remain unfinished. Others, already completed, close down operations. Still others are carried on because, after writing off losses which represent a waste of capital, operation of the existing structure pays at least something.
>
> (Mises 1928: 129–30)

The money rate of interest is pressured upwards back towards what would now be the relevant 'natural rate', not only because of the rising demand for present goods, but also because of the emerging inflation premium on interest rates. While critical of Irving Fisher's version of the quantity theory of money, Mises did endorse his theory of the influence of inflation expectations on the nominal, or money, rate of interest. Thus, as the general value of money declines, creditors demand compensation for the anticipated depreciation of the purchasing power of lent funds during the period of the loans (Mises 1928: 93–5; 1953: 225–34). If the monetary authority continues to increase the supply of fiduciary media in an attempt to maintain or increase the number of roundabout projects inconsistent with the actual real supply of savings, the increasing demand for present goods and the emerging inflation premium may be delayed or prevented from fully returning the rate of interest to the appropriate natural rate. The price of such a policy would be an unending inflationary spiral with the potential to eventually destroy the monetary system. Mises was convinced that he had presented a complete theory of the business cycle (Mises 1940b: 110).[10]

GUNNAR MYRDAL AND ERIK LINDAHL

In the interwar period, several Swedish economists took up the Wicksellian theme. This chapter focuses on two of the leading Swedish figures during this time, Gunnar Myrdal and Erik Lindahl. Both devoted attention to the problems of 'periods', 'plans' and expectations.

When, in 1926, Bertil Ohlin contributed an essay on 'Tendencies in Swedish economics', for a festschrift in honour of Lujo Brentano (a leading member of the German historical school), no mention was given to the role of expectations in economic analysis. Instead, he held that the focus of Swedish economic thought in the years following World War I had been the refinement of the existing body of 'marginalist' equilibrium theory, the application of theory to contemporary and historical situations, and debates over Wicksell's analysis of the influence of change in the money interest rate on prices in general (in light of the great inflations experienced during and after the war). He suggested that the next step in the development of economics would be a 'description of a time-consuming process, the real dynamics of economic science' (Ohlin 1927: 343–63).

The shift in emphasis apparently occurred a year later, in 1927, with the publication of Gunnar Myrdal's dissertation, *The Problem of Price Formation and Change*. Economic dynamics had two tasks, he argues. The first concerned an analysis of the sequential process by which one 'price situation is transformed into another price situation' due to the fact that any change in the 'data' and market prices during one period would be the causal elements in influencing new pricing configurations in following periods. Thus, a study of the forces creating a pricing pattern at a *moment of time* would give directional meaning to price movements *over time*. The task concerned an analysis of expectations, for it is expectations held about future events at a moment in time that would determine the present prices prevailing on the market. Since the sequence of price movements was dependent upon the expectations held at various points over the time sequence, 'an investigation of the former problem [price movements over time] requires the latter [formation of expectations over time] to be solved' (Lindahl 1929: 89–91).[11]

The next development of this train of thought came in Myrdal's *Monetary Equilibrium* (1939).[12] Myrdal says there were two primary purposes behind his analysis: first, to determine the conditions of a 'non-cumulative price situation', that is a position of equilibrium in which money serves as an intermediary for both present and intertemporal exchanges; second, to 'include anticipations in the monetary system', because it is discrepancies between actual and expected values in the market that are the source of the economic disturbances usually associated with a Wicksellian-type cumulative process. The tool Myrdal believed appropriate for analysing divergences between real and anticipated events is the distinction between *ex ante* and *ex post* (Myrdal 1939: 30–2, 47).

Wicksell laid down three requirements for a monetary equilibrium:

1 the natural rate was the rate of interest at which the marginal technical productivity of real capital equalled the money rate
2 the supply of and the demand for savings were equal
3 the price level (as measured in terms of consumer goods) was 'stable'.[13]

For the first condition – the equating of the marginal technical productivity of real capital to the money rate of interest – Myrdal shows that once there is more than one factor of production, it is necessary to express the relationships between the factors in value terms. However, when so expressing marginal productivities in value terms, the next step is to realize that the only relevant value expressions for capital-investment decision making are 'anticipated values'. Because it is 'expected profitability of an undertaking' which 'is decisive for entrepreneurs' programmes, not the profitability actually experienced during a past period'. The latter is important only 'indirectly as evidence of future profitability'. In equilibrium, the expected rate of profit on real investment must equal the money rate of interest for each firm, otherwise any *ex post* positive (negative) discrepancies between the two rates would, in the next *ex ante* period, set off a cumulative expansion (contraction) in economic activities, as entrepreneurs' actions tend to bring the two rates back to equality (Myrdal 1939: 49–68).

The second Wicksellian condition stated that, in equilibrium, the rate of interest must equalize the supply of and demand for saving. Since in non-stationary conditions the distinction between merely replacing existing capital and new investment becomes hazy, Myrdal reformulates the thesis in more general terms. Here:

> the money rate is normal, i.e., at its 'natural level', if it brings about an equality between gross real investment on the one side and saving plus total anticipated value-change of the real capital . . . on the other side.

These first two conditions, when they hold, assure that a cumulative process would not occur (Myrdal 1939: 95–6).

Cumulative processes can occur, Myrdal argues, under any of three conditions:

1 Where expectations of entrepreneurs rise (fall), with a given money rate of interest. With an elastic currency system, more (less) funds will be borrowed and incomes will rise (fall). This will result in higher (lower) prices for consumer goods and the raising (lowering) of profit expectations.

2 Where, given entrepreneurial expectations, the money rate of interest falls (rises). The rate of profit expected would tend to increase (decrease), again stimulating (retarding) investment. Incomes would rise (fall), with consumer goods prices then rising (falling) soon after, tending to reinforce the optimistic (pessimistic) expectations.

3 Where savings increased (decreased) but the rate of interest did not quickly adjust to reflect the new underlying conditions, consumer demand would have fallen (increased), lowering (raising) prices and profit margins that could be expected. Entrepreneurial investment activity would decline (expand), incomes would fall (rise) and consumption demand would fall (increase) even further, thus reinforcing the initial change (Myrdal 1939: 101–12).

As for Wicksell's third equilibrium condition (that the rate of interest must be such that the 'price level' is kept 'stable'), Myrdal argues that if the 'equilibrium price relations . . . are fulfilled, any movement of the absolute money prices consistent with them will leave monetary equilibrium undisturbed' (*ibid.*: 132). Equilibrium requires appropriate relative prices, and as long as relative prices are 'correct' and retained, the 'price level' and its height is secondary. However, as a practical matter Myrdal also says changes in the 'price level' can disturb the equilibrium price relationships if all prices, particularly wages, do not show easy and smooth flexibility. A falling price level in which some prices, such as wages, did not decline to the appropriate degree would degenerate cost–price discrepancies that would disturb monetary equilibrium. His conclusion was that 'A monetary policy aimed to preserve the equilibrium relations must . . . adapt the flexible prices to the absolute level of the sticky ones' if there was a danger of falling prices (*ibid.*: 134–5).

Finally, there is Myrdal's analysis of *ex ante* and *ex post* and their relation to 'periods'. For accounting purposes, *ex post,* there must always be a balance between savings and investment, but there is no reason for the *ex ante* savings and investment decisions to balance, and it will be the *ex ante* calculations and plans that will always be 'driving the dynamic process forward' (*ibid.*: 45–6). *Ex ante* calculations relate to the point in time at which they are made and to a period of time for which the calculation and plan is constructed. Any full analysis would contain two parts: an analysis of plans and expected values at one point in time, which are then compared with the *ex post* values at another point at the end of the specified period; and an analysis of the development of events between these two points in time, which are the factors that would generate a discrepancy between the *ex ante* estimates and the *ex post* results. A focus on the *ex ante* plans at the beginning of the period highlights the 'tendencies which must be studied as a preparatory step to the dynamic analysis proper which refers to the causal development in time up to the next point studied' (*ibid.*: 44–5, 54).

Our critical remarks will focus on three points: the meaning of 'periods' in Myrdal's approach; his analysis of investment patterns in the cumulative process; and his assumptions about the 'neutrality' of price level movements in the face of flexible prices and wages. First, concerning Myrdal's 'periods'.[14] His comparison of the *ex ante* plans with the *ex post* results set rigid limitations on consumption and production decisions during the period. All plans for the coming period – investment, production and consumption plans – must be made at the same moment at the beginning and must extend over the entire period. None of these plans can be revised during the period so that, for instance, what may happen during the first half of the period is not allowed to influence or modify any of the plans for the second half. Thus, what Myrdal constructs is not actually a sequence or process analysis through periods of time, but an analysis of outcomes in comparison to expectations that may change plans between periods.

When Myrdal outlines Wicksell's schema, he emphasizes that an integral aspect of the cumulative process is the shifting of factors of production from shorter to longer time-consuming investments. Indeed, he goes so far as to state that the

> shift in production thus brought about is the essential and necessary change keeping the cumulative process going as long as there is the drive for capital values enhanced by a discrepancy between the money rate of interest and the 'natural rate'.

> (Myrdal 1939: 26)

Yet, in his own exposition of the cumulative process, Myrdal almost totally ignores this influence, discussing instead the incentives for investment in general by emphasizing the larger rate of profit available. The essential ingredient in Wicksell's sequence of events – based as it is on Böhm-Bawerk's theory of roundaboutness – is that interest rate changes do not affect the profitability of all investments equally, i.e., changes in the money rate of interest can influence the structure of production because of the increased profitability of investments possessing a longer 'time-shape'.[15] Parts of Myrdal's analysis, therefore, collapse into a simple 'derived demand' process. Changes in expectations about the demand for consumer goods either stimulate or retard investment demand, *in general*. The Wicksell–Mises approach, on the other hand, recognized the influence of changes in and expectations about consumer goods, but offered a richer analysis precisely by pointing out that not all investment activities would be affected in the same way or to the same degree, and that as a result the 'structure of production' would be modified during and inseparable from the cumulative process.

Finally, there is Myrdal's assumption that as long as institutional rigidities did not prevent wages and prices from changing so as to maintain 'equilibrium values', monetary policies that 'stabilized' the 'price level' or moved it in a particular direction need have no distortive effect. This would be true under either of two conditions:

- all changes in aggregate monetary expenditures to influence the 'price level' occur proportionally and simultaneously in all sectors of the economy (thus assuring that money was 'neutral' in terms of the structure of relative prices)
- while a change in aggregate monetary expenditures does not affect the various sectors simultaneously, expectations on the part of the market participants are such that each one can correctly anticipate when, how and to what extent the change in monetary expenditure will impinge on his respective activities, so each individual is able to successfully distinguish 'real' from 'monetary' forces at work, and adjust market actions accordingly.

As neither of these two conditions is likely ever to be present, monetary policies that change the aggregate expenditure streams will necessarily affect the structure of relative prices – even when the policy goal is only 'price level' stabilization.

In *Monetary Equilibrium*, Gunnar Myrdal gave credit to Erik Lindahl for being one of the first to 'give a more systematic representation of certain parts of Wicksell's monetary theory' (Myrdal 1939: 7). In his early studies, *The Aims of Monetary Policy* (1929) and *Methods of Monetary Policy* (originally published 1930, reproduced in Lindahl 1939), Lindahl offered an extended elaboration of Wicksell's cumulative process by postulating alternative assumptions about perfect and imperfect knowledge, production periods and the existence of full or less-than-full employment, as well as the consequences of pursuing various 'price level' goals. In his later monograph, 'The dynamic approach to economic theory', Lindahl developed his more detailed theory of 'period' and 'plan' analysis (see Lindahl 1939).[16]

In both the earlier and later expositions, a common assumption is the idea of

periods of time so short that the factors directly affecting prices, and therefore also the prices themselves, can be regarded as unchanged in each period. All such changes are therefore assumed to take place at the transition points between periods.

Prices in these 'short periods' are set at the beginning of the period and supply and demand are determined by them (*ibid.*: 158–9).[17]

We will first consider Lindahl's analysis in his 1930 study. Following Wicksell, Lindahl emphasizes that, if starting from a position of equilibrium, the money rate of interest is lowered, there 'will be an increase in all capital values, which will of course be proportionally greater for relatively long-term investments than for relatively short-term ones' (Lindahl 1939:

164). The actual working of the cumulative process, he continues, will depend upon the subsidiary assumptions.

For our purposes we will consider two of Lindahl's cases, those that start with full employment and others that begin with idle resources. Under conditions of full employment, the lowering of the money rate of interest brings about a

> lengthening of the investment period which is now profitable . . . Factors of production will be transferred from direct production of consumption goods to the production of capital goods, the relative prices of which have increased. And in the capital goods industries the newly constructed equipment will be more durable than the old while the production process will itself occupy a longer period.
>
> (Lindahl 1939: 170–1)

Furthermore, the shift of resources to capital goods production will tend to reduce the supply of consumer goods; the prices of consumer goods will begin to rise because of the smaller supply and because of the higher money demand for goods due to the additional income generated via the borrowing at the lower money rate. The rising consumer prices raise entrepreneurial expectations further 'since capital values are partly determined by the anticipated prices of consumer goods' (*ibid.*: 171). The savings necessary to enable longer production processes to be undertaken is obtained through 'forced savings': the bidding of resources towards investment activity lowers the supply of consumer goods and 'forces' consumers to consume less (at higher prices) than they would if the lower money rate of interest had not acted as an investment stimulus (*ibid.*: 173–6). The cumulative process continues as long as the money rate is kept below the natural rate.

The other alternative is to assume that initially unemployed resources are available. The sequence of events will depend upon where in the economy the unemployed factors are located. If unemployment is in the capital goods sectors, the unemployed will be absorbed into investment activity, without having to diminish the supply of consumer goods. But consumer goods prices will still tend to rise because a given quantity of consumer goods will now be demanded by a larger work force. If resources are mobile between the consumer goods and capital goods sectors, when all idle resources have been finally absorbed in the investment sector, input factors will, finally, be bid away from consumer goods industries and consumer goods prices will rise even further as their supply diminishes.

If unemployment is initially in the consumer goods sectors, greater investment activity will result in a transfer of some of those unemployed factors into capital goods production; but as consumer goods demand begins then to rise, the prices for final output need not rise significantly at first, since the idle factors can be used to expand supply. Only when all unemployed resources are finally utilized will the continuing transfer of factors to capital goods production result in significant price increases for consumer goods.

Finally, if unemployment exists in both investment and consumer goods sectors, both will be able to expand, with the upward pressure on prices initially slowed. When one or the other becomes fully employed, the sequence of events will follow along the lines of the previous two cases (Lindahl 1939: 169–79). A money rate of interest above the 'natural' rate would set in motion a reverse set of events, with the additional complications that may arise from any wage or price rigidities that might prevail (*ibid.*: 183–6).

We see that in this early 1930 study, Lindahl had an income–expenditure framework; income is generated through the sale of factor services and influenced by the terms at which funds can be borrowed on the loan market. Earned income is then translated into savings and consumption expenditures in which it is discovered that the savings and consumption patterns of factor-income earners is incompatible with the attempts of entrepreneurs to carry through with various investment plans. The income–expenditure pattern, however, is also linked with the distribution of the real factors among their alternative uses and the effect of that distribution on the availability of consumer goods. In other words, Lindahl attempts to contain in one analysis both the *patterns of monetary expenditures* that appear as incomes with the *patterns of resource allocations* that generate those incomes. What is found to be insistent is the *ex post* availability of consumer goods in relation to capital goods, compared to the *ex ante* planned expenditures stream on consumer goods. This *ex ante–ex post* incompatibility has been caused by the way in which the real factors were initially allocated in the structure of production.

In his 1939 monograph, 'The dynamic approach to economic theory', Lindahl directs his attention to the changing pattern of plans and actions due to disappointed *ex post* results. The analysis attempts to explain future changes in planned actions in a determinant fashion based upon events in past and future periods. Lindahl argues that if we know the respective plans of the individuals at the beginning of the period; if we know how the individuals would change their plans under different future conditions; and if we have the knowledge of external conditions so that we know what events will impinge on individuals and make them revise their plans in particular ways, 'then it should be possible to provide a theoretical construction of the developments that will be the outcome of the initial position' (*ibid.*: 37–8).

A theory of planning is developed in which it is shown how present period plans act as constraints on future choices, while at the same time the different successful steps in each imagined plan would open future options that the alternative plans might exclude. Lindahl summarizes his approach in the following way: 'The dynamic process is divided into fairly short time periods, e.g., a day. All decisions about the business and consumption plans to be adopted, and all price changes, take place at the transition points between these periods.' For example, at the beginning of the 'day' sellers set their prices. Entrepreneurs and consumers combine this price information with their expectations of the future profitability or anticipated utility from alternative courses of action. They choose the ones that offer the highest returns, entrepreneurs proceed to purchase factors of production and consumers to buy various finished commodities. At the end of the 'day' each individual sums up his experiences based on the outcome of the period just passed (of either unexpected unsold inventories or unexpected orders in excess of supply), then sets the prices for the next 'day', given the quantities each now decides to supply (*ibid.*: 62–3).

A dynamic, ongoing process is thus created in which past period events influence present period expectations and plans, and, in turn – depending upon the compatibility of the interpersonal plans – set up the conditions under which future plans in future periods will have to be revised. Lindahl assumes no tendency for interpersonal plan coordination or equilibrium. Instead there is only a sequence of periods in which there may be temporary equilibrium or a pattern of disequilibrium situations. If equilibrium occurs it happens only 'sporadically' (*ibid.*: 64–9).

In the earlier 1930 study, Lindahl attempted to unify an analysis of expenditure patterns with an analysis of the pattern of the distribution of the factors of production. However, in this later monograph the focus shifts almost completely to income and expenditure flows during periods, and to their influence on changes in planned pricing and quantities supplied in the next 'short period'. Gone is any concern with the 'time-shape' of the structure of production and its importance for the stream of available goods *over periods*.[18]

A cumulative process in this new framework would take the general (and rather superficial) form of an excessive increase in aggregate money demand for quantities available at present period prices. The next period would see a rising of prices and the cumulative process would be continuing if, at these higher prices, money demands again exceed the quantities demanded. In terms of the Wicksellian framework that Lindahl used in 1930, this later approach passes over without discussion of the very elements of the cumulative process that Wicksell considered to be crucial.

Finally, while claiming to offer a more realistic analysis of dynamic processes, it is important to remember that the determinant steps in Lindahl's sequential periods are dependent upon the assumption of knowing not only the initial plans of the individuals, but how they will form concrete expectations when faced with a particular circumstance. What Lindahl does not offer is a theory of expectations formation that could serve as a guide to how individuals decide on a plan of action, when the actions they undertake must incorporate some anticipation of the likely actions of others if their own plans are to have a chance to succeed.

FRIEDRICH A. HAYEK

Friedrich A. Hayek was the most prominent proponent and refiner of the Wicksell–Mises business-cycle theory. Indeed, it is no exaggeration to say that the theory gained world renown among economists through him.[19] Yet Hayek's use of the Wicksell–Mises theory has a uniquely distinct twist to it. Both Wicksell and Mises had been interested in explaining how a discrepancy between the natural and money rates of interest set in motion a cumulative process of a general rise or fall in prices. The essential accompanying process through which this rise (fall) in prices is brought about is a distortion of the intertemporal allocation of resources from a shorter (longer) period of production to a longer (shorter) one.

Hayek makes the primary task of analysing discrepancies between the natural and money rates of interest an explanation of how changes in the supply of money must bring about modifications in the structure of relative prices, with any changes in the general value of money as an incidental result of this process. This is explained in his first book, *Monetary Theory and the Trade Cycle* (Hayek 1929) and in *Prices and Production* (Hayek 1935), as well as in his articles on 'Intertemporal price equilibrium and movements in the value of money' (Hayek 1928) and 'On "neutral money"' (Hayek 1933b). Hayek's criticisms of 'price level' stabilization was an analytical tool to demonstrate that stability or movement in the general level of prices was neither an indicator nor a benchmark for equilibrium in the economy.

In the later 1930s and 1940s, Hayek's research in this area led him to rethink what 'equilibrium' meant and what its existence required in terms of coordinating interpersonal plans in and across time. This theme was taken up especially in his essays on 'Price expectations, monetary disturbances and malinvestments' (Hayek 1933a: 135–56), 'Economics and knowledge' (Hayek 1937: 33–56) and 'The use of knowledge in society' (Hayek 1945: 77–91), and in the chapter on 'Equilibrium analysis and the capital problem' (Hayek 1941: 14–28).

In 'Intertemporal price equilibrium and movements in the value of money', Hayek attempted to demonstrate that equilibrium through time required prices of goods at each moment across time to consistently reflect the supply and demand conditions of those respective moments. Any attempt to 'stabilize' the price of a good or a set of goods at the same 'level' across time, in spite of differing market conditions across that time, must set in motion market reactions that would be 'destabilizing'. If, for example, the supply of a good was going to be greater in the future than today because of some productive innovation being introduced that would lower costs, and if equilibrium is to prevail in that future period as well as in the present period, then the price of that good in the future period (assuming given demand conditions) must tend to be lower than the price in the present period. If this good's future price was to be 'stabilized' across time at the 'level' that prevailed in the present, this would result in future expected profit margins being greater than if natural market forces normally were at work competing the price down to reflect the now lower costs of production. The 'stabilized' higher price in the future period would tend to induce an excess production of the good in comparison to what the 'real' supply and demand conditions would dictate, and this 'surplus' would eventually create a destabilizing effect in this market (Hayek 1928: 91–3).

What was true for any particular good would be true for a situation in which there were a general expansion of output due to falling costs across many markets. If each price in this situation were permitted to find its equilibrium level, the general 'price level' (as measured by some statistical averaging) would have declined, though the structure of relative prices will have been kept in equilibrium across time. However:

> if the money supply is increased just sufficiently to prevent a fall in prices, it must have basically the same effect on the structure of production as any other expansion in the quantity of money not 'justified' by an increase in output. By preventing the temporal gradation of prices determined by the 'goods situation' from being established, it gives rise to shifts in production which prevent the necessary equalization of the supply of goods as between different points in time. Moreover, at a later stage, when some of these shifts have already been irrevocably completed, it obliges much greater changes in prices which must result in the loss of some portion of the expenditures made.
>
> (Hayek 1928: 94)[20]

Thus, 'price level stabilization' through a policy of monetary expansion (contraction) can in fact be destabilizing. Stability on the monetary surface can hide disequilibrating forces beneath that surface (Haberler 1928: 434–49).

The task that Hayek saw for monetary theory was to analyse how the presence of money in the exchange process had the potential to undermine the 'normal' forces in the market which should tend to establish and maintain equilibrium relationships across the economy. Whereas in barter every change in any supply or demand tended directly to bring about the appropriate reciprocal actions from other suppliers and demanders, these direct links and reciprocal actions were not present in the same way in a money economy (Hayek 1933a: 93, 108). Instead:

> The necessary starting point for any attempt to answer the theoretical problem seems to me to be the recognition of the fact that the identity of demand and supply, which must necessarily exist in the case of bar-

ter, ceases to exist as soon as money becomes the intermediary of the exchange transactions. The problem then becomes one of isolating the one-sided effects of money . . . which will appear when, after the division of the barter transaction into two separate transactions, one of these takes place without the other complementary transaction. In this sense, demand without corresponding supply, and supply without a corresponding demand, evidently seem to occur in the first instance when money is spent out of hoards (i.e., when cash balances are reduced), when money received is not immediately spent, when additional money comes on the market, or when money is destroyed.

(Hayek 1935: 130)

The influence of money on 'real' factors is inseparable from the presence of money in the market process. Conceptually, 'monetary' forces can be distinguished from 'real' forces, but in a money-using economy any real changes are only transmitted in the form of money demands for and supplies of goods and services. Furthermore, a change in the supply of money that increases (decreases) individuals' cash balance positions directly influences the capacity for individuals to demand real goods and services. This modifies the actual structure of relative prices for as long as a change in the supply of money continues, or while its effects are still working through the economy (Hayek 1929: 104, 124–5). So, like Mises, Hayek considers the non-neutrality of money to be the cornerstone for analysing money's influence upon and relationship to the real economy. The primary task of monetary theory consequently becomes, in Hayek's view, the study of money's influence on relative prices and the structure of production (Hayek 1929: 116–17; 1935: 29).

Hayek's Austro-Wicksellian theory of the trade cycle is an application of this monetary approach to a particular problem, but with the following difference. Unlike some of the Swedes, Hayek's analysis never strays far from an emphasis on money's influence on the intertemporal structure of prices and production. The Hayekian triangles highlight the intertemporally interdependent relationships which permeate the economic order. The stages of production are connected and coordinated with each other through the network of prices which encapsulate the demand and supply for the various 'higher' and 'lower' order goods. The rate of interest is the governor mechanism. It ensures that the period of production and flow of consumer goods from it over time is effectively coordinated with the patterns of consumer preference for consumption goods per period and the preference for savings sufficient to maintain production processes of particular time durations (Hayek 1935: 32–100; Rothbard 1962: 273–386). Hayek argued that

An equilibrium rate of interest would then be one which assured correspondence between the intentions of the consumers and the intentions

61

of the entrepreneurs . . . [T]his would be rate of interest arrived at on a market where the supply of money capital was of exactly the same amount as current savings. If the supply of money capital is increased, by monetary changes, beyond this amount, the result will be that the rate of interest will be lowered below the equilibrium rate and entrepreneurs will be induced to devote a larger part of the existing resources to production for the more distant future than corresponds to the way in which consumers divide their income between savings and current consumption. At the time when entrepreneurs make this decision the consumers have no possibility of expressing their wishes with sufficient emphasis since their money incomes are as yet unchanged while the expansion of credit has increased the funds available for investment. The investment of these funds, however, must in the course of time increase total income by nearly the full amount of these funds, either because wages are raised in order to attract people away from producing consumers' goods towards producing capital goods, or because the funds are used to employ formerly unemployed workers. This will certainly tend to increase the intensity of the demand for consumers' goods . . . The entrepreneurs who have begun to increase their productive equipment in the expectation that the low rate of interest and the ample supply of money capital would enable them to continue and to utilize these investments under the same favourable conditions, find these expectations disappointed. The increase in the prices of all those factors of production that can be used also in the late stages of production will raise the costs of, and at the same time the rise in the rate of interest will decrease the demand for, the capital goods which they produce. And a considerable part of the newly created equipment designed to produce other capital goods will stand idle because the expected further investment in these other capital goods did not materialize.

(Hayek 1933b: 145–6, 148)

The question of the compatibility of expectations and intertemporal plans led Hayek in the mid-1930s to pursue the meaning of equilibrium and the level of knowledge that market participants would need for a coordination of plans to be possible.[21] In 'Economics and Knowledge', Hayek defined equilibrium as meaning that

the foresight of the different members of the society is in a special sense correct. It must be correct in the sense that every person's plan is based on the expectation of just those actions of other people which those other people intend to perform and that all these plans are based on the expectation of the same set of external facts, so that under certain conditions nobody will have any reason to change his plans.

(Hayek 1937: 42)

This conception of equilibrium, he argues, does not require any assumption that the knowledge of the agents is either perfect or extending into an infinite future. All that is required is that the agents have all the 'relevant' knowledge to assure that their plans are mutually compatible. The relevant knowledge in this case is all the knowledge that each of them 'is bound to acquire in view of the position in which he originally is, and the plans which he then makes' (Hayek 1945: 53). In other words, given that the agent may discover in the process of undertaking a plan that his expectations about the actions of others with whom he is interdependent is incorrect, the direction in which the inconsistency exists will provide the agent with the additional, new knowledge concerning how he should revise his plans so they are more compatible with the actions of those with whom he is interacting (Hayek 1941: 23). In elaborating some of the types of knowledge used by participants in the social system of division of labour, Hayek explains how the price system helps economize on the detailed information required by agents when coordinating their activities with others (Hayek 1945: 77–91). Furthermore, agents each coordinate their action with that of others to the greatest extent possible by continually adjusting their conduct to the changing price conditions in their respective corner of the market.

This conclusion brought Hayek back to where he started from in 1929 when he said that 'in the exchange economy, production is governed by prices, independently of any knowledge of the whole process on the part of individual producers' (Hayek 1929: 84–5). As long as individuals allow themselves to be guided in their actions by prices and any changes in prices 'relevant' to their particular activities, there need be no forces that can bring about systematic mistakes by a large number of market participants, especially entrepreneurs. This is likely to occur only if an exogenous disturbance is introduced into the system – such as a change in the supply of money that brings about a deviation of the money rate of interest from the natural rate.

This in no way solves the question of how individuals are to use the price information that comes their way. Either an actual price which is different from the one that was expected, or a quantity of some good actually sold which is greater/smaller than was expected to sell at that price, are both forms of knowledge that show plans need to be revised. But the plan revisions to be undertaken in these cases are ambiguous. The information provided by a frustrated plan in the present must be interpreted in the context of what it is suggesting about the shape of new plans oriented towards the future. In other words, Hayek's analysis of equilibrium and knowledge fails to provide a theory of expectations.[22]

RICHARD M. EBELING

LUDWIG VON MISES – AGAIN

By the late 1930s and 1940s, members of the Swedish school like Myrdal and Lindahl, and Austrians like Hayek, had reached the point at which periods, plans and expectations had come to be seen as central questions to be answered if economic analysis was to be taken further. Each had come to this point from a similar starting point: Wicksell's theory of a cumulative process induced by a discrepancy between the money and natural rates, and which set in motion intertemporal misallocations of resources and output mixes. Each had understood this process as the product of mutually inconsistent plans between consumers and producers, savers and investors, and these inconsistencies only manifested themselves at sequentially different times as different participants discovered that their respective plans could not be successfully consummated.

This led the Swedish economists to formulate various types of 'plan' and 'period' analyses. Lindahl, for example, postulated that prices are set at the beginning of the period, transactions are carried out during the period, and at the end of the period the registered quantities bought and sold at those prices are tabulated. Based on any disappointed expectations, revisions are made in pricing and production plans and these serve as the starting point for the events of the next period. Lindahl divides the sequential periods into arbitrarily 'short periods' during which the individual plans are postulated as unchanged.[23]

The Swedes were no better at solving the problem of expectations than Hayek. To say that plan disappointments in one period serve as the basis for plan revisions in the next period tells little about how individuals form expectations about what they should do in the next period. If, at the end of the present period, sales of a product are less than expected (because demand was not as great as had been expected), does it naturally follow that in the next period the planner should revise the production level downwards? Well, it depends. Is the level of sales experienced in the first period a temporary or a permanent change in demand? How might one's competitive rivals on the supply side be reacting to this actual level of demand? The answers not only influence the choice of the next period's output level, they may also influence investment decisions planned for several future periods. Hayek's emphasis on market price as an economizer of information – to which individuals should adjust their actions when price changes are experienced – has the same problem. An actual price different from an expected price informs the planner that plans should be changed, but expectations must still be formed on the basis of that price information so as to specifically know what to do.

In his later work, Ludwig von Mises suggested his own version of what 'periods' should mean in economic analysis and offered a theory of expectations formation (Mises 1949, 1957, 1962). In his earlier writings, there was an explicit sequence analysis: Mises' theory of the non-neutrality of money is, what he called, a 'step-by-step' analysis of the diffusion of a monetary change throughout the economy, during which relative demands, price relationships and resource allocations are sequentially and temporally impacted upon. It is only in his later writings that the problem of the meaning of periods and expectations are explicitly dealt with; and they can only be understood in the context of his wider theory of human action.

In Mises' view, man is above all else the being who acts. Man has intentionality and he pursues purposes. He designs plans to succeed in his endeavours and he applies means to bring them about. Possessing consciousness, man mentally projects himself into the future and imagines conditions or states of affairs that he would prefer to his actual or other potential circumstances. He tries to discover causal relationships and connections in the world in which he lives and selects the ones he thinks would be most effective for achieving his goals. In selecting between alternative courses of action, man must choose, and choice implies uncertainty: the actor believes that his actions can influence the future and thus the future, from his perspective, is not 'preordained'. At the same time, what individuals view as 'ends' to pursue, what they classify as 'means' for various tasks, what are the 'benefits' and 'costs' in the context of choices being weighed – these have intelligibility and meaning only when understood from the actor's perspective. It is a human mind that contemplates possibilities, that classifies, orders and arranges the physical things of the world into categories of meanings and relationships. As a result, it is how the human actor assigns meanings to things that determines what they are (in the context of the purposes and plans the actor has constructed) and which then guides his conduct towards those things in his environment. Looking at man in this manner is what Mises referred to as the 'subjectivist method'; the analyst understands the world from the actor's point-of-view.[24]

In this methodological subjectivist perspective, all action occurs in and is inseparable from time. All action implies a before and an after, a sooner and a later, a becoming and a became. This means that it is impossible, Mises says, for man to be indifferent to the passing of time. Indeed, it is in the contemplation of action that man becomes most conscious of time. And, in Mises' view, it is the potential for action that delineates the past from the present and the present from future (Mises 1957: 202–3, 287). He argued:

> That which can no longer be done or consumed because the opportunity for it has passed away, contrasts the past with the present. That which cannot yet be done or consumed, because the conditions for undertaking it or the time for its ripening have not yet come, contrasts the future with the past. The present offers to acting opportunities and tasks for which it was hitherto too early and for which it will be hereafter too late. The present qua duration is the continuation of the

conditions and opportunities given for acting. Every kind of action requires special conditions to which it must be adjusted with regard to the aims sought. The concept of the present is therefore different for various fields of action. It has no reference what ever to the various methods of measuring the passing of time by spatial movements. The present contrasts itself, according to the various actions one has in view, with the Middle Ages, with the nineteenth century, with the past year, month, or day, but no less with the hour, minute, or second just passed away. If a man says: Nowadays Zeus is no longer worshipped, he has a present in mind other than that of the motorcar driver who thinks: *Now* it is still too early to turn. And as the future is uncertain it is always undecided and vague how much of it we can consider as *now* and present. If a man had said in 1913: At present – now – in Europe freedom of thought is undisputed, he would have not foreseen that this present would very soon be a past.

(Mises 1949: 100–1)

In this conception of time, individuals pursuing various goals invariably operate simultaneously in terms of 'periods' of varying length. Each action has its own time horizon. For some plans, the actor is in the middle of the 'present' period; for other plans, the 'present' period is coming to a close; for yet other plans the 'future' period is just becoming the 'present'. For still other plans, the potentials for action are still in a 'future' period. Nor are these periods of equal length. For some actions, the 'present' period is an instant as measured by the movement of the clock, and then is gone; for other actions, the 'present' extends far into the future as measured by the clock. Each planning period would have its sub periods divided into 'past', 'present' and 'future' (for instance, 'Right now I'm working on my undergraduate degree' would have the sub period 'Right now I'm in my first year', which would have the sub period 'Right now I'm having lunch in between my morning and afternoon classes').

In the market changes usually do not impact simultaneously on all transactors. Instead, a change in market conditions originates at some point in the economic system. From this 'epicentre' the consequences of the change, in terms of changes in the actions and plans of those initially impacted, emanates out in a particular path-dependent sequential and temporal order. Some individuals in the social system of division of labour will be affected by this – to a greater or lesser extent – at a different time than others; some individuals may be impacted at the same time; some will be impacted sooner, others later. At each of those moments at which the change reaches each individual, each of them will have to weigh the meaning and significance of the change in terms of requiring a 'change in plans', that is in terms of when, how and how much.

How precisely shall the change be interpreted for deciding how plans should be modified? This brings us to Mises' theory of expectations formation (Ebeling 1994: 83–95; 1995b: 81–92). In developing his theory of expectations formation, Mises was influenced by Max Weber and by one of his own students, Alfred Schutz. Max Weber had defined action as 'all human behavior . . . insofar as the acting individual attaches a subjective meaning to it'. Social action was defined as action in which the actor 'takes account of the behavior of others and is thereby oriented in his course' (Weber 1922: 88). Social actions, including market interactions, are actions of mutual orientation, in which each participant is aware of others whose activities are relevant to one's own goals or purposes (Weber 1907: 109, 112).[25]

Mises states that the fundamental problem for the 'acting man' in the social arena is the problem of anticipating the future actions of others:

> How can a man have any knowledge of the future value judgments and actions of other people? . . . The task with which acting man, that is, everybody, is faced in all relations with his fellows does not refer to the past; it refers to the future. To know the future reactions of other people is the first task of acting man. Knowledge of their past value judgments and actions, although indispensable, is only a means to this end.

> (Mises 1957: 311)

The historian reconstructs the past by sorting and arranging the preceding actions of human actors. Everyday acting man, however, must anticipate the future actions of other men, without which the success of his own action may be impossible. This is done, Mises explains, on the basis of the knowledge we collect about other individuals and groups of individuals from our past interactions or accumulated information about them. This knowledge is 'acquired either directly from observing our fellow men and transacting business with them or indirectly from reading and from hearsay, as well as our special experience acquired in previous contacts with the individuals or groups concerned'. With this knowledge, 'we try to form an opinion about their future conduct' (*ibid.*: 313).

The method that men use to do this was conceptualized by Mises' student, Alfred Schutz, in the idea of the 'ideal type' (Schutz 1932, 1962). First we are all born into a common world of intersubjective meaning. These intersubjective meanings, which we learn from childhood, specify and define the meanings of actions and objects in the social world around us. They enable us to identify certain actions and things in most 'typical' situations as meaning one thing rather than another. They enable us to understand and mutually orient ourselves in the social arena. But besides these general meanings that define situations and activities as usually or 'typically' meaning 'this' or 'that', when a person is seen doing something or using something, there are also 'ideal types' we create in our minds of particular individuals or groups of individuals. The ideal type, in other words, is a composite image of an individual or a group of individuals created in an individual's mind for understanding other's actions in the past or anticipating them in the future. Or as Mises puts it:

> The characteristic mark of an 'ideal type' . . . is that it implies some proposition concerning valuing and acting. If an ideal type refers to people, it implies that in some respects these men are valuing acting in a uniform or similar way. When it refers to institutions, it implies that these institutions are products of uniform or similar ways of valuing and acting or that they influence valuing and acting in a uniform or similar way.
>
> (Mises 1957: 316)

Ideal types, Mises argues, enable an acting man to be 'the historian of the future' (*ibid.*: 322). Forming composite pictures or images of individuals in terms of characteristics, qualities, motives and meanings, ideal types enable an individual decision maker to project himself into the future, imagine that another individual or individuals is confronted or faced with a particular situation or change in circumstances, and then ask: 'How might these individuals respond?' on the basis of the behavioural typifications the decision maker has in his mind of them.

It is a peculiar fact that this part of Mises' writings – his suggestion for defining 'periods' in terms of 'potentials for action,' and his theory of expectations formation on the basis of 'ideal types' – has received practically no attention by Austrian economists. If integrated into the Austrian theory of entrepreneurship and the market process, intertemporal exchange and the structure of production, as well as the Austrian theory of money and the business cycle, it could potentially go a long way towards improving the internal consistency of the Austrian system, as well as increasing our practical knowledge about how the 'real world' works.

NOTES

1 For summaries of the 'Austrian' approach to economics, see Lachmann (1991: 17–39) and Ebeling (1991a: 1–40). On the 'Swedish' approach to economics, see Ebeling (1981: 1–12).
2 Böhm-Bawerk (1901: 401–13) rejects the later Keynesian-type arguments that the greater profitability of longer-term investment projects will be counteracted by the decline in effective demand for final output that results from an increase in savings. He also responds to the argument that, since consumers do not specify the future benefit they want from their acts of saving, the uncertainty of what might be profitable to produce for future consumption may counteract the incentives for long-term investment.
3 Wicksell's use of the concept of the 'natural rate' was not without ambiguity. Arthur W. Marget, for example, distinguished at least eight different meanings

that Wicksell assigns to the 'natural' rate (Marget 1942: 201–4). The difficulties of calculating a 'natural' rate in barter (that is, one without a unit of account with which to convert productive capabilities into value terms) was also emphasized by a number of Wicksell's followers (Mises 1932: 65; Lindahl 1939: 247–9; Myrdal 1939: 49–51).

4 A detailed breakdown of the Wicksellian 'periods' process under both 'stationary' and 'cumulative' conditions, as well as an analysis of some of the internal inconsistencies to be found in Wicksell's exposition, is given by Uhr (1962: 235–45).

5 Wicksell points out that it is 'not impossible for the rise in prices to be counteracted to a certain extent by an increase in production . . . if previously there had been unemployment' (1911a: 195).

6 Wicksell was under no illusion that 'constant price' expectations would long be in effect under these circumstances. The series of rising prices would, as he expressed it, 'create its own drought'. Entrepreneurs would begin making decisions not purely on present prices but based on anticipated future prices. Factor prices, in turn, would spiral upwards to reflect the expected higher final goods prices (Wicksell 1898: 96–7). In a criticism of those who have advocated a gently rising price level as a beneficial stimulus to economic activity, Wicksell remarks that 'if a gradual rise in prices, in accordance with an approximately known schedule, could be reckoned on with certainty, it would be taken into account in all current business contracts; with the result that its supposed beneficial influence would necessarily be reduced to a minimum' (*ibid.*: 3–4).

7 For a recent exposition and elaboration of Mises' regression theorem, see Selgin (1994: 808–26). For a comparison of Mises' cash balance approach with A. C. Pigou's Cambridge 'k' cash balance approach, see Ebeling (1992: 127–38).

8 In defining the purchasing power of money in this manner, Mises was following some of the classical economists (Viner 1937: 311–14).

9 Mises, like Wicksell before him, accepted that the availability of unemployed resources at the start of the sequence would delay this counteracting process from setting in as soon as would otherwise tend to be the case: 'At times, even on the unhampered market, there are some unemployed workers, unsold consumers' goods, and quantities of unused factors of production, which would not exist under "static equilibrium". With the revival of business and productive activity, these reserves are in demand right away. However, once they are gone, the increase in the supply of fiduciary media necessarily leads to disturbances of a special kind' (Mises 1928: 125).

10 However, see Kuznets' comments (1930: 148–51).

11 The quotes appear in Palander (1953: 9). See Thomas (1936: 66–74) and, for a detailed summary of Myrdal's analysis in this work, see Hansson (1982: 29–46).

12 It originally appeared as an article in *Ekonomisk Tidskrift* (1931) and was enlarged in a revised version two years later, appearing under the title, 'Der Gleichgewichtsbegriff als Instrument der Geldtheoretischen Analysis' [The equilibrium concept as a tool of analysis in monetary theory]. It was this essay, slightly revised, that was finally published in English in 1939 as *Monetary Equilibrium*.

13 It is not always easy to follow and summarize Myrdal's exposition. This is partly because, while he says that there are two ways of thinking about these problems – as purely theoretical problems and as practical problems requiring 'operational' content – he in fact shifts back and forth, sometimes combining and confusing the two.

14 The following remarks on this point rely heavily upon the arguments made by Palander (1953). See also Hansson (1982: 103–55).

15 Thus, I do not agree with the view of either Ellis (1940: 434–6) or Robinson (1939: 493–5) that Myrdal's analysis is plagued by the 'Austrian' notion of a 'period of production'. Quite to the contrary. Nor do I share Ellis's and Robinson's preference to see the concept of a 'period of production' dropped from economic theory.

16 *The Aims of Monetary Policy* appeared only in Swedish. *Methods of Monetary Policy*, on the other hand, was condensed and translated as Part II of Lindahl (1939: 139–268), under the title 'The interest rate and the price level'. The 1939 volume opens with a long monograph on 'The dynamic approach to economic theory' and it is in this essay that the 'period analysis' for which Lindahl is famous was given its most elaborate exposition. It also shows a definite change in Lindahl's approach to 'process analysis'. In the earlier work, Lindahl moved along strongly Wicksellian lines, focusing on changes in the production structure during the phases of the cumulative process. In the 1939 monograph, Lindahl abandons this mode of exposition for what is primarily an income–expenditure model in terms of periods and the influence of the results in previous periods on present and future periods.

17 The assumption that during the period prices are fixed and quantities demanded and supplied adjust to them distinguishes Lindahl's 'period analysis' from Hicks (1939: 115–40), who assumes quantity as fixed and prices the adjusting factor in the period. See Hicks' contrast between his own approach and that of Lindahl (Hicks 1956: 139–51). See also Bode (1943: 348–54).

18 Lindahl's use of 'fairly short periods', in which prices are set at the beginning and a summing up of plan successes or failures is not done until the end of the period, is open to criticisms raised by Myrdal: it ignores the fact that necessary adjustments may require more time than an analytical 'short period' allows for, and the outcomes of the process may well depend upon the 'time order' of the actual events in the period, and which are ignored by focusing only on beginning and end 'points of registration'. At the same time, Lindahl is open to the criticisms raised by Tord Palander against Myrdal. While it is true that Lindahl's approach offers a 'sequence analysis' over time that Myrdal's did not offer in his 'dynamic analysis', Lindahl's 'points of registration' at the point between periods take on little meaning once we realize that the relevant points and times for plan re-evaluation will depend upon the individual's particular plans and the time horizons in them. An appropriate time for comparing *ex ante* plans with *ex post* may, for some people, be some point within the 'short period', while for others the time for comparing *ex ante* plans with *ex post* outcomes may be outside the 'short period'.

19 Of course, Hayek was not the only proponent; there was a wide circle of economists in Austria, and especially in England, who accepted the theory and used it in their analyses of cyclical phenomena. Among the more important of them were Haberler (1932), Strigl (1934), Machlup (1934, 1940), Robbins (1934), and Phillips, McManus and Nelson (1937). For a listing of many other books and articles in the Austrian monetary tradition published during this period, see Ebeling (1985: 55–7).

20 See additionally Hayek (1935: 28). See also Haberler (1931); Fisher (1935a: 49–64; 1935b: 197–211); Machlup (1935: 280–7); and Ebeling (1991b: 481–99).

21 In fact, Hayek stated that his thoughts turned in this direction because of the criticisms by Swedish economists, like Gunnar Myrdal, that he had failed to incorporate expectations and uncertainty into his theory of the trade cycle

(Hayek 1933a: 155–6). Having turned his attention to these matters, when Hayek reviewed Lindahl's *Studies in the Theory of Money and Capital*, he said that 'the strongest impression [the volume] leaves with the reader is one of intense regret that Professor Lindahl's ideas should not have become more widely accessible when they were first outlined in Swedish some ten years ago . . . [Y]et, when at last they are made available to us in full, we find that not only have they lost most of the attraction of novelty but even that what might have been a revelation to us now mostly represents a stage through which we ourselves have passed, although considerably later than Professor Lindahl, yet some time ago' (Hayek 1940: 332–3). Hayek also admitted that it was the earliest essays included in the volume that had most attraction for him, in which 'Professor Lindahl remains closest to the views of his master Wicksell . . . Since then Professor Lindahl has taken an active part in the general movement away from "real" problems towards almost exclusive concern with the monetary aspects of economic problems, and indeed has become a leader in that movement.'

22 See Ebeling (1990a and also 1995a: 138–53), where I have discussed this shortcoming in Hayek's writings in another context.

23 It would be a false impression to assume that Lindahl's particular period analysis was one that all, or even most, Swedish economists during these years accepted or used. Other Swedish economists gave different meanings to 'periods'. Erik Lundberg (1937) stated that the relevant period depended upon the nature of the theoretical exercise. One had to first specify whether the focus of the analysis concerned 'production periods', 'periods of contract' or 'reaction or adjustment periods', and to analyse the total effect of a change it would be necessary to have a period long enough for everyone in the economy to have been affected. Björn Hansson (1982, 1989: 168–213) summarizes several of the alternative period and process models developed by different members of the Swedish school.

24 On Mises' theory of action and some of its implications, see Ebeling (1995c: 39–53). See also my introduction to *Money, Method and the Market Process, Essays by Ludwig von Mises* (Ebeling 1990b: ix–xxvi).

25 Mises refers to the exchange relation as 'the fundamental social relation', in which there is 'intentional mutuality' (Mises 1949: 195).

REFERENCES

Bode, K. (1943) 'Plan analysis and process analysis', *American Economic Review*, June.

Böhm-Bawerk, E. von ([1901] 1991) 'The function of savings', in *Austrian Economics: A Reader*, R. M. Ebeling (ed.), Hillsdale: Hillsdale College Press.

——(1959) *Capital and Interest*, 3 vols, South Holland: Libertarian Press.

Ebeling, R.M. (1981) 'The Stockholm school of economics: an annotated bibliography', *The Austrian Economics Newsletter*, 3 (2).

——(1985) 'Ludwig von Mises and the gold standard', in *The Gold Standard: An Austrian Perspective*, L.H. Rockwell Jr (ed.), Lexington: Lexington Books.

——(1990a) 'What is a price? Explanation and understanding', in D. Lavoie (ed.) *Economics and Hermeneutics*, London: Routledge.

——(ed.) (1990b) *Money, Method and the Market Process, Essays by Ludwig von Mises*, Norwell: Kluwer Academic Press.

—— (1991a) 'The significance of the Austrian economics in twentieth-century economic thought', in R.M. Ebeling (ed.) *Austrian Economics: Perspectives on the Past and Prospects for the Future*, Hillsdale: Hillsdale College Press.

——(1991b) 'Stable prices, falling prices and market-determined prices', in R.M. Ebeling (ed.) *Austrian Economics: Perspectives on the Past and Prospects for the Future*, Hillsdale: Hillsdale College Press.

——(1992) 'Variations on the demand for money theme: Ludwig von Mises and some twentieth-century views', in J.W. Robbins and M. Spangler (eds) *A Man of Principle: Essays in Honor of Hans Sennholz*, Grove City: Grove City Press.

——(1994) 'Expectations and expectations-formation in Mises's theory of the market process', in P.J. Boettke and D.L. Prychitko (eds) *The Market Process: Essays in Contemporary Austrian Economics*, Brookfield: Edward Elgar.

——(1995a) 'Toward a hermeneutical economics: expectations, prices and the role of interpretation in a theory of the market process', in D.L. Prychitko (ed.) *Individuals, Institutions, Interpretations: Hermeneutics Applied to Economics*, Brookfield: Avebury Publisher.

——(1995b) 'Cooperation in anonymity', in D.L. Prychitko (ed) *Individuals, Institutions, Interpretations: Hermeneutics Applied to Economics*, Brookfield: Avebury Publisher.

——(1995c) 'Austrian subjectivism and phenomenological foundations', in P.J. Boettke and M. Rizzo (eds) *Advances in Austrian Economics*, vol. 2A, Greenwich: JAI Press.

Ellis, H. (1940) 'Review: monetary equilibrium', *The Journal of Political Economy*, June.

Fisher, A.G.B. (1935a) 'The significance of stable prices in a progressive economy', *Economic Record*, March.

——(1935b) 'Does an increase in volume of production call for a corresponding increase in volume of money?', *The American Economic Review*, June.

Haberler, G, (1928) 'A new index number and its meaning', *The Quarterly Journal of Economics*, May.

——(1931) *The Different Meanings Attached to the Term 'Fluctuations in the Purchasing Power of Gold' and the Best Instrument or Instruments for Measuring Such Fluctuations*, official no., F/Gold/74, Geneva: League of Nations.

——([1932] 1990) 'Money and the business cycle', in R.M. Ebeling (ed.) *The Austrian Theory of the Trade Cycle and other Essays*, Auburn: The Ludwig von Mises Institute.

Hansson, B.A. (1982) *The Stockholm School and the Development of Dynamic Method*, London: Croom Helm.

——(1989) 'The Stockholm school and the development of dynamic method', in B. Sandelin (ed.) *The History of Swedish Economic Thought*, London: Routledge.

Hayek, F. A. ([1928] 1984) 'Intertemporal price equilibrium and movements in the value of money', in *Money, Capital and Fluctuations: Early Essays*, Chicago: University of Chicago Press.

——([1929] 1966) *Monetary Theory and the Trade Cycle*, New York: Augustus M. Kelley.

——([1933a] 1969) 'Price expectations, monetary disturbances and malinvestments', in *Profits, Interest and Investment*, New York: Augustus M. Kelley.

——([1933b] 1984) 'On "neutral money"', in *Money, Capital and Fluctuations: Early Essays*, Chicago: University of Chicago Press.

——([1935] 1961) *Prices and Production*, New York: Augustus M. Kelley.

——([1937] 1948) 'Economics and knowledge', in *Individualism and Economic Order*, Chicago: University of Chicago Press.

——(1940) 'Review: studies in the theory of money and capital,' *Economica*, August.

——(1941) *The Pure Theory of Capital*, London: Macmillan.

——([1945] 1948) 'The use of knowledge in society', *Individualism and Economic Order*, Chicago: University of Chicago Press.

Hicks, J.R. (1939) *Value and Capital*, Oxford: Oxford University Press.

——(1956) 'Methods of dynamic analysis', in *Twenty-Five Essays in Honor of Erik Lindahl*, Stockholm: Ekonomisk Tidsskrift.

Kuznets, S. (1930) 'Monetary business cycle theory in Germany', *The Journal of Political Economy*, April.

Lachmann, L.M. (1991) 'The significance of the Austrian school of economics in the history of ideas', in R.M. Ebeling (ed.) *Austrian Economics: A Reader*, Hillsdale: Hillsdale College Press.

Lindahl, E. (1929) 'Review: dynamic pricing', *Economic Journal*, March.

——([1939]) 1970) *Studies in the Theory of Money and Capital*, New York: Augustus M. Kelley.

Lundberg, E. ([1937] 1964) *Studies in the Theory of Economic Expansion*, New York: Augustus M. Kelley.

Machlup, F. (1934) *Führer durch die Krisenpolitik*, Vienna: Julius Springer.

——(1935) 'Inflation and decreasing costs of production', in H.P. Willis and J.M. Chapman (eds) *Economics of Inflation*, New York: Columbia University Press.

——(1940) *The Stock Market, Credit and Capital Formation*, London: William Hodge.

Marget, A.W. ([1942] 1966) *The Theory of Prices*, vol. 2, New York: Augustus M. Kelley.

Mises, L. von (1924) *Theorie des Geldes und der Umlaufmittel*, Munich/Leipzig: Duncker & Humblot.

——([1928] 1978) 'Monetary stabilization and cyclical policy', in *On the Manipulation of Money and Credit*, Dobbs Ferry: Free Market Books.

——([1932] 1990) 'The position of money among economic goods', in R.M. Ebeling (ed.) *Money, Method and the Market Process, Essays by Ludwig von Mises*, Norwell: Kluwer Academic Press.

——([1940a] 1990) 'The non-neutrality of money', in R.M. Ebeling (ed.) *Money, Method and the Market Process, Essays by Ludwig von Mises*, Norwell: Kluwer Academic Press.

——([1940b] 1978) *Notes and Recollections*, South Holland: Libertarian Press.

——([1949] 3rd edn, 1966) *Human Action, A Treatise on Economics*, Chicago: Henry Regnery.

——([1953] 1981) *The Theory of Money and Credit*, Indianapolis: Liberty Classics.

——([1957] 1969) *Theory and History*, New Rochelle: Arlington House.

——(1962) *The Ultimate Foundations of Economic Science*, Princeton: D. Van Nostrand.

Myrdal, G. ([1939] 1962) *Monetary Equilibrium*, New York: Augustus M. Kelley.

Ohlin, B. (1927) 'Tendencies in Swedish economics', *The Journal of Political Economy*, June.

Palander, T. (1953) 'On the concepts and the methods of the "Stockholm school"', *International Economic Papers*, vol. 3.

Phillips, C.A., McManus, T.F. and Nelson, R.W. ([1937] 1972) *Banking and the Business Cycle*, New York: Arno Press.

Robbins, L. (1934) *The Great Depression*, New York: The Macmillan Company.

Robinson, J. (1939) 'Review: monetary equilibrium', *Economic Journal*, September.

Rothbard, M.N. ([1962] 1970) *Man, Economy and State*, vol. 1, Los Angeles: Nash Publishing Co.

Schutz, A. (1932) *The Phenomenology of the Social World*, Evanston: Northwestern University Press.

——(1962) *Collected Papers, I: The Problem of Social Reality*, The Hague: Nijhoff.

Selgin, G. (1994) 'On ensuring the acceptability of a new fiat money', *Journal of Money, Credit and Banking*, November.

Strigl, R. ([1934] 1995) *Capital and Production*, Auburn: The Ludwig von Mises Institute.

Thomas, B. (1936) *Monetary Policy and Crises: A Study of Swedish Experience*, London: George Routledge & Sons.

Uhr, C. (1962) *Economic Doctrines of Knut Wicksell*, Berkeley: University of California Press.

Viner, J. ([1937] 1965) *Studies in the Theory of International Trade*, New York: Augustus M. Kelley.

Weber, M. ([1907] 1977) *Critique of Stammler*, New York: The Free Press.

——([1922] 1947) *The Theory of Social and Economic Organization*, New York: Oxford University Press.

Wicksell, K. ([1898] 1969) *Interest and Prices*, New York: Augustus M. Kelley.

——([1911a] 1935) *Lectures on Political Economy*, vol. 2, London: George Routledge & Sons.

——([1911b] 1958) 'Böhm-Bawerk's theory of capital', in *Selected Papers on Economic Theory*, London: George Allen & Unwin.

——([1914] 1993) 'Review: théorie des geldes', in B.B. Greaves and R.W. McGee, compilers, *Mises: An Annotated Bibliography*, Irvington-on-Hudson: Foundation for Economic Education.

4

SCHUMPETER'S WALRASIAN STAND IN THE SOCIALIST CALCULATION DEBATE

Willem Keizer

In the stream of Schumpeterian studies which accompanied the 1983 centenary celebrations of Schumpeter's birth and the fortieth anniversary of the publication of *Capitalism, Socialism and Democracy* (1947, henceforth *CSD*), one major aspect of his multifaceted work has been neglected. This is the particular stand he took in Part III (especially Chapters XVI and XVII) of the book on the famous 'socialist calculation debate' about the rationality of a hypothetical socialist economy. In modern evaluations of *CSD* all attention is focused on Schumpeter's 'grand vision' of the demise of corporate capitalism and the nature of the socialism he predicted would follow it. There was no discussion of his theoretical arguments concerning the rationality of a socialist economy. This chapter seeks to redress that omission by analysing the nature and causes of the particular arguments Schumpeter advanced to support his stand in the debate.

This chapter will discuss two related issues:

- Schumpeter's 'anti-Austrian' stand in the debate in the 1940s
- explanations for this in terms of his espousal of the Walrasian general equilibrium (GE) model.

In these two issues a number of paradoxes or anomalies can be found, which we shall discuss:

- Schumpeter's 'renegade' stand in the debate, defending a socialist economy he personally disliked against the 'Austrian' critique of Mises and Hayek
- his recourse to neoclassical GE theory to refute the Austrian charge, instead of his own 'Schumpeterian' arguments
- the paradox of Schumpeter's admiration for Walras and the GE theory, as compared with his own sociological and evolutionary bent of mind and his literary style.

This chapter will elucidate these two issues and the anomalies they comprise, attempt to explain them and examine their implications with a view to casting new light on Schumpeter and his role in the socialist calculation debate.

Schumpeter was a relative latecomer to the debate, which by 1942 had already been going on for two decades. It is well known that he argued in favour of a socialist economy against its Austrian critics, Mises and Hayek, with whom he shared a common intellectual and methodological background. He denied their charges of socialism's theoretical and practical irrationality (or, in the terminology of those days, its 'impossibility') and rebutted their arguments with the aid of Walrasian GE theory. In *CSD* he reasoned primarily in terms of partial equilibrium analysis, but a few years later in the *History of Economic Analysis* (1954, henceforth *HEA*), he argued solely in GE terms. In both instances he accepted the assumptions and derivations of static neoclassical welfare theory. He shared this methodological stance with such socialist opponents of the Austrians as O. Lange, H.D. Dickinson and A.P. Lerner.

It will be argued here that Schumpeter's 'renegade' stand (from the Austrian point of view) was largely the result of his admiration for Léon Walras, GE analysis and mathematical economics in general. This is paradoxical, as his own sociological way of thinking, his literary style and his evolutionary 'vision' were the very opposite of those of the mathematical school. Furthermore, it is peculiar that Schumpeter should refute the Austrian critique with arguments derived from GE analysis, instead of his own Schumpeterian theories. Explanations for these anomalies will be sought in his attitude towards mathematical economics and the GE model in particular. It was his faith in the scientific power of GE theory that made him side with the neoclassical socialists against his Austrian compatriots. This wrong position (as it ultimately proved to be) detracted from the credibility of his 'vision' on socialism in *CSD* and cost him some of his status as a great theoretical economist. Some authors even believe that the underlying Walrasian cause of this exacted a considerable toll from Schumpeter's performance as a theoretician in his later years.

SCHUMPETER AND THE SOCIALIST CALCULATION DEBATE

Brief survey of the debate

The famous 'socialist calculation debate' concerned the rationality of the centrally planned allocation of scarce means under state ownership of the means of production, as compared with that of the decentralized market under dispersed private ownership. In effect it was a challenge to socialists to provide a microeconomic theory of socialism, which apparently did not exist in 1920 when Mises published his famous critique.[1] The ensuing debate lasted for decades, shifting in the 1930s from Central Europe to Great Britain and from Mises versus Central European Marxists to F.A.

Hayek versus neoclassical economists with socialist convictions, such as H.D. Dickinson, O. Lange and A.P. Lerner, whom we can call 'neoclassical socialists'. The debate took a different direction with Hayek's two contributions of 1935, which said that socialism could not practically solve the 'millions of equations' required for a real-life GE model. The socialists saw this as a major retreat of the Austrians, from Mises' strong statement 'impossible, even in theory' to Hayek's weaker 'impossible in practice'. When Oskar Lange in 1936 countered the latter argument with his partial equilibrium model of 'market socialism', most economists were persuaded that the socialists had won the debate. It also became widely known that the Italian E. Barone had shown how the GE models of Walras and Pareto could be applied to a socialist economy – indeed, that they could only be applied under socialism. By the end of the 1930s the profession (with the exception of a few uncompromising Austrians) had become convinced that a socialist economy could 'calculate rationally' (that is, achieve a Pareto-optimal allocation) both in theory (proved by the GE models) and in practice (indicated by Lange's model of market socialism). This was the state of the debate in the early 1940s, when Schumpeter addressed the matter in *CSD* (Part III, Chapters XV–XIX) and again in *HEA* (Chapter 7, section 5).

The influence of Schumpeter's stand in the debate

Although he did not make any really original contributions to the debate, Schumpeter's writings were influential as far as the general consensus on the matter was concerned. His self-assured tone and confident conclusions in *CSD* were taken over by others and came to be regarded as authoritative statements on the debate. As far as the economic profession in general was concerned, Schumpeter's olympic pronouncements on the theoretical and practical possibility of socialism clinched the matter. For this reason Hayek calls him the 'original author of the myth that Pareto and Barone have "solved" the problem of socialist calculation' (Hayek 1949: 90, n. 1). Lavoie starts his survey of what he calls the 'standard version' of the debate with Schumpeter's account of it (Lavoie 1981: 46–9).[2]

Like all other professional economists, Schumpeter rightly admits the importance of Mises' critique and criticizes the orthodox socialists for not providing a theoretically sound reply. He says that proof of the logical unsoundness, or even failure to prove the logical consistency of the socialist economy, would in itself suffice to convict it of 'inherent absurdity' (Schumpeter 1947: 172). He also correctly ascribes the major theoretical responses to this critique to such non-socialist economists as Wieser, Pareto and Barone.

It is well known that Schumpeter rejected the Austrian charge of the irrationality of socialist calculation. His famous and often quoted pronouncements on the controversy form the opening sentences of Chapters XV and XVI of *CSD*: 'Can socialism work? Of course it can. No doubt is possible about that . . . the answer . . . is clearly Yes' (*ibid.*: 167); and 'The answer is in the affirmative. There is nothing wrong with the pure logic of socialism' (*ibid.*: 172).

In both *CSD* and *HEA* Schumpeter emphasizes that the formal theory of rational allocation is the same under capitalism (or 'commercial society') and socialism. Like Barone, he says that the economic categories of capitalism (such as money, scarcity prices and interest) would also have to exist in a rational socialist economy.

Schumpeter's 'renegade' position in the debate

There are several reasons why this pro-socialist stand in the calculation debate was a 'renegade' position to take for an Austrian-born and -bred economist. In the first place Schumpeter need not have held that a socialist economy would be rational, despite his 'grand vision' in *CSD* that capitalism was doomed and that some kind of socialism would succeed it. Without betraying this vision he could still have maintained that socialism, while inevitable, would nonetheless be irrational. Secondly, Schumpeter was decidedly not a socialist himself and had no reason to defend it on account of his political convictions.[3] According to Haberler he had an ingrained dislike of socialism and feared its apparently inexorable advent (Haberler, in Harris 1951: 45). Samuels says that Part III of *CSD* 'argues – regrettably, as it were, to Schumpeter – that socialism . . . can work' (J.W. Samuels, in Coe and Wilber 1985: 82). So Schumpeter actually argued *contre coeur* in favour of socialism.

As a third-generation member of the Austrian school who shared an 'Austrian' background and training with Mises and Hayek, one would have expected Schumpeter to side with his compatriots (as Haberler did). This raises the question whether he really was an 'Austrian' economist (see Simpson 1983: 1–18). Many authors have expressed doubts about Schumpeter's 'Austrian-ness' (for instance Haberler, in Harris 1951: 29; Samuelson, in Frisch 1981: 4) and call him more of a 'Walrasian' instead. Both Mises and Hayek denied Schumpeter's affiliation to the Austrian school, making reference to his early propagation of mathematical economics and GE analysis.

This authorized view of Schumpeter as a 'non-Austrian' was common in the first two decades after his death. Against this view it may be held that his great contributions to economics – such as the concepts of innovation, the entrepreneur and the dynamism of market capitalism – have a strong 'Austrian' flavour. Their assumptions of and accent on individualism, the power of the profit motive, rivalry between entrepreneurs, the dynamic nature of market competition and the causes of economic development, form an essential part of the Austrian paradigm. Boehm concludes that there is a strong case for challenging 'received scholarship' on Schumpeter's Austrian connection. He opines that Schumpeter's lasting contributions are precisely those which are most congenial to modern Austrian economics (Boehm 1990: 202–3). In sum, Schumpeter can certainly be classified as a major Austrian economist, albeit a maverick one (Kirzner 1990: 243; Simpson 1983: 15). His stand in the debate was certainly not determined by any principled rejection of the Austrian paradigm.

What is 'un-Austrian' in Schumpeter's theorizing on economic systems is his conviction that economic calculation under socialism could be rational; and his recourse to neoclassical equilibrium theory to prove it. Both points are causally connected. It was *because* of his early acceptance of neoclassical microeconomics (in its GE formulation by Walras) that Schumpeter concurred with the neoclassical socialists' rebuttal of the Austrian critique. It may be surmised that, had he not embraced GE analysis at an early stage in his career, he would probably not have taken this position in the debate and so not have contradicted Mises and Hayek in their critique of socialist (but actually of neoclassical) economics (Rothbard 1991: 60). This presents us with the multiple paradox of an 'Austrian' economist who opposes his fellow Austrians with neoclassical GE arguments and defends an economic system he personally dislikes.

For a more facile explanation, we can refer to the oft-documented fact that Schumpeter enjoyed taking up paradoxical positions and to *épater* not only *les bourgeois* but also his fellow economists (Haberler, in Harris 1951: 30). Sylos-Labini says that it was his love for paradoxes and for contradicting or shocking others that led Schumpeter to his favourable judgement on socialism (Sylos-Labini, in Scherer and Perlman 1992: 63). Haberler says that, just for argument's sake, Schumpeter would sometimes defend a position in which he did not believe (Haberler, in Harris 1951: 30).

So a non-theoretical reason for Schumpeter's 'anti-Austrian' stand would be that he defended socialism to *épater* his fellow Austrians who were then living in exile in that epitome of capitalism, the USA. However, there are more serious theoretical reasons for this stand, which we shall analyse below.

Possible 'Schumpeterian' arguments against the Austrian critique

If Schumpeter rejected the Austrian critique, one would have expected him to do so on his own 'Schumpeterian' grounds, such as the atrophying of the entrepreneurial function under managerial capitalism, as expounded in Chapter XII, section 1 of *CSD*. He could have used his own arguments about the growth and bureaucratization of successful enterprises, the obsolescence of the entrepreneur and the bureaucratization of his function into mere staff jobs for salaried professionals. Then he could have argued that modern managerial capitalism was not so efficient either and that it was debatable which system would be more 'irrational' in actual practice.

He also could have made a good case for the presumed inefficiency of giant capitalist corporations with separated management and ownership, in which salaried managers waste potential profits on private perquisites and 'X-inefficiency', uncontrolled by the 'mere rentier class' of absentee shareholders. At the time CSD was being written Berle, Means and Burnham had just discovered the 'managerial revolution' in modern capitalist economies. The implications of the principal-agent problem between shareholders and their managers, coupled with the then-current belief in the irrelevance of the former, as compared with the importance of the latter, could have made a good case against 'corporate capitalism'.

Continuing along this line, Schumpeter could have argued that the professional managers of modern corporations would probably function as efficiently under a socialist regime as they had done under a capitalist one, a point already made by Lange (1938: 109). If rentier shareholders no longer exercise effective control over their managers (as was then commonly believed), there would be no reason why the latter should not perform as well (or as badly) for the socialist state. This argument touches a weak spot in the Misesian critique, which then needs to be bolstered by modern property rights theories of shareholder control. But at the time CSD was written, most economists believed that socialism would be eminently compatible with managerial corporations. Schumpeter could have used this argument to prove his case for the rationality of socialism as compared with real-life corporate capitalism. Although he was aware of the managerial revolution, he omitted any reference to the principal-agent problem in his discussion of the performance of state managers under socialism (Seidl 1984: 201). Like Lange and the other neoclassical socialists of the time (as well as Hayek), Schumpeter is silent on this important institutional point (Keizer 1994: 223).

Schumpeter's Walrasian defence of socialist calculation

Schumpeter rejected the Austrian critique on purely theoretical grounds only, without referring to empirical facts. Wiles remarks that Schumpeter was quite incurious about real-life socialism as it existed in the USSR. He ignored facts about the Soviet economy and only discussed the hypothetical socialism of the debate (Wiles, in Heertje 1981: 154).[4] In his opinion the Austrian critique could only be refuted on the high level of pure theory, which to him meant GE analysis. According to Lavoie, Schumpeter paid 'disproportionate attention to the equilibrium argument' and spent most of his analytical energy on this (Lavoie 1981: 48). He starts his treatment of the debate in Chapter XVI of CSD by posing the problem in GE terms:

> given a socialist system . . . is it possible to derive from the data and
> from the rules of rational behaviour . . . equations which are independ-

ent, compatible . . . and sufficient in number to determine uniquely the unknowns of the problem before the central board or ministry of production?

(Schumpeter 1947: 172)

The real problem is precisely how this . . . can be done rationally, i.e. in a way which will result in a maximum of consumers' satisfaction subject to the limits imposed by the available resources, the technological possibilities and the rest of the environmental conditions.

(*ibid.*: 175)

From the start Schumpeter saw the problem of rational calculation under socialism as an exercise in what Hayek has called the 'pure logic of choice': as a problem of maximization subject to constraints. Hence he concludes that

there exists for any centrally-controlled socialism a system of equations that possess a uniquely determined set of solutions, in the same sense and with the same qualifications as does perfectly competitive capitalism, and that this set enjoys similar maximum properties.

(Schumpeter 1954: 988–9)

For Schumpeter, only Barone's centralist GE solution proves the theoretical possibility of rational allocation under socialism. In *CSD* he states that Barone's model had definitively solved the problem and he proceeds to give a verbal 'brief sketch' of this proof (Schumpeter 1947: 173–8). The exposition is apparently intended for the layman, for it is circumlocutory and adds nothing new to Barone's conclusions. Schumpeter says that he is 'proving' the case for socialism and speaks of '*our* solution', as if he is solving the problem for the first time (e.g. *ibid.*: 177), when in fact he is only paraphrasing Barone and Lange. His exposition of the rules for enterprise managers and the Central Planning Bureau (CPB) is less clear, logical and to the point than their original formulations. To a modern economist his tone is pedantic, with too much use of the *pluralis maiestatis*.

It strikes the reader that, although Schumpeter poses the problem in GE terms and refers repeatedly to Barone's model as its solution, he actually discusses the matter only in the simpler terms of the *partial* equilibrium models of Lange, Dickinson *et al.* It must be for this reason that Richter repeatedly refers to the Lange model as the 'Lange/Schumpeter argument' (Richter 1992: 190–1, 196). The exposition of the problem and the description of its solution only refers to individual markets, without mentioning the equations of a GE model. Schumpeter invokes this model for his proof, but in actual fact only discusses partial equilibria. There is no treatment of the functions and variables of Barone's system of equations, nor any proof that they fully describe the economy. In short, in *CSD* Schumpeter does not describe the GE model at all.

It is unclear whether at that time he really understood how a GE model solves the allocation problem in an economic system. He knew that a system of equations can be considered determinate or 'solvable' if there are as many equations as there are unknowns (see Schumpeter 1954: 1013), but he does not explain how this solution yields an optimal allocation under planned socialism. He does not say that the CPB has then determined the complete set of optimal prices and quantities for all goods and services, which are imposed on the firm managers as obligatory plan targets. Nor is it stated explicitly that this is a *centralist* solution, in which the CPB solves the 'millions of equations' itself, so that the managers only have to execute the resulting central orders. On the contrary, Schumpeter often writes as if they make decisions independently, as they do in Lange's decentralized model. Thus he says that the CPB could act as a 'clearing house' for information and could coordinate the decisions of the firm managers (Schumpeter 1947: 175, 186). He seems to be unaware that *if* the CPB has solved a GE model, then all allocative decisions have been taken. The managers do not have to decide any more – it has been done for them by the central solution of the model and laid down in directive plans.

Most of the space devoted to the debate in *CSD* is taken up with the discussion of other and more 'Schumpeterian' concerns, such as growth and investment, the motivation of workers and bureaucrats, income distribution and democracy under socialism. It shows that Schumpeter, while accepting the logical correctness of Barone's GE solution, was at that time either not well enough versed or not interested enough in GE analysis to set it out properly for the lay reader. In *HEA*, some years later, he does discuss socialist allocation in the context of the GE model only. Here Lange's partial equilibrium model is rather slightingly referred to as an 'addition of details and some further developments' (Schumpeter 1954: 987). But in *HEA* there is no exposition of Barone's model either. There are only statements to the effect that he had solved the problem and thus refuted the Austrian critique on a theoretical level. In the subsequent section on Walras, written shortly before his death, Schumpeter sets out the GE model in great detail and discusses some of its problems (such as the uniqueness and stability of equilibrium), but without applying it to a socialist economy (*ibid.*: 1006–9).

In *CSD*, Schumpeter makes light of Hayek's arguments about the 'practical impossibility' of the centralist GE solution. Like Lange, he believes this point to be the main issue 'on which most anti-socialist economists are at present inclined to retire after having accepted defeat on the purely logical issue' (Schumpeter 1947: 185). He believes that 'our solution to the theoretical problem will satisfy the reader that it is eminently operational . . . it not only establishes the logical possibility, but in doing so also shows the steps by which this possibility can be realized in practice' (*ibid.*: 185). The bureaucracy would have sufficient information 'to come at first throw fairly close to the correct quantities of output in the major lines of production, and the rest would be a matter of adjustment by informed trial and error' (*ibid.*: 185). These comments show that he believed Lange's decentralized institutions and rules to be capable of solving the planning problem in practice, after the centralist GE models had proved it to be solvable in theory.

In *HEA* this optimism about the practical feasibility of a centralist GE solution is more muted. After reasserting the theoretical possibility of constructing a GE model with socialist institutions, Schumpeter now remarks: 'We must not forget that . . . the pure theory of socialism moves on a very high level of abstraction and proves much less for the "workability" of the system than laymen (and sometimes theorists also) like to think' (Schumpeter 1954: 989). In his first book he had already expressed his belief that the practical applicability and usefulness of GE theory was small (Schumpeter 1908: xix). In *HEA* he says that questions concerning the relative optimality of socialism, its susceptibility to fluctuations and its conduciveness to progress are much more important than the GE issues of the model's logical determinateness or its rationality per se. He now finds it quite possible to accept the logic of GE models 'and yet to hold that the socialist plan, owing to the administrative difficulties involved or for any other of a long list of reasons, is "practically unworkable"' (Schumpeter 1954: 989). However, in a footnote to these doubts Schumpeter again rejects the argument he attributes to Hayek, Robbins and, wrongly, to Mises: that without private property there is no mechanism to *realize* the 'set of solutions of the equations that describe the statics of the socialist common-wealth. They can be realized by the method of "trial and error"' (*ibid.*: 989, n. 12). Here he seems to want it both ways: it is wrong to claim that solving the system of equations of GE is 'practically unworkable', and yet for a long list of reasons one may legitimately hold this view.

In both *CSD* and *HEA* Schumpeter invokes the partial equilibrium mechanisms of the Lange model to solve the 'millions of equations' of a real-life GE model. While stressing that the Walras–Barone model theoretically refutes the Austrian critique, he discusses the problem and its solution only in partial equilibrium terms. However, it is an inadmissible ploy to use a decentralized (and therefore partial equilibrium) model to 'realize' the solution of a GE model in practice. GE models demand *simultaneous* solution. It is theoretically inadmissible and practically impossible to successively equilibrate the individual markets using the *ceteris paribus* assumption, and by doing so equilibrate the entire system. In a GE model all markets must be brought into equilibrium simultaneously, which can only be done by solving the equations simultaneously. This brings us to Robbins's problem of the 'millions of equations' which must be solved simultaneously and (with ever-changing data) continuously. Lange's practical mechanisms and rules for attaining partial equilibria under the implicit assumption of *ceteris paribus* on all other markets cannot be used for this purpose. Schumpeter (like the neoclassical socialists of the time) does not seem to have realized this.

Like all neoclassical economists, Schumpeter assumes that the 'quantities of the means of production' are *given* and, for the time being, constant (Schumpeter 1947: 175). By this he means that *all* information is given, including all possible production functions and consumer preferences. Like the neoclassicists, he assumes that this information consists of objective 'data', which are known and can be communicated to the planners. The officials of the CPB 'would command sufficient information' to be able to establish a fairly optimal plan (*ibid.*: 185). Further on he speaks of the 'given data', which lead to determinate solutions for the problems of production (*ibid.*: 194). These statements show that Schumpeter did not differentiate between 'information' (or even more technically, 'data') on the one hand, and 'knowledge' on the other. He was not aware of what Kirzner called 'Hayek's knowledge problem', according to which it is not information or data that matters most, but knowledge. This knowledge has to be discovered, is dispersed over millions of people and often cannot be communicated to central planners in an objective way (Hayek 1949: 50–5, 79 ff.; Kirzner 1984: 409). Schumpeter fully embraced the epistemological assumptions of neoclassical theory, which led him to believe that the calculation problem could be solved by a centralized GE model. Hayek's epistemological critique of these neoclassical assumptions applies with equal force to Schumpeter (see Hayek 1949: 36, 77–91).

Schumpeter's further arguments against the Austrian critique

Schumpeter was well aware that the Walrasian equilibrium is a static one. To him 'statics' meant price and distribution theory, which he believed to be settled by the Walrasian GE model. Already in his first book, 'dynamics' had meant *economic development* to him, and he saw this as the most important phenomenon in economic life (Schumpeter 1908: 186). His concept of dynamics was a very different thing from the 'dynamics' meant by Hayek, to whom it meant the *process* by means of which coordination is sought between the dispositions of the individuals. Schumpeter's dynamics concerns socio-economic changes on a grand scale, the long-term secular processes of socio-economic change and development. In the Schumpeterian sense, Hayek's concept of dynamics is also 'static'. So instead of treating Hayek's 'dynamic' issue of the process by means of which equilibrium (or coordination) is sought, Schumpeter directs his treatment of dynamics under socialism towards the problems of economic progress and development (Schumpeter 1947: 178). He concludes that 'it cannot be held that socialism . . . would necessarily fail in the solution of the problems presented by "progress"' (*ibid.*: 178). But this was not the point of the Austrian critique. They had never charged that socialism could not generate economic growth. Schumpeter goes into considerable detail discussing saving and investment under socialism as prerequisites for growth, but this was not the 'dynamics' which Hayek meant. Schumpeter missed the point of the Austrian criticism of the staticness of neoclassical equilibrium models.[5]

In his own dynamic context Schumpeter believes that 'progress' under socialism would be achieved with less disturbance and loss than under capitalism (*ibid.*: 195). He says that socialism would have a 'superior rationality' because it would spread innovations more rapidly. Under capitalism innovations occur in individual firms and take time and meet resistance in their diffusion. Large numbers of firms may continue to cling to the old methods.[6] 'In the socialist order every improvement could theoretically be spread by decree and substandard practice could be promptly eliminated' (*ibid.*: 196).[7] In an uncharacteristic passage, Schumpeter even avows that this planned state dissemination of innovations would help to eliminate business cycles:

> But the planning of progress, in particular the systematic coordination and orderly distribution in time of new ventures in all lines, would be incomparably more effective in preventing bursts at some times and depressive reactions at others . . . it would eliminate the cause of the cyclical ups and downs, whereas in the capitalist order it is only possible to mitigate them.
>
> (*ibid.*: 194)

Coming from the author of the *Theory of Economic Development* (1934), this passage rings most untrue. It could be expected that orthodox socialists, untrained in economics, would hold such naive views, but it is amazing that the originator of the concepts of innovation and 'creative destruction' should share them in 1942.

In his dynamic theories Schumpeter uses the concept of equilibrium (or 'circular flow') only as a benchmark, to contrast his dynamic concepts of innovation and entrepreneurial action. 'Equilibrium' does not describe any real economy, but is a mental construct to distil the essential characteristics of development and evolution in real-life economies (Rothbard 1987: 101). But in the calculation debate Schumpeter appears to view (general) equilibrium as an actual state of the economy, which central planning will be able to achieve. Here he does not use the concept as a benchmark only, but as the description of a realizable ideal.

Schumpeter is oblivious to the nature of the *uncertainty* which plays such a big role in the Austrian critique. This is shown by his argument that socialist managers would have an 'easier task' than their capitalist counterparts, because the uncertainty over what their competitors would do and how general business conditions would be in future would be absent. They would be in a position to know exactly what their colleagues propose to do and could even get together for concerted action (Schumpeter 1947: 186).

The CPB could act as a 'clearing bureau' for information and could even coordinate their decisions. This would make a huge reduction in the amount of 'thinking work' managers would have to do, so that less intelligence would be required to run a socialist enterprise (*ibid.*: 186). Thus the task of the socialist managers will be easier than that of the captains of industry under capitalism (*ibid.*: 202). These beliefs again show that Schumpeter, under the influence of Walrasian GE analysis, wholly embraced the neoclassical knowledge assumptions. In this passage he clearly has no idea of what the Austrians meant by their concept of 'fundamental uncertainty'. Another reason he gives for the 'superior rationality' of socialism is that under oligopolistic capitalism, prices and output are theoretically indeterminate and decisions have to be taken in an atmosphere of uncertainty. This uncertainty and the resultant oligopolistic strategies would be absent under socialism, where everything is uniquely determined (*ibid.*:194). These statements show that, like the neoclassicists, Schumpeter completely misunderstood the nature of the fundamental uncertainty the Austrians had in mind.

Schumpeter discusses the problem of bureaucracy under socialism in some detail, but mainly to refute Mises' dire predictions on that score. He admits that socialism would be characterized by a huge and all-embracing bureaucratic apparatus: 'under modern conditions a socialist economy requires the existence of a huge bureaucracy' (*ibid.*: 206). Yet this need not horrify anyone who knows how bureaucratized economic life under contemporary capitalism has already become. Bureaucracy is an inevitable complement to democracy and modern economic development, and is therefore essential in a socialist society. Schumpeter dismisses Mises' argument that the great threat to rational allocation under socialism is the elimination of the profit and loss motive for the state managers, and with it the lack of personal responsibility for spending other people's money. In this matter he seems to be unaware of the property rights, principal-agent and motivational problems raised by Mises. More important for him are the stultifying effects that bureaucratic methods and the general atmosphere of a bureau have on creative minds. The bureaucratic machine gives little scope for initiative and much scope for smothering it (*ibid.*: 207). A typically Schumpeterian point, this is for him the real danger of bureaucratization under socialism. However, it is a danger which he believes also to be present in large-scale corporate capitalism, where it forms one of the reasons for the stagnation and ultimate demise of the system (*ibid.*: 133–4).

Although Schumpeter recognizes the danger of 'political interference' in a bureaucratized economy, he does not believe that politicians would interfere to an extent that would jeopardize its efficiency. Preconditions for this are that the bureaucrats are given sufficient power to make them independent of political control and that they are selected in such a manner as to form a meritocracy, with a strong *esprit de corps* (*ibid.*: 299). In this passage

Schumpeter manifests an idealized conception of bureaucracy, which is radically opposed to modern mainstream theories (Frey, in Frisch 1981: 133; Richter 1992: 198).

REASONS FOR SCHUMPETER'S STAND IN THE DEBATE

In this section I shall show that the reason for Schumpeter's particular stand in the socialist calculation debate was his early belief in the power of mathematical economics and his espousal of the Walrasian GE model. Together they predisposed him to reject the Austrian critique and to side with the neoclassical socialists.

Schumpeter's admiration for the Walrasian GE model

It is commonly known that Schumpeter was a great admirer of Léon Walras and his GE model. He thought Walras was the greatest economist in history and that his GE model was the pinnacle of economic theorizing. Some authors even go so far as to call him a 'Walrasian' on this account.[8] In his preface to the Japanese translation of the *Theory of Economic Development* (1934) Schumpeter said of himself that 'as an economist I owe more to Walras than to any other influence' (quoted by Smithies and Haberler, in Harris 1951: 18, 29). This admiration dates back to his earliest days as an economist, as is shown by the *In Memoriam* for Walras that he wrote in 1910 (Schumpeter 1952: 74–9). There it was expressed in fulsome literary terms. Nearly 40 years later this admiration, now couched in more scientific terms and better founded in an understanding of GE theory, was still undimmed. In *HEA*, Schumpeter devotes almost 30 pages to a detailed exposition of Walras's GE model (Schumpeter 1954: 998–1026). It abounds with praises for the model, such as: 'Walras, whose system of equations defining (static) equilibrium in a system of interdependent quantities, is the Magna Carta of economic theory' (*ibid.*: 242), and

> However, so far as pure theory is concerned, Walras is in my opinion the greatest of all economists. His system of economic equilib-rium . . . is the only work by an economist that will stand comparison with the achievements of theoretical physics . . . It is the outstanding landmark on the road that economics travels toward the status of an exact science and, though outmoded by now, still stands at the back of much of the best theoretical work of our time . . . his superb achieve-ment in pure theory.
>
> (*ibid.*: 827–8)

What is it that Schumpeter admired so much about the GE model? Schneider says it was that it showed the interdependence between all the variables of the economic system and that it integrated all microeconomic theories into a single comprehensive model. Schumpeter's admiration for Walrasian economics was derived from a deep respect for 'pure' or abstract theory, especially in a mathematical formulation. He believed that the scientific content of an economic theory was measured by its use of mathematics (Minsky, in Scherer and Perlman 1992: 366). It was because of his belief in the scientific rigour and power of mathematical economics that Schumpeter embraced Walrasian GE theory.

This explains the paradox of his use of the static Walrasian model to defend socialism against what was in essence a dynamic critique by the Austrians. We saw that 'dynamics' meant very different things to Mises/Hayek and to Schumpeter, but the latter's own dynamics does not only differ from, but is actually radically opposed to, the statics of Walrasian GE theory. It is therefore remarkable that he should defend a socialist version of it against a dynamic critique. Modern neo-Austrian surveys of the calculation debate interpret Mises' critique also as a fundamental attack on neoclassical equilibrium thinking (Lavoie 1985: 108–11). Although it could only deal with statics, Schumpeter still thought that GE analysis was the greatest achievement in economic theory and for that reason he defended it against this prong of the Austrian critique. We saw that he tried to introduce his kind of dynamics into the controversy by discussing economic growth, savings and investment under socialism. He always retained the hope that mathematical economics would some day produce a dynamic counterpart to the statics of the Walrasian system, which would integrate all of economic dynamics in the same way (Smithies, in Harris 1951: 15; Schneider 1970: 69, 77).

Anomalies of Schumpeter's attitude to GE analysis and mathematical economics

There are some curious anomalies in Schumpeter's admiration for Walras, GE analysis and mathematical economics. It would have been natural if he had been a good mathematical economist and GE theorist himself, but he and his kind of economics were the very opposite of Walras and his abstract theorizing. Schumpeter's convoluted literary style of expressing himself, his sociological and evolutionary bent of mind and his personal ineptitude in mathematics made him the counterpole of the mathematical economists he admired.

Schumpeter's style of writing (and therefore of thinking) was literary and, on occasion, even verbose. Haberler, who translated some of his articles into English, speaks of Schumpeter's 'baroque' and involved literary style, with its long sentences and many qualifying phrases. These characteristics are even more pronounced in the German originals (Haberler, in Harris 1951: 45). His early *In Memoriam* for Walras is a good example of this, even in Stolper's translation (Schumpeter 1952: 74–9). Schumpeter was a verbal (and in this early instance even a verbose) economist. As such, he was the stylistic opposite of the mathematical economists.

His praise for Walras and GE analysis would also have been understandable if he had had a systematic and mathematical mind himself. However, Schumpeter's work shows him to have had a historical, sociological and evolutionary bent of mind. The author of the concepts of innovation, the entrepreneur, 'creative destruction' and the sweeping historical vision of the demise of capitalism expounded in *CSD* stands in the German historical and sociological tradition of Marx, Weber and Sombart, not in the French 'engineering' tradition of Cournot and Walras. According to his colleagues and former students, Schumpeter was an unsystematic and erratic thinker. Haberler speaks of

> a certain lack of systematic arrangement and neatness in his writings which became more pronounced in his later years . . . The great wealth of ideas . . . made it very hard for him to present his views on any subject neatly and systematically. He was not always able to fully integrate his ideas, and he easily gave the impression of being undecided about important issues and even contradictory.
>
> (Haberler, in Harris 1951: 45)

In short, Schumpeter himself was the opposite of the mathematical theorists he admired so much. Haberler says that 'Schumpeter did not have an essentially mathematical mind but he extolled the use of mathematics' (*ibid.*: 29). According to his ex-student Minsky, 'Schumpeter lacked the mathematical quality of mind he admired in others' (Minsky, in Scherer and Perlman 1992: 366). Haberler and many others have remarked that Schumpeter's advocacy of mathematical methods in economics stood in stark contrast to the little use he made of it himself (Haberler, in Harris 1951: 29; Hammond, in Seidl 1984: 11). They all refer to his practical ineptitude in mathematical analysis. Samuelson says that 'he was quite aware of his own lack of facility with mathematical economics and cheerfully admitted the difficulties he had in mastering and retaining mathematical techniques' (Samuelson, in Harris 1951: 49). Despite his admiration for Walras and mathematical economics, Schumpeter himself was inept in explaining it. This contrast between his admiration for and advocacy of mathematical economics and econometrics on the one hand, and his personal ineptitude in them on the other, is a paradoxical aspect of Schumpeter's relationship to mathematical economics.[9]

Schumpeter's Walrasian toll

A number of authors have regretted the influence of Walras and the GE model on Schumpeter. Seidl calls Walrasian economics Schumpeter's 'Procrustean bed'. His faith in it was so great that any discrepancies between its logic and his own vision were solved by renouncing his own ideas. 'Schumpeter thus fell victim to his worship of Walrasian economics, which . . . demanded a high price from his basic economic message' (Seidl 1984: 197, 199). In matters such as his disinterest in the unemployment problem of the 1930s, his belief in complete price flexibility, a zero rate of interest in equilibrium and the assumption of malleable capital, Schumpeter dutifully followed the dictates of the Walrasian system. As there were no profits in the Walrasian GE, Schumpeter involved himself in an unnecessary controversy with Böhm-Bawerk over the existence of a zero rate of interest in a stationary state.[10] The same can be said for the position he took in the socialist calculation debate, where he contested the Austrian critique on the basis of his inferences from Walrasian GE analysis.

Both Haberler and Minsky remark on a certain deterioration in Schumpeter's work in his later years (Haberler, in Harris 1951: 45; Minsky, in Scherer and Perlman 1992: 367–8). Minsky says that Schumpeter's admiration for Walras may well have played a critical role in this. He explains this point with the aid of Schumpeter's own distinction between the 'vision' and the 'technique' of an economist (*ibid.*: 367–9). Ideally the two ought to match each other: an economist's technique should provide him with suitable instruments for formulating his 'vision' in a scientific way. This is the case for Schumpeter's socio-historical vision and his literary technique, and it also applies to the relationship between Walras's vision and technique. However, Minsky sees the visions of Schumpeter and Walras as completely different. Schumpeter's vision is essentially holistic, whereas that of Walras is reductionist or atomistic. So Walras's technique would be inapplicable to Schumpeter's vision, as Schumpeter's would be to that of Walras. Minsky believes that in certain instances Schumpeter's admiration for Walras led him to adopt Walras's technique (mathematical GE analysis), which was incompatible with his own vision.[11] This led to an inconsistency between the 'vision' he held and the 'technique' he employed.

Like Seidl, Minsky regrets that Schumpeter adopted Walras's technique, which was essentially unsuited to the problems he was interested in. His treatment of the calculation debate can be seen as an example of this: here Schumpeter applied the Walrasian paradigm to a problem better suited to his own 'literary' technique. The result was the paradoxical and erroneous stand he took in the debate, which now detracts from his stature as an economic theoretician.

According to Sylos-Labini one of the consequences of Schumpeter's overconfident statements in *CSD* on the rationality of the socialist economy was 'a rather widespread mistrust towards Schumpeter, that led several economists to refuse to accept not only his views on centrally-planned economies but also some of his very fertile theses'. Despite the recent revival of interest in Schumpeter's theoretical constructions, he believes that their influence is still limited with respect to their relevance. As the main reason for this relative neglect he sees Schumpeter's fallacious judgement on the functioning of the centrally planned economy (Sylos-Labini, in Scherer and Perlman 1992: 63). Thus, Schumpeter paid a high toll for his faith in GE theory and his stand in the debate, in terms of the credibility of his theoretical contributions in other fields.

It is significant that when appraising the importance of CSD at its fortieth anniversary, none of the authors discussed the sections devoted to the socialist calculation debate and the confident assurances Schumpeter made about:

- the theoretical rationality of the socialist economy
- the ease with which the calculation problem could be solved in a GE planning model
- the superior rationality of socialism in practice.

Yet these are some of the most important statements in the book, which at the time (and for at least a decade afterwards) were adopted and reiterated by almost the entire profession. In his assessment of CSD 40 years after its publication, Haberler calls Part III the 'most controversial and questionable part of the book'. He tries to rationalize Schumpeter's statements by saying that he only dealt with the logic of theoretical blueprints, and not the actual performance of real-life socialist economies (at the time only the USSR). Schumpeter's proclaimed 'superior performance' of socialism was only relative to that of the actual capitalist economies, which he saw as fettered by government regulation, large public sectors and heavy tax burdens (Haberler, in Heertje 1981: 87–8). When, in the 1980s, the Austrian critique was theoretically vindicated by a new generation of neo-Austrian economists, Schumpeter's stand in the debate was shown to have been fundamentally wrong. His overconfident statements quoted above now have a rather fatuous ring. It must be for this reason that present-day commentators on CSD ignore this major theme in the book, as if embarrassed by the erroneous pronouncements Schumpeter made in this particular matter.[12]

CONCLUSION

According to Ekelund and Hébert, Schumpeter's greatest contribution to economics was his destruction of the static framework of neoclassical orthodoxy. He was the first economist to give dynamics and processes of change common currency in economics (Ekelund and Hébert 1992: 567–8). His defence of socialist economics with the arguments of static neoclassical equilibrium theory is therefore paradoxical. This can be explained by looking at Schumpeter's relationship to mathematical economics in general and to the Walrasian GE model in particular. It stems from his innate belief in the power of mathematics to solve problems that his own 'literary' technique had not managed to do. It is therefore a pity that this eminent

Austrian economist, whose greatest contributions lay in the field of dynamics and evolutionary economics, should, due to the spell cast over him by the technical brilliance of the Walrasian GE model, take up a mistaken position in the socialist calculation debate and spend his energy arguing the case for a static equilibrium theory that his own theories had already demolished.

NOTES

1 For modern surveys and interpretations of the debate, see Vaughn (1980), Lavoie (1985), Keizer (1989, 1994).
2 However, Lavoie only summarizes Schumpeter's arguments and does not go into the nature and causes of his stand in the debate.
3 Stolper describes how Schumpeter, as Austrian Minister of Finance, was involved in financing an attempted *coup d'état* by aristocratic counterrevolutionaries against the Bolshevik regime of Bela Kun in Hungary in 1919 (Stolper 1994: 18–20).
4 As an expert on the Soviet economy, Wiles finds Schumpeter's chapters on the theoretical blueprint of socialism 'astonishingly jejune ... It is absolutely not enough to dish up a little welfare economics and assure us that the "planners' problem" is soluble.'
5 Schumpeter's misunderstanding of this point is shown by the first assumption of his example concerning new investment: 'Suppose that a new and more efficient piece of machinery had been designed for the productive process of industry X' (Schumpeter 1947: 178). Mises and Hayek would immediately have rejected this assumption. In the absence of a rational price system, how can one know whether a piece of machinery is 'more efficient', or the old ones 'less efficient'? They could even have used this example to demonstrate the essence of the calculation problem they pose.
6 This point had already been made and treated extensively by Lange (1938: 112–15).
7 True to his own ideas, Schumpeter immediately adds that he considers this but a minor advantage, as capitalism has very efficient methods of eliminating conservative firms.
8 Thus Gide and Rist proclaim that 'Schumpeter belongs to the school of Walras ... he showed himself the convinced and suggestive interpreter of the mathematical schools of France, Italy and England' (Gide and Rist 1948: 717). Seligman says that 'the major influence in his thinking was Walras, whom he considered the greatest of modern economists. So far as he was concerned, anyone who did not study and comprehend Walras was unlikely to become a good theorist' (Seligman 1971: 695–6).
9 Seidl explains his advocacy of mathematics in economics also by his ingrained desire to shock his Austrian colleagues. The two traditions he was educated in, the German historical school and the Austrian school, were both hostile towards mathematics, so any economist flaunting his love for mathematical economics in those days could be sure of shocking his Central European colleagues (Seidl 1984: 188–9). Schneider says that in Austrian academic circles before World War I, the young Schumpeter was considered an *enfant terrible* and a mathematical economist to boot (Schneider 1970: 13).
10 Samuelson has demonstrated that Schumpeter's Walrasian belief in a zero rate of interest in equilibrium is untenable. In conclusion he remarks that at the

end of his life Schumpeter was prepared to admit that even the giant corporations of modern corporate capitalism continue to make Schumpeterian profits, which is not possible in the Walrasian GE model. 'Schumpeter's final logic *ought* to have predisposed him to accord to Hayek the final victory over Lerner and Lange in the debate over whether a socialist state could play the game of parametric pricing . . . the letter of Walrasian equations achievable by Lerner–Lange auctioneers and bureaucrats serves as nothing compared to what Hayek's real-life speculators and profit receivers are led by the invisible hand of market competition to contribute' (Samuelson, in Frisch 1981: 15).

11 In his biography of Schumpeter, Khan also pointed out that Walras's influence on Schumpeter was on his technique and not on his ideas or 'vision' (Khan, as cited by Boehm 1990: 232, n. 2).

12 P.J.D. Wiles, an expert on the Soviet economy, says that Chapters XVI–XVIII are well below the standard of the others. He finds himself unable to take them seriously (Wiles, in Heertje 1981: 154).

REFERENCES

Boehm, S. (1990) 'The Austrian tradition: Schumpeter and Mises', in K. Hennings and W. Samuels (eds) *Neo-classical Economic Theory, 1870 to 1930*, Boston, MA: Kluwer Academic Publishers, 201–41.

Coe, R.D. and Wilber, C.K. (1985) *Capitalism and Democracy: Schumpeter Revisited*, Notre Dame, IN: University of Notre Dame Press.

Ekelund, R.B. and Hébert, R.F. (1992) *A History of Economic Theory and Method*, 3rd edn, New York: McGraw-Hill.

Frisch, H. (ed.) (1981) *Schumpeterian Economics*, New York: Praeger.

Gide, C. and Rist, C. (1948) *History of Economic Doctrines*, 2nd English edn, London: G. Harrap (1960).

Harris, S.E. (ed.) (1951) *Schumpeter, Social Scientist*, Cambridge, MA: Harvard University Press.

Hayek, F.A. (1949) *Individualism and Economic Order*, London: Routledge & Kegan Paul.

Heertje, A. (ed.) (1981) *Schumpeter's Vision. Capitalism, Socialism and Democracy after 40 years*, New York: Praeger.

Keizer, W. (1989) 'Recent reinterpretations of the socialist calculation debate', in J. Krabbe, A. Nentjes and H. Visser (eds) *Austrian Economics: Roots and Ramifications Reconsidered*, Manchester: MCB University Press, 63–8.

——(1994) 'Hayek's critique of socialism', in J. Birner and R. van Zijp (eds) *Hayek, Coordination and Evolution*, London: Routledge, 207–31.

Kirzner, I. (1984) 'Economic planning and the knowledge problem', *Cato Journal*, 4 (2): 407–17.

——(1990) 'Commentary' to Boehm (1990), in K. Hennings and W. Samuels (eds) *Neo-classical Economic Theory, 1870 to 1930*, Boston, MA: Kluwer Academic Publishers, 242–9.

Lange, O. (1938) 'On the economic theory of socialism', in B.E. Lippincott (ed.) *On the Economic Theory of Socialism*, New York: McGraw-Hill (1964).

Lavoie, D. (1981) 'A critique of the standard account of the socialist calculation debate', *The Journal of Libertarian Studies*, V (1): 41–87.

——(1985) *Rivalry and Central Planning*, Cambridge: Cambridge University Press.

Richter, R. (1992) 'A socialist market economy – can it work?', *Kyklos*, 15 (2): 185–207.

Rothbard, M.N. (1987) 'Breaking out of the Walrasian box: the cases of Schumpeter and Hansen', *The Review of Austrian Economics*, 1: 97–108.
——(1991) 'The end of socialism and the calculation debate revisited', *The Review of Austrian Economics*, 5 (2): 51–76.
Scherer, F.M. and Perlman, M. (1992) *Entrepreneurship, Technological Innovation and Economic Growth*, Ann Arbor, MI: University of Michigan Press.
Schneider, E. (1970) *Joseph A. Schumpeter*, Tuebingen: J.C.B. Mohr.
Schumpeter, J.A. (1908) *Wesen und Hauptinhalt der theoretischen Nationaloekonomie*, Leipzig: Duncker & Humblot.
——(1934) *The Theory of Economic Development*, Cambridge, MA: Harvard University Press (1949).
——(1947) *Capitalism, Socialism and Democracy*, 3rd edn, New York: Harper.
——(1952) *Ten Great Economists*, London: George Allen & Unwin.
——(1954) *History of Economic Analysis*, London: George Allen & Unwin.
Seidl, C. (ed.) (1984) *Lectures on Schumpeterian Economics*, Berlin: Springer Verlag.
Seligman, B.B. (1971) 'The thrust toward technique', *Main Currents in Modern Economics*, vol. 3, Chicago, IL: Quadrangle Books.
Simpson, D. (1983) 'Joseph Schumpeter and the Austrian school of Economics', *Journal of Economic Studies*, 4: 15–28, in J.C. Wood (ed.) *Joseph A. Schumpeter, Critical Assessments*, vol. IV, London: Routledge (1991), 1–17.
Stolper, W.F. (1994) *Joseph Alois Schumpeter*, Princeton, NJ: Princeton University Press.
Vaughn, K. (1980) 'Economic calculation under socialism: the Austrian contribution', *Economic Enquiry*, 18 (4): 535–54.

5

MISUNDERSTANDINGS AND OTHER COORDINATION FAILURES IN THE HAYEK– KEYNES CONTROVERSY

Bert Tieben

INTRODUCTION

In recent years several authors have discussed the controversy between Hayek and Keynes in the 1930s. These assessments critically compare their monetary views and business cycle theories (Nentjes 1989), their economic methodologies and social philosophies (Birner 1993; Steele 1993); discuss the reasons behind the Keynesian victory (Birner 1985; McCormick 1992) and the influence they had on each other (Nentjes 1989; Mongiovi 1990); and draw the lessons of the debate for contemporary business cycle theorists (Cochran and Glahe 1994).

However, there is one striking aspect of this controversy which has received comparatively minor attention in this literature, and that is the complete lack of understanding which characterizes the debate between Hayek and Keynes. This chapter aims to correct this omission and argues that from the perspective of the history of economic thought it is important to understand why two of the leading economists of this period failed to discuss their recent work in business cycle theory.

This aspect of the controversy has been neglected because the misunderstandings between Hayek and Keynes are often regarded as the too-obvious result of the fact that they represented (a) two different economic traditions, the Austrian school of economics and Cambridge economics respectively, and (b) two rivalrous academic institutions, the London School of Economics and Cambridge University (see McCormick 1992). Hayek descended from an Austrian tradition in economics that was in many respects different from the Cambridge economics represented by Keynes. A few of these distinguishing features are:

- a firm belief in the allocative efficiency of the market system and a rejection of interventionist policies of any form
- a theory of capital in which capital goods are heterogeneous
- methodological individualism as the preferred approach to economic theory (see Kirzner 1987: 148).

In contrast, Cambridge economics adopted the aggregate concepts of the quantity theory of money and lacked an explicit account of capital theory. From this point of view the Hayek–Keynes controversy can be described as 'a typical example of a clash between two opposing paradigms and its accompanying lack of communication' (Nentjes 1989: 143). For that reason it is important to consider these paradigmatic differences in some detail, and this will be the purpose of the first section.

The debate between Hayek and Keynes was above all a one-way-street affair. Their exchanges show that Keynes hardly bothered to respond to the extensive criticisms which Hayek delivered in a review of his *Treatise on Money*. Hayek published his comments in two parts in August 1931 and January 1932 (Hayek 1931b; Hayek 1932). Keynes responded only to the first part and one may surmise that he never even read the second part of Hayek's review.[1] Moreover, Keynes never seriously addressed the problems raised by Hayek, but responded instead by ridiculing Hayek's *Prices and Production* (1931a). Famous is Keynes's description of the book as

> one of the most frightful muddles I have ever read, with scarcely a sound proposition in it beginning with page 45 . . . It is an extraordinary example of how, starting with a mistake, a remorseless logician can end up in Bedlam.
>
> (Keynes 1931: 55–6)

After the publication of the second part of Hayek's review their correspondence soon ended.[2] In turn, a few years later Hayek never bothered to comment upon Keynes's *General Theory*.

So one may conclude that what characterizes the Hayek–Keynes controversy is the absence of debate. The second part of this chapter aims to explain this aspect of their exchanges. To this purpose the following details require attention:

- the chronology of the exchanges between Hayek and Keynes
- their arguments about the exact meaning of the definitions used in the analyses
- their different views on the proper rules of academic discourse.

These details hardly receive attention in the current interpretations of the Hayek–Keynes controversy. In that respect they must be considered an important supplement to the existing interpretations in terms of paradigmatic and institutional differences.

TWO MONETARY THEORIES OF THE BUSINESS CYCLE

The direct cause of the controversy between Hayek and Keynes was the publication of their respective books on the problems of the business cycle in the early 1930s. Keynes's two-volume *Treatise on Money* appeared in 1930

(Keynes 1930). A year later Hayek published a collection of lectures under the title *Prices and Production* (Hayek 1931a), to which an English translation of his *Geldtheorie und Konjukturtheorie* followed in 1933 (Hayek 1933). Despite their many differences in scope and content these books have a common starting point, which is Wicksell's analysis of a monetary economy. Hayek and Keynes both adopted his distinction between a natural and a market rate of interest and defined monetary equilibrium as the equality between these rates. From that stage onwards, their analyses part significantly, as they attribute a divergence between these rates to different causes. Based on the insights provided by the Austrian theory of capital, Hayek considered the elasticity of the credit system as a monetary cause of the real adjustments that take place in the capital structure of the economy. Keynes could not consider such changes, since his theory does not provide an explicit account of the capital structure that underlies the production of consumption and investment goods. The innovation of his theory is that it distinguishes between different kinds of assets. Keynes saw sudden shifts in speculative sentiments as the most important cause of cyclical fluctuations. He argues that investors shift resources between monetary and real assets and either disturb monetary equilibrium or prevent the real adjustments that are necessary to cope with a situation of disequilibrium.

So, Hayek and Keynes located the source of cyclical fluctuations at different places in the economy, respectively in the organization of its monetary institutions and the operation of its financial markets. Nentjes (1989) presents this difference as the main reason for their theoretical disagreements and lack of understanding. It is therefore important to consider these differences in some detail. To that purpose this section will provide a brief survey of their respective monetary business cycle theories.

The problem with Nentjes's discussion of the Hayek–Keynes controversy is that he accepts their failure to communicate as a given fact. By interpreting their controversy as a 'typical example of a clash between two opposing paradigms' (*ibid.*: 143), he simply rules out the possibility of a rational discussion between them. In this passage, he seems to adopt the Kuhnian view that paradigms are both methodologically and semantically incommensurable (see Boyd 1991). According to this view, paradigms are by definition mutually exclusive. This implies that, as representatives of different paradigms, Hayek and Keynes could not have been expected to exchange arguments about their disagreements in the first place. They would simply have lacked the means to do so. Given the semantic differences between their paradigms, they would have been, quite literally, unable to understand each other.

We find this explanation of the Hayek–Keynes controversy lacking. Cochran and Glahe (1994) show that, in contrast to Nentjes's assertion, there are important similarities between their business cycle theories. They argue that both treated the business cycle as a manifestation of the same problem, that of the coordination between saving and investment (*ibid.*: 74). They both realized that savers and investors are different groups of individuals whose decisions and actions are largely independent of each other.[3] In a decentralized economy the question arises how individual economic decisions are coordinated. That is the fundamental question which underlies their respective trade cycle theories.

These theories, then, are not incompatible in principle. This section will show that the coordination problem can serve as a background against which these theories can be fruitfully compared. The conclusion of this analysis will be that the Kuhnian definition of a 'paradigm' is inadequate to explain the misunderstandings and the lack of communication which characterized the Hayek–Keynes controversy. An analysis using this term assumes rather than explains the semantic and methodological differences between their work. The second section of this chapter focuses on a number of reasons which may account for these differences. It will be shown that both men held widely different views on the proper rules of academic discourse. These different styles of reasoning led to a heated debate about the correct interpretation of the definitions underlying their analyses. It was this fact which caused the misunderstandings and prevented a rational discussion of the real issue at stake in their controversy: the problem of coordination between saving and investment in a monetary economy.

Hayek's analysis of this problem was based on Wicksell's distinction between a natural and a market rate of interest. Wicksell had originally introduced this distinction as an explanation of the transmission mechanism between the quantity of money and the general price level. He called the 'rate of interest at which *the demand for loan capital and the supply of savings* exactly agree, and which more or less corresponds to the expected yield of newly created capital' the normal or natural rate of interest (Wicksell 1935: 193; emphasis in the original).[4] This rate, in other words, denotes the hypothetical value of the interest rate at which planned saving and investment exactly match each other. The market rate of interest, on the other hand, is determined by the demand and supply for loanable funds. This rate is not a notional concept, but denotes the actual interest rate observed in reality. According to Wicksell, a divergence between these two rate generates a cumulative process of price changes until the economy returns to a position of equilibrium. This may happen either indirectly, when the monetary authorities adjust the interest rate and return the volume of credit to an equilibrium level, or directly through a real-cash-balance effect (see van Zijp 1993: 20).

Hayek combined Wicksell's statement of the indirect mechanism between money and prices with the Austrian theory of capital. This construction allowed him to analyse the way in which money can produce fluctuations in output and employment. He treated the business cycle as a sequence of real changes, taking place between the different stages of the production, set in motion by a monetary disturbance. In a monetary economy the medium of exchange is a 'loose joint' between the decisions to buy and sell goods and is therefore a unique source of coordination problems and real disturbances (Garrison 1984). Such problems do not arise in a barter economy, where goods are exchanged directly. '[T]he automatic adjustment of supply and demand can *only* be disturbed when money is introduced in the economic system' (Hayek 1933: 101, emphasis added). By definition, the Hayekian business cycle is a problem of a monetary economy (Klausinger 1989: 62, 78). In the macroeconomic model, coordination failures may arise between the two main groups in the economy – firms and households – who supply and demand loanable funds. Here the banking system (comprising both monetary authorities and banks in general) becomes a disturbing factor. They are the only party able to upset the circular flow of expenditures between firms and households by changing the supply of (credit-)money.[5]

Hayek's general approach to the study of the phases of the trade cycle was the method of decreasing abstraction. Hayek argued that theorizing proceeds by assuming away the complexities of the real situation in order to isolate the essential forces operating in the economy. The influence of several complicating factors may subsequently be studied by comparing them to this ideal situation. By gradually adding more realistic details, the model must ultimately approach a true description of the causal mechanisms at work (e.g. Hayek 1933: 95–6; 1935: 36; 1941: 28).[6]

In Hayek's early business cycle theory, monetary equilibrium is a bench-mark which abstracts from the problem causing cyclical fluctuations, namely coordination failures between saving and investment. In this ideal situation, money is referred to as 'neutral' because it does not interfere with the coordination of decisions between buyers and sellers (Hayek 1933: 112; 1935: 129–31). Changes in the quantity of money that do occur are foreseen and do not affect the activities that individuals plan to undertake or, in equilibrium, monetary changes do not have real effects so that the distin-guishing characteristics of the business cycle do not arise. The disturbances and events which cause and constitute a cycle only manifest themselves in a disequilibrium situation.

The mechanism which coordinates the saving and investment decisions of firms and households in a monetary economy is the interest rate mechanism. Hayek's benchmark model assumes that in the absence of monetary shocks, market forces are able to secure and maintain equilibrium between the natural and the market rate of interest. The interesting aspect of this equilibrating mechanism is that it clearly anticipates Hayek's later ideas on the role of prices in disseminating information (see Hayek 1937, 1945). One may argue that the interest rate signals adjustments in the plans of particular parties in the economy, thereby spreading this information and allowing firms and households to dovetail their responses.

In equilibrium, the plans of these groups are coordinated. The equality of the market and natural rates of interest implies that the firms perceive intertemporal profit opportunities such that they allocate current resources between the production of consumption and investment goods in accordance with the intertemporal consumption preferences of households. Unforeseen changes in the external data will upset this equilibrium between saving and investment, but in the absence of changes in the money supply, the interest rate mechanism will lead savers and investors to gently revise their plans in the required direction and restore equality between the natural and market rates of interest. Shocks of this nature cause an information problem when they affect particular parties in the economy. Obviously a change in the rate of time preference is only perceived by consumers. It is only through their subsequent actions that the information of this change reaches investors and producers. A fall in this rate upsets monetary equilibrium because consumers now favour a date of consumption that is further in the future than was expected by producers. This causes the natural rate to fall below the market rate of interest, as households are planning savings in excess of investment.

However, when households carry out their plans to curtail current consumption and increase their savings, the excess supply of loanable funds lowers the market rate as well. The shift in consumer preferences has now visibly resulted in a price change, telling producers that the information on which they based their investment plans is no longer accurate. The fall in the interest rate also leads them to revise their plans in the correct direction; they are induced to adjust investment in accordance with the shift in consumer preferences and so real equilibrium is restored. First, the lower lending rates reduce the relative cost of producing investment goods. The production of consumption goods is less roundabout than the production of investment goods, involving processes which require less capital to complete and whose costs are therefore less affected by the fall in the interest rate. Second, on the revenue side, the fall in the interest rate is a signal that consumer preferences have shifted in favour of a demand for goods that is further in the future, leading investors to expect a higher yield on newly created capital. Both effects make investment in a more roundabout production structure an attractive option. Firms are thus induced to coordinate their plans with the desires of consumers. They reallocate resources between the different stages of production so that the time pattern of supply again matches the intertemporal preferences of consumers. As they curtail the production of consumption goods to free resources to finance their new investment plans, they remove the existing excess supply from the goods market and restore equilibrium between *ex ante* saving and investment.

In short, real shocks, causing the natural rate of interest rate to deviate from a given market rate, tend to be automatically corrected. Changing circumstances quickly manifest themselves in the interest rate, thus informing the parties concerned about the impact of this shock. It is this information which allows them to adjust their plans and to again coordinate their decisions. By spreading information, the price mechanism cushions the shock and prevents coordination failures from causing the dislocations associated with the business cycle.

In Hayek's theory, market failures cause the business cycle. These occur when

- the interest rate does not follow the change in the natural rate after a real shock, and
- when a monetary shock causes the market rate to deviate from a given natural rate.

In both cases, the banking system is the unique source of the disturbance. In a monetary economy, the banking system may expand or contract the circular flow of expenditures between the firms and households by lending more or less. Controlling the volume of (credit-)money available to the public, the banks may prevent a change in the interest rate by accommodating an excess demand or supply of loanable funds, or change the interest rate on their own accord.[7] If money is the 'loose joint' between buyers and sellers, then banks are the 'loophole' in the circular flow between firms and households.[8]

The typical Hayekian business cycle starts with an increase in the money supply which causes the market rate to fall below the natural rate of interest. The monetary shock here disturbs equilibrium prices and prevents the market from restoring equilibrium as long as it persists. Hayek implicitly assumes that it persists long enough to have an impact on the long-term commitments of investors, thus leading to the misallocation of resources which are the ultimate problem of the business cycle. Two effects induce firms to elongate the period of production and to start an investment boom which cannot be maintained, given the underlying propensity to save. First, the lower lending rates affect the costs of production and make the production of investment goods relatively cheaper. Second, as a consequence of the fall in the interest rate, firms are faced with a signal extraction problem. Unaware of the true cause of the lower interest rate, they may perceive this fall as a sign that the future demand for their products has changed. If an excess supply of savings is the cause of the lower interest rate, the fall indicates a shift in the time preference of consumers towards a demand for goods that is further in the future. Based on this expectation, firms decide to change the structure of production to match the time pattern of that demand.[9] Given that the shock persists long enough, both effects induce firms to increase their investment spending and to build a more roundabout structure of production. At this stage, the cycle is in its upward phase.

The investment boom contains all the seeds for the subsequent downfall. Given that the plans driving the boom are doomed to fail, the turning point is inevitable (Hayek 1933: 183; Klausinger 1989: 77). The upswing started when a lower interest rate made the producers expect a shift in the demand for goods towards a date further in the future. In anticipation of this change, they decided to curtail the production of consumption goods to free resources for an increase in investment spending. This reallocation of resources turns out to be unprofitable when the banks again contract the volume of credit and it appears that the intertemporal preferences of consumers have not changed at all.[10] Faced with a rising interest rate, the firms realize that the future demand they had anticipated is not forthcoming and that the yield they had expected on their newly created capital is over optimistic. At this stage, the cycle reaches its upper turning point as producers now try to reverse their plans, curtail their investments and again shorten the period of production.

Rigidities in the capital structure subsequently prevent a smooth return to equilibrium. Price signals again point in the right direction, but the problem is that capital goods currently being produced are not easily amortized without incurring great costs. Given that the production of investment goods involves a long-term commitment, it is inevitable that a certain amount of capital will be destroyed when firms try to return to a less capital-intensive method of production. In the downward phase of the cycle firms go bankrupt and workers, formerly employed by the now redundant capital goods, will be laid off. Capital destruction and unemployment characterize the typical Hayekian crisis, which lasts as long as it takes the firms to bring the time structure of production into conformity with the intertemporal preferences of consumers; that is, until planned investment is again coordinated with the planned saving of households.[11]

In the Hayekian business cycle, monetary shocks cause real changes in the capital structure. In a monetary economy, the banks are the ultimate source of cyclical fluctuations. They are able to expand the volume of credit and thus distort the relative prices which coordinate the intertemporal choices of producers and consumers. Here money is not neutral, but has real effects; it causes firms to change investment plans independent from changes in the propensity to save. The result is that real investment and real savings are no longer in equilibrium as the interest rate deviates from its natural level. So, the best cure for the trade cycle is to prevent the banks from expanding credit beyond the net demand for inactive balances. Banks should be required to keep a 100 per cent gold reserve against notes, while the monetary authorities should refrain from changing the stock of money in circulation. Hayek realized that the practical implementation of a constant money policy would be hard to achieve (Klausinger 1989: 66) and given that it would require the abolition of bank money, he considered a 100 per cent reserve requirement for banks 'purely Utopian' (Hayek 1933: 190).

Here the cure might be worse than the disease. Nevertheless, in spite of these problems Hayek advocated a fixed money supply as a second best option for monetary policy (Hayek 1935: 124–5).

There are some important differences between Keynes's explanation of the business cycle in the *Treatise on Money* and Hayek's trade cycle theory. These involve the following points:

- Keynes's use of the aggregate apparatus of the quantity theory of money
- the absence of a theory of capital in the *Treatise*
- Keynes's clear separation of price changes and output fluctuations in his analysis of the several phases of the cycle
- Keynes's explicit consideration of the store-of-value function of money.

The main problem of his theory, however, is the same as Hayek's. It studies the problem of coordination between intertemporal economic activities. The theory deals with the dynamics of the business cycle which arise when markets fail to fulfil their coordinating task. In contrast to Hayek, however, Keynes is concerned with the reasons for change in the natural rate of interest. This difference will be addressed below in a brief discussion of the main features of the *Treatise*.

In the late 1920s Keynes, like Hayek, became aware of the shortcomings of the quantity theory of money. Hayek's answer to these defects was to integrate monetary analysis with capital theory to account for the dynamics that constitute the business cycle. Keynes, however, came from a tradition that lacked an explicit theory of capital. He did not reject the quantity theory, but tried to remedy its shortcomings by using it as a starting point to develop a more disaggregated analysis of price changes. The *Treatise* therefore retains the strict separation between monetary changes and real effects that is characteristic of the quantity theory approach.

Keynes started his monetary analysis by defining the conditions for an equilibrium price level in two so-called 'fundamental' equations. These differentiate between short-term and long-term prices to distinguish permanent causes of price changes from temporary ones. Thus the long-period equilibrium norm of the purchasing power of money is given by the money-rate of efficiency earnings of the factors of production; while the actual purchasing power oscillates below or above this equilibrium level as the cost of current investment is running ahead of, or falling behind, savings. A principal object of the *Treatise* is to show that we have here the clue to the way in which the fluctuations of the price level actually come to pass, whether they are due to oscillations about a steady equilibrium level or to a transition from one equilibrium to another (Keynes 1930: 152, see also xvii, 120)

In other words, long-term and short-term price levels are determined respectively by the unit costs of production and the saving–investment relationship. Keynes states that his distinction between these price levels corresponds to Wicksell's distinction between the market and the natural rate of interest (*ibid.*: 139). Monetary disequilibrium arises when an excess demand or supply of savings causes a deviation between short-term and long-term price levels. Equilibrium between these is restored when saving equals investment. Like Wicksell's market rate of interest, Keynes's short-term prices are disequilibrium prices with regard to the equilibrium determined by the long-term costs of production (*ibid.*: 121–4).

Profits are the dynamic element of Keynes's monetary theory. They are 'the main spring of action' and explain how entrepreneurs respond to price changes and effect transitions between equilibrium states (*ibid.*: 141). An outstanding feature of his theory is that Keynes defined profits as windfall gains. In equilibrium, entrepreneurs are assumed to earn a 'normal' reward, but these are excluded from Keynes's definition of profits. Profits arise in a state of disequilibrium and are equal to the difference between savings and investment. They are realized gains that arise when the current-sale proceeds exceed the cost of production. In this connection saving and investment are also taken as *ex post* quantities (*ibid.*: 111).

Keynes's 'fundamental equations' assume a given level of output and hence determine nominal income. Output changes are addressed in a second stage of the analysis, when Keynes discusses how investment decisions may change as a result of price adjustments. The distinction between these stages gives the *Treatise* a distinctly Wicksellian flavour. They demonstrate that, like Wicksell, Keynes adopted a type of period analysis that exhibits the phases of the business cycle in distinct, sequential time intervals which are separately described (Shackle 1967: 177; Leijonhufvud 1981: 167).

The 'fundamental equations' are the main instrument of this method. They confront long-term and short-term prices with each other and therefore explicitly display the comparison of the now-realized with the formerly expected price level. In the first instance, Keynes assumes a constant level of output and distinguishes between three stages of changes in nominal aggregate income that arise during the cycle. These are due respectively to commodity inflation, profit inflation and income inflation. Commodity inflation arises during the start of an upward phase of the cycle, when investment expenditures outrun the value of savings. Unexpectedly, prices rise above their equilibrium levels, determined by the costs of production. This difference causes a windfall gain and profit inflation marks the second phase of the boom. Slowly the equilibrium price level adjusts in the direction of the short-term, disequilibrium price. As expectations adjust to the change in prices with a lag, factor costs rise and erode the windfall gains. Eventually, the earnings of the other factors catch up with the profit incomes and income inflation ends the boom. In the downward phase of the cycle this sequence of price changes is reversed (see Keynes 1930: chapter 18).

A second stage of the analysis informally discusses the consequences which these price changes have on the levels of output and employment. In Keynes's theory, (unanticipated) profits are the mainspring of action, so that changes in these levels take place when profit inflations and deflations are being experienced. In the upward phase of the cycle, windfall profits induce entrepreneurs to increase the output of all types of goods and hire more labour (if available). Production is reduced when lower prices face entrepreneurs with unexpected losses during a bust. In this case incomes are likely to fall as a result of these changes, leading producers to expect a further loss in revenue. Financial opinion turns 'bearish', which reduces investment spending and erodes the community's purchasing power still further. As pessimism spreads throughout the economy, the bust becomes a self-fulfilling prophecy. The reduction in output causes a fall in factor incomes and a lack of effective demand, increasing the downward pressure on prices and confirming the worst expectations of firms and the financial community. Ultimately, a sequence of wage and price reductions pushes the economy into a deep crisis with a steep fall in output and mass unemployment.

It must be stressed that Keynes presented this sequence of price and output adjustments as a typical example of a trade cycle. He argued that many other schemes are conceivable, given that circumstances are likely to change from case to case and depending on the origin of the cycle. Keynes's conception of business cycle theory is therefore different from Hayek's; he does not attempt to reduce the level of abstraction of his theories to develop an increasingly realistic picture of the cycle. Keynes's theories are not intended to give an accurate description of the events taking place during the cycle, rather they should be seen as heuristic devices which may help the economist to discuss the several phases of the cycle in a formal or informal way. They may be used to deduce the consequences of certain changes or to interpret prevailing economic conditions, and must help to construct and assess the validity of several future contingencies. Their own validity is judged in terms of the plausibility of these accounts, and not on the basis of their truth content.

Keynes's theories therefore lack the theoretical rigour which Hayek strives for. However, that does not mean that the *Treatise* did not introduce novel theoretical insights. The most important of these are

- the explicit consideration of the store-of-value function in the money demand equation, and
- an interest rate theory which acknowledges that investors may choose between different types of assets (see Nentjes 1989: 141).

Keynes allowed that stocks of assets may influence the interest rate in addition to the income flows which determine saving and investment (Leijonhufvud 1981: 161). Analysing the problem of interest-rate determination in terms of stocks *and* flows, he introduced expectations as a powerful source of economic fluctuations. The current prices of financial assets generally depend on the sentiments and expectations of the investors. When these prices influence the interest rate, sudden changes in expectations may seriously hamper its coordinating task. Keynes's attention to the relationship between the prices of assets and the interest rate gave him a reason to claim that disequilibrium between savings and investment may well persist for a while, even when the quantity of money in circulation does not change.

Differences between Hayek and Keynes are most significant at the policy level. Keynes claimed an important task for the monetary authorities in redressing monetary equilibrium and in doing so he fundamentally deviated from Hayek, who warned the monetary authorities to forego all intention to influence the money stock (Keynes 1930: 137, 262; Hayek 1935: 124–5). Evidently, Hayek had more faith in the capacity of the market to coordinate activities and to bring about the necessary adjustments to restore and maintain a state of monetary equilibrium. However, there is another reason which explains why their monetary policies deviated so much: Keynes's conclusions were derived on the basis of a theoretical innovation which Hayek apparently failed to understand. In the *Treatise*, Keynes developed a theory of the interest rate, explaining why the market could fail to coordinate activities appropriately. This theory deviates from Hayek's in that it considers how asset prices affect the flows of saving and investment. Hayek did not consider this relationship in his theory of the interest rate until the late 1930s. His earlier theories explain the interest rate in terms of the flows of saving and investment, identifying these flows with the supply and demand for loanable funds respectively. In contrast, Keynes argued that savings do not automatically constitute a supply of loanable funds. To substantiate this claim he differentiated between the decision to save current resources instead of consuming them and the decision to loan savings to investors (Keynes 1930: 127, 154–8; 1936: 165). The total volume of savings is then determined by the propensity to consume and the nominal aggregate income. In contrast to Hayek, Keynes realized that in a capitalist economy the public has the choice between a variety of financial assets – such as bonds, securities and money – to determine the form in which savings must command future consumption. In deciding what to do with savings, a person considers the yields on assets that compete with money and balances the advantages of keeping money assets and buying investments. Accordingly, the demand and supply of loanable funds are not independent, but are influenced by the operation of other financial markets.[12]

For this reason, Keynes argued that a theory of the interest rate should account for the relationships which exist between these markets in a modern economy. His insight was a major step towards a portfolio-balance approach to monetary theory, but it proved a main obstacle in his subsequent discussions with Hayek, for it claimed that the interconnections between financial markets are a vulnerable spot of a market economy. Keynes argued that, independent of the actions of the monetary authorities, financial markets transmit disturbances which are caused by shifting speculative sentiments. For that reason they may well seriously obstruct the coordinating task Hayek attributed to the interest-rate mechanism.

A typical case discussed by Keynes in the *Treatise* concerns a rise in the propensity to save (Keynes 1930: 233). This causes the natural rate of interest to fall below the market rate and should activate forces that lead to a re-establishment of monetary equilibrium, given that the banks supply a constant quantity of money. The innovation introduced by Keynes is that the expectations of investors are endogenous to this process of adjustment and may in fact prevent a fall in the interest rate. His analysis assumes that producers have the financial means to defer decisions and adjust their production plans when they are faced with a shift in the pattern of demand. Depending on their price expectations, producers may have an incentive to defend their market share when the shift in the propensity to save reduces the demand for, and hence the price of, consumer goods. Expecting a return to previous price levels, they decide to temporarily compensate for the loss of revenue by selling securities. In anticipation of this possibility, investors expect a fall in the price of securities and sell stock in exchange for money. In this case, Keynes argues, financial opinion turns 'bearish' *as a consequence* of the disequilibrium between saving and investment. He further assumes that this excess flow demand for cash balances is exactly matched by a demand for securities by the public. The implicit assumption here is that the public suffers from money illusion and does not anticipate the fall of the consumption price index which their higher savings effect. Accordingly they experience higher real-cash balances, which they neither expected nor disired. Given their price expectations and to restore equilibrium between their asset holdings, the public is now quite willing to supply the cash balances demanded by the speculators and producers in exchange for the securities they offer. This leads to the key result that the new savings are not supplied on the market for loanable funds but are traded against existing securities. In Keynes's theory, an excess of saving over investment does not necessarily bring about the fall in the interest rate and the real adjustments required to restore monetary equilibrium. Instead, adjustments take place on the financial markets, while decisions to increase real investment are being deferred. Producers do not shift resources from the production of consumer goods to the investment goods industry, but continue to produce the same amount of consumer goods as before, as long as they expect that prices will rise again in the future or that competitors will perish before they do.

Speaking in 1933 about Hayek's and Keynes's respective trade cycle theories, Dennis Robertson observed that 'a difference of terminology seems to conceal an essential similarity of analysis' (Robertson 1940: 98). The similarity he refers to and that he subsequently explored in his 'Industrial fluctuation and the natural rate of interest' (1934) is the fact that both theories adopt Wicksell's definition of monetary equilibrium as the equality between a natural and a market rate of interest. They both analysed the business cycle in terms of the same problem – that of coordination between saving and investment in a monetary economy. However, the foregoing analysis has shown that this question was analysed in theories which seriously depart when they address the origin of a divergence between the natural and market rates of interest, and when they study how shocks are propagated throughout the economy. Nentjes claims that these differences are the main reason for the mutual misunderstandings that caused the breach between Hayek and Keynes in the early 1930s. He sees their lack of communication as the typical result of a clash between two opposing paradigms (Nentjes 1989: 143). In the Kuhnian sense, paradigms are both methodologically and semantically incommensurable and therefore lack the basis on which a rational choice between them can be made. The Kuhnian notion of a paradigm leaves the whole idea of theory-assessment without a foundation. Theories belonging to competing paradigms can never be compared, since they must be considered incompatible by definition.

Evidently, the methodological and theoretical differences between Hayek and Keynes are substantial and crucial for a proper understanding of their controversy, but the drawback of using the term 'paradigm' to denote these differences is that it forecloses all chances to explore the 'essential similarity of analysis' referred to by Robertson. In the rest of this section it will be argued that this drawback is indeed a liability and that there are ways to reconcile the two business cycle theories, indicating that they cannot be seen as incompatible in principle. Faced with this possibility, it becomes important to find additional reasons for the lack of understanding which characterizes the Hayek–Keynes controversy. To undertake that task, the next section addresses the exchanges between them in more detail.

To escape the conclusion that paradigmatic differences rule out reconciliation by definition, it may be useful to consider their theories as differing, not in principle, but in substance. It then becomes apparent that these theories are not mutually exclusive, but were devised to account for a different class of phenomenon. They refer to different aspects of the same process and can be compared as such. Referring to the points of disagreement noted above, these differences can be stated as follows.

Concerning the origin of the cycle, it appears that Hayek is mainly interested in the consequences of bank policies which influence the money supply and cause the market rate to deviate from the natural rate of interest. His life-long preoccupation with the dangers of inflation led him to isolate the monetary system as the vulnerable spot of the market economy. In Hayek's early business cycle theories it is a change in the money supply which upsets monetary equilibrium and causes the interest rate to give a false signal to investors who, doubting the true nature of the shock, are led to misallocate resources and distort relative prices, thus giving motion to the upward phase of the cycle. In Keynes, the most likely source of disturbance is found elsewhere. Likely to have been influenced by his own experiences as a speculator, Keynes recognized that, in a modern economy, the financial markets are important sources of fluctuation in the interest rate, independent of any action by the monetary authorities. The main difference between his interest theory and Hayek's is that it considers a broader range of assets as possible sources of change in the flows of saving and investment. In Keynes's theory, the public holds bonds and securities alongside money, making these assets a stock of wealth capable of expanding or contracting the circular flow of expenditures between households and firms. In that regard the analysis can be considered complementary to Hayek's theory, studying the case in which, for a given money supply, a change in the demand for money as a store of value upsets the coordinating function of the interest rate.

A similar shift in emphasis is relevant to the second point of disagreement: the propagation of a shock in the economy. Again, it appears that Hayek and Keynes broached different questions which, however, need not necessarily conflict. In his early work Hayek is mainly concerned with the disturbances that monetary disequilibrium causes in the capital structure of the economy. Cyclical fluctuations are real changes taking place in the time structure of the production. Displaced from its equilibrium level, the interest rate gives investors a false signal which distorts relative prices and leads to a misallocation of resources between the different stages of production. Keynes had no theoretical tools to account for such changes in the capital structure and could not even begin to consider the questions that formed the core of Hayek's concerns. The main focus of his interests is the relationships between financial markets. Treating expectations as endogenous to the changes taking place during the different phases of the cycle, he argues that substitution between assets may well obstruct the coordinating function of the interest rate. Anticipating a fall in the price of securities in response to higher real savings, speculators shift the money-demand curve which changes the interest rate and prevents the alignment of real investment in the direction required to restore equilibrium. Here, shocks are not propagated in the capital structure but in the financial markets, while real adjustments are being deferred. Keynes discusses real changes in a subsequent stage of the analysis to allow for the specific circumstances of the case considered. Although it separates nominal and real changes, there is no reason why this theory could not be supplemented with the capital-theoretic considerations of Hayek's business cycle theory, explaining the adjustments taking place between the different stages of the production structure when a change in the flow of expenditures between households and firms has either upset monetary equilibrium or has prevented a timely adjustment of the interest rate.

With regard to these questions, then, there are several possible ways of reconciling these theories. They should not, therefore, be regarded as methodologically incommensurable. Accordingly, there is a reason to argue that paradigmatic differences are not a sufficient explanation of the disagreement between Hayek and Keynes on the subject of trade cycle theory. In the next section it will be argued that an explanation of their controversy requires a careful consideration of the following aspects:

- the chronology of their exchanges
- their use of definitions in economic theory
- the differences in their approach to scientific discourse.

MISUNDERSTANDINGS IN THE HAYEK–KEYNES CONTROVERSY

The most obvious cause of misunderstandings in the communication of ideas is the use of language itself. It is therefore rather surprising that this aspect has never received much attention from commentators on the Hayek–Keynes controversy, particularly as the work of economists in the early 1930s is often said to be characterized by the complexity of their writing. Referring to Keynes's *Treatise*, Hicks remarked that it looked like 'a work written in a foreign language' and that one 'has to learn the language before one can read it' (Hicks 1967a: 189). He recalled that he found the *Treatise* 'very hard to understand' (Hicks 1982a: 8). Similar comments are made about Hayek's work. Of his *Prices and Production* Hicks remarked that it

> was in English, but it was not English economics. It needed further translation before it could be properly assessed . . . what emerged, when we tried to put the Hayek theory in our own words, was not Hayek. There was some inner mystery to which we failed to penetrate.
> (Hicks 1967b: 204–5)

Such remarks echo Hayek's complaint about the obscurity of Keynes's *Treatise*. His assessment of the book was that, even after careful scrutiny, it remains 'entirely unintelligible'. He regarded the exposition of its main arguments so 'difficult, unsystematic, and obscure, that it is extremely difficult for the fellow economist who disagrees with the conclusions to demonstrate the exact point of disagreement and to state his objections' (Hayek 1931b: 2). This passage in the introduction to the first part of Hayek's review of the *Treatise* is important for a proper understanding of the controversy because it shows that from the beginning Hayek doubted whether a discussion of his disagreements with Keynes was possible at all. His concluding remarks of this opening section make it clear that he found it very difficult to articulate these differences because of Keynes's obscure use of language, for '[i]t is only with extreme caution and the greatest reserve that one can attempt to criticise, because one can never be sure whether one has understood Mr. Keynes aright' (*ibid.*).

So it appears that from the start there was a problem of communication between Hayek and Keynes. Such problems are often interpreted as a result of the semantic differences that characterize competing paradigms, but in the case of the Hayek–Keynes controversy this interpretation seems insufficient. Hicks's remarks demonstrate that he found both Keynes's *Treatise* and Hayek's *Prices and Production* difficult to understand due to their particular and idiosyncratic use of language. This feature of their writings may have well arisen from a characteristic that their respective paradigms shared.

This claim is supported by Andvig (1991), who tries to explain the remarkable obscurity of theoretical macroeconomics in the 1920s and 1930s. He suggests that there was a conflict between the essentially verbal methods adopted by economists in this period and the very complex issues they addressed. In the 1920s, for instance, Austrian economists tried to integrate value theory and monetary theory (Mises 1924; Hayek 1933). Hicks and Keynes had similar objectives in the 1930s (Keynes 1936; Hicks 1982b). In the field of trade cycle theory the need for a dynamic analysis of cyclical fluctuations was widely recognized (Keynes 1930: xvii, 120; Hayek 1939: 137). To this purpose Hayek aimed to integrate capital and monetary theory, while Keynes's interest rate theory dealt with endogenous expectations to account for shifts in speculative sentiments. The connection between monetary disturbances and real adjustments was another topic that featured high on the research agenda of many economists throughout the 1920s and 1930s. Andvig claims that such questions led to a conflict between theoretical aims and the verbal analytical tools applied by economists. These were inadequate and unsuited to dealing with such complex issues, while more advanced mathematical techniques were not yet available or also unsuited. Hicks recalls that in 1932 he was asked by Robbins to develop a mathematical model of Hayek's business cycle theory, a task he failed to complete because the theory's complex dynamics simply resisted an adequate mathematical treatment (Hicks 1982a: 6). In the light of these problems, macroeconomists became interested in reducing the complexity of the issues they were addressing, so that analysis could be conducted verbally. This, according to Andvig, led to a method of reasoning that was bound to create confusion and may be held responsible for the relative obscurity and inaccessibility of the economic texts of this period.

Andvig discusses several methods which may help reduce complex questions to more manageable problems. Evidently, the number of variables studied can be reduced by using partial equilibrium models, but Andvig argues that a more pronounced method of simplification was what he calls a 'definitional mode of thinking' (Andvig 1991). This method is nothing more than a shrewd way to circumvent the difficult questions by redefining variables in terms of other variables. Obscuring the exact relationship between the basic postulates and the conclusions of a theory, such definitions can create the suggestion that it explains certain events. A typical example of this practice is the restriction of the analysis to questions of sums and differences, instead of more general functional relationships. For instance, the claim that A and B determine some interesting variable X can be stated in terms of the general function: $X = f(A,B)$. But instead of specifying this functional relationship, one may be tempted to define X in terms of A and B, such that X really consists of two things: one part due to A, called X^A, and another part due to B, called X^B. Adopting these new definitions, the general function $X = f(A,B)$ can now be reduced to the much more tractable equation $X = X^A + X^B$. Obviously, equations that just consist of sums and differences have the benefit that they can easily be solved with the help of some basic algebra.

An example from the *Treatise* may illustrate this strategy of explaining variables by redefining them in terms of other variables. Keynes stated that the purpose of his trade cycle theory was to explain variations in the general price level during the several phases of the cycle (Keynes 1930: 249). With this in mind he made a classification of the total quantity of money into deposits used for the purposes of industry – which he called the industrial circulation – and deposits used for purposes of finance – called the financial circulation. He subsequently defined the industrial circulation as the sum of income deposits and business deposits A, where A serves to distinguish this part of the business deposits from the part that belongs to the financial circulation. This part of the quantity of money in circulation is defined as the sum of saving deposits and business deposits B (*ibid.*: 217–18). However, saving deposits also fall into two categories and a further division distinguishes between saving deposits A and B respectively (*ibid.*: 223).

These divisions and subdivisions serve to permit discussion of the factors that influence the general price level. They relate variations in prices to changes in the velocity and the quantity of money that circulates in different parts of the economy. However, it is still unclear how one should distinguish between business deposits A and B, or between saving deposits A and B. Such definitions beg for clarification and just invite another round of classifying variables. Trying to establish the meaning of a term will lead to an infinite regress, as one must continually clarify the meaning of each new defining variable. It seems that by redefining the variables of his basic theory, comprised in his two fundamental equations, Keynes was able to increase the number of variables it handles arbitrarily. As a result, the classification not only becomes very difficult to understand, it can also be used to 'explain' almost anything.

Hayek certainly had a point when he complained that, by using so many different definitions, the theory would become virtually immune to logical criticism.[13] In his review of the *Treatise* he pointed at numerous terms which required clarification to clear up some of the more important ambiguities. Hayek appeared especially puzzled by the Keynesian definition of investment, for the question 'But what does Mr. Keynes mean by investment?' appears frequently, as do references to the obscurity of that term (Hayek 1931b: 4, 6, 7, 8, 9, 10, 14 (twice); 1932: 65, 70). Hayek goes on to cite other examples of Keynes's 'rich' and 'varied' terminology, for instance

> his terms for the alternatives which are commonly called 'hoarding' and 'investing' are 'bank deposits' and 'securities'. But instead of 'bank deposits' or 'saving deposits' or 'inactive deposits', the terms 'liquid assets', 'hoarded money' or 'hoards' are frequently used, while the 'securities' become 'non-liquid assets'. 'Active deposits' correspond, of course, to 'current accounts' or 'demand deposits'.
>
> (Hayek 1932: 75)

Hayek ridiculed this maze of terms by tracing their changes over a few pages. Unable to discover 'what Mr. Keynes means by investment' he finally concedes: 'I am afraid that it is not altogether my fault if at times I feel altogether helpless in this jungle of differing definitions' (Hayek 1931b: 11). Much would be improved 'if he only stuck to his definitions. But, of course, he does not' (*ibid.*: 15).

It was not just Hayek who fell over Keynes's inconsistent use of terms and definitions. Most major journals such as the *American Economic Review*, the *Journal of Political Economy*, *Economica* and the *Economic Journal* published discussions about the peculiar definitions and concepts of the *Treatise*.[14] In a similar vein the *General Theory* provoked heated debates about the definitions used by Keynes. Moreover, Keynes was not the only economist to base his theories on an unintelligible maze of definitions. Andvig discusses several other examples of this 'definitional style of thinking' in the work of Frisch, Myrdal and Robertson and says that this practice was quite common in the interwar period (Andvig 1991: 438–49). This raises the question of why definitions came to play such an important role in the first place. It was already observed that redefining variables could reduce the complexity of the questions addressed by economic theory and that a clever choice of definitions could help economists fit the theory to the facts. A subtle shift in the meaning of a term or the introduction of a different definition for a variable may well be of use in the 'explanation' of certain events. In fact, such practices may allow a theory to explain almost any event (*ibid.*: 437, 452). It would be too far fetched to suggest that such motives were the reason behind the practice of economists in this period to use many and often differing definitions of their terms, but it is without question that Hayek accused Keynes of such sly intentions.

A prime example of such an allegation is Hayek's rejection of the Keynesian argument that the market mechanism may break down in a monetary economy. The capacity of the market economy to automatically restore equilibrium between saving and investment may be regarded as the key theoretical issue at stake in their dispute (Cochran and Glahe 1994: 73). In that respect Hayek was one of the first to recognize that the potential for coordination failures in a market economy lay at the heart of the Keynesian system (Skidelsky 1992: 454–5). Nevertheless, Keynes's theory did not convince Hayek of the validity of this thesis. Above all, he most forcefully rejected the Keynesian proposition that market forces do not automatically establish equilibrium between the market and the natural rate of interest, even when the quantity of money in circulation remains constant. In his review of the *Treatise* Hayek contends that Keynes does not offer a shred of evidence for this proposition which was in complete opposition to the conclusions of his own monetary theory.

> The most characteristic trait of Mr. Keynes' explanation of a deviation of the actual short-term rate of interest from the 'natural' or equilibrium rate is his insistence on the fact that this may happen independently of whether the effective quantity does, or does not, change. He emphasizes this point so strongly that he could scarcely expect any reader to overlook the fact that he wishes to demonstrate it. But, at the same time, while he certainly *wants* to establish this proposition, I cannot find any proof of it in the *Treatise*. Indeed, at all the critical points, the assumption seems to creep in that this divergence is made possible by the necessary change in the supply of money.
>
> (Hayek 1932: 66; emphasis in the original)

Hayek means that it is not a result which can be deduced from Keynes's theory. In his opinion this would even be impossible, since what Keynes presents as the heart of his theoretical system – his so-called 'fundamental equations' – are nothing but mere truisms. He therefore maintains that Keynes assumes from the outset what he wants to prove, namely that an increase in the rate of saving will not induce entrepreneurs to expand the production of investment goods, thus restoring monetary equilibrium (*ibid.*: 72). Keynes does not demonstrate the potential for coordination failures in a monetary economy, but arrives at this proposition by a clever manipulation of the terms used in the analysis. Referring to his claim that a difference between saving and investment may persist, Hayek writes that 'by arbitrarily changing the meaning of familiar concepts, Mr. Keynes has succeeded in making plausible a proposition which nobody would accept were it stated in ordinary terms' (*ibid.*: 73). Keynes's conclusion that the monetary authorities should intervene to correct monetary disturbances was, in Hayek's view, completely unfounded and in fact based on an illegitimate use of definitions.

However, his conclusion that Keynes's definitions deceive his readers is, in turn, misleading. Hayek was a bit too eager to undermine an argument that was anathema to his own ideas and he ignored the main theoretical innovation of the *Treatise*. Keynes had argued that the stocks of existing assets also influence the interest rate, in addition to the flows of income that finance the production of new investment goods. He contended that changes in these stocks account for the fact that disequilibrium between saving and investment may well persist for a while. According to Keynes, there is no reason to assume that producers will always invest savings in the production of new capital goods. It is evident, he reasoned, that in an economy with developed financial institutions investors have other options at their disposal. They may use the new savings offered by the public to enlarge their money stocks or invest in other financial assets. In these cases higher savings finance the expansion of monetary assets rather than the production of new investment goods. Such choices, in other words, defer the real adjustments that are necessary to restore equilibrium between saving and investment.

Hayek conceded that Keynes's study of the relations between bank credit and the stock market was 'in many respects, the most interesting part of his theoretical analysis', but he considered the difficulty of its exposition an obstacle to a serious discussion of its merits (Hayek 1932: 75). He doubted whether 'anybody could gather, from the text of the *Treatise* alone, the exact meaning of the author's theory on this point' (*ibid.*) and he subsequently ignored Keynes's explanations of how stock prices affect the interest rate.

At this point it is interesting to note that Hayek's discussion of the Keynesian interest rate theory is entirely based on the conclusions of his *own* monetary theory. In his review of the *Treatise*, Hayek consistently used his own theory as the yardstick against which he measured the deficiencies of the Keynesian system. His own theory states that, in the absence of changes in the money supply, the interest rate establishes and maintains equilibrium between saving and investment. It then follows that

> under the existing monetary organisation, where all changes in the quantity of money in circulation are brought about by more or less money being lent to entrepreneurs than is being saved, any change in the circulation *must* be accompanied by a divergence between saving and investing.
>
> (Hayek 1931b: 19, emphasis in the original)

Criticizing the *Treatise* on the basis of this theory, Hayek wrongly attributed to Keynes the assertion that any divergence between saving and investment must arise from, and be equal to, changes in the effective supply of money made available to the public by the banks (Nentjes 1989: 142; Mongiovi 1990: 134), as Keynes himself was quick to point out.[15] It is therefore not surprising to find that he rejected its main proposition. Since his theory does not account for the presence of financial assets other than money, it cannot deal with the effects that existing stocks of assets have on the interest rate. Confining his attention to the domain of inquiry covered by his own monetary analysis, Hayek could never assess the market failures addressed by the Keynesian theory.

In brief, Hayek did not review the *Treatise* in the sense that he discussed its merits in their own right. Instead he professed not to understand its main theoretical innovation and subsequently ignored the arguments presented by Keynes in support of his position. Finally, he repeated the conclusions of his own theory as the only valid answer to the problems addressed by Keynes.[16]

Keynes proved just as short sighted when he discussed the Austrian explanation of the interest rate in the *General Theory* a few years later. Like Hayek he did not judge his opponent's theory upon its own merits, but attacked his own 'straw man' version of it. To be able to criticize the Austrian theory of capital, he translated its concepts into the concepts of his own theory. To start with, he replaced the Austrian notion of the natural rate of interest with his own schedule of the marginal efficiency of capital (MEC), an innovation which he introduced in the *General Theory*. His own version of the Austrian theory then runs as follows.

> By a somewhat drastic simplification the marginal efficiency of capital is taken as measured by the ratio of the supply price of new consumers' goods to the supply price of new producers' goods. This is then identi-fied with the rate of interest.
>
> (Keynes 1936: 192)

Keynes argued that, according to the Austrians, a fall in the interest rate is favourable to investment because the prices of consumer goods fall relatively to the prices of producers' goods. But in the *General Theory* a lowering of the schedule of the MEC has exactly the opposite effect. According to Keynes, investment is stimulated when, for a given interest rate, the schedule of the MEC is raised. The result predicted by the Austrian theory must then be considered erroneous or, as Keynes concludes, '[a]s a result of confusing the marginal efficiency of capital with the rate of interest, Professor Mises and his disciples have got their conclusions exactly the wrong way round' (*ibid.*: 193). But the Austrians never 'confused' the interest rate with the schedule of the MEC. They would in fact never have used this schedule in their capital theories, since they fundamentally oppose the use of such aggregate concepts in economic analysis. In their view, these merely conceal the causal mechanisms at work in the economy (e.g. Hayek 1931b: 7). It was Keynes himself who, as a 'drastic simplification', interpreted their theory in terms of this schedule. By doing so, he attributed to the Austrians a theory which was completely anathema to their tradition. Evidently, Keynes just tried to score points against a straw-man version of the Austrian interest-rate theory.[17]

So it appears that both Hayek and Keynes showed a remarkably low degree of understanding for the theories advanced by each other and this was partly due to unfamiliarity with the peculiar terminology they employed. Keynes used a complicated system of definitions in the *Treatise* and these led to frequent misunderstandings, while Hayek introduced an Austrian capital theory to the English-speaking world, which anyone unfamiliar with the continental tradition found difficult to understand. Famous in this regard is Keynes's exclamation that 'God knows what the Austrians mean by "period of production". Nothing in my opinion' (Keynes to Robertson, 20 February 1935, in Keynes 1973: 517). Nevertheless, the numerous references to the Austrian theory of capital in his notes and the preparatory material for the *General Theory* testify that he tried to answer Hayek's critique that the *Treatise* lacked a proper capital-theoretic foundation relating price adjustments to output fluctuations (see Keynes 1979: 73–6, 116–20, 155–7). But, as the above remark suggests, Keynes found the Austrian notion of capital incomprehensible and so in the *General Theory* he retreated to a familiar line of defence by claiming that he had no idea what the Austrians meant by this notion since they had never clearly defined this term.[18]

It can be concluded that a debate between Hayek and Keynes never took place. Unable or unwilling to find the exact meaning of each other's theories, they avoided discussion about the issues that really mattered, such as the need to integrate monetary and real factors in an explanation of the business cycle or the different causes of coordination failures in a monetary economy. Instead they quarrelled about the definitions they used, which only added to the confusion surrounding their theories. Hayek's review of the *Treatise* offers many examples of this practice. Keynes, in turn, was keen on exposing the fallacies behind the Hayekian notion of forced savings. His correspondence with Hayek in the winter of 1931–2 shows that he constantly pressed him to explain the meaning of this term (see Keynes 1973: 257–66), but despite an at time frantic exchange of letters (see, for instance, the two letters written on Christmas Day 1931) he remained unconvinced by Hayek's elaborate elucidations. Furthermore, both economists showed great unwillingness to seriously consider the arguments advanced by the other. Discussions and reviews of each other's theories frequently involve misleading accounts of these theories. Thus Hayek rejected the Keynesian argument that the interest rate may fail to establish and maintain equilibrium between savings and investment in a monetary economy, even with a given money supply, because his own monetary theory could not account for this. Likewise, Keynes exposed the fallacies of an 'Austrian' theory of the interest rate which the Austrians would not have dreamed of inventing themselves. Evidently, both authors were talking at cross purposes.

For this reason, it is not surprising that the debate did not last very long. The exchanges started in August 1931 when Hayek published the first part of his review of the *Treatise* (Hayek 1931b) and ended in March 1932 with a letter by Keynes informing Hayek that he saw no point in continuing their discussions (letter of 29 March 1932, in Keynes 1973: 266). Even more telling is the fact that Keynes published a short reply to the first part of Hayek's review (Keynes 1931), but never bothered to respond to the second part, published in January 1932 (Hayek 1932).

There seem to be two reasons for Keynes's silence after his first and final reply. These point to a difference in argumentative styles between Hayek and Keynes. First, Keynes strongly objected against the interpretation which Hayek gave of his 'fundamental equations'. As noted above, Hayek had argued that a gap between savings and investment in these equations is equivalent to a change in the money flow. Regarding this claim, Keynes sarcastically retorted that

> I could never have expected . . . that a competent economist could read my *Treatise* carefully and leave it with the idea that it was *my view* that the difference between saving and investment could be exactly measured by changes in the quantity of money.
>
> (Keynes 1931: 53, emphasis in the original)

Given this interpretation of the *Treatise*, it was no wonder that Hayek found many of its conclusions inconsistent with its 'fundamental' propositions. Before this problem was cleared up Keynes saw no reason to discuss the 'irritating terminology' which provoked most of Hayek's comments (*ibid.*: 51).

Second, it appears that Hayek's lengthy and at times teasing discussion of the terms used in the *Treatise* made Keynes aware that their differences would indeed be very difficult to bridge and that it would be best to avoid discussing these matters altogether. This may be inferred from a remark which Keynes pencilled on his personal copy of Hayek's review in which he complained about Hayek's lack of goodwill. It states that

> Hayek has not read my book with that measure of 'good-will' which an author is entitled to expect of a reader. Until he can do so, he will not see what I mean or know whether I am right. He evidently has a passion to pick on me, but I am left wondering what this passion is.
>
> (Keynes 1973: 243)

According to Keynes 'good-will' was required in order to gain an intuitive understanding of what a theory is all about. Keynes attached great importance to such intuitive judgements because economics could never be stated in precise mathematical terms. He argued that the definitions of economic terms are different from the postulates or axioms of mathematics. In contrast to these, economic definitions are not tautological. The terms defined are not mere truisms, but are derived from or refer to events or phenomena that exist in economic reality. They are also abstractions from that reality. Theorizing always proceeds by abstracting from the many details of economic life that may be considered irrelevant for the problem at hand. This is what Keynes meant when he said that definitions in economics are always fairly vague and capable of several interpretations (Keynes 1979: 36). He reasoned that economics is not an exercise in pure logic and its definitions are therefore never 'precise'. They do not adhere to the rules of logic in the same way as the definitions of mathematics do.

> Thus theoretical economics often has a formal appearance where the reality is not strictly formal. It is not, and is not meant to be, logically watertight in the sense in which mathematics is. It is a generalisation which lacks precise statement of the cases to which the generalisation applies. Thus it is exceedingly dependent on the intelligence and goodwill of the reader or hearer, whose object should be to catch the substance, what the writer is at. Those writers who try to be strictly formal generally have no substance.
>
> (*ibid.*: 37–8; see also Keynes 1973: 470)

Keynes argued that, since economic terms are abstract notions, it is inevitable that conflicts concerning their exact meaning will arise. That is why he attached so much importance to intuitive judgements in economic discourse. He realized that an economic theory can never offer an exact description of reality but that, as an abstraction, it suggests the detailed variety of the world that is familiar to the reader. 'Goods' are not the homogenous stuff economists assume them to be. The reader knows that the goods referred to in an economic text are not just an analytical term; they stand for daily groceries that can be bought at the market. The reader therefore uses intuition to understand that the meaning of economic terms goes beyond their proper definition. The problem in economics is that, when such intuitive appeals fail to convince the reader, it is always tempting to ask what a term really means. Keynes argued that such questions do not always help to convey the true meaning of a theory. More details may of course be added, but there is no reason to assume that a lower level of abstraction will improve its explanatory power. Moreover, a less abstract theory uses more analytical terms, which makes it less accessible for those unfamiliar with its formulations. That is why an economist requires a fair amount of goodwill from his readers. They must be willing to use their intuition in order to understand the meaning of a theory. Further questions concerning the exact definitions of the terms employed may only muddle the argument the author tries to make and will therefore only add to the confusion.

Evidently, Hayek broke this unwritten rule of scientific discourse. He did not show the required measure of goodwill and cooperation but chose 'to pick over the precise words I have used with a view to discovering some verbal contradiction or insidious ambiguity' (Keynes 1931: 50). According to Keynes, this illustrated his failure to understand the intuitive meaning of the ideas conveyed in the *Treatise*. Consequently, he saw no point in a discussion with Hayek about the critical points on which their opinions parted. The importance which Keynes attached to intuitive judgements, together with his view that definitions in economics are by their very nature vague and imprecise, appear to have been important reasons for his refusal to engage in a debate with Hayek about their business cycle theories.

In sum, arguments about the use and abuse of definitions play a part in the Hayek–Keynes controversy at the following stages:

1 In his review of the *Treatise* Hayek argued that an inconsistent use of definitions made it virtually impossible to understand and criticize Keynes's theory.
2 Hayek claimed that many of Keynes's so-called 'proofs' were nothing but the result of a clever manipulation of terms. Keynes did not offer a theoretical explanation of the possibility of coordination failures in a monetary economy, but arrived at this conclusion by redefining variables in terms of other variables.
3 Hayek wrongly attributed to Keynes the proposition that a difference between saving and investment was equivalent to a change in the money flow. This view allowed him to demonstrate certain 'inconsistencies' between the conclusions and the fundamental propositions of the *Treatise*.
4 Keynes tried to score points against a straw-man version of the Austrian theory of interest. As a 'drastic simplification' he discussed a version of this theory which used his own schedule of the MEC and then concluded that the Austrians had got it all wrong.
5 Keynes strongly disagreed with Hayek's interpretation of the *Treatise* and refused to discuss their disagreements as long as he retained this view.
6 Hayek violated Keynes's unwritten rules of scientific discourse. His elaborate discussion of the terminological inconsistencies in the *Treatise* showed that he lacked the goodwill to grasp the intuition behind the theory. This, in Keynes's view, precluded a fruitful exchange of arguments and made discussion with Hayek a waste of time.

These points bring together the several threads of our argument. They show that an explanation of the lack of communication between Hayek and Keynes requires consideration of the following details:

• the chronology of their exchanges
• their use of definitions in economic theory
• the differences in their approach to scientific discourse.

In the first place, points 5 and 6 above contain the reasons for Keynes's short and sharp response to the first part of Hayek's review of his *Treatise*. They also explain why he never bothered to comment upon the second part. Second, points 1–4 are further reasons that stand in the way of a critical debate. They show how the use and abuse of definitions in theoretical constructions could lead to heated disputes about the exact meaning of terms. The Hayek–Keynes controversy is a prime example of this practice. Third, points 1 and 6 point to differences in argumentative styles that may explain why Hayek and Keynes failed to communicate. Hayek had a tendency towards the use of deductive methods and logical rigour in scientific analysis (Colonna 1990: 54). That is the reason why he stressed the need for clear and consistent definitions in economic theorizing and criticized Keynes's obscure and sloppy use of definitions in the *Treatise*. Keynes on the other hand attached great value to intuitive judgements in economic reasoning on the grounds that in economics definitions are necessarily vague and imprecise. He considered Hayek's elaborate discussion of the terminological inconsistencies in the *Treatise* as a lack of the goodwill required to reach agreement on an intuitive level. Hayek, in Keynes's view, split too many hairs and failed to grasp the essence of the analysis presented. This meant that there was no basis on which a debate with Hayek could be fruitful. Further efforts to try and persuade him would be a waste of time and energy.

CONCLUSION

It may be concluded that the reference to paradigmatic differences provides only a partial explanation for the lack of communication which characterizes the Hayek–Keynes controversy. Employing the term 'paradigm' to denote the differences between their respective approaches to business cycle theory draws the dividing line between their positions too sharply. It is true that there are important differences between their business cycle theories; they give different explanations of the origin of monetary disequilibrium and the subsequent propagation of shocks throughout the economy, but these disagreements do not rule out discourse by definition. Even though they must have contributed to the misunderstandings discussed, they do not preclude comparison and can be reconciled in terms of a common problem, that of coordination between individual decisions in a decentralized economy. This is a reason to see their theories as complementary rather than supplementary. It indicates that Keynes and Hayek account for different classes of phenomena which are not mutually exclusive, but refer to different aspects of the same process. Here it might be unfruitful to speak of different paradigms, conjuring up the penumbra of methodological and semantic incommensurabilities.

Stated in these terms, there is nothing worth explaining about the Hayek–Keynes controversy, since the potential for discourse between competing paradigms is precluded by definition. To escape this conclusion, there should be other reasons why Hayek and Keynes never explored the common ground of their interests in the monetary causes of the business cycle. Such reasons can be found in several details of their debate, such as the chronology of their exchanges, their disagreements concerning the exact meaning of the definitions employed and their different views on the proper rules of scientific discourse, which show that they were talking at cross purposes and never seriously addressed their substantial disagreements. Instead, they misinterpreted and misrepresented each other's theories and quarrelled about the definitions they employed. It was this aspect of their controversy which led to the misunderstandings which characterize their dispute and caused the breach between them.

NOTES

1 See the second quotation in note 2 below. For Hayek's brief comment to this reply, see his 1931b.

2 Twelve letters of the Hayek–Keynes correspondence during the period December 1931–March 1932 have survived (Keynes 1973: 257–66). They largely deal with the exact meaning of Hayek's definition of forced savings. Hayek's extensive elucidations, however, failed to convince Keynes of its meaning and relevance. On 11 February 1932, Keynes professed to have the same confusion about this notion as when he first broached the question: 'Going back to the point at which our correspondence started, I am left where I began, namely in doubt as to just what you mean by voluntary saving and forced saving as applied to the real world we live in' (*ibid.*: 265). On 29 March 1932 he ended the correspondence and informed Hayek that '[H]aving been much occupied in other directions, I have not yet studied your *Economica* article as closely as I shall. But . . . I doubt if I shall return to the charge in *Economica*' (*ibid.*: 266).

3 As Hayek remarked, 'Only in comparatively few cases will the people who have saved money and the people who want to use it in production be identical. In the majority of the cases, therefore, the money which is directed to new uses will first have to pass in other hands' (Hayek 1935: 84; see also 1939: 144–5). Likewise, Keynes observed that 'It is not surprising that saving and investment should often fail to keep step. In the first place . . . the decisions which determine saving and investment respectively are taken by two different sets of people influenced by different set of motives, each not paying very much attention to the other' (Keynes 1930: 250).

4 In *Interest and Prices* (first published as *Geldzins und Güterpreise* in 1898) Wicksell referred to this rate as the interest rate that would exist if all lending were effected in the form of real capital goods (Wicksell 1936: 102). Hayek adopted this same definition in his *Prices and Production* (Hayek 1931a: 23), which provoked severe criticism by Sraffa who, quite correctly, argued that there is no single rate of interest in a barter economy (Sraffa 1932: 92; see also Hayek 1933: 210; and Blaug 1985: 639). For a recent review of the Hayek–Sraffa exchange see Lawlor and Horn (1992).

5 It is by no means true that Hayek considered monetary disturbances the *only* cause of cyclical fluctuations. There are many other factors which 'may at any time increase the profitability of any group of enterprises' and start an investment boom in those sectors (Hayek 1933: 182–3). The point he wishes to emphasize is that 'the modern economic system cannot be conceived without fluctuations ascribable to monetary influences; and therefore any other factors which may be found necessary to explain the empirically observed phenomena will have to be regarded as causes *additional* to the monetary cause' (*ibid.*: 186, emphasis in the original).

6 This is one of the main reasons why Hayek defined equilibrium as an intertemporal concept in his early study on 'Intertemporal price equilibrium

and movements in the value of money' (Hayek 1928). In economics the assumption of equilibrium is a useful fiction because it abstracts from the problems caused by the element of time in the analysis. However, Hayek (1928) argues that the validity of this assumption may be questioned, given the observation that all economic activity is carried out through time. So, 'it becomes evident that the customary abstraction from time does a degree of violence to the actual state of affairs which casts serious doubt upon the utility of the results thereby achieved' (*ibid.*: 72). According to Hayek, a realistic economic theory, which purports to explain the causal mechanism operating in a monetary economy, cannot abstract from the element of time. Hence, if the assumption of equilibrium is to be retained as a 'methodologically valuable fiction' it should be modified to incorporate this element. By defining an intertemporal conception of economic equilibrium which can serve as the basis for a more realistic, less abstract theory of a monetary economy, Hayek (1928) addresses this task (see also Hayek 1939: 139).

7 In the three-sector macroeconomic model that includes banks, firms and households, the supply of loanable funds consists of private and business savings plus bank credit. The total demand for loanable funds equals the sum of the investment demand and the net demand for purposes of hoarding inactive balances. Planned saving therefore equals planned investment when the inactive balances exactly absorb the net credit creation. This means that, by determining the supply of credit, the banks have the ability to change the interest rate (Blaug 1985: 641).

8 Adding a financial sector to a basic two-sector macroeconomic model allowed Hayek to give an endogenous explanation of the business cycle. He did not rest content with ad hoc changes in the money stock causing cyclical disturbances. More important was the case in which such changes arise endogenous to the operation of a monetary economy (Cottrell 1994: 200). 'The situation in which the money rate of interest is below the natural rate need not, by any means, originate in a *deliberate lowering* of the rate of interest by the banks . . . The decisive significance of the case quoted is . . . due to the fact that . . . it *must inevitably recur* under the existing credit organization' (Hayek 1933: 147–8, emphasis in the original). The determining cause of the cyclical fluctuation is the elasticity of bank credit (*ibid.*: 179–80).

9 The fact that entrepreneurs accept the interest rate as a reliable guide for the prediction of future demand explains why they should all simultaneously make mistakes in the same direction (Hayek 1939: 141). In this regard Hayek's equilibrium mechanism depends on a certain type of rule-guided behaviour: the rule that a lower (higher) interest rate warrants an increase (decrease) in investment spending. But entrepreneurs will only accept this rule because, on average, it proved a reliable guide in their past decisions. In other words, Hayek's monetary theories already point at the crucial relationship between the role of knowledge in the economy and the equilibrium mechanism that governs it; an issue that would occupy him more and more in later years (see Desai 1994).

10 The boom caused by the credit expansion will, in the end, force the banks to raise their lending rates. Inflation continues to increase the demand for credit which, for a given amount of cash reserves, impairs the liquidity of the banks. Ultimately the growing drain on their cash balances forces them to check further credit expansion (Hayek 1933: 175–6; Klausinger 1989: 19).

11 For a more detailed exposition of the Hayekian business cycle the reader is referred to Klausinger (1989), Colonna (1990), van Zijp (1993) and Cottrell (1994).

12 It is very likely that Keynes's monetary ideas reflect his own personal experiences, first as a civil servant and government advisor during the war of 1914–18 and later as a speculator in the City of London (e.g. Leijonhufvud 1981: 161; Skidelsky 1992: 316). Familiar with the actual operations of financial markets, Keynes argued that the interest rate is determined on the Exchange, not by the banking system. Accordingly, in the *Treatise* the demand price for capital goods is determined by supply and demand in the market for securities (Keynes 1930: 128, 226). Later in the *General Theory* he shifted the emphasis from the Exchange to the money market and claimed that the supply and demand for money determine the interest rate.

13 Leontief also criticized the sloppy use made by Cambridge economists of the definitions they adopted in their analyses. He said that Cambridge economists had acquired the bad habit of never explicitly defining the terms they used in their theories. They merely implied that a relation existed between the basic postulates and the variables they set out to explain; a habit which he called 'implicit theorizing'. He argued that the implicit use of definitions made their theories immune to criticism, for it was never precisely clear to a critic what a theory involved (Leontief 1937: 345).

14 For a discussion of the reception of the *Treatise* see Dimand (1989).

15 Referring to the above quotation from the first part of Hayek's review, Keynes writes that '[i]t is essential to [my] theory to deny these propositions – which Dr. Hayek puts in *my* mouth' (Keynes 1931: 51, emphasis in the original).

16 However, Hayek later recognized the relevance of the portfolio approach to monetary theory and in his *The Pure Theory of Capital* (1941) treated liquidity preference as a determinant of the short-run money rate of interest (Hayek 1941: 37, 359; see Nentjes 1989: 145).

17 A similar attempt is made in Chapter 16 of the *General Theory*, where Keynes tries to undermine the Austrian notion of roundaboutness (see Mongiovi 1990: 147–8).

18 'It seems probable that capital formation and capital consumption, as used by the Austrian school of economists, are not identical either with investment and disinvestment as defined above or with net investment and disinvestment. In particular, capital consumption is said to occur in circumstances where there is quite clearly no net decrease in capital equipment as defined above. I have, however, been unable to discover a reference to any passage where the meaning of these terms is clearly defined' (Keynes 1936: 76).

REFERENCES

Andvig, J.C. (1991) 'Verbalism and definitions in interwar theoretical macroeconomics', *History of Political Economy*, 23 (3): 431–55.

Birner, J. (1985) 'Keynes versus Hayek: interne en externe factoren in een controverse in de economie', *Kennis en Methode*, IX (1): 26–48.

——(1993) 'A tale of two foxes: an essay on intellectual styles and the life of ideas', Research Memorandum, Limburg University.

Blaug, M. (1985) *Economic Theory in Retrospect*, 4th edn, Cambridge: Cambridge University Press.

Boyd, R. (1991) 'Confirmation, semantics, and the interpretation of scientific theories', in R. Boyd, Ph. Gasper and J.D. Trout (eds) *The Philosophy of Science*, Cambridge, MA: MIT Press, 3–35.

Cochran, J.P. and Glahe, F.R. (1994) 'The Keynes–Hayek debate: lessons for contemporary business cycle theorists', *History of Political Economy*, 26 (1): 69–94.

Colonna, M. (1990) 'Hayek on money and equilibrium', *Contributions to Political Economy*, 9: 43–68.

Cottrell, A. (1994) 'Hayek's early cycle theory re-examined', *Cambridge Journal of Economics*, 18: 197–212.

Desai, M. (1994) 'Equilibrium, expectations and knowledge', in J. Birner and R.W. van Zijp (eds) *Hayek: Co-ordination and Evolution*, London: Routledge, 25–50.

Dimand, R.W. (1989) 'The reception of Keynes's *Treatise on Money*: a review of the reviews', in D.A. Walker (ed.) *Perspectives in the History of Economic Thought*, vol. II, Aldershot: Edward Elgar, 87–96.

Garrison, R. (1984) 'Time and money: the universals of macroeconomic theorizing', *Journal of Macroeconomics*, 6: 197–213.

Hayek, F.A. (1928) 'Intertemporal price equilibrium and movements in the value of money', in R. McCloughry (ed.) *Money, Capital and Fluctuations*, London: Routledge & Kegan Paul, 1984, 71–117.

——(1931a) *Prices and Production*, 1st edn, London: Routledge & Kegan Paul.

——(1931b) 'Reflections on *The Pure Theory of Money* of Mr. J.M. Keynes (I)', *Economica*, 11 (August): 270–95, in J.C. Wood and R.N. Woods (eds) (1991) *Friedrich A. Hayek. Critical Assessments*, vol. I, London: Routledge, 1–23.

——(1931c) 'A rejoinder to Mr. Keynes', *Economica*, 11 (November): 398–403, in J.C. Wood and R.N. Woods (eds) (1991) *Friedrich A. Hayek. Critical Assessments*, vol. I, London: Routledge, 60–4.

——(1932) 'Reflections on *The Pure Theory of Money* of Mr. J.M. Keynes (II)', *Economica*, 12 (February): 22–44, in J.C. Wood and R.N. Woods (eds) (1991) *Friedrich A. Hayek. Critical Assessments*, vol. I, London: Routledge, 65–85.

——(1933) *Monetary Theory and the Trade Cycle*, New York: Kelley, 1975.

——(1935) *Prices and Production*, 2nd edn, London: Routledge & Kegan Paul.

——(1937) 'Economics and knowledge', *Economica*, 4: 33–54.

——(1939) 'Price expectations, monetary disturbances and malinvestments', in *Profits, Interest and Investment*, New York: Kelley, 1966, 135–56.

——(1941) *The Pure Theory of Capital*, London: Routledge & Kegan Paul.

——(1945) 'The use of knowledge in society', *American Economic Review*, 35 (4): 519–30.

Hicks, J.R. (1967a) 'A note on the *Treatise*', in *Critical Essays in Monetary Theory*, Oxford: Clarendon, 189–202.

——(1967b) 'The Hayek story', in *Critical Essays in Monetary Theory*, Oxford: Clarendon, 203–15.

——(1982a) 'LSE and the Robbins Circle', in *Money, Interest and Wages*, Oxford: Blackwell, 3–10.

——(1982b) 'A suggestion for simplifying the theory of money', in *Money, Interest and Wages*, Oxford: Blackwell, 46–63.

Keynes, J.M. (1930) *A Treatise on Money: I The Pure Theory of Money, The Collected Writings of John Maynard Keynes*, vol. V, London: Macmillan, 1971.

——(1931) 'The Pure Theory of Money. A reply to Dr. Hayek', *Economica*, 11 (November): 387–97, in J.C. Wood and R.N. Woods (eds) (1991) *Friedrich A. Hayek. Critical Assessments*, vol. I, London: Routledge, 50–9.

——(1936) *The General Theory of Employment, Interest, and Money, The Collected Writings of John Maynard Keynes*, vol. VII, London: Macmillan, 1973.

——(1973) *The General Theory and After: Part I Preparation, The Collected Writings of John Maynard Keynes*, vol. XIII, London: Macmillan.

——(1979) *The General Theory and After: a Supplement, The Collected Writings of John Maynard Keynes*, vol. XXIX, London: Macmillan.

Kirzner, I.M. (1987) 'The Austrian school of economics', *The New Palgrave Dictionary of Economics*, London: Macmillan, 145–51.

Klausinger, H.J. (1989) *Theorien der Geldwirtschaft*, Berlin: Duncker & Humblot.

Lawlor, M.S. and Horn, B.L. (1992) 'Notes on the Sraffa–Hayek Exchange', *Review of Political Economy*, 4 (3): 317–40.

Leijonhufvud, A. (1981) 'The Wicksell connection; variations on a theme', in *Information and Coordination*, Oxford: Oxford University Press, 131–202.

Leontief, W. (1937) 'Implicit theorizing: a methodological criticism of the neo-Cambridge school', *Quarterly Journal of Economics*, 51: 337–51.

McCormick, B.J. (1992) *Hayek and the Keynesian Avalanche*, Hemel Hempstead: Harvester Wheatsheaf.

Mises, L. (1924) *Theorie des Geldes und der Umlaufsmittel*, 2nd edn, Leipzig: Duncker & Humblot.

Mongiovi, G. (1990) 'Keynes, Hayek and Sraffa: on the origins of chapter 17 of the *General Theory*', *Economie Appliquée*, 43: 131–56.

Nentjes, A. (1989) 'Hayek and Keynes: a comparative analysis of their monetary views', in J.J. Krabbe, A. Nentjes and H. Visser (eds) *Austrian Economics: Roots and Ramifications Reconsidered*, Bradford: MCB University Press.

Robertson, D.H. (1934) 'Industrial fluctuations and the natural rate of interest', *Economic Journal*, 44: 650–6.

——(1940) *Essays in Monetary Theory*, London: Staples Press, 1948.

Shackle, G.L.S. (1967) *The Years of High Theory*, Cambridge: Cambridge University Press.

Skidelsky, R. (1992) *John Maynard Keynes, vol. 2: The economist as savior, 1920–1937*, Harmondsworth: Penguin, 1995.

Sraffa, P. (1932) 'Dr. Hayek on money and capital', in J.C. Wood and R.N. Woods (eds) (1991) *Friedrich A. Hayek. Critical Assessments*, vol. I, London: Routledge, 86–96.

Steele, G.R. (1993) 'Philosophical perceptions and the precepts of political economy: Friedrich von Hayek and John Maynard Keynes', *Scottish Journal of Political Economy*, 40: 88–103.

Wicksell, K. (1935) *Lectures on Political Economy*, vol. II, London: Routledge & Kegan Paul.

——(1936) *Interest and Prices*, New York: Kelley, 1965. First published as *Geldzins und Güterpreise*, Jena: Gustav Fischer, 1898.

Zijp, R.W. van (1993) *Austrian and New Classical Business Cycle Theories*, Aldershot: Edward Elgar.

6

CRITICAL REALISM
Marx and Hayek
Steve Fleetwood

On initial reflection, Marx's work on value and Hayek's work on order not only appear to be different projects, they seem to be grounded in different philosophical and methodological perspectives. This initial reflection is, I believe, mistaken. The source of the error lies in a misunderstanding of the philosophy and method adopted by each thinker respectively, which is then carried over into a (mis)identification of their central projects. The similarities between Marx and Hayek in terms of philosophy and method, and of their central projects, become partially obscured, and are thereby apt to be overlooked.

This chapter attempts to correct this mistaken reflection, by pursuing primary and secondary, although inextricably linked, objectives. The primary objective is to develop an understanding of the similar philosophy and method adopted by Marx and Hayek. The secondary objective is to use this understanding to correctly identify their central projects and highlight the similarities that lie within these projects. When these similarities are made visible, the way is then open for a dialogue between Austrians and Marxists.

Pursuing these objectives is done in three parts. The first section introduces the philosophical and methodological perspective of *critical realism* (CR). Section two argues that in his work on order, and on social rules of conduct and the telecommunications system, the mature Hayek (post 1960) adopts a quasi-CR perspective.[1] The final section argues that in Marx's work on value, utilizing social structures in the form of relations of production, commodities and the value form, he adopts a CR perspective.

CRITICAL REALISM

While empiricist philosophy and methodology, typically, prioritize epistemological questions (for instance, 'How can one gain reliable knowledge of what exists?'), CR prioritizes ontological questions (such as 'What is the nature of existence?'). Prioritizing ontological matters does not, of course, mean ignoring epistemological ones. It means recognizing that the nature of the world determines the way one can actually go about obtaining knowledge of it – which is, typically, the reverse of the positivist economist's *modus operandi*.[2] So what, according to CR, is the nature of the world? The next two subsections illustrate that from the CR perspective, the world is *layered* and *transformational*. The final subsection highlights the switch in the mode of theorizing encouraged by this layered and transformational ontology.[3]

Layered ontology

Bhaskar establishes the possibility of a layered ontology via an inquiry into the practice of science, with particular emphasis upon the notion of laws.[4] Laws are, typically, presumed to be of the Humean variety, that is based upon the presumption of constant conjunctions of events and styled here as: 'Whenever event X, then event Y.' Bhaskar makes two key observations from this understanding of law, identifies two key problems, then draws implications for ontology. First, almost all the constant conjunctions of events that are of interest to science do not occur spontaneously, but in experimental situations.[5] The point of experiment is to *close the system* by creating a particular set of conditions that will isolate the interesting causal mechanism from all those that are not of interest. The interesting causal mechanism is then allowed to operate unimpeded and the results, the constant conjunctions, are recorded. Hence, the Humean law is more accurately styled as: 'Whenever event X, then event Y, *under conditions Z.*' Second, the results obtained from experimental situations where conditions Z exist (that is, in closed systems) are often successfully applied outside experimental situations (in open systems).

Two problems follow. First, if Humean law is based upon a constant conjunction of events, and such constant conjunctions are, typically, not found outside closed systems, then one must conclude that there are no laws outside closed systems.[6] Second, if Humean law is based upon a constant conjunction of events, and such constant conjunctions are, typically, not found in open systems, then the question of what governs events in open systems is left unaddressed. Moreover, it leaves the observation that the results obtained from closed systems are often successfully applied in open systems without any valid explanation.

If events manifesting themselves as constant conjunctions are, typically, not found in open systems, whence Humean law cannot govern or explain them, then something else must govern and explain them. The governing mechanism cannot be predicated upon a constant conjunction of events because whatever does govern events does so even when the events do not manifest themselves in constant conjunctions. The mechanism (gravity) which governs the fall of the autumn leaf does not cease to govern when the leaf fails to conform to any empirical regularity - that is when the leaf is acted upon by a series of other (possibly counteracting) mechanisms such as aerodynamic and thermodynamic mechanisms. This has implications for ontology.

There appears to be an ontological domain where events actually occur, a domain where they are experienced and a domain where the mechanisms and structures that govern these events are operative. This *layered* ontology is represented by Lawson (1994c: 263) in the table below.

The best way of understanding what this layered ontology entails is via an example:

1 *Domain of the empirical.* One might perceive agents engaging in satisfactory transactions, that is exchanging goods or services without resort to swindling or theft.
2 *Domain of the actual.* Most agents actually do engage in satisfactory transactions.
3 *Domain of the deep.* There are 'deep structures' such as the rules of private property that causally govern this actuality.

These domains are, typically, *unsynchronized* or *out of phase with one another.* For example, although most of the time most agents participate in satisfactory transactions, occasionally some do not. This deviant action occurs irrespective of whether or not it is perceived and in spite of the fact that the rules of private property persist throughout. Being out of phase means that structures existing in the domain of the deep, such as rules of private property, might (a) only be indirectly observable, and (b) act *transfactually.* The indirectly observable nature of deep structures implies that science has to take the domain beyond the actual and empirical seriously.

The transfactual nature of deep structures carries two implications, both of which assist in the explanation of the non-existence of constant conjunc-

Domain	Entity	
Empirical	Experience Impression Perception	
Actual	Events and actions	These three domains are, typically, 'out of phase' with one another
'Deep'	Structures[7] Mechanisms Rules Powers Relations	

tions of events. Transfactuality implies that deep structures such as the rules of private property continue to govern the flux of events even when the events

- are not manifest *at all* in the domains of the actual or empirical, or
- are not manifest as constant conjunctions.

This is because other, countervailing structures (such as high rates of poverty) might also be governing the behaviour of the agents engaged in the transaction. Typically, then, one will not be able to make the empirical observation that all transactors, at all times, engage in satisfactory transactions. The actual events depend upon the interplay of a range of causally governing structures.

Although the discussion has been couched in terms of natural science, it can readily be extended into social science by making the following claims about human agency. If human agency is real, then (a) human agents could always have acted otherwise, and (b) human action must make a difference to the social world.[8] The implication arising from these claims is that the social world is open. The conclusions derived from an investigation of the practice of natural science, therefore, hold for social science. The social world constitutes an open system and the social ontology is layered.

Transformational ontology

Not only is the ontology adopted by CR layered, it is also transformational. Bhaskar establishes the possibility of a transformational ontology from an investigation into the nature of society.[9] While, traditionally, most commentators recognize that society consists (in some sense) of agents and structures, the debate centres upon the way they interact. With the Transformational Model of Social Action (TMSA), Bhaskar enjoins this debate. He proceeds to identify, and retain, the correct parts of the three traditional social ontologies, synthesizing them to form a new position.

From the reificationist position represented by Durkheim,[10] Bhaskar retains the notion that structural elements exert constraint upon agents. From the voluntarist position represented by Weber,[11] he retains the notion that social material is concept dependent; it depends upon the intentional and meaningful behaviour of individuals. From the 'dialectical' position represented by Berger,[12] Bhaskar retains the notion that the other two positions are reductionist; the task of social theorists is to find a way of avoiding the Scylla and Charybdis of reification and voluntarism while elaborating a *meaningful* interaction or relation between agents and structures.

Nothing happens out of nothing. Agents do not create or produce structures *ab initio*. Instead, they *re*create, *re*produce and/or *transform* a set of pre-existing structures. Society continues to exist only because agents reproduce and/or transform those structures that they encounter in their social actions. Every action performed requires the pre-existence of some social structures which agents draw upon to initiate that action, and in doing so they reproduce and/or transform those structures. For example, communicating requires a medium (language) and the operation of the market requires the rules of private property. This ensemble of social structures, according to Bhaskar, simply *is* society. As Bhaskar observes:

> [P]eople do not create society. For it always pre-exists them and is a necessary condition for their activity. Rather society must be regarded as an ensemble of structures, practices and conventions which individuals reproduce and transform, but which would not exist unless they did so. Society does not exist independently of human activity (the error of reification). But it is not the product of it (the error of voluntarism).
>
> (Bhaskar 1989: 36. See also 1987: 129)

So, the transformational principle centres upon the mechanisms and structures that are the ever-present condition, and the continually reproduced and/or transformed outcome, of human agency. Agents, acting purposefully or consciously, draw unconsciously upon these mechanisms and thereby reproduce the structures which govern their actions in daily life. People do not marry with the conscious aim of reproducing the nuclear family, yet this is nevertheless an unintended consequence of, as well as a necessary condition for, their activity.[13]

Switch in the mode of theorizing

Operating with a layered and transformational ontology, the emphasis of investigation necessarily switches (ontologically speaking) from the domains of the empirical and actual, to the domain of the deep and the deep structures that govern these events/actions. With the recognition that the events/actions of experience are not manifest in the form of constant conjunctions, the notion of Humean law becomes untenable. As a consequence, the axiomatic deductive mode of theorizing is also rendered untenable. When this is combined with the further recognition that something must govern the events/actions of experience, then the mode of theorizing, if it is to bear fruit, must switch.

Although the consequences of particular events/actions *cannot* be deduced, one does not have to abandon 'scientific' or systematic investigation: the conditions for the possibility of these events/actions *can* be excavated. The deep structures which act with transfactual necessity to govern the events/actions given in sense experience can be uncovered and their operation illuminated and explained. Hence the domain of the deep is where investigation must focus. As Bhaskar says:

Looked at in this way [TMSA] . . . the task of the various social sciences [is] to lay out the structural conditions for various conscious human actions – for example, what economic processes must take place for Christmas shopping to be possible – but they do not describe the latter.

(Bhaskar 1989: 36)

Metaphorically speaking, then, the correct *modus operandi* of economics is *not* to move (horizontally) between actions/events, trying to ascertain or generate constant conjunctions, but to move (vertically) from events/actions to the deep structures which govern them. Economics, from the CR perspective, proceeds by inquiring into, illuminating and explaining the conditions (the reproduction and/or transformation of deep structures) necessary for the existence of some observed socio-economic activity. Illumination and explanation supplant deduction and prediction.[14]

HAYEK

What has just been adumbrated is extremely important if one is to understand that Hayek's explanation of the market process is an example of a transformational principle. Once a layered and transformational ontology is recognized, and the alternative mode of theorizing that is engendered by it is adopted, the possibility is open to replace the principle of equilibrium with the transformational principle of order – which is what Hayek does after about 1960.[15]

An equilibrium is an end state; a state where all that is going to happen has happened.[16] A theory of equilibrium focuses upon and defines the spatio-temporal coordination of some events/actions; its ontological orientation is upon the domains of the actual and empirical. A transformational order, by contrast, is a process; a process involving the mechanisms and structures that are the ever-present condition and the continually reproduced and/or transformed outcome of human agency. A theory of transformational order focuses not on the outcome of events/actions, but on the conditions that make these events/actions possible; its ontological orientation is upon the domain of the deep. Since the source of the 'order' lies with the mechanisms and structures, the task of economics is to illuminate and explain what these mechanisms and structures are, and how they are reproduced and/or transformed.

The objective of this section is to establish the claim that Hayek appears to accept this philosophy and methodology, ontology, mode of theorizing and task of economics. It will demonstrate how the interpretation of Hayek as a quasi CR allows one to identify the essential nature of his notion of order. The subsection on Hayek's quasi TMSA remains at a high level of abstraction, laying out Hayek's layered and transformational ontology, while the following subsection charts the switch in Hayek's mode of theorizing stemming from it. The last two subsections proceed to more concrete matters by elaborating upon Hayek's understanding of social rules of conduct and their articulation with the telecommunications system in the market process leading to the formation of a transformational order.

Hayek's quasi TMSA

According to the Hayekian quasi TMSA presented here, the socio-economy is the ensemble of resources (knowledge), mechanisms (telecommunications system) and structures (rules). However, these elements are not merely thrown together in a heap; there is a principle of organization in operation, and that principle is transformation. These elements are the ever-present condition and the continually reproduced outcome of human agency.

Agents, who are equipped with the cognitive apparatus that facilitates rule-following action, who have resources in the form of localized 'knowledge of time and place' (Hayek 1945: 527)[17] and who are motivated by the desire to increase their own welfare, initiate courses of action and attempt to bring about certain desired consequences. This action necessitates the drawing upon, and thereby reproduction and/or transformation of, social rules of conduct. In the absence of formal mechanisms which facilitate the production, communication and storage of knowledge (such as the trade press), access to a sufficient quantity of knowledge would be severely limited. In the absence of informal mechanisms, the telecom system being central, communication would (allegedly) be so cumbersome that no one would know enough about relatively distant economic activity to coordinate their plans and actions with others. However, in the absence of social rules of conduct, no social action of any kind would be possible, as agents can only act by following these rules. Agents cannot initiate meaningful social action without working with resources, mechanisms and structures, and in working with them, they are reproduced and/or transformed

Switch in the mode of theorizing

With the adoption of something approaching a CR ontology, an extremely important development in Hayek's method appears to occur. His mode of theorizing switches from what he refers to as 'narrow technical economics' (Hayek 1964a: 91), that is, from what might be described as a focus upon the domains of the actual and empirical to the domain of the deep.[18] It switches from a preoccupation with events/actions given in sense experience, to a preoccupation with the deep structures that govern them. Economics, for Hayek, becomes an inquiry into, and explanation of, the various resources, mechanisms and structures that are drawn upon, reproduced and/or transformed in establishing socio-economic order. Although Hayek does not, of course, explain his *modus operandi* with this terminology, it appears to be a perfectly acceptable interpretation. It fits with his rejection of the notions of equilibrium and (Humean) law, and explains why, as an economist, he needs to focus upon social rules of conduct.

The evolution of Hayek's problematic

Although 'Hayek's work' appears to undergo what Lawson refers to as a 'continual transformation' (1994c), two significant sea changes can be detected. While the possibility of a change, dated from the publication of 'Economics and knowledge' (1937), is recognized,[19] the second, dated from the publication of *The Constitution of Liberty* (1960), is not. It appears that Hayek sets out *the* crucial question for economics in 1937 but cannot answer it satisfactorily until 1960. The question is this: How can the socio-economic activity of millions of unconnected individuals be coordinated when this requires the prior coordination of their plans, which in turn requires the discovery, communication and storage of an enormous quantity (and quality) of knowledge that exists only as a decentralized and fragmented totality?[20]

The answer comes in two temporally divided parts. In a 1945 paper, Hayek argues that coordination occurs due to the discovery, communication and storage of knowledge being facilitated by the telecom system – Hayek's term for the price mechanism. By itself, however, the telecom system cannot perform this facility since, as Hayek is aware, there is a range of knowledge that is discovered, communicated and stored by mechanisms other than the telecom system.[21] In his work after 1960 Hayek argues that the discovery, communication and storage of knowledge is facilitated not by the telecom system *alone*, but by the telecom system articulating with, and embedded within, a dense web of social rules of conduct.[22] As Hayek puts it:

> [It] is mainly changes in price that bring about the necessary adjust-ments. This means that, for [the price system] to function properly, it is not sufficient that the rules of law under which it operates be gen-eral rules, but that their content must be such that the market will work tolerably well. The case for a free system is not that any system will work satisfactorily where coercion is confined by general rules, but that under it such rules can be given a form that will enable it to work . . . [The] efficiency of the system will depend on the particular content of the rules.
>
> (Hayek 1960: 228–9, see also 350)

Hayek, it appears, comes to recognize that the telecom system alone cannot facilitate the discovery, communication and storage of the knowledge necessary for socio-economic order to occur, yet occur it does. Some other knowledge-facilitating device must therefore be in operation, and this something else turns out to be social rules. This raises the following question: What properties do rules possess that enable them to articulate with the telecom system to facilitate the discovery, communication and storage of knowledge? In one place Hayek writes:

> In such spontaneous formations [as a market society] is embodied a perception of the general laws that govern nature. With this cumulative embodiment of experience in tools and forms of action will emerge a growth of explicit knowledge, of formulated generic rules that can be communicated by language from person to person.
>
> (Hayek 1960: 33)

Hayek describes an historical, evolutionary process of trial and error whereby agents discover new rules or modify existing ones, using them as a basis for action. The reason rules can serve as a basis for action is because they embody the collected wisdom of the society.[23] As Hayek puts it:

> Like all general purpose tools, rules serve because they . . . help to make the members of the society . . . more effective in pursuit of their aims . . . The knowledge that has given them their shape . . . is knowledge of the occurrence of certain problem situations.
>
> (Hayek 1973: 21)

> [By] guiding the actions of individuals by rules . . . it is possible to make use of knowledge which nobody possesses as a whole.
>
> (*ibid.*: 49)

> Most knowledge . . . is obtained . . . in the continuous process of sifting a learnt tradition . . . The tradition is the product of a process of selection . . . which without anyone knowing or intending it, assisted in the proliferation of those who followed them . . . The process of selection that shaped custom and morality could take account of more factual circumstances than individuals could perceive, and in consequence tradition is in some respects superior to, or 'wiser' than human reason.
>
> (Hayek 1988: 75)

By embodying the collected wisdom of society, knowledge becomes available to all individuals, giving what Butler refers to as an 'instant and unconscious summary of how to act' (Butler 1983: 23).[24]

With the nature of Hayek's problematic firmly understood, it is now possible to demonstrate that the market process *just is* the process of reproduction and/or transformation of the deep structures and mechanisms (the social rules and telecom system) which facilitate the discovery, communication and storage of knowledge and make coordinated socio-economic activity possible.

STEVE FLEETWOOD

The market process or catallaxy

Whereas the term 'economy' might refer to a planned system (which could even be an individual agent), the term 'catallaxy' contains no such constructivist connotations. A catallaxy is the order spontaneously 'brought about by the mutual adjustment of many individual economies in the market' (Hayek 1976: 108–9) and has four key characteristics.

First, while the individuals that populate the catallaxy are isolated, they are not *asocial* but *social* individuals. They are situated within, and depend for their ability to act upon, a web of social rules of conduct. Hayek offers a social theory rather than a set of claims about the behaviour of (fictitious) atomized individuals.

Second, each agent possesses differing fragments of knowledge. The precise extent of their knowledge is dependent upon the type of knowledge they have, lack, or seek. For example, an agent may have fairly extensive knowledge of the immediate environment, be virtually ignorant of the remote environment and radically ignorant of the future.

Third, agents have expectations, formulate plans and subsequently initiate courses of action to pursue their own goals – perhaps selfishly, perhaps with great altruism, the motive makes no difference. The point is, there is no one mind in control directing agents to initiate certain actions, to pursue certain goals, so there is no one mind attempting to make the agents' actions and goals compatible with one another.

At first glance this looks like a recipe for chaos: isolated individuals with small parcels of localized, fragmented and partial knowledge, who are occasionally ignorant, pursuing their own (perhaps) self-serving goals and have no conscious coordinating agency in control. It is the fourth important characteristic which, according to Hayek, prevents this slide into chaos and holds the key to establishing socio-economic order, namely the social rules of conduct. Since agents are only able to initiate social action (including reacting to price signals) by drawing upon social rules, their actions are simultaneously individually motivated and socially sanctioned. According to Hayek:

> What reconciles the individuals and knits them into a common and enduring pattern of a society is that . . . they respond in accordance with the same abstract rules . . . What . . . enables . . . men to live and work together in peace is that in the pursuit of their individual ends the particular monetary impulses which impel their efforts . . . are guided and restrained by the same abstract rules. If emotion or impulse tells them what they want, the conventional rules tell them how they will be able and be allowed to achieve it.
>
> (Hayek 1976: 12)

A catallaxy is thus the special kind of spontaneous order produced by the market through people acting within the rules of the law of property, tort and contract.

(ibid.: 109)

So, where *in*compatibility appears to be the more likely outcome, a high degree of compatibility of actions and consequences is ensured by the existence of a set of deep structures in the form of social rules of conduct.[25]

Social rules have two important characteristics: they relate not to specific but to general action, and are more often than not limiting in the sense that they forbid certain classes of action. The kind of rules Hayek has in mind do not specify that a particular commodity must sell at a particular price, or that a certain distribution of income must be maintained, or that a particular bankruptcy must be avoided.[26] These would be examples of constructivist rules; they are consciously designed and implemented. The rules Hayek does have in mind appear as a complex web of rules for the laws of property, tort and contract, although a series of tacit rules such as integrity, honesty and keeping promises are equally important for him.

While the complex web of rules acts to decrease uncertainty in general, it will almost inevitably increase uncertainty in particular instances. Rules can only ensure that agents have the potential to interact in a potentially fruitful manner, they cannot guarantee that they will do so: 'But all that rules can achieve in this respect is to make it easier for people to come together and to form [a] match: abstract rules cannot actually secure that this will always happen' (Hayek 1973: 99). This increase in local uncertainty is germane with respect to price, though it initially appears paradoxical. By following rules, agents are able to utilize the knowledge content of prices and thereby decide upon a course of action. However, the rules do not extend as far as stating what the price should be.

> The abstract rule of conduct can (and, in order to secure the formation of a spontaneous order, should) thus protect only the expectations of command over particular physical things and services, and not the expectations concerning their market value.
>
> (Hayek 1976: 124)

> It may at first appear paradoxical that in order to achieve the greatest attainable certainty it should be necessary to leave uncertain so important an object of expectations as the terms at which things can be bought and sold.
>
> <div align="right">(<i>ibid.</i>: 125)</div>

Prices have a very important temporal aspect to them, captured in Jevons's phrase 'bygones are forever bygones' (*ibid.*: 121). Only current prices are important, since they inform on what action ought to be taken in the present, that is they inform on how much time, effort and resources it is currently worth putting into a product. Resources already expended cannot be recovered if, over the passage of time, conditions which were thought stable actually change. In this case, there is a likelihood that the action will lead to disappointed expectations. So, prices will typically be the 'wrong' ones – they will contain the 'wrong' information.

Considering prices, along with social rules of conduct, there appears to be a complex interaction between the social structures of rules and the mechanisms of the telecom system. According to Ioannides:

> The price mechanism is not however the only knowledge-dispersion system in a market society . . . the *rules of conduct and the social institutions which have evolved through centuries . . . themselves constitute a knowledge disseminating system.* Through them, the knowledge of the legal, political and moral framework of any social activity is conveyed to all market participants.
>
> There is thus a major difference between the information disseminating functions of the price system and those rules and institutions. The knowledge dispersed by the former is of a dynamic nature, in the sense that it leads individuals to a constant revision of their plans. The knowledge dispersed by the latter is stabilizing, in the sense that it constantly affirms the stability of the social framework in which individuals act.
>
> (Ioannides 1992: 38, emphasis added)

Ioannides recognizes not only that social rules are structures that facilitate the discovery, communication and storage of knowledge in their own right, but also that there is a concatenation or articulation between them and prices. This places social rules on an equal footing with the telecom system vis-à-vis production, discovery and communication of knowledge, and makes it necessary for *economists* interested in the operation of the market to understand social structures.

Hayek appears to be arguing that, while following abstract, general rules and monitoring price signals, agents proceed by trial and error. This must inevitably involve a constant stream of disappointed expectations for a number of them. The continual process of trial and error, disappointed expectations and the communication of failure to others triggers a process of adaptation as agents strive to correct them. Once certain plans or expectations are shown to be false, then the consequences are perceived by other agents who might attempt to avoid acting on the same false expectations. As Lachmann puts it: 'Nobody can profitably [or one might add unprofitably] exploit his knowledge without conveying hints to others' (Lachmann 1976: 59).

However, since the ability of the mechanisms and structures that facilitate the discovery, communication and storage of knowledge are far from perfect, socio-economic coordination must also be far from perfect, efficient or optimal. Activity in the market place, proceeding by trial and error and therefore via the never-ending necessity of continual successes and disappointment, generates a socio-economic order which is far from mere chaos, even though it cannot be described as an equilibrium or perfect coordination of actions. If the socio-economy is neither perfectly coordinated nor chaotic, some alternative principle of organization must be in operation, and the most likely candidate is some form of transformational principle along the lines described here.

The mature Hayek appears to adopt a *transformational principle of spontaneous socio-economic order*. The conditions for socio-economic order: resources in the form of knowledge; mechanisms such as the telecom system that facilitate the discovery, communication and storage of this knowledge; and structures in the form of social rules of conduct are the ever-present conditions, and continually produced outcomes, of market-based action. Hayek's elaboration of the market process or catallaxy is the substantive manifestation of this transformational social ontology.

MARX

This third section will demonstrate how the interpretation of Marx as a CR allows one to identify the essential nature of his labour theory of value, namely that it is a theory of socio-economic order. The subsection 'Marx's critical realist ontology' remains at a high level of abstraction, laying out Marx's CR, layered and transformational ontology. The next subsection proceeds to more concrete matters by elaborating upon Marx's understanding of relations of production, the commodity and the value form, and the last two subsections focus respectively on the theory of value and Marx's mode of theorizing. The aim is to identify Marx's labour theory of value as

- a theory of socio-economic order, and
- an application of CR perspective.

Marx's critical realist ontology

Marx is well known for distinguishing between essence and appearance, that is between a realm where phenomena are operative and a realm where phenomena are manifest. This can quite easily be translated into CR terminology as a *layered* ontology. The following is a brief sketch of Marx's layered ontology, and this sketch will become clearer as the section unfolds.

1 *Domain of the empirical.* The social relations that coordinate the labouring activity between human beings *appear* as relations between things, between commodities. Social relations appear in the fetishized form of material relations between commodities.

139

2 *Domain of the actual.* Under specifically capitalist conditions, social relations do take the form of material relations between commodities because this is actually the only way labouring activity can be coordinated.

3 *Domain of the deep.* There are 'deep structures', specifically relations of production coordinating labouring activity. These relations causally govern the actuality and appearance.

Not only is Marx's ontology layered, it is also *transformational*. According to the Marxian TMSA presented here, society is the ensemble of material–technical and socio-economic relations. However, these relations are not thrown together in a heap; there is a principle of organization, and that principle is transformation. The relations are treated as the ever-present condition and the continually reproduced outcome of human agency. Pre-empting CR terminology, Marx stated:

> The conditions . . . of the direct production process . . . are themselves equally moments of it, and its only subjects are the individuals, but individuals in mutual relationships, which they equally reproduce and produce anew. The constant processes of their own movement, in which they renew themselves even as they renew the world of the wealth they create.
>
> (Marx 1973: 712)

Relations and historical specificity: two key factors[27]

This section will now attempt to put flesh on the bones of Marx's layered and transformational ontology sketched out above. Contrary to popular belief, the labour theory of value is not *primarily* concerned with prices, or for that matter with exploitation. Instead, it is concerned with the key relations which people necessarily enter into in a capitalist socio-economic formation so that production and reproduction occurs. According to Perlman:

> Political economy deals with human working activity, not from the standpoint of its technical methods and instruments of labour, but from the standpoint of its social relations which are established among people in the process of production . . . political economy is a study of social relations, a study of culture . . . [it] asks how the working activity of people is regulated in a specific, historical form of economy.
>
> (Perlman, in Rubin 1990: x)

Marx recognizes that human working activity (production) has material–technical and socio-economic aspects, and that both need to be grasped if one is to understand how socio-economic order is ensured.[28] At the basis of human life is a material–technical transformation. Work is an activity whereby matter is transformed from one state to another, more useful, state. This material–technical process is characterized by the following points:

- it is spatio-temporally universal
- it results in the production of a physical object and therefore relates to the domain of use value
- it requires material–technical coordination, that is raw materials and machinery must be spatially and temporally coordinated
- this coordination is ensured if and when material–technical relations are established, and this is what Marx has in mind when he refers to the material relations between things.

If, however, material–technical transformation is to occur, isolated producers must enter into production relations to coordinate and regulate their labouring activities. This entails a socio-economic process. As Marx puts it in the famous passage from the *Critique*:

> In the social production of their existence, men inevitably enter into definite relations, which are independent of their will, namely relations of production appropriate to a given stage in the development of the material forces of production. The totality of these relations of production constitutes the economic structure of society.
>
> (Marx 1970: 20–1)

This socio-economic process is characterized by the following points:

- Material transformation occurs by humans coordinating and regulating their socio-economic activities. Thus, material–technical relations necessarily imply socio-economic relations.
- Not only are various material entities produced and reproduced, so too are the relations into which people have entered.
- The socio-economic process captures social relations between people as opposed to material relations between things.
- Socio-economic relations are spatio-temporally specific, in that the mode of coordination of humans differs fundamentally in space and between epochs.

While the material–technical relations are spatio-temporally universal, socio-economic relations are spatio-temporally particular. This prompts Marx to inquire into the essential nature of a specifically capitalist socio-economic formation and gives rise to the following question: Given that coordination of production requires a greater quantity (and quality) of knowledge than is available to any one conscious agency, how is production coordinated and regulated under capitalism? It is here that Hayek's inquiry into the production, communication and storage of knowledge becomes interesting for Marxist economists, since this is exactly what Hayek wants to know. (See p. 134 above.)

I have taken the liberty of transposing Hayek's term the 'telecom system' into the Marxian framework because, although Marx never used this terminology, it is arguably quite in keeping with his thoughts. Marx's project and central question appear to be the same as Hayek's. For Marx, it is only via the telecom system that the abstract labour 'embodied' in a commodity becomes socially validated, socially sanctioned or, as Marx puts it, recognized as socially necessary. In other words, it is *essentially* via the market (understood in terms of Hayek's articulation of telecom system and rule network) that one isolated producer comes to obtain knowledge about the productive conditions of the multiplicity of other producers. As Marx puts it:

> The owners of commodities . . . find out that the same division of labour which turns them into independent private producers also makes the social process of production and the relations with the individual producers to each other within that process independent of the producers themselves.
>
> (Marx 1990: 202)

Marx recognizes that the function performed by the market is to produce, communicate and store sufficient quantities of knowledge to enable commodity production to continue relatively uninterrupted, thereby enabling the relations of production to be reproduced. How well or how badly the market actually does this is irrelevant for the purposes of this chapter; the point is merely that the market *is* the process by which this reproduction occurs.

For the purposes of understanding the labour theory of value as a theory of socio-economic order under capitalism, it is useful to proceed by comparing relations under a non-capitalist system to relations under a capitalist system. Consider a stylized, non-capitalist system such as a slave society, feudal society, Stalinist planned economy or even a capitalist enterprise consisting of spatially differentiated production sites.

Production takes place on isolated, unconnected production sites and requires the existence of a conscious agency (slave owner, feudal lord, central planner or manager) to design and oversee a production plan. Although the actual administration of the plan might be very difficult (or even impossible), the principle is quite straightforward. This conscious agency, possessing knowledge of the material–technical properties of things and production sites, ensures that labour, semi-finished objects and raw materials are spatio-temporally distributed in accordance with the technical requirements of the various stages of the productive processes.

Things flow from production site A to B to C (and so on) because the conscious agency, knowing a range of material–technical properties, knows that each subsequent site has the technical ability to transform the thing into some other thing that is more useful. By issuing instructions based only upon material–technical properties, relations are established between the sites. The relations that ensure the uninterrupted coordination of things are *permanent*, *direct* and *social*.

1 They are permanent because once they are established by the conscious agency, they endure until removed or altered.
2 They are direct because they are established without the intervention of any other vehicle. The connection is directly between plant and plant at the behest of the conscious agency.
3 They are social because the central agency has already 'socially sanctioned' the products and thereby the human labour expended upon them. Sanctioning occurs, typically, in the interests of the central agency.

So, under this stylized non-capitalist system, things move between productive stages because some conscious, central agency, possessing knowledge of material–technical properties of things and production sites, is able to establish a set of permanent and directly social relations to coordinate production. However, the things themselves are unimportant for the establishment of the relations which coordinate the processes that produce them – the importance of this will become clear in a moment.

Contrast this with a stylized capitalist system, whereby the three production sites are now owned by completely different firms. Things still circulate between independent production sites, but now for different reasons. Things pass from A to B, not *because* of any technical ability possessed by B to transform that object into something useful (although this is an obvious presupposition), but because a sum of money passes from B to A. Firm A is no longer interested in firm B's material–technical ability to transform things, they are no longer merely given away, but are now sold. Things cease to be mere things and become *commodities* produced solely for exchange on the market. They cease to be mere use values and become, in addition, *exchange values*.

There are no *permanent* production relations between A and B initiated at the behest of a conscious agency. Production relations are now only established through the successful exchange of commodities. The following points capture the changes involved when a non-capitalist formation gives rise to a capitalist one:

1 The relations are established not directly via a conscious agency, but *indirectly* via the commodity adopting the form of exchange value and successfully entering into an exchange for money.
2 The relations, while now indirect, remain *social*, but two important changes have occurred:
   (a) The temporal location where the 'social sanctioning' takes place has changed vis-à-vis the production process, from a priori to a posteriori.

It is now not in production but exchange that the labour embodied in the commodity is recognized as socially necessary – or not.

(b) The person(s) who do the sanctioning have changed from the conscious agency to 'society' at large.

3 The now indirectly social relations only endure as long as commodity exchange endures, hence the relations are *transient* and in need of continual renewal or reproduction.

In sum, only if the commodity finds a buyer on the market can the socio-economic relations and thus the material–technical relations be established. Failure to sell results in failure to establish relations of production and thereby failure of production and reproduction. The things themselves (the commodities) and the form in which they appear (exchange values) are now important for the establishment and maintenance of the relations, and therefore for the coordination of the very process, which produces them. Unlike non-commodity production, commodity production is based on a curious system whereby it is the very existence of the product as a *bona fide* commodity appearing in the form of an exchange value that creates the conditions for the reproduction of that commodity.

Making sense of the labour theory of value

Under capitalism, the process of producing and continually reproducing a set of useful objects requires the coordination and regulation of physical objects and human labouring activity, which in turn requires the establishment of relations of production, knowledge about the production processes of others and the wishes of consumers. This comes about via the production of a product which takes the forms of a commodity, and a value.

The successful completion of this chain of events rests upon the moment of successful valorization, that is the moment of exchange, whereby the level of human labouring activity expended is known to be socially necessary. Because value is the form taken by labouring activity, successful valorization conveys knowledge about the conditions under which that activity was expended, that is whether socially necessary labour has been performed or not. Only if such labour has been performed will reproduction of the commodity occur, and with it the reproduction of the material–technical and socio-economic relations upon which the capitalist socio-economic formation rests.

Marx, it would appear, understands that successful valorization is the key to the successful reproduction of the relations of production. Having explained how the successful valorization and reproduction of the relations of production is brought about, he has also explained how the capitalist form of socio-economic order is produced and re-produced – he has also, of course, laid the basis of an explanation of how and why this order may fail to be reproduced. The labour theory of value, then, is a theory of socio-economic order. Moreover, concentrating as it does upon the conditions necessary for the reproduction of relations of production, one could quite easily refer to the theory of value as a transformational theory of socio-economic order.

Marx's mode of theorizing

Marx appears to start from the 'stylized fact' that under capitalism, in contrast to all other modes of production, the products and human labouring activity appear in the form of commodities. In fact, volume I of *Capital* opens with the words: 'The wealth of societies in which the capitalist mode of production prevails appears as an immense collection of commodities; the individual commodity appears as its elementary form. Our investigation therefore begins with the analysis of the commodity' (Marx 1990: 126). Marx then proceeds to inquire into the conditions of possibility for such a society. In other words, he asks the following transcendental question: What conditions or essential relations might exist that would explain how and why human labouring activity appears in the form of a commodity? Marx proceeds by retroducing to a set of relations and their forms which, when combined, can explain the phenomena that appear in sense experience.[29]

So, for Marx, political economy involves an explanation of the deep structures, specifically the socio-economic and material–technical relations, that are drawn upon, reproduced and/or transformed in establishing socio-economic order. Furthermore, it involves an explanation of the forms taken by these relations as they manifest in the domain of the empirical – the commodity, the value and ultimately the money forms. Hence Marx unites essence and appearance, or in more CR language, the domains of the deep and the empirical. Although Marx does not, of course, explain his *modus operandi* in these terms, it appears to be a perfectly acceptable, if not well-known interpretation in Marxist circles. According to Sayer:

> Marx's object is the social forms assumed by economic phenomena . . . His 'analytic' consists of an excavation of the conditions that must be supposed for the phenomena to assume such forms, that is, of the essential relations that must exist if the world as experienced is to be possible. Marx's reasoning is thus eminently transcendental, although *pace* Kant, his is a transcendental realism.
>
> (Sayer 1979: 37)

Once one understands Marx's philosophy and method, and thereby his *modus operandi*, one is better placed to understand exactly the essential nature of his project, and hence the exact point of his theory of value. Moreover, once the labour theory of value is seen as a transformational theory of socio-economic order, the similarities with Hayek's project are striking.

CONCLUSION

If the interpretation offered here is valid, and both Hayek and Marx adopt something approaching a CR philosophy and methodology, then by extension they reject empiricism and its positivist variants. Yet one problem remains: many of their followers in the Austrian and Marxian camps respectively, do not follow Hayek and Marx in shifting towards a CR perspective and abandoning empiricism – or at least they do not follow sufficiently. There are two kinds of evidence for this claim. First, there are some who take Hayek's insights and attempt to weld them to a positivist/neoclassical framework (for instance, the search for a Hayekian notion of equilibrium).[30] Second, there are some who take Marx's insights and attempt to weld them to a positivist/Sraffian framework (for instance, the treatment of value theory as a version of general equilibrium theory).[31]

While any Austrian/Marxian dialogue is already clouded by dense ideological fog, visibility is restricted even further by this failure to abandon positivism. Failing to appreciate the philosophy and methodology used by Hayek and Marx leads on the one hand to many contemporary *Austrians* failing to understand (a) Hayek's central project and (b) Marx's central project. On the other hand, too many contemporary *Marxists* fail to understand (a) Marx's central project and (b) Hayek's central project. The result is not only that Austrians and Marxists respectively fail to see what their own paradigm has to offer, they also fail to see what the 'opposition' has to offer.

NOTES

1 The term 'quasi' in this sense means 'something approaching', and implies that Hayek does not actually adopt the entire corpus of CR, although I cannot elaborate here upon this point.
2 See Lawson (1994c: especially 257–61).
3 A CR ontology, or something approaching it, is implicitly presupposed in certain aspects of the works of Kaldor (Lawson 1989), Marx (Pratten 1993), post-Keynesians (Lawson 1994a) and Commons (Lawson 1994). Peacock (1993), Lawson (1995) and Fleetwood (1995) have also noted Hayek's possible CR credentials.
4 Bhaskar (1978: chapters 1, 2 and postscript); Collier (1994: chapter 2).
5 Hayek's discussion of 'complex phenomena' (by which he means primarily social phenomena) indicates his recognition that there are no constant conjunctions of events to be found in the social world and hence no Humean laws – though he does not, of course, put matters this way (1955: 3–4, 8–9). For a more detailed discussion, see Fleetwood (1995: chapter 2).
6 Note that the move into statistical theory does not overcome the problem that event regularities cannot be discovered. The 'Whenever X then Y' format is

essentially the same as the 'Whenever X then Y on average' or some such. Stochastic closure is still closure. On closure, see Lawson (1996).

7 The term 'structures' or 'deep structures' is a generic term to connote all phenomena of this domain. For instance, rules are deep structures. The term 'deep' is metaphoric.

8 Henceforth, and in recognition that the social scientific analogue of the natural scientific term 'event' is 'action', I shall refer to 'events/actions'.

9 Bhaskar (1987: 104–36; 1989: chapter 2).

10 'Reification' refers to the notion that society exists independently of human action. Put bluntly, agents' actions are merely the result of them being buffeted by social structures. Schematically: structures → (create) → agents' actions.

11 'Voluntarist' here refers to the notion that agents merely produce society in their actions. Not only are constraints on action not taken seriously, structures that *enable* action are also ignored. Schematically: agents' actions → (create) → structures.

12 'Dialectical' here refers to the notion of reciprocal causality where agents' actions cause structure which then causes agents' actions and so on. Schematically: agents' actions → (create) → structures → (create) → agents' actions etc. On all this, see Bhaskar (1989: 27–44).

13 It is important to note that, while social structures are necessary for action, that is they facilitate or causally govern action, they do not determine it. Social conventions may put pressure on people to marry but they do not determine whom they should marry. By using this conception CR is able to maintain an active role for human agency while at the same time avoiding the error of voluntarism and retaining constraining (and enabling) structures.

14 This is merely to claim that the mode of inference switches from deduction to retroduction. For a comparison of deduction and retroduction see Lawson (1994c) and for an elaboration of retroduction see Collier (1994: 160–7). See also note 29 below.

15 For a detailed exposition of Hayek's reorientation from equilibrium to order, see Fleetwood (1995: chapter 5, part 2).

16 See Hayek (1937: sections V–IV; 1946: 92–4).

17 The dates for Hayek's work will refer to the date of presentation or publication – whichever is earliest.

18 Hayek appears to think of himself, prior to the late 1930s, as a positivist – and therefore an empirical realist on my definition. In 1942 he writes: 'I myself originally approached my subject thoroughly imbued with the belief in the universal validity of the method of the natural sciences. Not only was my first technical training largely scientific in the narrow sense of the word but also what little training I had in philosophy or method was entirely in the school of Ernst Mach and later of the logical positivists' (Hayek 1942: 57–8).

19 There is something of a debate on this transformational interpretation. See Hutchison (1981: 210–18), Caldwell (1988), Zijp (1993: chapter 4), Lawson (1994b) and Foss (1995).

20 'Clearly there is here a problem of the Division of Knowledge which is quite analogous to, and at least as important as, the problem of the division of labour' (Hayek 1937: 49).

21 I shall cite just one example: 'Their knowledge of the alternatives before them is the result of what happens on the market, of such activities as advertising etc, and the *whole organisation of the market* serves mainly the need of spreading the information on which the buyer is to act' (Hayek 1946: 96, emphasis added). Hayek's reference to the 'whole organisation of the market' indicates

his awareness that there are institutions other than the telecom system that facilitate the discovery, communication and storage of knowledge.

22 This periodization is often missed by commentators who look for both the question *and* answer in Hayek's early work. They fail, therefore, to see the relevance of his more sophisticated (yet still economic) mature work on rules (see Desai 1994).

23 The idea that rules embody knowledge is not unique to Hayek. Institutionalist economists have long known of what one leading thinker calls the 'informational function of institutions' (Hodgson 1993: 7, 10; see also 1988: chapter 6).

24 For further elaboration of his work on rules, see Hayek (1962, 1964a, 1964b, 1967, 1970 and the 1979 epilogue).

25 Hayek's use of the term 'catallaxy' is extremely illuminating here. The word derives from ancient Greek and means not only to exchange, but more importantly 'to change from an enemy into a friend' (Hayek 1976: 108). The harnessing of a potentially destructive force lies at the heart of Hayek's spontaneous socio-economic order.

26 Hayek (1976: 4, chapters 7 and 10; 1960: chapter 4; 1962: 57; 1988: 12).

27 This section draws heavily on Rubin's (1990) interpretation of Marx, especially chapters 1 and 2.

28 The following section is based on Marx (1982: 42–8).

29 On Marx's use of retroduction see Wilson (1991: chapter 6). See also note 14 above.

30 See Vaughn (1992) for an overview of this kind of debate.

31 While all Sraffian-inspired Marxism suffers disastrously from the effects of positivism, one of the most misguided contributions is that by Hollander.

REFERENCES

Bhaskar, R. (1978) *A Realist Theory of Science*, Hemel Hempstead: Harvester Wheatsheaf.
——(1987) *Scientific Realism and Human Emancipation*, London: Verso.
——(1989) *The Possibility of Naturalism*, Hemel Hempstead: Harvester Wheatsheaf.
Butler, E. (1983) *Hayek: His Contribution to the Political and Economic Thought of Our Time*, London: Temple Smith.
Caldwell, B. (1988) 'Hayek's transformation', *History of Political Economy*, 20 (4).
Collier, A. (1994) *Critical Realism: An Introduction to Roy Bhaskar's Philosophy*, London: Verso.
Desai, M. (1994) 'Equilibrium, expectations and knowledge', in J. Birner and R. van Zijp (eds) *Hayek, Co-ordination and Evolution*, London: Routledge.
Fleetwood, S. (1995) *Hayek's Political Economy: The Socio-Economics of Order*, London: Routledge.
Foss, N. (1995) 'More on Hayek's transformation', *History of Political Economy*, 27 (2).
Hayek, F.A. (1937) 'Economics and knowledge', *Economica*, 4 (February).
——(1942) 'The facts of the social sciences', in F. Hayek, *Individualism and Economic Order*, London: Routledge & Kegan Paul, 1949.
——(1945) 'The use of knowledge in society', *The American Economic Review*, 35 (4) (September).
——(1946) 'The meaning of competition', in F. Hayek, *Individualism and Economic Order*, London: Routledge & Kegan Paul, 1949.
——(1960) *The Constitution of Liberty*, London: Routledge & Kegan Paul.

——(1962) 'Rules, perception and intelligibility', in F. Hayek, *Studies in Philosophy, Politics and Economics*, London: Routledge & Kegan Paul, 1967.
——(1964a) 'Kinds of rationalism', in F. Hayek, *Studies in Philosophy, Politics and Economics*, London: Routledge & Kegan Paul, 1967.
——(1964b) 'Kinds of order in society', *New Individualist Review*, 1 (3).
——(1967) 'Notes on the evolution of systems of rules of conduct', in F. Hayek, *Studies in Philosophy, Politics and Economics*, London: Routledge & Kegan Paul.
——(1970) 'The errors of constructivism', in F. Hayek, *New Studies in Philosophy, Politics and Economics*, London: Routledge & Kegan Paul, 1978.
——(1973) 'Rules and order', in F. Hayek, *Law Legislation and Liberty*, London: Routledge & Kegan Paul, 1982.
——(1976) 'The mirage of social justice', in F. Hayek, *Law Legislation and Liberty*, London: Routledge & Kegan Paul, 1982.
——(1979) 'The political order of free people', in F. Hayek, *Law Legislation and Liberty*, London: Routledge & Kegan Paul, 1982.
——(1988) *The Fatal Conceit: The Errors of Socialism*, London: Routledge & Kegan Paul.
Hodgson, G. (1988) *Economics and Institutions*, Cambridge: Polity.
——(1993) 'The economics of institutions', *European Association for Evolutionary Political Economy Newsletter*, July.
Hollander, S. (1981), 'Marxan economics as general equilibrium theory', *History of Political Economy*, 13 (1).
Hutchison, T. (1981) *The Politics and Philosophy of Economics*, Oxford: Basil Blackwell.
Ioannides, S. (1992) *The Market, Competition and Democracy*, Aldershot: Edward Elgar.
Lachmann, L. (1976) 'From Mises to Shackle: an essay on Austrian economics', *Journal of Economic Literature*, 54 (March).
Lawson, C. (1994) 'The transformational model of social activity and economic analysis: a reinterpretation of the work of J.R. Commons', *Review of Political Economy*, 6 (2).
Lawson, T. (1989) 'Abstraction, tendencies and stylised facts: a realist approach to economic analysis', *Cambridge Journal of Economics*, 13.
——(1994a) 'The nature of post Keynesianism and its links to other traditions: a realist perspective', *Journal of Post-Keynesian Economics*, 16 (4) (summer).
——(1994b) 'Realism and Hayek: a case of continuous transformation', in M. Colonna and H. Hageman (eds) *Capitalism, Socialism and Information: The Economics of F.A. Hayek*, Aldershot: Edward Elgar.
——(1994c) 'A realist theory for economics', in R. Backhouse (ed.) *New Directions in Economic Methodology*, London: Routledge.
——(1995) 'A realist perspective on contemporary economic theory', *Journal of Economic Issues*, 29 (March).
——(1996) *Economics and Reality*, London: Routledge.
Marx, K. (1970) *A Contribution to the Critique of Political Economy*, M. Dobb (ed.), Moscow: Progress Publishers.
——(1973) *Grundrisse: Foundations of the Critique of Political Economy*, Harmondsworth: Penguin.
——(1982) *The German Ideology*, London: Lawrence & Wishart.
——(1990) *Capital: A Critique of Political Economy*, vol. I, Harmondsworth: Penguin.
Peacock, M. (1993) 'Hayek, realism and spontaneous order', *Journal for the Theory of Social Behaviour*, 23.
Pratten, S. (1993) 'Structure, agency and Marx's analysis of the labour process', *Review of Political Economy*, 5 (4).
Rubin, I. (1990) *Essays on Marx's Theory of Value*, Montreal: Black Rose Books.

Sayer, D. (1979) 'Science as critique', in J. Mepham and D. Hillel-Ruben (eds) *Issues in Marxist Philosophy Vol. III: Epistemology, Science, Ideology*, Hemel Hempstead: Harvester Press.

Vaughn, K. (1992) 'The problems of order in Austrian economics: Kirzner vs. Lachmann', *Review of Political Economy*, 4 (3).

Wilson, H. (1991) *Marx's Critical Dialectical Procedure*, London: Routledge.

Zijp, R.W. van (1993) *Austrian and New Classical Business Cycle Theories*, Aldershot: Edward Elgar.

7

AUSTRIAN ECONOMICS AND THE ABANDONMENT OF THE CLASSIC THOUGHT EXPERIMENT[1]

Laurence S. Moss

I cannot imagine an Austrian economics without 'thought experiments'. And so I was not at all surprised to find that Peter J. Boettke and David L. Prychitko include this 'method of imaginary constructions' among the five distinguishing characteristics of Austrian economics (Boettke and Prychitko 1994: 289–90). Boettke and Prychitko likened this method to the *gedankenexperiment* in the natural sciences that allows scientists to (apparently) discover empirical information from experiments that have not been performed – they have only been imagined (*ibid.*: 289). The older Austrian economists used thought experiments to rule out certain claims and conjectures about the organization of society, especially those advanced by the socialist writers.

Contemporary Austrian writers hark back to Carl Menger's *Principles of Economics* (1950) for insights about information, ignorance and uncertainty, but they have kept a cautious distance from the several classic imaginary constructions that have guided the Austrian school throughout much of its history. Menger's account of the origin of money – what Nozick termed the 'invisible-hand explanation' of the origin of social institutions – now serves as the prototype for much contemporary Austrian model building (Nozick 1994).[2] The contemporary effort is to appreciate how spontaneous social formations can outperform conscious design and produce coordinative market outcomes. The emphasis has shifted towards the conjectural history that we find in Adam Smith and the other Scottish social theorists of the eighteenth century and away from the logical search for the necessary and sufficient conditions needed to sustain an organized society that was characteristic of the thought of Friedrich von Wieser, Eugen von Böhm-Bawerk, Ludwig von Mises, Israel Kirzner, Murray Rothbard and others. In this chapter I shall demonstrate that thought experiments were important features of the theorizing of the older Austrian economists. It seems to me that a paper stressing the importance of imaginary constructions for Austrian economics has long been overdue.

LAURENCE S. MOSS

THE GREATEST AUSTRIAN THOUGHT EXPERIMENT
OF THEM ALL

Wieser's benevolent dictator model

In his *Social Economics*, Friedrich von Wieser distinguished what he called the 'simple economy' from the complex economy of everyday experience (Wieser 1967: 18–21). Apparently, what made an economy 'simple' was the assumption that the conflicts and conditions that typically accompany the 'formation of socio-economic powers' were absent. Power relationships, including monopoly and fraud, are assumed to be absent. What remains is an economy that is large, equipped with technological knowledge and stocked full of people and resources but devoted to satisfying consumer utility only. Monopoly profits and the uncertainties due to asymmetrical information are assumed away completely. This 'broad economy', Wieser explained, is 'guided by a single mind' (*ibid.*: 19). The single mind or 'director', to use Wieser's term, 'foresees ends, weighs them without error or passion and maintains a discipline which ensures that all directions are executed with the utmost precision and skill and without the loss of energy' (*ibid.*: 20). The masses respond to the director's orders 'cheerfully as though enlisted in their individual interest' (*ibid.*). In short, in the simple economy all agents are assumed to have personal incentives perfectly aligned with those of the director or, as I shall call this person, the 'benevolent dictator'.[3]

Wieser contrasted the simple economy under the control and direction of the benevolent dictator with a modern economy. In the modern economy, exchange is conducted not only to satisfy the needs of the household but also to increase wealth. Furthering economic activity takes place under conditions of economic compulsion, intentional misinformation, ignorance and error. In this world, market prices no longer reflect utility but instead are shaped by force, fraud and other types of power (Wieser 1967: 168, 236, 380). One source of power is the 'large-scale capitalistic enterprise' which can force market prices to deviate from the utility values they would otherwise reflect in the simple economy under the command and control of the benevolent despot (*ibid.*: 380). In his 1926 work, *The Law of Power*, Wieser continued his examination of the economy as a system of power (Wieser 1983).[4]

Warren Samuels has perceptively noted that this emphasis draws out themes already present and partially developed in Wieser's earliest work, *Natural Value*, published in 1889 (Wieser 1956). In *Natural Value*, the notion of the simple economy is used in a particularly compelling way. The simple economy is supposed to be the ideal version of the communist state in which all property is held by society but managed for the good of the people. Wieser quickly dismissed the criticism that such an arrangement can never exist by remarking that it is enough that we can *imagine* it. We use our imagination to think of the prices that would emerge in our present economy 'if we could think away private property, as well as all the troubles which are a consequence of human imperfection' (*ibid.*: 61n.). Wieser remarks that the communistic state is the 'perfect state' because

> everything will be ordered in the best possible way; there will be no misuse of power on the part of its officials, or selfish isolation on the part of its individual citizens; no error or any other kind of friction will ever occur.
>
> (*ibid.*: 61)

Wieser is not always clear about the methodological purpose this model of communism plays in his economics. However, a careful review of the several contexts in which he invokes the pure communist model is consistent with the following interpretation.

In a world where the consumer is sovereign, all resources would be valued according to their marginal contribution towards the production of consumer utility. In such an economy production would be conducted efficiently. Only some, not all, of the productive instruments would command exchange value in a communistic state. Wieser's main interest is to discover what price relationships would exist in the ideal communistic state. Consider what Wieser concluded about land rent.

Wieser noted Ricardo's claim that, in a private property economy, differential rents arise because farmers compete to obtain the rights to harvest the most fertile lands when less fertile lands are also needed.[5] Without differential rent there would be no effective way of getting farmers to choose to harvest less fertile land. Farmers would flock only to the most productive lands. In a communist state, competition among farmers to obtain leaseholds has been eliminated and land is allocated by central direction, perhaps by a minister of agriculture appointed by the benevolent dictator. Under these novel institutions it is interesting to consider whether land would be allocated towards production in a different manner than what had occurred under private property and also whether the imputation of differential land rent would still be needed for the rational pricing of agricultural output. After examining the efficiencies associated with satisfying consumer wants, Wieser concluded that if the communist dictator 'tries to manage the property economically, and to have an effectual control over his servants [then] it will be impossible for the communistic state to act differently from any large landowner of the present day' (Wieser 1956: 116). In short, by pricing corn uniformly, regardless of the grade of land from which it originated, differential gains would be automatically generated and imputed to the different grades of land.

Wieser's main point in *Natural Value* bears repeating. In the communistic state where the production of consumer utility is the main objective of economic organization, it would be insane to price commodities according to the labour theory of value and disregard differential rents (Stigler 1959: 158–78). Any regime that encourages production at the lowest opportunity cost will guarantee that aggregate output is produced on a combination of lands with differing degrees of fertility. So long as all corn has the same price, differential rents will accrue. The labour theory of valuation operates against social arrangements that allow for differential rent. Based on this, Wieser concluded that the labour theory has 'introduced into theoretic political economy the greatest errors that have ever been perpetrated within its sphere' (Wieser 1956: 185).

Böhm-Bawerk's Positive Theory of Capital

In 1888, Böhm-Bawerk published the first edition of his remarkable *Positive Theory of Capital* which, according to some, is the greatest single accomplishment of the Austrian school in the nineteenth century (Schumpeter 1951: 190). Böhm-Bawerk developed Ricardo's ideas about capital and wages in exciting new directions. This resulted in a macroeconomic model of interest and wages, and a well-defined structure of production (Dorfman 1959; Blaug 1968). As he established the basic relationships that adhere to any market system, Böhm-Bawerk invited his readers to join him in a thought experiment.[6]

Böhm-Bawerk asks us to 'imagine' a socialist state (Böhm-Bawerk 1959, vol. II: 341). In this socialist state all private property and private ownership of capital has been abolished. The benevolent dictator is in charge of the means of production, and can allocate them in whatever manner is required by the interests of the community. Exactly as we have seen in Wieser, Böhm-Bawerk asks us to assume that the leaders of the community and the workers put the public interest above their respective private interests. In this setting, he asks if the causes that produce interest in an 'individualist community' will still function to cause interest to emerge in a socialist state.

Böhm-Bawerk's main finding is that the 'causes [of interest] are still present' (Böhm-Bawerk 1959, vol. II: 341). In a socialist community time does not stand still. The passing of time means that the leaders will notice that present goods are more valuable than future goods. They are more valuable because present goods can be used to extend the period of production and that raises annual output and consumer utility.

Let me emphasize that the same discounting of future goods must occur under socialism as it does under private ownership. Böhm-Bawerk asks us to imagine what would happen if the central authority 'did not place a lower valuation on future goods' (*ibid.*: 342). If he did not apply the discount, the existing means of production would always be invested towards the production of goods that accrue at later dates. However, the masses cannot survive on mere promises of future consumption goods and as a result they will suffer a 'present dearth' and suffer immense 'distress' (*ibid.*: 342). Somehow the supply of goods devoted to future production must be both limited and allocated efficiently. A benevolent dictator in charge of a socialist commonwealth cannot escape this management responsibility because the problem is a *technological one* that remains regardless of how the property rights structure of modern society is altered.[7]

According to Böhm-Bawerk, we are told that the socialists describe income from capital as an exploitation-like gain, a predacious deduction from the product of labour (*ibid.*: 343). Now a realignment of the relationship of the ownership of the means of production would certainly change the cast of characters who receive the interest payments, but it would not eliminate the necessity that interest be paid. Böhm-Bawerk explained that interest is emphatically not a 'fortuitous "historico-juridical" category which appears in our individualist and capitalist society, and which would disappear again with that society' (*ibid.*: 346). Not that at all! Rather, interest is an 'economic category which arises from elemental economic causes and hence will appear everywhere, irrespective of the type of social or juridical organization, provided there exists an exchange of present for future goods' (*ibid.*).

Mises' challenge to the socialists, 1920

Mises' 1920 challenge to the socialists was a formidable one and sparked one of the most famous controversies in modern economics. The economic calculation debate has spawned an enormously rich literature that I shall not attempt to summarize here (Vaughn 1994). In Mises, it is no longer merely a matter of proving that a socialist ministry would have to duplicate the sort of calculations associated with market systems. Mises' challenge was far more devastating than the ones offered by Wieser and Böhm-Bawerk. Mises claimed that even the most benevolent socialist dictator would find it impossible to make rational production decisions once the market for capital goods was abolished. By definition, socialism proposed to abolish the market for capital goods and, therefore, socialism would sink the economy into poverty and despair.

According to Mises, the benevolent socialist dictator cannot calculate rationally, no matter how pure his or her heart, or how brilliant his or her mind. Mises' words are as follows:

> Calculation *in natura*, in an economy without exchange, can embrace consumption-goods only; it completely fails when it comes to deal with [capital] goods . . . And as soon as one gives up the conception of a freely established monetary price for [capital] goods . . . rational production becomes completely impossible. Every step that takes us away

from private ownership of the means of production and from the use of money also takes us away from rational economics.

(Mises 1920: 104, emphasis in the original)

Without a competition for the means of production there is no practical way of knowing whether one method of production, say, technique A, is preferable to another technique of production, technique B. Without the measuring rod of competitive prices, the socialist commonwealth would soon find it difficult to feed its population and economic chaos would be the inevitable consequence.

Mises did qualify his provocative findings in one important respect. He explained that under *static* market conditions, economic calculation is no longer needed. Under static equilibrium, where tomorrow's flows of demand and supply are exactly like today's, 'we might . . . conceive of a socialist production system which is rationally controlled from an economic point of view' (Mises 1920: 109). Mises went on to point out that this conceptual possibility is of no use to socialist planners because 'a static state is impossible in real life' (*ibid.*). Under normal market conditions, Mises continued,

all economic data [change] in such a way that a connecting link with the final state of affairs in the previously existing competitive economy becomes impossible. But then we have the spectacle of a socialist order floundering in the ocean of possible and conceivable economic combinations without the compass of economic calculation . . . .in the socialist commonwealth . . . [t]here is only groping in the dark. Socialism is the abolition of rational economy.

(*ibid.*: 109–10)

And so in Mises' famous 1920 article, the socialists were challenged to explain how the central planners will simulate the role that capital-goods markets play under dynamic market conditions. Mises continued the Wieser–Böhm-Bawerk tradition by invoking the benevolent dictator construct and drawing conclusions by the thought experiment method. This time Mises used his imagination to reach an ironic result. The socialist minister cannot do even what he knows he must do because socialism has abolished competitive market pricing of the means of production. The benevolent dictator–manager is left groping in the dark so to speak.

Hayek and the demise of the benevolent dictator model

In 1941, Hayek offered a qualified macroeconomics as the centrepiece of *The Pure Theory of Capital* (Hayek 1941). In the first chapter, Hayek explained his conceptual method in painstaking detail. A short quotation will serve to capture his commitment to both equilibrium analysis and the thought experiment. Hayek wrote:

> The use of the equilibrium method here then means constructing an *imaginary* state in which the plans of the different people (entrepreneurs and consumers generally) are so adjusted to one another that each individual will be able to sell or buy exactly those quantities of commodities which he has been planning to sell or buy.
>
> (Hayek 1941: 26)

Let us examine how Hayek applied this method to the investigation of the sequence of events that had to occur if an act of real saving were to give rise to a permanent increased flow of real income.

Hayek asked us to consider the case of a 'centrally directed communist society' (*ibid.*: 26–7).[8] As in Wieser and Böhm-Bawerk, the purpose of Hayek's invocation of the benevolent dictator model is simply to fix our attention on important matters that must accompany rational economic calculation regardless of who owns the means of production. Hayek was quite apologetic about adducing the aid of such an aggregative model since the confusions of aggregative analysis was one of the leading topics of discussions during the 1930s debates about capital theory (Hayek 1972; Lachmann 1978). He explained that the purpose of the imaginary centrally planned economy was purely pedagogic and only a temporary modelling device that would be useful in Part 2 of his book but was soon to be discarded in Part 3 (Hayek 1941: 156, 247, 267).

How does the benevolent dictator increase real income for all the citizens? According to Hayek, the central planner must either reduce current consumption or else draw down stocks of current consumption goods that can now be traded for claims to future goods. These present consumption goods can then be traded for other claims and new capital-using methods of production will come on line. The claims to the future goods could be stock certificates in firms that are starting up more roundabout methods of production. The benevolent dictator will, through directed accumulation efforts, eventually bring about a new state of affairs in which average income will be higher.[9]

I remarked that Hayek promised his readers a full account in Part 3 of his book of how, in a decentralized market system, the self-regarding actions of individuals could bring about essentially the same pattern of events that occur under central planning. This demonstration was not forthcoming. Surely, if many private households save by cutting back on present consumption and, in addition, the saving is used by either the households or financial intermediaries to finance the start up of organizations bent on extending production, then per capita income can rise (Hayek 1941: 247–305). But in a decentralized market system something can happen that cannot occur in a central planned economy. Each household may rely on other households to save and therefore either not save at all or else not save enough.[10] This is a prisoner's dilemma-type situation having to do with aggregate saving levels turning out to be less than it would be if the households had some certainty that free riding could not occur.

Hayek never reached this conclusion about less-than-preferred levels of saving in decentralized markets as compared with central planning. This conclusion is implied by the logical structure of his 1941 work, especially in light of the examples he selected. His sympathies may have been more in line with those of his Austrian forebears who refused to grant any merit whatsoever to communist methods and techniques, even though the communist systems apparently had a better chance of facilitating capital accumulation.[11] Hayek's application of the benevolent dictator model did not continue much past his *Pure Theory of Capital*, and the promised subsequent elaboration on dynamic economics never materialized (Hayek 1941: v). I have argued elsewhere that sometime prior to 1944, Hayek realized that the thought experiment involving the benevolent dictator was fundamentally flawed as a device for organizing thought experiments about the market system. The flaw is that the market system is not analogous at all to a household economy under the direction of a single patriarch whose preference ordering can represent the entire group (Moss 1994).

Austrian thought experiments in the service of neoclassical economics

It is necessary to stop for a moment and recognize the significance of the benevolent dictator to Austrian economics. It was perhaps the longest-running thought experiment in the history of economics. The point of that experiment was to facilitate an understanding of the market system by assuming away its most troublesome institution — private property in the ownership of the means of production. The word used by Austrian writers time and time again is 'imagine'. Apparently, it is from the imagination that practical information about the economy is obtained. This information has to do with the discovery of which characteristic patterns of behaviour are fundamental to social organization and which are not. By 'fundamental' I mean necessary if society is to reproduce itself and survive to see another day. These essential primordial features of social and economic organization cannot be eliminated by legislation or the visionary dreams of social reformers. To try to put any 'social will' ahead of objective reality will produce a society that ends in defeat, frustration and poverty. The fact that modern economics had discovered essential features of social organization that could not be eliminated by the popular struggles of political parties or by the reshuffling of property rights was the great contribution of the older Austrian economists to mainstream economics. The method of persuading readers about this fact was the imaginary construction or fiction of the benevolent dictator.

During the latter half of the nineteenth century and certainly until World War II, the basic elements of what we today call neoclassical economics were established. It is clear that neoclassical economics benefited greatly from the fundamental principles laid down by the older Austrian writers. Perhaps the most stunning feature of the neoclassical paradigm was the claim that free competitive markets would lead to the maximization of national output. If factors of production were substitutable then the 'marginal rates of factor substitution' between any two factors of production in all industries must be equal if social production is to be at a maximum. When the equality between marginal rates of factor substitution holds, it will be impossible (given the state of the arts and assuming full employment) to reshuffle any factor of production to increase the output of one industry without necessarily decreasing the output of some other industry. Among consumers, marginal rates of commodity substitution needed also to be made equal and ultimately linked to the rate at which one commodity can be transformed into another by reshuffling resources among sectors. Resources employed in this way are said to be 'efficiently allocated'. This efficiency was part of a body of economics that Francis Bator described as 'antiseptically independent of institutional context' (Bator 1957: 22–59).

THOUGHT EXPERIMENTS ABOUT GENERAL EQUILIBRIUM

Mises' ill-fated evenly rotating economy

The demise of the benevolent dictator model after 1941 did not put an end to imaginary experiments in Austrian economics. The construct of the evenly rotating economy (ERE) emerged in Mises' *Human Action* and became a leading feature of Austrian economics in America (Mises 1963: 244–50).[12] The construct provided insights in the operation of the market system as a whole and it was endorsed by Murray N. Rothbard and other Austrians as a measured alternative to the more popular Arrow–Debreu model now widespread among neoclassical economists. I remarked that, as early as 1920, Mises criticized the socialist writers for confusing the necessary tool of *static* equilibrium with proposals for a blueprint on which to plan the socialist economy. This elementary confusion was to prove costly to the socialist experiments in economic organization that took place in Russia, China, Cuba and other places during the twentieth century. Mises was interested in static equilibrium not because it was descriptively realistic but because it was a clever method for obtaining insights about the market system. Mises' position was subsequently refined in his major work, *Human Action,* published in 1949 (Mises 1963).

There are a variety of models of general equilibrium (GE) extant in the literature.[13] The great majority of these GE models posed a particular technical question about the price system and proposed to answer that question by abstract mathematical reasoning. They ask whether, in a world where traders try to maximize utility and resource owners maximize their wealth, it is possible to imagine a set of commodity and resources prices that will allow (a) all trading parties to consummate their trades at once, and (b) all trading parties to improve their welfare simultaneously. A positive demonstration of this possibility depended on many artificial assumptions, such as that the state of technological knowledge was available to all, that consumer preferences were constant and unchanging and that supplies of resources were available under competitive conditions. The answer also depended on the rules followed by traders when seeking out and consummating their trades with others. In my opinion, GE analysis is the grandest thought experiment in all of economics and there are now a number of useful histories on this subject.[14]

The fact that something is conceptually possible – that is, the fact that it can be imagined – does not prove that what has been imagined is realistic or even discoverable using ordinary statistical research methods. Therefore, it is not surprising that many modern Austrian economists complain that (a) the majority of neoclassical economists spend endless futile hours discussing the characteristics of equilibrium and neglect other more important questions in economics, and (b) economists who analyse problems using the techniques of pre-reconciled choice are wasting their time because a GE state of affairs is unrealistic and will never happen. The first criticism is about the duties of economists in pursuing their professional obligations. The second is a clear normative judgement about the significance of the research priorities now in place.

When all is said and done there is something disingenuous about these modern Austrian criticisms of how neoclassical economists conduct their research. Why should upholders of subjectivism in economics – that is, those who uphold the claim that *understanding the market process* is more important than *prediction and control* – strenuously object to the elaborate thought experiments carried out by the GE economists? These exercises in abstract reasoning may not provide much grist for the mills of modern Austrians who, according to Karen Vaughn, find that Austrian insights about real time and ignorance do not 'adapt well to neoclassical language' (Vaughn 1994: 167). Even so, GE reasoning is a self-proclaimed source of inspiration to its neoclassical devotees and that needs to be respected by contemporary Austrians.

Neoclassical economists ask questions about what is or is not logically possible in a fiction-free world of pre-coordinated markets and find that rhetorical exercise downright insightful and intellectually exciting (Weintraub 1985). Apparently, contemporary Austrians do not find the question or its answer intellectually exciting at all. These differences are a matter of taste and not methodological principle. David L. Prychitko summarized Austrian criticisms of neoclassical economics as follows:

> general equilibrium theory has developed an abstract model to an abstract question: can a decentralized economy converge into a general equilibrium? Yes, provided that, among other things, individual agents behave atomistically, while enjoying full and complete information, facing perfect certainty, reacting in formal, logical time.
>
> (Prychitko 1994: 79)

The abstract question posed by the neoclassical economists is one that contemporary Austrians simply do not find interesting *any longer*. Things were different in the past.

Contemporary Austrians are interested in explaining phenomena in historical time, where the future is uncertain and not predetermined, and where incentives must be aligned because information is not in a single location. But where are we to draw the line? If we rule out neoclassical modelling as misleading, wasteful and unrealistic, then perhaps, to be absolutely consistent, Austrians should dispense with abstract reasoning altogether. Austrian economics might specialize in existential descriptions of reality, as suggested by the phenomenology movement in philosophy. All thought experiments should then be rejected because imagination is frivolous fantasy and relies on subjectively perceived streams of consciousness not 'hard fact'. Indeed, this seems to be the attitude guiding some contemporary Austrian writers whose displeasure with neoclassical economics is strong enough to rule out important features of the earlier Austrian tradition. Consider the attack by Cowen and Fink against Mises' ERE (Cowen and Fink 1985).

The attack by Cowen and Fink

Cowen and Fink point out that Mises was ambivalent, if not hopelessly confused, about the exact role this GE construct was supposed to play in his economics. On the one hand there is evidence that Mises and especially his students, Rothbard and Kirzner, believed that the ERE showed the *direction* in which the entire economy was heading at any point in time. The metaphor of a ship can be used here to examine his thoughts about the usefulness of GE constructions.

Imagine the economy to be like a ship adrift at sea. A lightning-calculating navigator can plot the ship's heading if enough data are available. This is not a prediction in the common-sense use of the term. No one expects the navigator's calculations to come to pass, because the ship moves first in one direction and then in another. As the winds shift, the ship changes course. Still the navigator's calculations are not altogether useless.

161

At any moment in time, the navigator can anticipate that, if present winds continue (and we expect that they will not continue), the ship will head in exactly one direction. Now the same metaphor can be applied to the idea of the 'circular flow', which again shows the direction in which the economy is heading and nothing more. This is precisely how Rothbard understood Mises' ERE:

> the ERE is the goal (albeit shifting in the concrete sense) toward which the market moves . . . The ERE is the condition that comes into being and continues to obtain when the present, existing market data (valuations [i.e. preferences], technology, resources) remain constant. It is a theoretical construct of the economist that enables him to point out in what directions the economy tends to be moving at any given time.
>
> (Rothbard 1962, vol. 1: 306)

Cowen and Fink dismiss this claim:

> all that the Rothbard–Mises analysis implies is that there is a tendency towards equilibrium *in a world with frozen data*. Of course, this implies little or nothing about whether there is a tendency towards equilibrium in a world where the data are not frozen . . . the Rothbard–Mises analysis does not succeed in establishing a real world tendency towards equilibrium.
>
> (Cowen and Fink 1985: 867)

In short, the ERE fails as a thought experiment in proving any tendency whatsoever towards equilibrium under modern market conditions.

The second use of GE ideas

There was another, and perhaps more interesting, application of the ERE construct within Mises' writings and in the subsequent Mises wing of the Austrian school. According to Mises, the ERE represents a style of argument in economics that he termed *argumentum a contrario* (Mises 1963: 250). Suppose the economist wants to show that money is needed precisely because the future is uncertain. Start by assuming an obviously false situation such as the one provided by the ERE. As Mises explained:

> The evenly rotating economy is a fictitious system in which the market prices of all goods and services coincide with . . . final prices. There are in its frame no price changes whatever; there is perfect price stability. The same market transactions are repeated again and again . . . The system is in perpetual flux, but it remains always at the same spot. It revolves evenly round a fixed center, it rotates evenly. The plan state of rest is disarranged again and again, but it is instantly re-established at

the previous level. All factors, including those bringing about the recurring disarrangement of the plain state of rest, are constant. Therefore prices – commonly called static or equilibrium prices – remain constant too.

(*ibid.*: 247)

Next, assume that money exists, but show that this assumption produces a logical contradiction. Mises wrote that 'in the imaginary construction of an [ERE] the very notion of money vanishes into an unsubstantial calculation process, self-contradictory and devoid of any meaning' (*ibid.*: 417). And so we arrive at this result: that money has no place in the ERE. From this result we deduce that money exists because the future is uncertain. We have established the importance of money by using a venerable mode of demonstration that, according to some accounts, was first used by Pythagoras of Samos in 570 BC – proof by contradiction (Rescher 1991).

Mises did not deny that the ERE thought experiment made unreal assumptions and was anti-historical in its principal description of the market system. Still, despite its lack of realism Mises claimed that studying the ERE would focus the mind on selected features of actual market systems which highlight the essential roles that entrepreneurship, money and interest rates play in common everyday market life. According to Mises, we can better understand the conditions needed to sustain organized society by examining a world in which radical change and uncertainty are absent. As Mises stated, 'There is no means of studying the complex phenomena of action other than first to abstract from change altogether' (Mises 1963: 248).[15] The ERE serves as the mental benchmark for understanding and appreciating those modern institutions that help individuals navigate the shoals of uncertainty. In addition to money, Mises used the ERE to explain the nature of both the entrepreneurial function and interest deductions from the contributions of other resources. I shall not recount these explanations here since my point is only to show how important the ERE thought experiment was to Mises' entire theoretical project.

Cowen and Fink concluded by insisting that Mises' and Rothbard's preference of the ERE over the more advanced GE models of the 1970s was a poor choice because the later models are more 'internally consistent'.

Must a thought experiment be 'internally consistent'?

Is internal consistency the only thing we look for in valuing thought experiments? I think not. A good thought experiment stimulates thought, and that is its primary function. Much like a catalyst which facilitates the production of a chemical substance, it may not actively appear in the final product. However, the fact that the catalyst is filtered out of the final product does not make it unimportant. Apparently, for the older Austrian writers the ERE had a certain heuristic effect on their reasoning and helped promote their understanding of the market process. I speculate that there is a correlation between contemporary Austrian warnings – about the stunted understanding of the market process that happens when an economist exclusively studies only equilibrium conditions to the neglect of disequilibrium processes at work in economic life – and Mises' ERE theory (Kirzner 1985). It is not the tools of economics that should be attacked, but the poor uses and inappropriate conclusions drawn by practising economists from the tools themselves.

Several younger Austrians appear to have lost their interest and (I suspect) tolerance for thought experiments in economics. The canonical general equilibrium, experiment is as follows. Isolated individuals are asked to economize in the face of a series of systematically altered external conditions and their reactions are recorded. The aggregate behaviour of a collection of independent economizing individuals is then constructed, based on the findings about the microbehaviour of the isolated individuals. The individuals whose combined behaviour is now charted need not have an appreciation or understanding of the aggregate behaviour under examination. This method of analysis, which is known as the resolutive compositive method, was pioneered by Thomas Hobbes in the social sciences and named 'methodological individualism' by Joseph Schumpeter in 1908. Apparently, it was also used by Menger who bequeathed the approach to all subsequent generations of Austrians. It remains the heart of all GE constructions in economics.

In a belated response to Mises' 1924 challenge – that what he termed his regression theorem was the *only* logical method to understand how individuals could evaluate their cash balance requirements – I suggested that Don Patinkin's 'thought experiment' carried out along the lines of the GE procedure sketched above is a bone fide counter example (Moss 1974). Furthermore, by focusing on a hypothetical individual's 'estimation of worth' it met basic subjectivist criteria. Several of my critics were quite alarmed that I should have dared to evaluate Mises' theoretical argument by invoking either Patinkin or, more broadly speaking, GE patterns of reasoning. One of my several critics, Matthew B. Kibbe, dismissed my approach based on abstract reasoning, explaining that my main concern should be with *explaining* the real world. According to Kibbe, taking Mises at his word was inappropriate because 'the real question is whether or not Patinkin's "solution" helps explain how the value for money is determined by real individuals in the real world' (Kibbe 1994). Is Kibbe suggesting that any realistic description of market behaviour is preferable to abstract analysis?

THE CONJECTURAL HISTORY EXPERIMENT

Menger's insights about the origin of institutions

Contemporary Austrians quickly pass over Menger's celebrated examination of equilibrium price formation in the first part of his *Principles of Economics* (1950). I have wondered why Austrians pay such short shrift to what has been declared a momentous contribution to economic theory. It was Menger's account that spawned Böhm-Bawerk's later analysis of the 'marginal pairs', and these developments together contributed to the fruitful development of neoclassical economic reasoning (Böhm-Bawerk 1959, vol. II: 215–56; Stigler 1959; Blaug 1968; Moss 1978). Contemporary Austrians have other styles of reasoning in mind and seldom write about those parts of the older heritage that made Austrian economics important. Of far greater significance to these writers are those other places in the *Principles* where Menger offered a remarkable account of the origin of money rather than perfecting formal equilibrium analysis. At these places, Menger demonstrated the role that spontaneous social formations play in coordinating economic activity (O'Driscoll 1986).

Consider just a short summary of Menger's theory of the origin of money. Menger explained why individuals who are searching for marketable commodities form the opinion that some commodities are likely to be more marketable than others. This search has the unintended effect of actually making certain commodities more marketable than others. The snowballing reputation of some commodities as 'very marketable' is what metamorphosizes some commodities into money commodities. By this selection process the interactions of market participants produce a result that 'apparently only could arise by conscious design' (Moss 1978: 21; Nozick 1994). The origin of money did not take place by conscious design at all; rather it was the unintended consequence of economizing activity in the market.[16]

Conjectural history as the core of Austrian theory

We can appreciate the significance of an institution by way of a thought experiment about a possible historical sequence that could have occurred 'just so' to create and reinforce the continued existence of that institution. The historical account is conjectural – not necessarily based on facts – although the facts about the market are shown to be consistent with the account offered. The purpose of the exercise is to explore the positive function that an institution such as money plays in human organization by outlining a logical sequence through which the institution (might have) emerged. The fact that the institution emerged to assist individuals in pursuit of their interests also lends a certain moral legitimacy to the institution. For many Austrians, the conjectural historical account somehow *legitimatizes* the institution and suggests that any ill-considered tampering with spontaneously formed customs may result in major economic inconveniences, if not grave losses in efficiency (Raico 1994).

Contemporary Austrians follow the Scottish Enlightenment and claim that they can account for the origin of law and language in much the same way as Menger succeeded in accounting for the origin of money. Other financial institutions that can be modelled in a more or less similar fashion include the various security-enhancing devices used in commerce (loan collateral and reputational marks such as trademarks and service marks), as well as instruments of commerce (bills of exchange and letters of credit) (O'Driscoll 1986; Moss 1992). Perhaps the greatest novelty of all was Robert Nozick's conjectural account showing how it is possible for a dominant (that is, monopoly) protection agency to arise out of anarchism by 'legitimate steps' if the individuals in society pursued mutual protection agreements only (Nozick 1974; Mises 1963: 405-8).

Each of these conjectural stories about the origin of a particular institution displays a certain leaning towards the conceptual framework that has proven so useful in biology to explain the selective adaptation of certain traits possessed by specific life forms. When the consequence of a certain process is in fact the entire reason, or a major part of the reason, that the process is taking place, then we have a pattern explanation in economics which resembles a form of teleology that has proved immensely useful in modern biology (Lennox 1992). The fact that this pattern of explanation is undoubtedly 'scientific' and yet appears to be entirely different from the 'covering law' model of scientific explanation emboldens modern Austrians to assert their methodological differences with mainstream economic thought.[17]

My own purpose here is not to explore the scientific value of this pattern of reasoning in economics, but to decide if conjectural history is indeed a veritable 'thought experiment' on the same level as the venerable benevolent dictator model or Mises' ERE. My inclination is to say that contemporary Austrians have largely abandoned the classic Austrian-style thought experiment for another entirely different style of argument – conjectural history. Conjectural history is indeed a species of hypothetical reasoning in economics, but it is a poor substitute for the classic Austrian thought experiment. The Austrian thought experiment tried to isolate the necessary and sufficient conditions needed to sustain a modern capital-using system. The spontaneously evolved institutions which promote economic life are not proved to be the only possible social institutions imaginable. Conjectural history cannot decide what is absolutely necessary for successful community life. At best, conjectural history demonstrates that useful customs and economical institutions can arise – spontaneously – without centralized guidance and direction (Cowan 1994). However, this is not the sum and substance of what the older Austrian school tried to offer with their remarkable 'thought experiments'. The age of the great Austrian thought experiment has come to an end, and to a rather abrupt end at that. The Austrian revival, about which so many recent scholars write (Vaughn 1994), has not resurrected the grand theorizing of the older Austrian school.

CONCLUSION

This chapter has been devoted almost entirely to one of the five distinguishing characteristics of Austrian economics (Boèttke and Prychitko 1994). Older Austrian writers excelled at the creation and explication of 'imaginary constructions' and the more controversial practice of drawing logical lessons from those mental constructions. The recent vintage of contemporary Austrians seem less comfortable and hostile to this older approach. In an effort to detach Austrian economics from its historical moorings in both the classical (Ricardian) and neoclassical traditions, the pendulum seems to have swung towards conjectural history and away from the isolation and appreciation of necessary and sufficient conditions. What is favoured by many contemporary Austrians is a sophisticated *description* of the evolution of the market process. This description must meet several rigid specifications; it must refer to individuals carrying on rational activities in historical time without being able to fully anticipate future market conditions. In this manner, existential descriptions of the market process have replaced the clever logical arguments that once confronted all serious students of Austrian economics. I maintain that they were at the core of the writings of Wieser, Böhm-Bawerk, Mises, Kirzner and Rothbard.

Going one step beyond Boettke and Prychitko, I conclude that the method of imaginary constructions is in rapid retreat among contemporary Austrians. Austrian economics in its contemporary suit of clothes seems to be quite different from the Austrian economics of the past.

NOTES

1 This paper was prepared for the 'Conference on Austrian Economics: Austrians in Debate' held at the Free University Amsterdam, 19–20 January 1995. My thanks to Professors Keizer, van Zijp and Tieben of the Austrian School Research Group for organizing this conference and preparing the conference volume. Professor Horowitz's criticisms were also helpful.

2 In a recent contribution to monetary economics, authors George A. Selgin and Lawrence H. White mention that 'the revival of Austrian economics' consists, at least in part, of the study of 'institutional orders formed spontaneously without central design' and do not mention 'thought experiments' or anything of that sort (see Selgin and White 1994). See also Koppl (1994), where the subject of 'thought experiments' is completely ignored. Indeed, despite Boettke's listing of 'thought experiments' as one of the five distinguishing characteristics of Austrian economics, his edited *Elgar Companion to Austrian*

Economics, which covers every conceivable topic and enlists the aid of scores of contemporary Austrians, fails to make meaningful references to 'thought experiments' (Boettke 1994). This ambivalence is what helps to distinguish traditional Austrian school methods from the contemporary variant.

3 I have decided to use the expression 'benevolent dictator' rather than 'communist leaders' or 'minister of production' for two reasons. First, because the whole point of the thought experiment is surely to substitute the visible hand of the ruler for the invisible or impersonal mechanisms of the market. Second, to emphasize the point that a single mind is at work. The single mind assumption is what eventually leads Hayek after 1941 to drop this metaphor and its various associations, as I argue elsewhere (Moss 1994).

4 According to Warren Samuels (1983), this book contains 'elements of the intertwining themes of the psychology of power and the role, including the manipulation, of ideas and belief systems in the operation and evolution of society, polity and economy' in his introduction to *The Law of Power* (Wieser 1983: xxix).

5 See Wieser (1956: 117), where he recounts Ricardo's theory and at the same time concurs with Ricardo that the 'natural principles of imputation are found to be in perfect agreement with the rules [Ricardo] has laid down for the formation of contract[ual] rent'.

6 Böhm-Bawerk started the section entitled 'Interest under socialism' by inviting his readers as follows: 'Let us imagine the socialist state actually consummated in its purest form. All private ownership of land and capital will have been abolished, all means of production concentrated in the hands of the community at large, all members of the nation enrolled as workers in the service of the commonwealth, and the national product distributed to all according to the measure of labour performed. What is the situation there with respect to the functioning of those causes which in an individualist economy produce interest?' (Böhm-Bawerk 1959, vol. II: 341).

7 Böhm-Bawerk offers a simple example. Consider two workers. The first worker labours a whole day to bake bread and produces a batch of bread with a combined market value of, say, $10. The second worker works just as hard and for exactly one day plants saplings on a reforestation project. In 20 years (without any additional labour) these saplings will grow into mature trees worth about $50 each or $5,000 in total. The second worker produces (future) output worth $5,000 while the first worker's output is worth only $10.00, yet they each work as hard and as long. If the socialist manager were to pay the forest worker the full $5,000, all the nation's labour would flock into reforestation activity and the bread would disappear from the shops creating hardship for all. Böhm-Bawerk insists that the socialist manager really has no choice but to pay $10 to all workers. The competition principle in a market economy also assures that all workers earn the same wage of $10, and that is why Böhm-Bawerk concluded, somewhat ironically, that the socialist manager would be compelled by the logic of the situation to engage in exactly the 'same "exploitation" that is practiced by the capitalist entrepreneurs of today. Therefore, it is . . . just as true of the socialist state as it is of our capitalist society that *owners of present goods derive interest through the labour of those who are producing a future product*'. There is, however, a difference between the market system and the socialist economy. In the former, the interest payment is received in large quantities by a 'small number of owners' while in the latter socialist community the interest payment is received by many 'co-owners with equal shares'. In both societies, interest must be included in the assessment of

relative wages, and that was Böhm-Bawerk's main point (Böhm-Bawerk 1959, vol. II: 345, emphasis added).

8 In a long note, Hayek readily acknowledges that this method of analysis was a 'device . . . used most systematically by F. Wieser' and more recently by A.C. Pigou (Hayek 1941: 27).

9 'We shall assume that what the dictator aims at is to produce the greatest possible income stream which remains constant in size' (Hayek 1941: 157).

10 This behaviour, if generalized, can result in zero capital accumulation, or even capital consumption. Apparently, Hayek stumbled upon the merciless logic of the prisoner's dilemma problem or what Garret Hardin most eloquently termed the 'tragedy of the commons' problem. The argument can be stated another way. Suppose that my act of saving an extra $1 makes possible a permanent rise in average living standards for all the other, say, one million citizens, but only in the amount of one cent ($0.01) per capita. Clearly, it is in the public interest that I commit this extra dollar to saving and a benevolent dictator would so order this saving. But is it not also possible that, from my personal self-interested point of view, the extra benefit of my saving an extra dollar may not justify giving up the consumption opportunities represented by that extra $1? In other words, the extra private saving will not happen at all. In the presence of positive externalities such as the above example, the socialist managers might indeed be able to achieve results that are not possible, or at any rate not probable, in a decentralized market system.

In the private decentralized economy, the investment sector might underinvest compared with the hypothetical benchmarks established in a pure communist state. And so the conclusion that actually follows from Hayek's particular use of the benevolent dictator model is not about what a socialist commonwealth must do to raise living standards. Rather, the conclusion that seems to follow is that a benevolent dictator, by centralizing investment and capital goods construction, can internalize any troublesome externalities and therefore outperform decentralized markets in raising living standards.

11 See Dobb (1963).

12 See the excellent evaluation of the Misesian ERE in Vaughn (1994: 81–5). Vaughn's text and my discussion below have been stimulated by the publication of Cowen and Fink (1985).

13 My judgement is that Mises' ERE most closely resembles the 'circular flow' model offered by Joseph A. Schumpeter in 1912 (Schumpeter 1961). Schumpeter's model was inspired by the mathematical formulation of the problem by Léon Walras, though Karl Marx remained a major influence on Schumpeter as well. See Goodwin (1993).

14 I have found E. Roy Weintraub's accounts particularly informative, though not without some idiosyncrasies of their own. See Weintraub (1979, 1985, 1991). A recent and particularly original treatment of Walras's system can be found in Van Daal and Jolink (1993).

15 The passage continues to suggest that the ERE can be of some use in what is called comparative static exercises, but Vaughn strenuously disagrees that Mises' abstract fiction could have much use in comparative static exercises. See Vaughn (1994: 81–5).

16 G.M. Hodgson questioned the coherence of Menger's account of the origin of money by pointing out that (a) it is inconsistent with its evolutionary foundations to claim that one commodity *finally* emerges as the 'money commodity' and (b) the spontaneous process by which a money commodity emerges and is maintained can proceed without activist government

intervention to catch the coin clippers, counterfeiters and so on. See Hodgson (1993: 109–20).

17 Hayek stated, 'It would then appear that the search for the discovery of laws is not an appropriate hall-mark of scientific procedure but merely a characteristic of the theories of simple phenomena' because with complex phenomena 'economic theory is confined to describing kinds of patterns which will appear if certain general conditions are satisfied, but can rarely if ever derive from this knowledge any predictions of specific phenomena' (Hayek 1969: 35, 42).

REFERENCES

Bator, F. (1957) 'General equilibrium, welfare, and allocation', *American Economic Review*, 47 (March): 22–59.

Blaug, M. (1968) *Economic Theory in Retrospect*, Homewood, IL: Richard D. Irwin.

Böhm-Bawerk, E. (1959) *Capital and Interest,* 3 vols, South Holland, IL: Libertarian Press.

Boettke, P.J. (ed.) (1994) *The Elgar Companion to Austrian Economics*, Aldershot: Edward Elgar.

Boettke, P.J. and Prychitko, D.L. (1994) 'The future of Austrian economics', in *The Market Process: Essays in Contemporary Austrian Economics*, Aldershot: Edward Elgar.

Cowan, R. (1994) 'Causation and genetic causation in economic theory', in Boettke (1994).

Cowen, T. and Fink, R. (1985) 'Inconsistent Equilibrium Constructs: The evenly rotating economy of Mises and Rothbard', *American Economic Review*, 75: 866–9.

Dobb, M. (1963) *Economic Growth and Underdeveloped Countries*, New York: International Publisher.

Dorfman, R. (1959) 'Waiting and the period of production', *Quarterly Journal of Economics*, 73 (August): 351–72.

Goodwin, R.M. (1993) 'Walras and Schumpeter: the vision reaffirmed', in A. Heertje and M. Perlman (eds) *Evolving Technology and Market Structure*, Ann Arbor, MI: University of Michigan Press, 39–49.

Hayek, F.A. (1941) *The Pure Theory of Capital*, London: Routledge & Kegan Paul.

——(1969) 'The Theory of Complex Phenomena', in *Studies in Philosophy, Politics and Economics*, New York: Simon & Schuster.

——(1972) *The Tiger By the Tail: The Keynesian Legacy of Inflation*, London: Institute of Economic Affairs.

Hodgson, G.M. (1993) *Economics and Evolution: Bringing Life Back Into Economics*, Cambridge: Polity Press.

Kibbe, M.B. (1994) 'Mind, historical time and the value of money: a tale of two methods', in Boettke and Prychitko (1994).

Kirzner, I. (1985) *Discovery and the Capitalist Process*, Chicago, IL: University of Chicago Press.

Koppl, R.G. (1994) 'Invisible hand explanations', in Boettke (1994), 192-6.

Lachmann, L. (1978) *Capital and its Structure* (1st edn, 1956), Menlo Park, CA: Cato Institute.

Lennox, J.G. (1992) 'Teleology', in E.F. Keller and E.A. Lloyd (eds) *Keywords in Evolutionary Biology*, Cambridge, MA: Harvard University Press.

Menger, C. (1950) *Principles of Economics* (1st edn, 1871), Glencoe, IL: Free Press.

Mises, L. von (1920) 'Economic calculation in the socialist commonwealth', in F. A. Hayek (ed.) *Collectivist Economic Planning*, London: Routledge & Kegan Paul, 1963.

——(1963) *Human Action: A Treatise on Economics* (1st edn, 1949), New Haven, CT: Yale University Press.

Moss, L.S. (1974) 'The monetary economics of Ludwig von Mises', in *The Economics of Ludwig von Mises: Toward a Critical Reappraisal*, Mission, KA: Sheed Andrews & McMeel, 13–49.

——(1978) 'Carl Menger and Austrian economics', *Atlantic Economic Journal*, 6 (September): 17–30.

——(1992) 'Harmony, conflict, and culture: an essay about the praxeological ideas of Ludwig von Mises', *Cultural Dynamics*, 5: 371–91.

——(1994) 'Hayek and the several faces of socialism', in M. Colonna, H. Hagemann and O. Hamouda (eds) *Capitalism, Socialism and Knowledge: The Economics of F.A. Hayek*, 2 vols, Aldershot: Edward Elgar, vol. II: 94–113.

Nozick, R. (1974) *Anarchy, State and Utopia*, New York: Basic Books.

——(1994) 'Invisible-hand explanations', *American Economic Review, Papers and Proceedings*, 84 (May): 314–18.

O'Driscoll, G. Jr (1986) 'Money: Menger's evolutionary theory', *History of Political Economy*, 18 (Winter): 601–16.

Prychitko, D.L. (1994) 'Praxeology', in Boettke (1994), 77–83.

Raico, R. (1994) 'Classical liberalism and the Austrian school', in Boettke (1994), 320–28.

Rescher, N. (1991) 'Thought experimentation in presocratic philosophy', in T. Horowitz and G.J. Massey (eds) *Thought Experiments in Science and Philosophy*, Savage, MD: Rowman & Littlefield.

Rothbard, M.N. (1962) *Man, Economy, and State: A Treatise on Economic Principles*, 2 vols, Princeton, PA: D. Van Nostrand.

Samuels, Warren (1983) 'Introduction', in Wieser (1983).

Schumpeter, J. (1951) 'Eugen von Boehm-Bawerk', in *Ten Great Economists From Marx to Keynes*, New York: Oxford University Press.

——(1961) *The Theory of Economic Development* (1st edn, 1912), trans., 1934, New York: Oxford University Press.

Selgin, G.A. and White, L.H. (1994) 'How would the invisible hand handle money?', *Journal of Economic Literature*, 32 (December): 1718–49.

Stigler, G. (1959) *Production and Distribution Theories: The Formative Period*, New York: Macmillan.

Van Daal, J. and Jolink, A (1993) *The Equilibrium Economics of Léon Walras*, New York: Routledge.

Vaughn, K.I. (1994) *Austrian Economics in America: The Migration of a Tradition*, New York: Cambridge University Press.

Weintraub, E.R. (1979) *Microfoundations: The Compatibility of Microeconomics and Macroeconomics*, Cambridge: Cambridge University Press.

——(1985) *General Equilibrium Analysis: Studies in Appraisal*, New York: Cambridge University Press.

——(1991) *Stabilizing Dynamics: Constructing Economic Knowledge*, New York: Cambridge University Press.

Wieser, F. von (1956) *Natural Value* (1st edn, 1889), New York: Kelley & Millman.

——(1967) *Social Economics* (English edn, 1927), New York: Augustus M. Kelley.

——(1983) *The Law of Power* (1st edn, 1926), trans. by W.E. Kuhn, Lincoln, NE: Bureau of Business Research.

8

THE THEORY OF ENTREPRENEURSHIP IN AUSTRIAN ECONOMICS

J. Patrick Gunning

In their writings on entrepreneurship, the Austrian economists were latecomers. Menger had little to say about the subject. Böhm-Bawerk acknowledged it as one of the two important problems remaining to be dealt with following Menger's theory of prices, but chose to tackle the second problem – that of interest.[1] Schumpeter, in 1911, was the first Austrian to use the general equilibrium framework to define the entrepreneur. However, this had already been done by earlier American writers, particularly J.B. Clark (1899). Schumpeter did not add anything of methodological significance and perhaps took a step backwards. Hayek wrote several papers about knowledge and competition, but seems to have gone out his way to avoid using the term 'entrepreneur'.[2]

Truly original Austrian contributions to the theory of entrepreneurship began with Mises' 1940 *Nationalökonomie* (Mises 1966). In that book, Mises put entrepreneurship at centre stage.[3] He regarded its elucidation (and the incentive to act entrepreneurially – profit and loss) as the fundamental task faced by anyone who wants to describe and understand economic interaction. Mises defined entrepreneurship, in its functional sense, as the embodiment of all behaviour in the market economy that is *distinctively human*. In other words, it encompasses all behaviour that cannot be expressed in a model of robots which operate according to maximizing algorithms.

Mises did not express his ideas in precisely these terms, yet his meaning is clear. He entitled the English version of his magnum opus *Human Action* and he pointed out that economics is the theory of human action (praxeology) under the conditions of the market economy (Mises 1966: 232–4). Because readers may not be accustomed to using the term 'human action' in Mises' sense, this chapter uses the term *distinctly human action* to refer to Mises' concept. An advantage of this term is that the word 'distinct' suggests that one must have in mind a procedure for distinguishing between action, which is human, and other behaviour.[4] Mises called the procedure for doing this the *method of imaginary constructions*.

In recent years Israel Kirzner, a student of Mises, has used the term 'entrepreneur' to refer to the central idea in his 'market process analysis'.

Partly as a result of this, Kirzner has been a major figure in the renewed professional interest in the entrepreneur. The publication of five books in the 1980s on the concept of the entrepreneur[5] is in no small measure due to his persistent argument that neoclassical economics puts too little emphasis on entrepreneurship.[6] In spite of Kirzner's professional success as an Austrian economist, I believe that he has promoted a non-subjectivist concept of entrepreneurship and has neglected what is best in Mises' writing on entrepreneurship.

I believe that the best parts of the Austrian theory of entrepreneurship are two recognitions by Mises. The first is that the role of the entrepreneur encompasses all distinctly human action in the market economy. The second is that, to define and elucidate the role of the entrepreneur, one must use the imaginary construction of the static general equilibrium model, or evenly rotating economy (ERE), to make a contrast. The ERE is a comprehensive, yet actionless, image of the saving-factor supplying–producing–consuming nexus of a pure market economy. In this image the savers, factor suppliers, producers and consumers are robots. To understand how distinctly human actors interact to cause saving, factor supplying, producing and consuming actions, one must contrast the robot behaviour with what one knows intuitively and through experience about how distinctly human actors will act under the conditions specified in the definition of the market economy. Thus, the ERE is an essential part of the procedure that enables economists to build an image of the market economy.

The basis for my beliefs is a continuing decade-long study of the economics of Mises. The tangible results have been two books on Mises and a few papers.[7] The first book (Gunning 1990) attempted to describe and extend Mises' work in a positive way. The second focused on contradictions and errors in his work.

This chapter is divided into three main sections plus a conclusion. The first section presents the new subjectivist theory of entrepreneurship in summary form. The second briefly discusses and assesses Schumpeter's theory, while the longer third section presents and evaluates Kirzner's argument that we should define entrepreneurship as 'alertness'. It strongly opposes that view and maintains that it threatens to undermine Mises' most important contribution to economic theory.

THE NEW SUBJECTIVIST ELUCIDATION OF ENTREPRENEURSHIP

The method economists must use to study the branch of human action that we call economic interaction is *subjectivism*. This does not say very much because this term has been used in a variety of ways. I am concerned here with what I called the *new* subjectivism (Gunning 1990), which I believe can be derived from Mises' work. To understand this, we must begin with what I call the 'old' subjectivism, as proposed by Carl Menger. The typical references to Menger's work regard him mainly as one of several founders of a consumer-based marginal-utility theory of value. Although Menger's contribution to this theory was one of his greatest accomplishments, an equally important achievement was that he defined an economic good (and, therefore, all relevant economic phenomena) in terms of the viewpoints of the subjects for whom the good is relevant in their choices or actions. Especially significant is Menger's assumption that, for a thing to be a good, some person or set of persons must have knowledge of its causal connection to the satisfaction of wants.[8]

The subjectivism in Menger's work is thus twofold. He required descriptions of economic interaction, on the one hand, to trace the price of goods to the *consumer role* and, on the other hand, to incorporate knowledge of causal connections among goods of different orders. From the standpoint of the history of the new subjectivism, the most important developments in the 70 years following Menger were the refinements that occurred in how economists came to represent these two aspects of Menger's work.

These developments were not made by Austrians but by other subjectivists, the most important of whom were J.B. Clark (1899), P.H. Wicksteed (1910), H.J. Davenport (1914), and F. Knight (1921). There is insufficient space here to describe this history. It is perhaps sufficient to say that, in one way or another, each of the authors helped to show that the concept of the entrepreneur, suitably defined in relation to the ERE, could be used to represent the two aspects.[9] However, it was not until Mises' *Human Action* (*Nationalökonomie*) that the *method* used by these authors was clearly identified.

The key to understanding Mises' contribution is to understand how he uses a combination of a priori assumptions and the evenly rotating economy to elucidate the relationship between the consumer and the entrepreneur roles. Consider the a priori assumptions. We know a priori that regardless of any particular wants or technical (supply) conditions, human beings make choices among alternative means of satisfying their ends. Moreover, we know that these choices have a time dimension, in the sense that choosers consider their anticipated future ends and their prospects for achieving them. Finally, for a variety of a priori reasons, individuals are uncertain about the outcomes of their choices.[10] In economic interaction, the significant type of uncertainty is intersubjective – uncertainty about the wants, abilities and knowledge of other actors.[11] To elucidate the relationship between the consumer and entrepreneur roles, we introduce the concept of the entrepreneur 'function'.

The entrepreneur 'function'

The 'function' of entrepreneurship embodies all that can be deduced about how time and uncertainty are relevant to the choices to identify and use factors of production to satisfy consumers' wants.[12] There are three inseparable parts to acting entrepreneurially: appraisement, undertaking and uncertainty-bearing.[13] *Appraisement* means identifying means (factors of production) and determining the profitability of using them to help satisfy consumers' wants. Thus, appraisement captures the knowledge of the causal connections among goods that was stressed by Menger. It adds to this the assumption that entrepreneurs operate in the environment of a market economy, where calculations are made in terms of money by individuals who differ in their judgements.[14] *Undertaking* means performing the act of will that directs the factors to their specific employments.[15] This, of course, is necessary for any production (and ultimately for any satisfaction of consumer wants) to occur. *Uncertainty-bearing* refers to the prospect of loss that results when one provides funds, or guarantees the funds provided by others, that are necessary to cause this production to occur. Mises showed that uncertainty is a necessary characteristic of action[16] and that the uncertainty which is relevant in a market economy is intersubjective uncertainty.[17]

In other words, appraisement refers to the entrepreneur's use of specialized knowledge of the causal connections among goods to attach prices to factors and decide whether the factors offered for sale by others are worth buying and employing. A market economy would not be possible without this. Undertaking refers to the actual decision to hire and employ factors. Uncertainty-bearing refers to the assumption that every undertaking entails the prospect of loss because of the uncertainty inherent in trying to predict how other people will act. Since economics is the study of action in the market economy, uncertainty-bearing is a property of every relevant undertaking. And every relevant undertaking by distinctly human actors requires appraisement.

Although Mises did not neatly lay out these three inseparable characteristics, he clearly indicated the method one must use to do so. It consists of using the ERE to conceptually strip, or extract, the distinctly human action from economic behaviour. Mises pointed out that such an imaginary construction is necessary in order to elucidate, by contrast, the role of the entrepreneur.[18] Perhaps because Mises did not clearly lay out these characteristics, his descriptions of entrepreneurship in the market economy seem not much different from (and in some ways inferior to) those of earlier writers on entrepreneurship. I believe that it is mainly for this reason that his contribution has gone unrecognized.

It is useful to have a precise definition of entrepreneurship. I have defined it in the following way: entrepreneurship refers to the willingness to bet one's time and/or money that one's appraisals of factors are superior to the appraisals of others. To fit this definition into the saving–production–consumption nexus, we must add that the bet contributes in some way to the production of goods to satisfy consumers' wants.

Entrepreneurship as the distinctly human part of human action

I have argued that the highest point in our understanding of entrepreneurship was achieved when entrepreneurship came to be associated with the distinctly human part of human action in the market economy. Following the logic of my 1990 book this argument can be defended as follows. First, Mises defined action as having the characteristics of ends and means, time and uncertainty (Mises 1966: chapters 4, 5 and 6). These characteristics – or 'properties of the category of action', as Mises called them – comprise the distinctly human parts of human action. What makes them distinctly human? We can only determine this by using our intuition and experience to contrast our personal understanding of our own means and ends with what might otherwise be called the means and ends of robots or animals.

For a simple Crusonean consumption–production action I have shown that the distinctly human parts are:

- identifying factors
- estimating net benefits of using a prospective factor according to a production plan
- making the actual decision to use the prospective factors in the plan
- uncertainty-bearing.[19]

Constructing an image of the market economy

The problem of economics is to incorporate these characteristics into an image of a market economy. Thus the second step is to define these terms so that they refer to saving, factor-supplying, producing and consuming under the conditions of private property rights, specialization and the use of money. We can accomplish this by means of definition and separation. We define saving as the *behaviour* of setting aside goods or factors for the satisfaction of future wants. We define factor-supplying as the *behaviour* of using one's factors to help produce a good. We define producing as the *behaviour* of using items that are regarded as factors of production to satisfy wants. We define consuming as the *behaviour* associated with using a first-order good (or goods, as opposed to factors) to meet the ends. We can imagine this behaviour being performed by robots in a routine fashion, or by animals according to imprinting and 'learning'. However, we reserve the term 'entrepreneurship' to refer to the distinctly human parts of using means to satisfy ends through time under the conditions of the market economy. Thus, we reserve the term 'entrepreneurship' to refer to the four distinctly human parts of action mentioned in the last paragraph, as they come to be expressed under the conditions that we assume to exist in the market economy.

The third step is to construct an image of the relationship between the prices of goods and the factors of production that includes the behaviour of saving, supplying factors, producing and consuming, but no entrepreneurship. This is the ERE. It gives us the means of elucidating the distinctly human action in the market economy. We ask what characteristics of human behaviour related to saving, supplying factors, producing and consuming cannot be represented in an image of robots. These characteristics are the entrepreneur actions. Referring to the characteristics of entrepreneurship described earlier, robots do not appraise (identify factors and estimate net benefits), make decisions (as opposed to selecting on the basis of algorithms) or bear (intersubjective) uncertainty.[20]

The fourth step is to construct an image of pure entrepreneurial interaction. We do this by conceiving of the *pure entrepreneurial economy*. This contains robot savers, factor suppliers, consumers and producer–managers who carry out the directives of the entrepreneurs. However, these robots do not make judgements or act. They operate according to routines, or algorithms. All economic interaction occurs among pure entrepreneurs. They use their own wealth to finance their bidding for the factors of production. Each bears the uncertainty connected with a particular enterprise. We use this image to describe:

* pricing
* competition (including copying and innovating)
* the appraisement of appraisement ability in others
* how people select themselves, others and objects to perform various functions in satisfying consumers' wants
* how people allocate the bearing of what they perceive to be uncertainty.[21]

This step enriches our definition of entrepreneurship in the market economy.

The fifth step is to use this enriched understanding of the entrepreneur function to refer to particular actions of real human actors who act in the role of savers, factor suppliers, producers and consumers under the conditions specified in the definition of the market economy. In other words, we use it to help us build an image of the pure market economy.[22]

A note on entrepreneurship in *Human Action*

After Mises had described the functional concept of the entrepreneur in *Human Action*, he made what I believe was the serious mistake of discussing a 'narrower' image of the entrepreneur concept, that reflects how '[e]conomics . . . always did and still does use the term "entrepreneur"' (Mises 1966: 254–5). This concept of the entrepreneur is based on the observable fact (datum) that individuals differ in the accuracy of their appraisals and in their willingness to bear uncertainty. Mises used the terms 'promoter' and 'promoting entrepreneur' to refer to this concept. It refers to 'those who are especially eager to profit from adjusting production to the expected changes in conditions, those who have more initiative, more venturesomeness, and a quicker eye than the crowd, the pushing and promoting pioneers of economic development' (*ibid.*).[23]

I have argued that using this notion of the entrepreneur was not only a serious mistake in judgment, it actually led Mises into error.[24] The important point here is that this chapter is about Mises' functional concept.

SCHUMPETER

J.A. Schumpeter was the first Austrian economist to explicitly develop what might be called a theory of entrepreneurship. In his 1911 book he elucidated entrepreneurship by contrasting his image of a real market economy with the static general equilibrium. He defined the latter as containing interaction, but no invention and innovation ('the carrying out of new combinations').[25] He used the term entrepreneur to represent these activities. Although Schumpeter wrote extensively after this, he did not develop the concept of entrepreneurship further. As far as I am aware, there were no other significant Austrian contributions until Mises.

Let us compare descriptions of economic interaction using Schumpeter's entrepreneur with descriptions using the 'new subjectivist entrepreneur'. Consider some examples. Suppose that a lender outbids his competitors by offering a lower cost loan to a prospective producer. The new subjectivist represents this as a competition among entrepreneurs for the right to the profit from the producer's future activities. A producer who outbids his competitor for some factor of production and an employee who offers to do a particular job for a lower price than his competitors are also regarded as competing entrepreneurs. An employment compact is a competition among entrepreneurs (the buyer and the seller of work) for the right to the product of the employee's work. Finally consider a person who agrees to pay part of a future loss in exchange for the right to part of what would otherwise be someone else's future business profit. The buyer of that right is really an entrepreneur who outbids his competitor (the seller of the right). The 'competitor' is not harmed, of course, but benefits from this competition because he or she happens to own the resources for which the bidding occurs. The unifying feature of all of these examples is that they can be expressed in terms of competition among individuals in their capacity as entrepreneurs. The subjectivist can form an understanding of these kinds of phenomena theoretically, simply by using his image of the pure entrepreneurial economy.

Schumpeter's descriptions are more cumbersome. For example, to describe phenomena like judgements of future wants, uncertainty-bearing, credit, underwriting and even competition, he must refer to producers, capitalists, businessmen and workers. By adopting this mode of description, one runs the risk of confusing the distinctly human category of entrepreneurship with various behaviours that are not entrepreneurship. Because he did not identify the entrepreneur function, he could not reason as abstractly as a new subjectivist. Consequently he could not easily shift back and forth between abstract theoretical reasoning and concrete description.

Schumpeter's limited conception of entrepreneurship stems directly from the problem with which he was concerned. He wanted to write about economic development, which he associated with new combinations, so he defined the entrepreneur as the discoverer and actuator of those combinations. Having appropriated the term entrepreneur to refer to this phenomenon, he had no other term with which to describe economic interaction in the abstract.

Correctly understood, economic development is a special application of the general theory of economic interaction. One asks: 'What would be the effect of changing a particular set of laws so that the real society conforms more (or less) closely to the imaginary construction of the pure market economy?' One outcome of changing from a socialist economy to a pure market economy would be the apparently greater number of what historians would call new products and methods of production, or the opening of new markets. But the motivation for this and the sequence of events that has this result are no different from those involved in the satisfaction of wants generally (with the use of 'old' combinations, for example).

In fact, Schumpeter's entrepreneur is not a subjectivist concept. In the market economy, what constitutes a 'new' combination is a subjective judgement. No one knows all of the combinations and thus no one can be certain whether a combination is 'new' or 'old' – and, of course, no one cares. No one will finance or undertake what he thinks is a new combination (or, for that matter, an 'old' combination) unless he judges that he can earn a profit. It is this judgement and the decision to act on it which constitute the important phenomena to the economist, not whether the combination is regarded as old or new.

The difference between the concept of the static equilibrium used by Schumpeter and the evenly rotating economy of the new subjectivism parallels this. Schumpeter uses static equilibrium to define old combinations. The new subjectivism uses the ERE not as a model of human beings who only produce and consume the fruits of old combinations, but as a model of robots who do not and cannot perform distinctly human action. The absence of distinctly human action, not the absence of new combinations, is the distinguishing feature of the ERE.

J. PATRICK GUNNING

KIRZNER'S ENTREPRENEUR

Kirzner's treatment of 'entrepreneurship' is extensive. Some of it uses a concept of the entrepreneur which is not too different from that used by Schumpeter in relation to equilibrium. However, the distinguishing feature of Kirzner's work concerns what he calls 'the entrepreneurial element in human decision-making, or alertness'. This section will focus mainly on Kirzner's idea of entrepreneurship as alertness. Towards the end of the section, I will discuss his departures from this usage.

Alertness as entrepreneurship

The fundamental concept in Kirzner's definition of entrepreneurship is 'alertness'. Alertness leads individuals to make discoveries of information that is valuable in the satisfaction of wants. It is subconscious, unplanned and completely unexpected. Because discoveries are unexpected, the discoverer is not able to prepare for them or to promote them. In Kirzner's terms, a discovery is like realizing that a free $10 bill which has already been discovered is resting in one's hand (Kirzner 1973: 47).

The discoveries due to alertness can be contrasted with another type of discovery. Like the captains of the first European ships which sailed to the New World, an individual can make a discovery which, while not planned for precisely, would nevertheless be expected in some measure at the outset of a particular plan of action. Using Kirzner's analogy, one can go searching for money and, with luck, find a $10 bill in one's hand. Kirzner is not talking about this kind of discovery. Discoveries due to 'alert entrepreneurship' are totally unexpected. The alertness of which he speaks is either totally unrecognized by the individual or, if it is recognized, he can do nothing to promote it.

The relevance of alertness

There can be no doubt that discoveries of the type that Kirzner describes do occur. We know this from inspecting our own actions. The issue I wish to raise is why such discoveries are relevant to economics. Given that they are totally unknown and unknowable to the actor, their relevance can only be derived from the action that occurs *after* the discovery. Suppose someone discovers that an item which was previously not a factor of production can be profitably used as such. If neither she nor someone else acts on this knowledge, it is irrelevant. Let us consider the case where this knowledge is accompanied by an incentive to act. Following the discovery, suppose that the discoverer comes to appraise the item and other factors of production differently than previously. She then proceeds to change her plans by buying factors and producing a saleable good. In this case the discovery is relevant.

We conclude that in the relevant case, the discoverer of a factor must bet that her discovery can earn a profit. She must be willing to bet that her appraisals of factors are superior to those of other appraisers. In terms of this chapter, alertness is relevant if it leads to discoveries that *entrepreneurship* regards as relevant to its choice. But then Kirzner uses the term 'entrepreneur' to describe 'alertness'. Although he surely would agree with the ideas expressed in this paragraph, he could not use these words to express them.

Alertness, entrepreneurship and maximizing

If we use the term 'entrepreneurship' to refer to alertness, what term should we use to describe the action of betting that one's discovered knowledge is correct by using one's wealth or factors of production to produce a saleable good? In his initial work, Kirzner contrasted the alert discoverer of knowledge with a Robbinsian maximizer. However, to date, he has said nothing about Mises' entrepreneur function as contrasted with the maximizing robots of the ERE.

Mises would have regarded the discoveries that result from alertness as data.[26] In a proper subjectivist analysis, data enter through the choosing minds of the subjects studied. To be relevant to economics they must be accounted for by appraising and uncertainty-bearing entrepreneurship. The economist may refer to data by showing how they are perceived by entrepreneurship. For example, if lenders incorporate a belief that business borrowers will have subconscious, unplanned and unexpected windfalls, they will act differently than if they do not have such a belief. Speculators may even buy and sell stock on the basis of their respective beliefs about the probable windfalls that will occur in the various businesses. However, if the prospect for windfalls is not taken into account by anyone, it does not belong in economics. To call the alertness that results in windfalls 'entrepreneurship' is tantamount to calling attention 'choice'.

Alertness as a real phenomenon

It is so unusual for a student of Mises to appropriate the term entrepreneurship in this way that one is naturally led to ask why he did it. Kirzner provides answers of sorts in two of his books (Kirzner 1979, 1992). In his 1979 book he seems to give two answers, the first being that alertness is a real phenomenon.

> The truth surely is that, of the mass of knowledge, beliefs, opinions, expectations, and guesses that one holds at a given moment and that inspire and shape action, only a fraction can be described as being the result of deliberate search or learning activity. Surely a very great vol-

ume of one's awareness of one's environment, and of one's expectations concerning the future, is the result of learning experiences that *occurred entirely without having been planned*.

(Kirzner 1979: 142)

One can hardly deny that much of our expectations of the future have resulted from experiences that were not planned by us. Even if we exclude experiences planned by others, such as schooling and 'socialization', there still appears to be a range of experiences that were not planned and which yielded knowledge that we regard as useful in predicting the future. Moreover, we have quite a bit of knowledge that we are normally unaware of and only call upon when we encounter an unfamiliar situation Notwithstanding these facts, the important question is how we should include the unplanned knowledge or discoveries in our images of economic interaction. The sun rises every day but this does not mean we should regard it as an important economic phenomenon and call it 'entrepreneurship'.

Desirability of institutions to generate unplanned learning

Kirzner's second answer of sorts is that institutions differ in the extent to which they generate subconscious discoveries. Thus alertness has policy relevance. He says:

I contend that the market performs a crucial function in discovering knowledge nobody knows exists; that an understanding of the true character of the market process depends, indeed, on recognizing this crucial function; and, finally, that contemporary economists' unawareness of these insights appears to be the result of otherwise wholly laudable attempts to treat knowledge objectively.

(Kirzner 1979: 139)

[I]t must appear highly desirable to choose among alternative social institutional arrangements those modes of organization that minimize this kind of ignorance – that is, those modes of organization that generate the greatest volume of spontaneous undeliberate learning.

(*ibid.*: 147)

The market process

It is important to realize that the 'market process' as Kirzner uses the term in the first quotation above, does not refer to individuals *deliberately* positioning themselves or making contractual arrangements, so that they can benefit from the actions or behaviour of others. It means 'a process of *spontaneous* discovery of the plans of other market participants' (*ibid.*: 148, emphasis added). 'Spontaneous' means subconscious and unplanned.[27] He assumes that the soon-to-be discoverers of plans are completely unaware of their prospect for gain. It follows that part of the statement under consideration can be rewritten as: 'I contend that the market performs the important function of inducing subconscious learning about others' plans.' The 'market' in this statement presumably refers to the conditions of private property rights and freedom of contract.

Alertness and instincts

At first glance, this is a remarkable claim. Since spontaneous learning is not a conscious process, it apparently falls into the category of an instinct (Mises 1966: 27). Instincts are either the consequence of a genetic accident or natural selection. Let us suppose that the relevant instincts are due to natural selection. Then they would have developed and have been selected for during times of species or group stress. And they would be suitable mainly for enabling the species or group to survive similar stressful situations. If we accept this, then instinctual curiosity and imitation would have arisen during periods of survival stress for pre-human and early human groups.

In the market economy such instincts may be more of a liability than an asset. Human actors who studied such instincts in others could potentially prompt behaviour that is contrary to the others' interests. For example, a stock promoter who knows that a new stock is worthless might expect some people to buy out of instinctual curiosity. As a result, he or she could gain at their expense. Similarly, recognizing an instinct for copying, a wise stock market speculator may sell his or her stock when he or she thinks that instinctual imitators have bid the price to an artificially high level. In these cases the wise speculator gains at the expense of the person with the instinctive behaviour.

Institutions and alertness

Can institutions effect alertness? The converse of Kirzner's argument is that socialism would stifle alertness. Is this true? It would surely stifle the betting that people do on their knowledge, subconscious or otherwise. But if people had an instinct for discovering wants and the means for satisfying them, how could socialism stifle it? Kirzner provides no help on this issue, as far as I am aware. One could make the argument that in the market economy parents deliberately promote alertness in their children to prepare them for success. But Kirzner does not speak about alertness that can be promoted through 'socialization', and for good reason. A parent who can stimulate the alertness in his or her child could presumably also stimulate alertness in him- or herself.

This is not to deny, of course, that the institutions of the market economy give individuals an incentive to utilize all knowledge, regardless of source, for the purpose of satisfying others' wants. My argument is that if there is a relationship between market institutions and subconscious discoveries, it is not direct and in any case is not relevant to action – and therefore economics – defined as a branch of praxeological theory. Alertness is relevant only to history or applied economics; since those disciplines require one to construct images based on realistic assumptions about all relevant facts.[28]

Kirzner's 1992 paper

In a more recent paper, Kirzner deals among other things with what he calls the radical subjectivist critique of his claim that economists should study how the 'entrepreneurial process' leads to equilibrium (Kirzner 1992: 12–14). The concept of alertness plays a role in his argument. He says:

> The writer's attempt to develop a theory of systematic entrepreneurial equilibrating tendencies that is rooted in creative entrepreneurial alertness is pronounced to fail because the 'subliminal teleology' implicit in notions of equilibration is thoroughly inconsistent with creativity.
>
> (*ibid.*: 17–18)

Kirzner defends his attempt by pointing out that by equilibrating tendencies, he means tendencies towards coordination; and the tendencies he has in mind are those envisioned and re-envisioned by individual actors as time passes. The wording of his defence is critical, and quotations are necessary to avoid misunderstanding. He says:

> Once we acknowledge the meaningfulness of endeavouring to imagine the future more correctly, we can hardly refuse to recognize the quality of 'alertness' (or of more correctly fertile imagination, or of greater prescience – call it what one will) in human beings. We must, that is, recognize something like 'entrepreneurial ability', understood as the capacity independently to size up a situation and more correctly reach an imagined picture of the relevant (as yet indeterminate) future.
>
> (*ibid.*: 26)

> [W]hat the alertness of the entrepreneur strives to notice and correctly to imagine are (what will turn out to be) future realities, and it is the *prospective gain offered by these realities* which 'switches on' entrepreneurial alertness.
>
> (*ibid.*: 27)

> The entrepreneur is not so much choosing a course of action that shall be appropriate to the 'realities' as he is choosing among alternative imaginable realities that his prospective action may be initiating.
>
> (*ibid.*)

it is the imagined *reality* . . . which inspires and shapes the entrepreneur's decision.

(*ibid.*: 32)

different imaginable realities may simultaneously exercise their influence on the entrepreneurial nose for profit.

(*ibid.*: 33)

These statements seem equivocal to the reader who is interested in whether Kirzner's reference to the entrepreneur is to conscious action or to subconscious processes. The imagined reality to which Kirzner refers must be part of consciousness. The individual constructs an image of a future reality and chooses what he regards as the best course of action. Thus, the 'entrepreneurial ability' to which Kirzner refers on page 26 would seem to be part of a conscious choice. On page 27, however, he does not say that an individual strives to notice prospective gain, he says that *the alertness of the entrepreneur* strives to notice this gain. Since he has consistently used the concept of alertness in previous work to refer to a subconscious process, Kirzner is presumably referring to that subconscious process here. This appears to be confirmed by the next quotation, to the effect that entrepreneurial alertness is *switched on* (notwithstanding that in the same sentence he says that the entrepreneur strives to notice and correctly imagine future realities).

In the next statement, again on page 27, he speaks of the entrepreneur choosing among imaginable realities. Choosing is presumably a conscious process. (It is noteworthy, however, that Kirzner uses the term 'imaginable' and not 'imagined', suggesting that perhaps he is not referring to what the entrepreneur imagines. There seems to be a certain slipperiness here, although one cannot be sure.) On page 32, Kirzner says that the imagined reality 'shapes' the entrepreneur's decision, while on page 33, the imaginable realities exercise their influence on the entrepreneurial 'nose for profit'. Is Kirzner speaking here of instincts?

Admittedly such a close scrutiny of anyone's work might lead us to conclude that his ideas are inconsistent. However, the point I want to make is that if we assume Kirzner is talking about conscious action, his argument is consistent with the new subjectivism. In this case he is talking about the method of imaginary constructions used by the appraising, undertaking and uncertainty-bearing entrepreneur. However, Kirzner's failure to use the term entrepreneur in the functional sense results in metaphors that are best avoided. On the other hand, if he is referring to subconscious processes, his argument fails. Subconscious behaviour cannot be driven by realities that are imagined by the one who behaves. And it cannot be driven by the individual's prospect for profit.

Recognition of conscious, planned action

It would be incorrect to say that Kirzner ignores the characteristic feature of the new subjectivist entrepreneur – namely betting on one's judgements. Quite to the contrary, he reminds us in his 1982 paper that he dealt specifically with this issue in his original work on the subject.[29] He points out to critics who had objected to his stress on alertness as opposed to uncertainty and speculation, that his emphasis was deliberate and intended to help illustrate the 'market process':

> All human action is speculative; my emphasis on the element of alertness in action has been intended to point out that, far from being numbed by the inescapable uncertainty of our world, men *act upon their judgments* of what opportunities have been left unexploited by others.
> (Kirzner 1973: 86–7; 1982: 141, emphasis in original)

In a related statement earlier in the same paragraph, Kirzner says that he has 'of course recognized that in a world of uncertainty every entrepreneur decision, no matter how much alertness it reflects, must to some extent constitute a gamble' (Kirzner 1973: 86).

On the basis of these statements one can hardly maintain that Kirzner ignored appraisement and uncertainty-bearing. My argument is first that his emphasis on alertness distracts attention from intersubjective uncertainty, as other writers have pointed out.[30] Second, and more important, his effort to appropriate the term 'entrepreneur' obscures what I believe is the most important contribution to economics made by an Austrian economist during this century. There is no hint in Kirzner that a new subjectivist revolution could have occurred.

CONCLUSION

To my mind the theory of entrepreneurship is the single most important contribution to economic theory during this century. The Austrians were really latecomers, though a case can be made that non-Austrian contributions can at least partly be traced to Menger's subjectivist theory of prices. Mises' contribution superseded those of the non-Austrians. Yet, to date, the Mises story is a tragic one.

He was the first to recognize the true significance of entrepreneur function. Moreover, he provided the epistemological underpinnings necessary to defend his view of that significance. He did this in steps in *Human Action*. First, he identified economics as a type of knowledge that differs from logic, mathematics, psychology, physics or biology (Mises 1966: 1). He then showed that economics is really just a branch of a broader type of knowledge which also differs from the other types. The broader type is praxeology – the theory of distinctly human action (*ibid.*: 3). Next, he told us that the starting point of economics is to construct an image of the pure market economy (*ibid.*: 238), that the method of praxeology and economics is the method of imaginary constructions (*ibid.*: 236), that the entrepreneur means 'acting man' in regard to changes in market data (*ibid.*: 254) and that, to comprehend the entrepreneur function, it is essential to use the imaginary construction of the evenly rotating economy (*ibid.*: 248).

In my previous work I have tried to elaborate and expand these ideas in an effort to construct an image of entrepreneurship that we can trace directly to distinctly human action. I wanted a concept of entrepreneurship that embodies all of the distinctly human action in the market economy. This is the kind of concept that I believe Mises had in mind when he wrote about the function of the entrepreneur. I have called this the 'new subjectivist' concept of the entrepreneur.

In this chapter, I outlined the procedure that one must follow to develop this concept. Two other notable Austrian writers who used the term 'entrepreneur' proceeded in different directions. On the one hand, Schumpeter associated entrepreneurship with assumed new combinations and disregarded subjectivism entirely. On the other hand, Kirzner has associated it with the unplanned, subconscious discoveries that he calls 'alertness'. In doing so (and to the extent that he has not revised his definition in recent years), he has not only tried to elevate a non-subjectivist idea to the status of a critical concept for our understanding of the market economy, but he has distracted those who might otherwise be interested in exploring the true meaning of the entrepreneur in *Human Action*. The tragedy is that the Austrian contribution to the most important idea of the century is in danger of being missed.

NOTES

1 See the introduction to Böhm-Bawerk (1959, vol. 1: 6–7).
2 See especially his papers of 1937 and 1945.
3 Lachmann (1951) seems to have recognized this clearly.
4 The term 'human', as used by Mises in his title, is redundant. In his book, he defines action as the conscious use of means to accomplish ends (Mises 1966: 92). This rules out other behaviour. I have retained the redundancy in this chapter for the sake of continuity.
5 See Casson (1982); Hébert and Link (1982); Reekie (1984); Barreto (1989); Wu (1989).
6 See particularly Kirzner (1973, 1979).
7 Gunning (1988a, 1988b, 1990, 1991, 1992a, 1992b, 1994, and 1997).
8 The role of knowledge in Menger's system was explored by Kirzner and by Lachmann in a symposium on Menger which was published in 1978. Streissler has especially emphasized it (see Kirzner 1978; Lachmann 1978; Streissler 1990).
9 The history of the entrepreneur concept as it pertains to the new subjectivism is discussed in Gunning (1992a).
10 See Mises (1966: chapters 4, 5, and 6, respectively).

11 Strictly speaking, intersubjective uncertainty cannot be derived a priori in the same way as uncertainty in general (see Gunning 1990: 42–4).

12 Mises did not define the term entrepreneur so clearly. He said:

> When economics employs the [following] terms it speaks of catallactic categories. The entrepreneurs, capitalists, landowners, workers, and consumers of economic theory are not living men as one meets them in the reality of life and history. They are the embodiment of distinct functions in the market operations.
>
> (Mises 1966: 251–2)

> Economics, in speaking of entrepreneurs, has in view not men, but a definite function. This function is not the particular feature of a special group or class of men; it is inherent in every action and burdens every actor. In embodying this function in an imaginary figure, we resort to a methodological makeshift. The term entrepreneur as used by catallactic theory means: acting man exclusively seen from the aspect of the uncertainty inherent in every action. In using this term we must never forget that every action is embedded in the flux of time and therefore involves a speculation. The capitalists, landowners, and the laborers are by necessity speculators. So is the consumer in providing for anticipated future needs.
>
> (*ibid.*: 252–3)

> In the context of economic theory . . . (e)ntrepreneur means: acting man exclusively seen from the aspect of [intersubjective] uncertainty inherent in every action . . . In the context of economic theory the meaning of the terms concerned is this: Entrepreneur means acting man in regard to the changes occurring in the data of the market.
>
> (*ibid.*: 254)

13 Gunning (1990: chapter 6). Appendix 5 of that book supports my argument that these parts were identified by Mises.

14 Mises says: 'Appraisement must be clearly distinguished from valuation. Appraisement in no way depends upon the subjective valuation of the man who appraises. He is not intent upon establishing the subjective use-value of the good concerned, but upon anticipating the prices which the market will determine. Valuation is a value judgment expressive of a difference in value. Appraisement is the anticipation of an expected fact' (Mises 1966: 332).

It would appear from this statement that Mises is making a distinction between the consumer role, which evaluates, and the entrepreneurial role, which appraises. But he does not actually say this. In fact, there is not a distinct and direct link in Mises between appraisement and the function of the entrepreneur. The link is indirect. To appreciate it, one must sort through Mises' prolix discussions, after coming to appreciate his unique contribution to methodology.

15 Regarding undertaking, Mises says: 'The specific entrepreneurial function consists in determining the employment of factors of production' (Mises 1966: 290–1). He also says: 'The function of the entrepreneur cannot be separated from the direction of the employment of factors of production for the accomplishment of definite tasks. The entrepreneur controls the factors of production' (*ibid.*: 306). Finally, he says: 'The entrepreneur determines alone, without any managerial interference, in what lines of business to employ capital and how much capital to employ. He determines the expansion and contraction of the size of the total business and its main sections. He determines the enterprise's financial structure' (*ibid.*: 307).

16 Mises (1966: 105–6).
17 Mises does not refer specifically to intersubjective uncertainty. The validity of this point must be inferred from his discussion of how dealing with uncertainty involves *understanding*: 'understanding is the only appropriate method of dealing with the uncertainty of future conditions' (Mises 1966: 118). And: 'A prospective entrepreneur does not consult the calculus of probability which is of no avail in the field of understanding. He trusts his own ability to understand future market conditions better than his less gifted fellow men' (*ibid.*: 299).

The scope of understanding is the mental grasp of phenomena which cannot be totally elucidated by logic, mathematics, praxeology and the natural sciences: 'The *understanding* establishes the fact that an individual or a group of individuals have engaged in a definite action emanating from definite value judgments and choices and aiming at definite ends, and that they have applied for the attainment of these ends definite means suggested by definite technological, therapeutical, and praxeological doctrines. It furthermore tries to appreciate the effects and the intensity of the effects brought about by an action; it tries to assign to every action its relevance, i.e., its bearing upon the course of events' (*ibid.*: 50, emphasis added).
18 Mises (1966: 248).
19 See Gunning (1990: chapter 5).
20 See Gunning (1990: chapter 6).
21 Mises (1966: 256) constructed such an image for the purpose of defining the pure entrepreneur but did not take the next step of describing abstract entrepreneurial interaction.
22 I used this procedure in Gunning (1990) and laid it out in summary form in chapter 1 of Gunning (1994).
23 These two definitions are explored in greater detail in Gunning (1994).
24 See Gunning (1994: chapters 4 and 5).
25 Schumpeter (1934: 66) presents a five-item list of characteristics.
26 'For praxeology data are the bodily and psychological features of the acting men, their desires and value judgments, and the theories, doctrines, and ideologies they develop in order to adjust themselves purposively to the conditions of their environment and thus to attain the ends they are aiming at. These data, although permanent in their structure and strictly determined by the laws controlling the order of the universe, are perpetually fluctuating and varying; they change from instant to instant' (Mises 1966: 646).
27 Note the difference between this meaning of spontaneous and the meaning attached by Hayek. For Hayek, 'spontaneous' meant 'not planned by a central authority'. See Hayek (1967).
28 See Gunning (1991) for the relevance of different kinds of assumptions to economic theory.
29 According to the title, this paper is about Misesian entrepreneurship. But it is really about Kirznerian entrepreneurship. There are only a few references to Mises and no serious contextual interpretation. Nevertheless, Kirzner argues that his work provides a deeper understanding of the Misesian entrepreneur. In some passages, he attributes his idea of alertness to Mises (see, for example, Kirzner 1979: 158). I could find no evidence that Mises used the term entrepreneurship in this way. To Mises entrepreneurship always exists in a market context and always involves intersubjective uncertainty. I can only guess that he was misled by Mises' unfortunate decision to write extensively about the entrepreneur as 'promoter'.

30 See Kirzner (1982: 140–2). The most authoritative criticism is that of Rothbard (1985) who apparently understood the importance of uncertainty to Mises. However, Rothbard did not quote Mises and I could find no hint in Rothbard's other works that he envisioned what I have called the 'new subjective revolution'. The comment on entrepreneurship closest to the new subjectivist concept is in a paper on Marxism by Grinder and Hagel (1977). They identified the second two characteristics – undertaking and uncertainty-bearing – clearly enough. However, instead of appraisement, they referred to 'alertness to price discrepancies', a very Kirznerian term. Their paper was not about entrepreneurship, so they did not try to defend their definition. Also, given Kirzner's definition of alertness, it is far from clear whether they had the new subjectivist notion of appraisement in mind.

REFERENCES

Barreto, H. (1989) *The Entrepreneur in Microeconomic Theory: Disappearance and Explanation*, London: Routledge.

Böhm-Bawerk, E. (1959) *Capital and Interest* (vol. 1 first published in 1884, vol. 2 first published in 1889, vol. 3 first published in 1912), trans. by George D. Huncke and Hans F. Sennholz, South Holland, IL: Libertarian Press.

Casson, M. (1982) *The Entrepreneur*, Totowa, NJ: Barnes & Noble.

Clark, J.B. (1899) *The Distribution of Wealth: A Theory of Wages, Interest and Profits*, New York: Macmillan.

Davenport, H.J. (1914) *Economics of Enterprise*, New York: Macmillan.

Grinder, W.E. and Hagel, J. (1977) 'Toward a theory of state capitalism: ultimate decision-making and class structure', *Journal of Libertarian Studies*, 1 (1): 59–79.

Gunning, J.P. (1988a) 'Mises on the evenly rotating economy', *Review of Austrian Economics*, 3.

——(1988b) 'Caldwell on Mises on methodology', *Review of Austrian Economics*, 3.

——(1990) *The New Subjectivist Revolution: An Elucidation and Extension of Ludwig von Mises' Contribution to Economic Theory*, Savage, MD: Rowman & Littlefield.

——(1991) 'Praxeology, economics, and ethical philosophy', in R.M. Ebeling (ed.) *Austrian Economics: Perspectives on the Past and Prospects for the Future*, Hillsdale, MI: Hillsdale College Press.

——(1992a) 'The meaning of entrepreneurship in economic theory: historical perspective', *Entrepreneurship, Innovation, and Economic Change*, June.

——(1992b) 'The new subjectivist elucidation of entrepreneurship', *Entrepreneurship, Innovation, and Economic Change*, September.

——(1994) *The Failure of the New Subjectivist Revolution: A Critical Essay on the Economic Theory of Ludwig von Mises*, Ft Myers, FL and Taipei: Nomad Press.

——(1977) 'Ludwig von Mises's transformation of the Austrian theory of value and cost, *History of Economics Review*, summer.

Hayek, F.A. (1937) 'Economics and knowledge', *Economica*, 4: 33–54.

——(1945) 'The use of knowledge in society', *American Economic Review*, 35 (4): 519–30.

——(1967) 'The results of human action but not of human design', chapter 6 in *Studies in Philosophy, Politics, and Economics*, Chicago, IL: University of Chicago Press.

Hébert, R.F. and Link, A.N. (1982) *The Entrepreneur*, New York: Praeger.

Kirzner, I. (1973) *Competition and Entrepreneurship*, Chicago, IL: University of Chicago Press.

——(1978) 'The entrepreneurial role in Menger's system', *Atlantic Economic Journal*, September.

——(1979) *Perception, Opportunity, and Profit*, Chicago, IL: University of Chicago Press.

——(1982) 'Uncertainty, discovery, and human action: a study of the entrepreneurial profile in the Misesian system', chapter 12 in I. Kirzner (ed.) *Method, Process, and Austrian Economics*, Lexington, MA: D.C. Heath & Company.

——(1992) *The Meaning of the Market Process: Essays in the Development of Modern Austrian Economics*, London and New York: Routledge.

Knight, F. (1921) *Risk, Uncertainty, and Profit*, New York: Houghton Mifflin.

Lachmann, L. (1951) 'The science of human action', reprinted in *Capital, Expectations, and the Market Process*, Kansas City, KS: Sheed Andrews & McMeel, 1977.

——(1978) 'Carl Menger and the incomplete revolution of subjectivism', *Atlantic Economic Journal*, September.

Mises, L. von (1966) *Human Action: A Treatise on Economics*, Chicago, IL: Henry Regnery Company. (An earlier version was originally published in German in 1940, under the title *Nationalökonomie.*)

Reekie, W.D. (1984) *Markets, Entrepreneurs and Liberty: An Austrian View of Capitalism*, Brighton: Wheatsheaf Books.

Rothbard, M.N. (1985) 'Professor Hébert on entrepreneurship', *Journal of Libertarian Studies*, 7 (2, fall): 281–6.

Schumpeter, J.A. (1934) *The Theory of Economic Development* (first published 1911), translated R. Opie, Cambridge, MA: Harvard University Press.

Streissler, E.W. (1990) 'Menger, Böhm-Bawerk, and Wieser: the origins of the Austrian school', in K. Hennings and W.J. Samuels (eds), *Neoclassical Economic Theory, 1870 to 1930*, Boston, MA: Kluwer Academic.

Wicksteed, P.H. (1910) *The Common Sense of Political Economy*, London: Lu nd Humphries, 1933.

Wu, S. (1989) *Production, Entrepreneurship, and Profits*, Cambridge, MA: Basil Blackwell.

9

ENTREPRENEURSHIP, INTERDEPENDENCY AND INSTITUTIONS

The comparative advantages of the Austrian and post-Keynesian styles of thought

Emiel F.M. Wubben

In this chapter, we will address the comparative advantages of the styles of thought ingrained in Austrian and post-Keynesian economics. The unease of post-Keynesian economics for any affiliation with Austrian economics may be exemplified by the following poignant illustration. The 1993 Leeds conference entitled 'Keynes, knowledge and uncertainty' brought together a variety of post-Keynesians, historians of economic thought and methodologists. Following his speech, the guest speaker Brian Loasby was confronted with the observation that the ideas he presented echoed the views of Hayek. The substance of Loasby's reaction was that he had mixed feelings on this comment. He would like to feel flattered by the observation, if only it was not meant as a condemnation.

The comment was not meant to be complimentary. However, other participants of this Keynes-related conference did not feel annoyed by this marked affinity with Austrian economics. Moreover, discussions between Austrians and post-Keynesians take place at various conferences, such as the meetings of the History of Economics Society and the European Association for Evolutionary Political Economy. A different light is cast on the inclusive or exclusive behaviour of the two styles of thought if one scrutinizes the index on authors in related companions. The *Elgar Companion to Austrian Economics* (Boettke 1994) offers an entry on Sraffians or neo-Ricardians, but not on its family members; for instance the 12-page index does not list Michal Kalecki, Jan Kregel or Paul Davidson. The *Biographical Dictionary of Dissenting Economists* (Arestis and Sawyer 1992) does not include Kirzner, Hayek, Lachmann or any other Austrian economist. This circumstantial evidence presents in a nutshell the present relationship between Austrian economics and post-Keynesian economics. It suggests that the line of demarcation between them, which is manifest in formal portrayals, is indistinct and includes relations in the personal and theoretical domains.

In this survey, the term 'style' is to be preferred to the term 'school'. A style may first and foremost be recognized by the dominant problem, the vision or ideals which one wants to realize as well as the techniques that are used (Zuidema 1986: 189). Moreover, a style creates order in the theoretical compositions and it creates a tradition through the related scientific learning processes. A number of styles may coexist. Because all classifications are somehow disputable, the most useful, that is the most suitable, classification may be introduced. Given this approach, it is no longer tempting to merely search for the largest common denominator and thus run the risk of neglecting deviating opinions within a school. Furthermore, the homogeneity implied when focusing on schools of economic thought artificially stresses the differences between groups of scientists. It will be claimed in this chapter that fruitful mutual exchanges of thought may take place between scientists committed to different sets of ideals. Neither Schumpeter (1954) nor Blaug (1985) portrays schools as closed groups of authors comprising a master and his disciples who subscribe to a closed theoretical pattern with which they typify the world and which tends to generate (over-)standardized solutions (Zuidema 1986: 184–5).

This chapter pleads in favour of local cross fertilization of Austrian and post-Keynesian economics. We shall first present a survey of the course of Austrian economics and this will be followed by that of post-Keynesian economics. A few bilateral exchanges will be discussed next, in particular the Hayek–Keynes macro debate and the Sraffa–Hayek duel. The inferences will be that these styles of thought (a) were talking at cross purposes, and (b) held different priorities regarding their position in economics. Our focus will then change from these early disputes to contemporary research topics. We shall look at:

- time, decision making and entrepreneurship
- interdependency and instability
- monetary theories
- pricing theories
- institutions
- methodology.

Clearly with regard to these themes another set of questions unfolds. Are the Austrian and post-Keynesian styles of thought substitutes or complements? Are they encompassing or exclusive? It will be argued in this chapter that the two styles of thought may fruitfully work together in a number of fields, such as those of understanding human behaviour, interdependency and institutions.

EMIEL F.M. WUBBEN

AUSTRIAN ECONOMICS

The style of reasoning inherent in Austrian economics was developed in Vienna and first fully manifested in the 1871 publication of Carl Menger's *Grundsätze der Volkswirtschaftslehre*. Menger emphasized subjectivism as the preferred approach to economic theory and presented the notions of higher order goods, marginal utility and roundaboutness as the core concepts of his economics. He started a tradition in economic theory that was further developed by his successor at the University of Vienna, Friedrich von Wieser and the former finance minister, Eugen von Böhm-Bawerk. They represent the older Austrian school which, together with the Austro-Hungarian monarchy and liberalism in general, faced its demise in the course of World War I.

In the interwar period there were at least three circles of Austrian economics in Vienna: one around Menger's Mathematical Colloquium; a second around Hans Mayer, who succeeded his teacher Wieser and which included Leo Schönfeld-Illy, Paul Rosenstein-Rodan and Oskar Morgenstern; and a third circle related to the *Privatseminar* of Ludwig von Mises, which existed from 1923 to 1934. The latter group would become the best-known circle of Austrian economists and included Alfred Schutz, Felix Kaufmann, Gottfried Haberler, Friedrich Hayek, Fritz Machlup and, again, Rosenstein-Rodan and Morgenstern. Mises, a student of Böhm-Bawerk, had a 'rare quality and intellectual stimulus of a high order' (Robbins 1971: 108), which, for example, persuaded Lionel Robbins to foster the ambition to 'hitch LSE's wagon to the Viennese star' (Thomas 1991: 389).

In 1930, Robbins invited Hayek for a series of lectures to the London School of Economics. Hayek's subsequent appointment as a professor at the LSE gave the Austrian tradition such a boost in popularity that within two years the LSE was described as a suburb of Vienna (Coats 1982: 25). But in Vienna political problems caused the dispersion of Mises' circle, with Mises emigrating to New York. With Hayek, the torch of Austrian economics was handed over to London where it burned for a short but potent period. Then a contradictory situation unfolded. On the one hand, economists of the Austrian style believed in the successful absorption of Austrian ideas into mainstream economics (Kirzner 1992: 64), but on the other hand severe criticisms were raised against Austrian viewpoints. As a consequence, Austrian economics experienced an almost fatal drop in scientific popularity.

By the end of the interwar period Hayek and Ludwig M. Lachmann were the solitary Hayekians at the LSE. Disillusioned, Hayek left London and pure economics for Chicago and political philosophy. Lachmann kept on publishing after he took a chair at the University of Witswatersrand in South Africa, but 'the fortunes of Austrian economics were at low ebb' (Lachmann 1956: viii). Austrian economists would experience almost three decades in the academic wilderness. At New York University, Israel M.

194

Kirzner succeeded his teacher Mises and created an important nucleus awaiting the revival of the fortunes of Austrian economics, which indeed occurred in the 1970s. This revival of what was by then transformed into neo-Austrian economics was initiated when, in 1967, Hicks reopened the debate on money and the trade cycle. Hayek's 1974 Nobel lecture on 'The pretence of knowledge' boosted the historical and theoretical interest in the neo-Austrian ideas on socialism, knowledge and information.

Real efforts to augment this momentum were made by Kirzner, Lachmann and Murray N. Rothbard. Kirzner elaborated upon the theme of competition as a discovery process, Rothbard and his Mises Institute became the advocates of a radical libertarian ideology, while Lachmann, inspired by Rosenstein-Rodan and Hayek, made the subjectivism of expectations a key theme in his work. Their efforts resulted in the rise of a new generation of economists advocating the Austrian style of theorizing. This generation comprises – among others – Mario Rizzo, Gerald O'Driscoll, Stephan Boehm, Jeremy Shearmur, Norman Barry, Peter Boettke, Karen Vaughn, Christopher Torr, Richard Langlois, George Shackle, Ulrich Witt, Jack High, Don Lavoie and Roger Garrison. Among them we find both narrow- and broad-minded scientists, holding different predilections with respect to the preferred innovative research stratagems. As a result the term Austrian economics is nowadays known as either (a) a historical term, (b) an understanding of the market process as the disequilibrium foundation of equilibrium economics, (c) a libertarian ideology or (d) a subjectivist stance which stresses the autonomous position of preferences and expectations in an open-ended and irreversible stream of knowledge (Kirzner 1992: 67–9).

POST-KEYNESIAN ECONOMICS

With the advantage of hindsight one may state that the onset of post-Keynesian economics took place around 1932 in Cambridge as the production approach came to predominate over the pure exchange views in the *Cambridge Circus* (Pasinetti 1991: 22–7). The first post-Keynesians are 'those one-time associates of Keynes' (Eichner and Kregel 1975: 1293), in particular Michal Kalecki (Polish), Joan Robinson (British), Piero Sraffa (Italian) and Sidney Weintraub (American) (Arestis and Skouras 1985: 1–2). While the '"Keynesian revolution" went off at half-cock' (Hicks 1976: 289), these economists inspired a variety of scientists to elaborate upon this style of reasoning. As became clear in the 1970s, there emerged a diversity of loosely linked approaches in which Keynes's ideas are taken as a source next to those of these first post-Keynesians.

First, in America, there emerged a line of thought followed by Weintraub, Lori Tarsis, Hyman Minsky, Paul Davidson, Jan Kregel and Alfred Eichner, which develops the *monetary production economy* with the investment–production connection as its key determinant (Kregel 1991: 79–81). The

Berkeley-trained UCL professor Victoria Chick personifies the Anglo-Saxon bonds with British economists, such as Philip Arestis, the then heterodox Nobel prize winner John Hicks, Tony Lawson, George Shackle, Bill Gerrard and the representatives of the Stirling school, such as Sheila Dow, Peter Earl and Brian Loasby. A main feature of this group's style of reasoning is that they see the economy as a process in historical time. They claim that uncertainty with regard to the future explains why expectations (together with economic and political institutions) significantly influence economic events and outcomes (Davidson 1980: 158).

The second tradition in post-Keynesian economics is known as the neo-Ricardian, or Sraffian. This style of reasoning has been developed most notably by Piero Sraffa, Luigi Pasinetti, Edward Nell, Pierangelo Garegnani, Wynne Godley, John Eatwell, Murray Milgate, Krishna Bharadwaj, Geoffrey Harcourt, Alessandro Roncaglia, Paolo Sylos-Labini, Charles Goodwin, Bertram Schefold and Ian Steedman. These contributors are united in a search for persistent forces at work in an economic system in order to investigate its long-term evolution (Pasinetti 1983: 127; Lavoie 1992b: 50). Adherents of both traditions cooperated in several projects, but as Davidson acknowledged, the joint establishment of the *Journal of Post-Keynesian Economics* created strange bedfellows.

Joan Robinson, herself strongly influenced by Sraffa and Richard Kahn, outgrew her early theoretical and methodological viewpoints, her political affinities, and her optimism for and faith in both any *complete theory* and any long-period theory. She came to stress the inadmissibility of long-term comparisons for describing processes (Harcourt 1986). There is a contradiction in any assessment of Robinson's contribution to economics. On the one hand, her idealism and her proclivity for polemics, politics and self-criticism have, for many, reduced her contribution to merely another bag of unpleasant surprises. On the other hand, her shrewd mind, sharp tongue and rigour in argumentation, inspired by a passion for justice and equality, made her eligible for the Nobel Prize. She finally called the famous 'reswitching' debate unimportant (Robinson 1975) and her own contributions to economics insignificant, proclaiming the usefulness of Kalecki's approach and economic thought. In line with this view, we do not hold Robinson for a patron in post-Keynesian economics, but consider her as a sounding board for post-Keynesians in general and for Kaleckians in particular.

The legacy of Michal Kalecki (representing the third strand) sustains, for instance, that investment – as the driving force of the economic process (Harcourt and Hamouda 1988: 220) – together with the degree of monopoly directs the distribution of national income and the level of price/cost mark ups. Among the proponents of this strand are Amitava Dutt, Athanasios Asimakopulos, Joseph Steindl, Thanos Skouras, Peter Groenewegen, Malcolm Sawyer, Roy Harrod, Robert Rowthorn, Jerzy Osiatynski, Keith Cowling, Nicholas Kaldor and Amit Bhaduri. The popularity of the more recent series of (non-linear) growth models of cumulative causation (e.g. in Romer 1986), with growth sustained by the Verdoorn Law but curbed by technological and/or institutional lock-ins, may explain part of the current revival of the Kaleckian tradition.

We should close this section by realizing that several of these economists, such as Hicks and Sukamoy Chakravarti, defy classification within a single style of reasoning. This may appear intrinsic to the whole post-Keynesian approach.

INTERACTIONS

Those years of high theory (Shackle 1967), which also saw the genesis of post-Keynesian economics, mark the period of the first antagonistic exchanges of thought between the main protagonists of the different styles of economic thought. Even when we limit ourselves to the Austrian and post-Keynesian styles of thought, one may list some significant exchanges of thought. Just think of the famous Hayek–Keynes macro debate and the well-known Sraffa–Hayek duel. There was also the Cambridge–LSE *Times* letters on expanding public works (McCormick 1992: 69), the Robbins–Keynes debate in the Macmillan committee on oversaving and monetary mismanagement, following up Hayek's 'Paradox of saving' (1931a), the joint LSE/Cambridge seminars and the Hayek–Kaldor case on the capital controversy, which would transform into the debate on the Ricardo effect. Important questions that can be raised here are:

- What was discussed in these debates?
- How did these exchanges evolve?
- In what respect did they foreshadow future mutual behaviour?

The Hayek–Keynes macro debate

First, we consider the Hayek–Keynes macro debate which followed the publication of Keynes's *Treatise on Money* (1930). This dispute began with 'a scathing attack' by Hayek (Butos 1994: 470), went through a series of articles and finally dwindled to a series of letters, which resulted in a grave disappointment to Hayek. Butos is right in his claim that the substance of the debate was 'the self-adjusting and coordination properties of a market economy' (*ibid*.: 470). Keynes (1930) had defined the discrepancy between *ex post* investments and savings as unanticipated profits. Expectations are respectively satisfied or frustrated when savings match or exceed investments, which results in a steady state evolution and a cumulative contraction, respectively. In the absence of third party intervention market economies contain no effective endogenous self-correcting mechanism to neutralize the disequilibrium conditions. Hayek, however, would refer to the intertemporal unwinding of monetary disturbances, with temporary fluctuations in the relative prices of products produced in more versus less roundabout production processes.

Keynes conceded to Hayek the need to develop the required capital theory, but he never carried out his promise. His restless and volatile character decisively frustrated Hayek's continuous efforts to convince him by means of rigorous argumentation. Ultimately Keynes flatly stated that he had now shifted his attention towards other and more interesting subjects. Hayek's conclusion was of little surprise considering his strict views on serious argumentation: he resolved never to initiate another direct confrontation with this 'erratic' person, as he came to characterize Keynes. This example of personal animosity epitomizes the fundamental disagreements between Austrian economics and post-Keynesian economics.

The Sraffa–Hayek duel

One finds several poignant examples of such disputes which lay bare the partial interests, inherent miscommunication and also the often more inimical than critical attitudes. As an example, one can place the 1931–2 'Sraffa–Hayek duel' in line with the better-known Hayek–Keynes macro dispute (Lawlor and Horn 1992). This duel links up with Hayek's *Prices and Production* (1931b), which was based on his 1930 Tooke Lectures at the London School of Economics. *Prices and Production*, and related writings, offer a combination of Wicksell's views about relative prices and interest rates and Böhm-Bawerk's theory of capital. They suggest that changes in monetary policy influence relative prices and production. Keynes came to qualify *Prices and Production* as a 'frightful muddle' and, probably following up an invitation by Keynes to review the book, Sraffa promptly delivered a trenchant 12-page commentary. It must be noted that Sraffa was already widely known for his incisive analysis and his rare appearances in print. Moreover, by then he was already at work on Ricardo, had expertise in price theory and an appropriate background in monetary theory.

Sraffa's critique called into question Hayek's neglect of money as a store of value and a standard for stability 'in terms of which debts and all kind of other obligations, habits, opinions, conventions, in short all kinds of relations between men, are more or less rigidly fixed' (Sraffa 1932: 43). Hayek (1931b) took money as something neutral in itself, and thus considered only its function as a medium of exchange. In his reply to Sraffa, Hayek (1932) admitted that he had assumed an equilibrium barter economy, that is a flexprice Walrasian system (Desai 1982). In this respect it is significant that, to Hayek, 'equilibrium' meant a market-clearing equilibrium, whereas for Sraffa 'equilibrium' meant a long-run cost-of-production equilibrium (Lachmann 1986: 228–9).

Another important point of criticism concerned Hayek's emphasis on quantitative changes in the money supply as the sole cause of the economic depressions during the interwar period (Sraffa 1932: 44). Hayek considered money perfectly neutral only if its supply was kept constant. Sraffa argued that Hayek's analysis emasculated the role of money, begging the question of the other factor that really explains the problem of the interwar economies.

The prevalent feeling among fellow economists was one of bewilderment, which is conspicuous in Frank Knight's remark (found twice in his letters) that he could not make head or tail of the duel (the Sraffa–Hayek duel may very well have inspired Knight's own attack on the very foundation of Hayek's business cycle theory, his theory of capital (Lawlor and Horn 1992: 318, n1)). Even now one may find no less than five distinct views on the clash of irreconcilable convictions in the Sraffa–Hayek duel. Some maintain that Hayek's *Prices and Production* had a profound impact on contemporary economists. It held a promise of originality and significance in its explanation of the business cycle as a monetary disequilibrium phenomenon. Other economists claim almost the opposite. They interpret Sraffa's review plus rejoinder (his sole publications in 25 years) as the opening shots in the neo-Ricardian counter revolution (Lachmann 1986: 226–7, 238) and also of the Keynesian revolution. Lachmann, the determined Austrian who joined Hayek at the LSE in the 1930s, concluded that it was the Sraffa–Hayek duel that divided the Austrian ranks. It was this controversy that marked the start of the decline of Hayek's renown as a theoretical economist in the 1930s (*ibid.*: 240).

Other exchanges

In 1931 Keynes and Hayek were the main economists competing for the allegiance of their fellow economists. Many of them – and especially those related to the LSE – were soon fascinated by Austrian economics, but the severe depression of the 1930s and the heated debates undermined most of their convictions. At the LSE, the open-minded younger assistants – Lerner, Kaldor, Hicks – and the research students – Shackle and Scitovsky – were soon swept away on the Keynesian tide. And yet the Keynesian onslaught could hardly have *converted* them from *Hayekism*, 'for Keynes was discussing deflation and Hayek was describing inflation' (Shackle 1966: 55). Eventually even Robbins was to admit that his own policy recommendations during the 1930s had been as unsuitable 'as denying blankets and stimulants to a drunk who has fallen into an icy pond, on the grounds that his original trouble was overheating' (Robbins 1971: 154). Hayek's views were considered absurd and his idea of an excessive accumulation of capital equipment due to *easy credit* was at odds with reality. At the end of these years of high theory Austrian economics was discredited, as these debates laid bare new theoretical gaps and enlarged conceded gaps instead of reducing them (Kaldor 1942: 359).

One of the unmistakable inferences to be drawn from the exchanges of thought between Austrian economists and the early post-Keynesians is that the proponents of these two styles of thought were talking at cross purposes. Recall the debate on the Ricardo effect. O'Driscoll (1977) argues that this debate had all the ingredients of a case of grave miscommunication (see also Moss and Vaughn 1986; Zijp 1993). Kaldor based his analysis upon comparative–static equilibrium positions, whereas Hayek was analysing capital investment decisions in a disequilibrium situation. Furthermore, Kaldor discussed some 'representative' firm, while Hayek distinguished between the individual firm and the economy as a whole. The distinction between the two is important, as a key feature of Hayek's view is the potential for coordination failures on a grand scale. However, the British economists appeared unwilling to lend their ears to what Hayek had to say, if only because they considered Böhm-Bawerk's analytical framework, with which Hayek underpinned his business cycle theory, to be eccentric (Hicks 1967: 204–5). Hayek had a talent for being misunderstood.

Another inference is related to the priority given to economic theory or to the pressing problems of the economy. Austrian economists presented 'puzzles' (as Hayek once labelled it) at a time when most economists were less interested in academic problems than in mass unemployment. The Austrians were primarily interested in the puzzle of how a market economy could operate as one enormously complex organism and also preserve human freedom at the same time. Individual human freedom was too important to them to see it sacrificed for the sake of what Hayek deemed to be, at most, insignificant material improvements. Hayek wanted social scientists to wait until they knew what the final consequences of their recommendations would be. With the rise of generations of policy-oriented economists, this attitude of most Austrian economists was clearly atypical, with their active participation in advice committees limited to Robbins's involvement in the Macmillan committee. It was here that the Robbins–Keynes debate unfolded: the sometimes scholastic debate on oversaving and monetary mismanagement. In contrast to the Austrians, the post-Keynesians were both theoretically and politically involved. Their writings carried policy-related undertones, with the intention to raise the welfare for the masses. The wartime evacuation of the LSE to Peterhouse in Cambridge symbolized the dismantling of this Austrian stronghold and brought Hayek and Lachmann into intellectual isolation.

From World War II onwards, there are few serious exchanges of thought worth mentioning. The single disagreement worth mentioning in the context of this chapter is the Hayek–Hicks debate on capital theory. In contrast to the interwar period, areas of economic thought overlapping both Austrian and post-Keynesian economics now developed. Under the influence of writings by Lachmann, Hayek and Shackle we witness a strong infusion of subjectivism in both post-Keynesian and Austrian economics. As a result there has emerged an intermediate field of research, concerning interdependent decision-making processes and the role of institutions in the economy. It also links up with themes related to time, uncertainty, entrepreneurship, instability, pricing theories, monetary theories, theory of the firm, game theory and methodology. In consequence we will shift our focus from tractable, isolated exchanges of thought to the dominant theoretical stances on some of the themes just mentioned.

TIME, DECISION MAKING AND ENTREPRENEURSHIP

As lists of their characteristics indicate, post-Keynesian and Austrian economics concur in their concern with historical time, information problems and institutions. Post-Keynesian economics has been characterized by the following elements:

- the economy is a process in historical time
- in such a world of uncertainty, expectations have an unavoidable and significant effect on economic outcomes
- economic and political institutions play an important role in determining economic outcomes (Davidson 1980: 158–64).

The characteristics of Austrian economics may be summarized by the following basic propositions:

- individuals perceive a decision-making environment
- these perceptions take place in a world of uncertainty
- individual perceptions are not always correct
- there is a tendency towards the coordination of individual activities (Rizzo 1982: 53–73).

Historical, dynamic or endogenous time, which Bergson called *la durée* (duration), is not to be seen as some homogenous quantity or as isolated points, but as a flow of events, of novel experiences (O'Driscoll and Rizzo 1986: 255; Hamouda 1990). The perspective of the individual changes with his or her experiences or, put more aptly, with novelty. The twofold aspects of historical time are (1) its irreversibility and (2) the generation of unpredictable changes. As a corollary of the second effect we may state that information is inherently incomplete. We need institutions to preclude incessant stalemates and to enable conscious action in a world of uncertainty. Uncertainty means that the past is unchangeable, while the future is inherently unknown. It implies both the endogeneity of the source of uncertainty and the perceived unlistability of all the potential outcomes of a course of action. O'Driscoll and Rizzo, who build on the ideas of older generations of the Austrian tradition, stress the importance of genuine uncertainty, which entails an open-ended set of possible outcomes (O'Driscoll and Rizzo 1985: 71). It is telling that genuine uncertainty is also brought to prominence by Davidson, the eminent post-Keynesian: 'Uncertainty involves ignorance about forthcoming prospects' (Davidson 1994: 93). Even within the limits of the possible, the number of possibilities is unlimited.

The future is not something to be filled in, but one of many possible futures yet to be created. A fundamental presupposition of the Austrians is that freewill gives humanity the ability to act or not to act; human behaviour is purposeful (Mises 1962: 4–6; Rizzo 1982: 57). Evidently, the freedom to choose only makes sense when the decision-making processes leave room for deliberation and command the making of choices. Therefore, given autonomous and/or creative decision making, the future state of the world is not wholly determined by the present state of the world. The environment is both physically and situationally open. Moreover, even when the decision maker's aims, interests and objectives are known, the socio-economic environment still does not uniquely determine any particular course of action (Latsis 1976: 21). 'Behaviour does not qualify as "action" unless the agent in question has the choice of actually not doing X, although it follows from his explanation schema that he should do X' (*ibid.*: 6). Both the Austrian and the post-Keynesian style of reasoning recognize the crucial importance of these multi-exit decision situations.

Memory of the past and anticipation of the future are the structural components of historical time. They connect successive periods through their non-deterministic, continuous influence on individual perceptions. The perception of time is not causally inert, but changes as one's memory evolves. On the one hand, Austrian economics most strongly denounces the use of any expectation-generating model, and on the other it denounces the use of social conventions to predict expectations. Expectations may diverge from individual to individual. Because of the prevalence of uncertainty, we find among Austrian economists and the Anglo-Saxon style post-Keynesians an emphasis on (a) the formation of expectations and (b) the coordination of individual plans. Post-Keynesians stress the social formation of expectations (the macrofoundation of microeconomics), while the Austrians underscore the importance of the coordination of the individual plans. This is exemplified by Hayek, who hardly examined the question of how expectations are formed. He concentrated on the second question; on how the market mechanism effectively disseminates local information (Hayek 1948: 45).

We find the theme of the acquisition and dissemination of knowledge in many writings of Austrian authors, notably those of Hayek, Lachmann and Kirzner (Boehm 1982: 47). Learning from experience results in changes of memory and knowledge, and thus of anticipations and expectations. 'As soon as we permit time to elapse we must permit knowledge to change'

(Lachmann 1959: 73). However, the coordination of economic activities, individually decided upon, is far from self-evident, given both the dispersion of knowledge and its volatile content. One wonders how coordination might prevail when errors exist which are related to past decisions and uncertainty as to future developments. Each individual has to interpret information and execute judgement with regard to his expectations. As a consequence there is no use for such terms as 'complete knowledge' or 'perfect foresight'.

A number of Austrian economists rely on the panacea of the unhampered market mechanism to yield the solution to the coordination problem. Market prices are presumed to be means of communicating scattered information and improving the coordination of plans. 'Modern Austrians have converged on the notion of *coordination* as the key to normative discussion. As we shall see, this notion fits naturally into the Austrian understanding of the market process' (Kirzner 1988: 11). Likewise, Hayek simply assumed that agents somehow learn from their past mistakes. He does not distinguish between information and knowledge, but takes inductive learning for granted (Boland 1986: 37). Concurrently, other Austrian and post-Keynesian subjectivists doubt whether markets always coordinate. For example, Lachmann stressed the possible relevancy of discoordination tendencies. This led the subjectivists to evolutionary explanations to clarify market processes.

INTERDEPENDENCY AND INSTABILITY

With regard to the (in)stability of the economic system it will be argued that Austrian economics may profit from cooperation with the post-Keynesians. Austrian economists are divided on the determinacy of the market process towards equilibrium; post-Keynesians take into account the possibility of an indeterminate process. They put forward good reasons for investigating the instability, be it temporary and abrupt, of an economic system. Note that in developing our argument we will not enter here in the wider-ranging terminological disputes on fuzziness, determinacy, stability and chaos. It may be informative, however, to elaborate on the added value of mathematical modelling when discussing the possible instability of the economic system. It is argued that there is no need for disregarding its instrumental usefulness.

Different groups within the Austrian and post-Keynesian styles of thought have taken different positions with regard to the opportune data set. 'We may describe the evolution of subjectivism from Menger through Mises to Shackle as an evolution from a subjectivism of given wants through one of given ends to that of active minds' (Lachmann 1982: 39). But for Mises, Kirzner and related Austrians, creativity was and is excluded from subjectivism. 'Market entrepreneurship reveals to the market what the market did not realize was available, or, indeed needed at all' (Kirzner 1979:

181). According to them, subjectivism brings about a 'spontaneous order', as the alert entrepreneur exploits a set of as yet unforeseen opportunities. Kirzner thus advocates the coordinating tendencies of the market (Clark 1987: 270). The use of the analytical device of entrepreneurial alertness enables him to see how human creativity discovers opportunities that are *waiting* to be discovered.

> Since each of the current decisions (which together generate the future course of events) is motivated and guided by entrepreneurial alertness, we can confidently assert that such alertness *is* able successfully to tend to link current decision of the 'underlying realities'.
>
> (Kirzner 1995: 21)

Note that Kirzner needs diverse qualifiers, thereby blurring the distinction between epistemology and ontology. It is a far cry from providing what Kirzner considers to be the task of economists: 'to explain the observed tendencies to coordination' (*ibid.*: 20). A clear critique of this 'coordinative alertness' has been given by Shackle: 'Were Dante, Michelangelo, Shakespeare, Newton, and Beethoven merely alert?' (Shackle 1983: 8). Paradoxically, this example both weakens and strengthens Kirzner's position. On the one hand, it is indeed convincingly shown that originality and real innovation can hardly be introduced with his concepts. On the other hand, the uniqueness of the creativity of these persons is a far cry from most entrepreneurial actions.

What is the post-Keynesian position on coordination and instability? First, within post-Keynesian economics it is generally presumed true that the economy is not automatically coordinated (Brown 1981: 448). Second, the microeconomic basis does not require the assumption of perfect information or foresight on the part of individual decision-making units (Dow 1982: 435). Expectations of prospective gains from investment, related to Keynes's Marginal Efficiency of Capital (MEC), depend on one's hopes and fears about the future. The MEC must be seen as dependent on these volatile expectations. Its variability is the cause of changing investments. Expectations can change overnight and may therefore cause violent fluctuations in the amount of investment – the factor 'most prone to sudden and wide fluctuations' (Keynes 1937: 121) – which in turn alters the course of the economic system.

In general, post-Keynesian economists reject the Austrian belief that the free market process is inherently stable. They stress indeterminacy, imagination and novelty instead of ignorance, alertness, search and signalling. An economic system may contain forces which endogenously create instability and fluctuations in the level of economic activity (Brown 1981: 458). Put even more strongly, one may also hold that 'In an uncertain world no equilibrium position can be known with certainty' (Lachmann 1956: 240). We conclude that economic judgements may pertain to both coordinating and discoordinating tendencies, the relative weights of which are situation-dependent and mediated institutionally.

The following two distinct insights about the economic world may be useful in typifying the contrasting positions: (a) 'human action is purposeful', and (b) 'there is an indeterminacy and unpredictability inherent in human preference, human expectations, and human knowledge' (Kirzner 1976: 42). The first tenet of Austrian methodology is stated to be sufficient to make the world intelligible in terms of human action. Economics must involve a theory of market activity as a learning process characterized by ignorance and alertness, where entrepreneurs attempt to correct past errors and coordinate future behaviour. Kirzner and his disciples consider entrepreneurship to be more of a stabilizing than a disruptive element in the economy (O'Driscoll and Rizzo 1986). But if the second tenet holds, 'we shall no longer be able to say in which particular direction knowledge changes, and we can no longer postulate a determinate process toward equilibrium' (Kirzner 1976: 49). It is true that the groups of Austrians and post-Keynesians related to Lachmann and Davidson respectively consider creativity as too important to be disregarded, even though it might result in serious economic discontinuities. *Movements along curves* are no longer neutral in a given situation. 'The growth of knowledge is the endogenous force that endlessly propels the system' (O'Driscoll and Rizzo 1985: 62). As a consequence, there should be scope for surprise and for creative evolution. The main characteristic of such so-called *process economics* is the absence of both a stable endpoint and a unique path to be followed (*ibid.*: 5).

Should we infer from that characteristic of process economics that there is no (instrumental) usefulness in mathematical modelling? On the contrary. To remain informative, a more complex analysis requires the use of effective means that add a minimum of *noise* themselves. So, those economists who normally abstain from mathematical modelling may find added value in the instrumental use of it for specific purposes. With the exception of Littlechild and Owen (1980), Austrian economics has hardly tried to model its insights. Moreover, it is part of the style of Austrian economics to deprecate mathematical modelling.

Post-Keynesians are more eclectic in using mathematics for the sake of enhancing their understanding of theoretical concepts and economic practices (we may refer to Kaldor, Hicks, Goodwin, Chakravarti, Minsky, Young and many others). In this respect, Kaldor may be put forward as an example. His mathematics fits neatly with the essence of his view of the economy as a system without equilibrium (Marcuzzo 1995: 454). His starting point is a microeconomic foundation that reflects the market structure of the economy concerned, usually an oligopoly-cum-price leadership. Furthermore, this system contains the elements of increasing returns and technical progress. It is technical change and not savings that drives economic growth. Institutions are indispensable for underpinning the whole system. Institutions, especially the state, can both *curb* and *cause* instability through their influence on, say, effective demand. It is usually assumed that the money supply is endogenously determined.

Kaldor, Myrdal and others have also modelled circular, cumulative causation. This substantiated their view of economic development as characterized by polarizations rather than by convergence. Elaborations of such models may also accommodate deadlock situations, path dependency, stalemate problems and strange attractors. Further research may be done on how payment structures influence behaviour and the stability of the system. Norms to curb a cumulative process of destabilization are also taken into account. A useful instrument may be the technique related to theorizing about dissipative structures, which 'emerge at some distance from equilibrium' (Fehl 1986: 77, n18). These theoretical structures reflect the concerted activities of the Schumpeterian and the Kirznerian entrepreneurs. One may conclude that it is necessary and fruitful to discuss the possible instability of economic systems, for which purpose mathematical modelling may carry some instrumental usefulness.

MONETARY THEORIES

Austrian and post-Keynesian economics both offer an essentialist view of money within a historical time continuum. It is worth taking seriously the advice to synthesize the two approaches combining the 'Austrian emphasis upon the money pricing-process and the post-Keynesian highlighting of the money-contract payment structure' (Wynarczyk 1992: 20; see also Wynarczyk 1990).

For Austrians money is essentially a veil, or at most a 'kind of loose joint in the self-equilibrating apparatus of the price mechanism, which is bound to impede its working' (Hayek 1941: 408). This looseness allows for a certain amount of intertemporal discoordination to go unobserved for a period of time (Garrison 1984: 207). Sraffa, in his review of Hayek (1931b), had already criticized this emasculation of money (see 'The Sraffa–Hayek duel' above). Hayek disregarded money as a store of value and therefore as a standard for stability. Moreover, his account of intertemporal relations was confined to monetary disturbances under perfect foresight and correct expectations (Hicks 1979: 359), which implies that the economy would be in equilibrium and that money is held to be neutral. Under a fractional-reserve system, an initial credit expansion due to extra central bank lending may bring about a boom in capital goods industries via a money-multiplicative process. However, as the credit creation is slowed down, the boom will be followed by a bust in which expectational errors are corrected and factually unprofitable investments will be eliminated. It will finally result in a stable situation, awaiting a new cycle in credit availability.

Austrians have come to stress the need for some neutral role of money, because money cannot lift the economy to a higher growth path. As Leland Yeager illustrates with reference to the gold standard, money should enhance stability in the economy (Chapter 2 in this volume). Nonetheless, Austrian economics does not infer the need for an institution such as the central bank for safeguarding the neutral role of money as much as possible.

Post-Keynesians hold it as evident that money is and cannot be neutral. They put forward the following four arguments to substantiate their claim:

1 Investment decisions and profits are considered in money terms, and not in terms of the output to be produced or the employment to be created. In consequence, even some stable constellation of financial market forces may fail to work well on the derived real variables such as innovativeness, employment and production capacity (Kregel 1983: 40–1).
2 In equilibrium, the subjectively held liquidity premium of money must be equal to the marginal efficiency of capital.
3 The existence of explicit money contracts provides a means of creating some assurance as to the possible future outcomes. It creates a kind of stability or 'stickiness' in a market economy.
4 Money itself opens up the possibility of a flexible response, whether this involves taking advantage of yet unforeseeable future opportunities, or protecting oneself against misfortune (Davidson 1988: 333–5). Although it offers a store of wealth and acts as a substitute for foreknowledge, money does not deliver any foreknowledge. It predicts no future and neither could its price, the interest rate, provide a pointer to the correct actions (Shackle 1972).

Keynes regarded money as a link between the present and the future. According to him money facilitates the way in which changing views about the future influence the present situation (Keynes 1936: 293). 'One must introduce uncertainty, before one can introduce money' (Hicks 1982b: 7). Shifts from favourable to unfavourable views about the future occur in response to specific economic events and sentiments. Such shifts create uneasiness as to possible future developments and cast doubts about the future creditworthiness of borrowers (Minsky 1986: 118). They increase the feeling of uncertainty and exacerbate the difficulties inherent in decision making. A depressed general state of expectations or an excessive state of liquidity preference may lead towards hoarding and an underemployment equilibrium. Businessmen and bankers live in the same expectational climate and therefore 'the governor mechanism by way of financing terms is often dominated by positive, disequilibrating feedbacks' (*ibid.*: 228). It may therefore be concluded that monetary and real forces are intimately connected (Davidson 1980: 164).

Post-Keynesian economics stresses the public nature of money. It carries forward the idea of money, not as some net worth – as exemplified in the

IS/LM model – but as credit money, the creation of a banking system. Money is created as by-product of commercial bank lending. 'Money is credit-driven and demand-determined' (Arestis 1992: 201). It is also considered important that contracts are normally written in monetary terms. Therefore, confidence in money as a means of exchange and unit of calculation must be established and consolidated. To stabilize the economic system there is a need for a monetary controlling authority which has the duty to promote trust in currency by means of its monetary policy. That the monetary authority is a public organization is a precondition for the 'uncomplicated enforcement' of financial and contractual activities (Davidson 1977: 281). The relevance of the post-Keynesian approach is strengthened by the growing dissociation between financial and physical flows.

Evidently, the arena of international monetary relations and speculation may be analysed more fruitfully from the post-Keynesian perspective than from the Austrian loose-joint standpoint. The post-Keynesian stress on trust is critical for such fragile networks where arbitration, speculation and propagation perform balancing acts with regard to the pricing or valuation of money. However, it is widely agreed that there are no simple and final answers to the problems of our capitalist system. 'Instability, put to rest by one set of reforms will, after a time, emerge in a new guise' (Minsky 1986: 333).

PRICING PROCESSES AND PRICING THEORIES

Austrian economists emphasize the role played by money in the pricing process. For example, Hayek's price theory 'may be interpreted as an extension of his business cycle theory' (O'Driscoll 1977: 9). Mises also criticized the economists' disregard for the non-neutrality of the denominator: 'they do not comprehend that money prices are the only vehicle of economic calculation' (Mises 1949: 202). Austrians see the market structure as some cheap communications network which functions as a system of signals (Hayek 1937: 45; 1945: 87). There is no better possible framework for guiding competitors than the price system. Prices are the result of judgements. Such judgements involve the conditions of output markets, the conditions of resource markets, the profit motive and one's experience in and gut feelings for assessing market conditions (High 1994: 154). Without pretending that it attains perfect adjustment, it is claimed that only by means of the price mechanism can a multitude of individuals use dispersed specific information. What is commonly called the 'normal level' of prices and interest rates is 'determined by what are believed to be permanently operative forces' (Lachmann 1977: 78). Although prices may reflect discoordination, they still *signal* opportunities for profitable adjustments in plans (Ikeda 1994: 27). Contrary to standard economic argumentation (such as Grossman and Stiglitz 1976), individuals do not glean all the relevant information from market prices, but may economize on their informational requirements because prices reduce the amount of the required detail.

Post-Keynesian economics is widely respected for advancing research, not so much on the pricing process, but on the principles of pricing theories, most notably on cost-plus pricing. This is where the predominance of formal and informal institutions, which direct behaviour and stabilize an economy, comes in. Post-Keynesians hold that rivalry between firms centres on the expected rate of return and thus on investments or discretionary expenditures, rather than on the price variables. So, the nominal wage is held to be determined largely exogenously to any optimization processTogether with the widespread use of cost-plus pricing practices it offers an instrumental variable for influencing the aggregate price level (Kregel 1980: 46–7).

Both theoretical implications and empirical evidence lend support to the conclusion that the concept of cost-oriented pricing depicts business practices better than profit maximization (Eichner and Kregel 1975; Okun 1981). Based on the assumption that marginal costs are constant up to the standard operating ratio or the normal degree of capacity utilization, cost-plus pricing constitutes a convenient rule of thumb in our complex world of uncertainty (Lavoie 1996). One is reminded of the fact that there are at least five roles to be attributed to prices. Next to their well-known allocative role, prices also perform the conductive, positional, strategic and financial roles. As a consequence, 'there can be various messages contained in a price-signal and different interpretations can be placed on the meaning of such signals' (Sawyer 1995: 54). Pricing theories are also important to post-Keynesians, because microeconomic pricing behaviour links up with industrial organization at the meso level and directs the categorical macroeconomic income distribution.

It is more than significant to find that post-Keynesian pricing theories are fundamentally alike, given that there is a long history of and an ongoing debate comprising a variety of contributors with widely differing opinions. Common elements in the post-Keynesian, including Sraffian (Lavoie 1992a: 146–7), pricing theories are the limited impact of (changes in) demand prices, that output instead of prices adjust to satisfy demand and that the approaches relate to conditions of imperfect competition.

The major originators of post-Keynesian pricing theories are Means, Hall and Hitch, Kalecki, and Sweezy. The essence of their contributions is that they establish empirical distinctions in pricing behaviour. Means, for instance, introduced the distinction between market-dominated and administration-dominated prices. Another important contribution was made by Kalecki who stressed the importance of the contrast between cost-determined and demand-determined prices. It was this contrast which later became the basis of Hicks's well-known distinction between flex-price markets and fix-price markets (Hicks 1965).

The current literature has established the empirical validity of at least three variants of the post-Keynesian cost-plus pricing theories, namely mark-up pricing, full-cost or normal-cost pricing and target-run pricing (Lee 1994, 1996; Downward and Reynolds 1996). None of these is related directly to marginal cost pricing and to the concept of profit maximization (Sawyer 1992: 76), nor are they designed to clear the market. They exemplify the post-Keynesian conviction that the choice of the proper trade-off between descriptive adequacy and theoretical rigour should be problem driven. It is along this line of thought that Austrians may benefit from post-Keynesian research on pricing theories.

INSTITUTIONS

It is intrinsic to the Austrian and post-Keynesian styles of thought to stress the importance of organizations and institutions for economic activities. It is standard practice in neoclassical economics to discuss human behaviour at the level of the isolated individual. In doing so, there is considerable danger of ignoring the role of formal and informal institutions. However, the economic system deals with ignorance and uncertainty via the actors agreeing on norms, regulations, contracts and standardized prices. Austrians and post-Keynesians agree that rules and institutions (laws, property rights, systems of markets) influence (but do not fully determine) individual decision making. Rules and institutions constitute patterns that serve as guidelines for individual and group decisions. Evidently, opinions are divided when the element of third-party interventions in economic practices enters into the discussion. Post-Keynesians are more inclined to third-party intervention, whereas Austrians are predisposed to a laissez-faire approach.

Austrians have been particularly prone to underscore the importance of institutions. They acknowledge the static and transformational importance of, for example, vertically integrated companies, market segmentation, marketing, market concentration, economic power, anti-trust policy, taxation laws and technological support policies. Austrians claim primarily that institutions must be arranged in such a way that the discovery and exploitation of socially advantageous opportunities turn into personal advantages. The imperfection of individual knowledge, in practice, makes the decentralization of decision making unavoidable, and a continuous communication and acquisition of knowledge a necessity. Competition is a process that supplies us with knowledge of the alternative commodities or services and their best supplies. In accordance with their position in the socialist calculation debate, Austrians think it impossible that formally organized non-market institutions can arrange economic activities in such a way that they are to be preferred to spontaneous arrangements related to decentralized decision making (see Wubben 1995: 124, 131).

Aspects of these Austrian views may be welcomed by post-Keynesians, including the claim that human action is important for economic developments. They should agree on the position that governmental regulations must promote a competitive industry. Furthermore, post-Keynesians may admit that laissez-faire capitalism works, but only under the qualifying remark that it need not give rise to socially desired or even tolerable results with regard to employment and wages. A crucial point of divergence, however, concerns the importance of levelling the agents' initial starting positions. Austrians assume it is either undesirable and/or impossible to equalize the initial point of departure for all economic agents. Strongly put, we might state that Austrian economists in general rank personal freedom from unwanted interference higher than the equality of opportunities. Post-Keynesians rank equality of opportunities above individual freedom from external interference.

Post-Keynesian economics considers it necessary that a sufficiently strong government ensures minimum standards of living and guards against the deterioration of working conditions. Government intervention in markets may be needed to curb potentially destabilizing market forces, to help in cases of market failure, to curtail fluctuations in aggregate profits and to manage externalities. More principally, governmental and monetary policies cannot be considered neutral and ineffective in economic affairs, if only because implemented policies affect economic institutions: policies change the patterns of individual behaviour. The objectives and behaviour of individuals can be moulded or reinforced by institutions. The acceptance of bounded rationality, limited information and societal constraints obfuscates the distinction between micro- and macroeconomics.

For post-Keynesians, institutions and policy 'can contain the thrust of instability' (Minsky 1986: 10). Aggregate intervention in the economy is often to be preferred to detailed interventions; programmes for full employment, price stability and greater equity are better than the emphasis on investment and economic growth, if only because the latter results in unstable performance (*ibid.*: 292–3). Consider the case of the banking system. The exposure of banks to uncertainty has traditionally been constrained by customer and collegiate surveillance. Customer surveillance diminished as the view gained adherents that protection by the regulatory authorities would make it redundant. Collegiate surveillance takes place in terms of differential interbank lending rates. Reserve deficiencies are handled via the lender of the last resort, the central bank. This function of central banks will involve them in guiding the evolution of financial practices along non-disruptive routes. Post-Keynesians argue that, as a result, major central bank interventions must be possible to prevent or, if necessary, contain and offset financial disruption (Minsky 1982: 185–90; Davidson 1990: 72). When discussing the more common and stable systems of economic practices, post-Keynesians argue that economists should not advance isolated or incremental changes (that is, discrete policies), but promote theoretically based and practically feasible systems of social–economic improvements. It is with regard to these more stable periods, that they may learn from Austrian economics.

METHODOLOGY

It is possible to reflect on a number of other themes, such as the theory of the firm and economic methodology. With regard to the theory of the firm we recommend economists from the post-Keynesian and Austrian styles of economic thought to integrate and build upon G.B. Richardson's writings on industrial organization, Shackle's subjectivist view of economics and Neil Kay's pioneering work on industrial organization (for instance, as done by Langlois, Earl and Loasby).

With regard to methodological questions we would advise Austrian and post-Keynesian economists to further the more philosophically sophisticated and realistic parts of economics (Boettke 1994: 611). Because of their realist propensities, Austrian and post-Keynesian economics may be in an advantageous position here. Both practically and principally it is fruitless to waste further economic resources on building an all-encompassing theory. Economists, widely defined, should face the facts of our dismal science and advance constructions based on realistic assumptions derived from observation of the world (stylized facts). For an example, think back to the section on pricing models. Both induction and deduction is needed, for either is insufficient by itself. Economists should always ask themselves *before* building, testing and applying specific theories, whether they are appropriate to the problem at hand. One should use different theories for different purposes, what Dow (1985) calls a 'horses for courses' approach.

With regard to methodology, Austrian economics has harboured a variety of opinions throughout its history. Since the revival of interest in Austrian economics in the 1970s, there has evidently evolved a heterogeneity of opinions among Austrians. Themes open for dispute are the usefulness of equilibrium models, the proper extension of Menger's subjectivism and the nature of human choice (Boettke 1994: 3). Likewise, post-Keynesian economics lacks a single organizing principle and offers a pluralistic approach to the subject.

Many Austrian and post-Keynesian economists share the methodological principle of radical subjectivism. However, in both Austrian and post-Keynesian styles of thought there are also adherents of gravity centre models. Those more inclined to subjectivism emphasize non-ergodic constructs and systems indeterminacy. Put in other terms, they encompass adherents of historical time models and of cumulative causation. Both Austrian and post-Keynesian economics stress the subjective elements in economic behaviour, but to Austrians these subjective elements seem to play an essentially equilibrating role, while for most post-Keynesians they play an essentially disequilibrating role. Such differences are better understood as being more relative than absolute. The stress on the role of (sensible) expectations is present in particular styles within both traditions of economic thought. One can mention Lachmann, O'Driscoll and Rizzo on the one hand and the Anglo-Saxon post-Keynesians like Shackle, Minsky and Davidson on the other.

At the same time, other economists in both traditions analyse the working of the economy in terms of gravity-centre models (Carvalho 1984). Examples are Hayek and Kirzner (for the Austrians), and Sraffians/neo-Ricardians such as Eatwell, Milgate and Pasinetti (for the post-Keynesians). Hayek held high trust in the ability of unhampered market processes to eventually overcome problems of dispersed and incomplete knowledge. As Loasby asserts, in Austrian economics 'certainty is thus preserved at the system level' (Loasby 1989: 12). Neither in *Prices and Production* (1931b), nor in *Profits, Interest and Investment* (1939), nor in his later work where expectations feature prominently, does Hayek discuss the possibility that the economy may destabilize or break down (Boehm 1992: 9).

In the case of the post-Keynesians, a gulf separates the Sraffian theorists from the others, like Shackle, who emphasize problems of uncertainty and argue that the economy cannot be apprehended in a static analysis (Hodgson 1989). This difference involves the portrayal of the economy at system-level requirements versus a focus on the *human predicament*. This distinction in post-Keynesian economics itself may also be presented as the difference between methodological collectivism and methodological individualism. One may analyse a set of ontological entities emphasizing either the collective or the individual point of view. Austrians generally employ the methodological individualist perspective. We propose to recast these alternative approaches towards long-term developments as perspectives on which one may build alternative scenarios: as images of possible futures, one of which is eventually to realize itself. A static approach may therefore be used to enhance our understanding of the evolving reality.

FINAL REMARKS

Contrasting opinions exist with regard to the future relations between Austrian and post-Keynesian economics. In a postscript to the Kluwer volume on tensions in, and directions for, Austrian economics, Lawrence White dismisses suggestions for a closer interaction of Austrian economics with post-Keynesian economics: 'Greater gains are to be expected from interacting with Neoclassical economists than with post-Keynesians and old-style Institutionalists' (White 1992: 265). In contrast to post-Keynesians, Austrians and neoclassicists are said to share at least the appreciation for the coordinative properties of the market.

In the same volume – but in meaningful contrast to White – Rizzo concludes that Austrian economics still belongs to the outskirts of the academic world and is facing its demise (Rizzo 1992: 246). A run for shelter under neoclassical economics is illusory. Any attraction to the neoclassicists 'is based merely on linguistic similarities' (*ibid.*: 247). Austrians have regard for (a) true surprise, (b) alert entrepreneurs and (c) an economic world in flux, all of which are in conflict with the views of the neoclassicists. The latter cling to stochastically foreseen outcomes, optimizing agents and a world of structurally stable equations respectively. According to Rizzo, Austrian economics is not a list of sacrosanct free market slogans but a way of looking at the world and of framing questions, including refutable propositions. He fully recognizes that the choices of individuals are bound by institutions, or 'methods of action arrived at by habituation and convention generally agreed upon' (*ibid.*: 250). As a consequence (and in the good company of Langlois) he welcomes post-Keynesians, new and old institutionalists, to join the debate on a sounder foundation for economic analysis.

Having gone through a period of intense *self-analysis* in the 1980s, post-Keynesians seem to surface as rather open-minded economists looking towards various sources for their inspiration to improve their often inefficient trial-and-error research. There are mixed feelings on their side towards crossing the border with Austrian economics, on the presumption that there actually is any discernible border.

In sum, Austrian and post-Keynesian economists might agree on the common grounds comprising the following principles:

- knowledge is dispersed, incomplete and sometimes wrong
- complex roundabout structures of production are often the most productive (Loasby 1992: 152).

Research acknowledging these principles will most probably be profitable at the meso or industry level, and much less so at macro or micro level. As discussed above, research encompasses such topics as the formation and transformation of formal and informal institutions, mechanisms on stability and dynamism in markets, networks and value chains and the theory of expectation formation.

To draw a parallel with the economic integration in the European Union, we note that over the past decades, animosities between the formerly independent territories have declined in importance with the rise of their interdependence, propelled by the need to combine against common economic enemies. Likewise, the styles of economic thought presented here have shown fewer animosities since there has grown an awareness that they may fruitfully combine strengths against common enemies in economics. The distinct characteristics of the various styles of thought have lost much of their sharpness. Austrians, post-Keynesians and related styles of economic thought may use their comparative advantages not for the sake of enhancing the trade in books, but for enhancing their cross-fertilization in specific fields of economic thought. The parallel interests presented above make one confident that they will end up not with disputes, but with discussions. It would therefore be ill advised to close the Austrian post-Keynesian borders.

REFERENCES

Arestis, P. (1992) *The Post-Keynesian Approach to Economics*, Aldershot: Edward Elgar.

Arestis, P. ånd Sawyer, M. (eds) (1992) *A Biographical Dictionary of Dissenting Economists*, Aldershot: Edward Elgar.

Arestis, P. and Skouras, T. (eds) (1985) *Post-Keynesian Economic Theory. A Challenge to Neoclassical Economics*, Brighton: Wheatsheaf Books.

Blaug, M. (1985) *Economic Theory in Retrospect*, 4th edn, Cambridge: Cambridge University Press.

Boehm, S. (1982) 'The ambiguous notion of subjectivism: comment on Lachmann', in I.M. Kirzner (ed.), 41–52.

——(1992) 'Austrian economics between the wars: some historiographical problems', in B.J. Caldwell and S. Boehm (eds), 1–30.

Boettke, P.J. (ed.) (1994) *Elgar Companion to Austrian Economics*, Aldershot: Edward Elgar.

Boland, L.A. (1986) 'Methodology and the individual decision maker', in I.M. Kirzner (ed.), 30–8.

Brown, E.K. (1981) 'The neoclassical and post-Keynesian research programs: the methodological issues', *Review of Social Economy*, 39 (2): 111–32. Reprinted in B. Caldwell (ed.) (1984), 438–59.

Butos, W.N. (1994) 'The Hayek–Keynes macro debate', in P.J. Boettke (ed.), 471–7.

Caldwell, B. (ed.) (1984) *Appraisal and Criticism in Economics. A Book of Readings*, London: Allen & Unwin.

Caldwell, B. and Boehm, S. (eds) (1992) *Austrian Economics: Tensions and New Directions*, Dordrecht: Kluwer Academic Publishers.

Carvalho, F. (1984) 'Alternative analyses of short and long run in post-Keynesian economics', *Journal of Post-Keynesian Economics*, 8 (2): 214–34.

Clark, C.M.A. (1987) 'Equilibrium, market process and historical time', *Journal of Post-Keynesian Economics*, 10 (2): 270–9.

Coats, A.W. (1982) 'Economics at LSE in the 1930s: a personal view', *Atlantic Economic Journal*, 10 (1): 18–30.

Davidson, P. (1977) 'Post-Keynesian monetary theory and inflation', in S. Weintraub (ed.) *Modern Economic Thought*, University of Pennsylvania Press, 275–94.

——(1980) 'Post-Keynesian economics: solving the crisis in economic theory', *The Public Interest*, 58: 151–73.

——(1988) 'A technical definition of uncertainty and the long-run non-neutrality of money', *Cambridge Journal of Economics*, 12: 329–37.

——(1990) 'Shackle and Keynes vs rational expectations theory and the role of time-liquidity and financial markets', in S.F. Frowen (ed.), 64–80.

——(1994) *Post-Keynesian Macroeconomic Theory*, Aldershot: Edward Elgar.

Desai, M. (1982) 'The task of monetary theory: The Hayek–Sraffa debate in a modern perspective', in M. Baranzini (ed.) *Advances in Economic Theory*, New York: St Martin's Press.

Dow, S.C. (1982) 'Substantive mountains and methodological molehills: a rejoinder', *Journal of Post-Keynesian Economics*, 5 (2): 304–8. Reprinted in B. Caldwell (ed.) (1984), 433–7.

——(1985) *Macroeconomic Thought. A Methodological Approach*, Oxford: Basil Blackwell.

Downward, P. and Reynolds, P. (1996) 'Alternative perspectives on post-Keynesian price theory', *Review of Political Economy*, 8 (1): 67–78.

Eichner, A.S. and Kregel, J.A. (1975) 'An essay on post-Keynesian theory: a new paradigm in economics', *Journal of Economic Literature*, 13 (4): 1293–1314.

Fehl, U. (1986) 'Spontaneous order and the subjectivity of expectations: A contribution to the Lachmann–O'Driscoll problem', in I.M. Kirzner (ed.), 72–86.

Frowen, S.F. (ed.) (1990) *Unknowledge and Choice in Economics*, London: Macmillan.

Garrison, R.W. (1984) 'Time and macroeconomics: The universals of macroeconomic theorizing', *Journal of Macroeconomics*, 6 (2): 197–213.

Grossman, S. and Stiglitz, J. (1976), 'Information and competitive price systems', *American Economic Review*, 66: 246–53.

Hamouda, O.F. (1990) 'Time, choice and dynamics in economics', in S.F. Frowen (ed.), 129–55.

Harcourt, G.C. (1986) *Controversies in Political Economy. Selected Essays of G.C. Harcourt*, editor O.F. Hamouda, London: Wheatsheaf Books.

Harcourt, G.C. and Hamouda, O. (1988) 'Post-Keynesianism: from criticism to coherence?', *Bulletin on Economic Research*, 40: 1–33. Reprinted in C. Sardoni (ed.) (1992) *On Political Economists and Modern Political Economy. Selected Essays of G.C. Harcourt*, London: Routledge, 209–32.

Hayek, F.A. (1931a) 'The paradox of saving', in *Profits, Interest and Investment*, London: Routledge & Kegan Paul (1939).

——(1931b) *Prices and Production*, London: Routledge (2nd edn, 1935).

——(1932) 'Money and capital. A reply to Mr. Sraffa', *Economic Journal*, 42: 237–49.

——(1937) 'Economics and knowledge', *Economica*, IV: 33–54. Reprinted in F.A. Hayek (1948), 33–56.

——(1939) *Profits, Interest and Investment*, London: Routledge.

——(1941) *The Pure Theory of Capital*, London: Routledge.

——(1945) 'The use of knowledge in society', *The American Economic Review*, XXXV (4): 519–30. Reprinted in F.A. Hayek (1948), 77–91.

——(1948) *Individualism and Economic Order*, Chicago, IL: University of Chicago Press.

Hicks, J.R. (1965) *Capital and Growth*, Oxford: Clarendon.

——(1967) 'The Hayek story', in J.R. Hicks *Critical Essays in Monetary Theory*, Oxford: Clarendon Press, 203–15.

——(1976) 'Time in economics', reprinted in J.R. Hicks (1982a), 282–300.

——(1979) 'The formation of an economist', reprinted in J.R. Hicks (1983), 355–64.

——(1982a) *Collected Essays on Economic Theory*, vol. II: *Money, Interest, and Wages*, Oxford: Basil Blackwell.

——(1982b) 'Introductory: LSE and the Robbins circle', in J.R. Hicks (1982a), 3–10.

——(1983) *Collected Essays on Economic Theory*, vol. III: *Classics and Moderns*, Oxford: Basil Blackwell.

High, J. (1994) 'The Austrian theory of price', in P.J. Boettke (ed.), 151–5.

Hodgson, G.M. (1989) 'Evolution and institutional change', unpublished ms, Newcastle upon Tyne Polytechnic.

Ikeda, S. (1994) 'Market process', in P.J. Boettke (ed.), 23–9.

Kaldor, N. (1942) 'Professor Hayek and the concertina effect', *Economica*, 14: 359–93.

Keynes, J.M. (1930) *Treatise on Money*, reprinted in J.M. Keynes *The Collected Writings of John Maynard Keynes*, vols V and VI, London: Macmillan, 1971.

——(1936) *The General Theory of Employment, Interest and Money*, reprinted in J.M. Keynes *The Collected Writings of John Maynard Keynes*, vol. VII, London: Macmillan, 1973.

——(1937) 'The general theory of employment', *The Quarterly Journal of Economics*, reprinted in J.M. Keynes *The Collected Writings of John Maynard Keynes*, vol. XIV: *The General Theory and After: Part II, Defence and Development*, London: Macmillan, 1973, 109–23.

Kirzner, I.M. (1976) 'On the method of Austrian economics', in E.G. Dolan (ed.) *The Foundations of Modern Austrian Economics*, Kansas City, KS: Sheed & Ward, 40–51.

——(1979) *Perception, Opportunity, and Profit. Studies in the Theory of Entrepreneurship*, Chicago, IL: University of Chicago Press.

——(ed.) (1982) *Method, Process, and Austrian Economics. Essays in Honor of Ludwig von Mises*, Lexington, MA: Lexington Books.

——(ed.) (1986) *Subjectivism, Intelligibility and Economic Understanding. Essays in Honor of L.M. Lachmann on his Eightieth Birthday*, London: Macmillan.

——(1988) 'The economic calculation debate: lessons for Austrians', *Review of Austrian Economics*, 2: 1–18.

——(1992) *The Meaning of the Market Process. Essays in the Development of Modern Austrian Economics*, London: Routledge.

——(1995) 'The subjectivism of Austrian economics', in G. Meijer (ed.) *New Perspectives on Austrian Economics*, London: Routledge, 11–22.

Kregel, J.A. (1980) 'Markets and institutions as features of a capitalist production system', *Journal of Post-Keynesian Economics*, 3 (1): 32–48.

——(1983) 'Post-Keynesian theory: an overview', *The Journal of Economic Education*, fall: 32–43.

——(1991) 'The organizing principle in post-Keynesian economics. A comment on Sawyer', in W.L.M. Adriaansen and J.T.J.M. van der Linden (eds) *Post-Keynesian Thought in Perspective*, Deventer: Wolters-Noordhoff, 79–81.

Lachmann, L.M. (1956) *Capital and its Structure*, Kansas City, KS: Sheed, Andrews & McMeel (2nd edn, 1978).

——(1959) 'Professor Shackle and the economic significance of time', *Metroeconomica*, 11: 64–73.

——(1977) *Capital, Expectations, and the Market Process. Essays on the Theory of the Market Economy*, Kansas City, KS: Sheed, Andrews & McMeel.

——(1982) 'Ludwig von Mises and the extension of subjectivism', in I.M. Kirzner (ed.), 31–40.

——(1986) 'Austrian economics under fire: the Hayek—Sraffa duel in retrospect', in W. Grassl and B. Smith (eds) *Austrian Economics. Historical and Philosophical Background*, London: Croom Helm, 225–42.

Latsis, S.J. (1976) 'A research program in economics', in S.J. Latsis (ed.) *Method and Appraisal in Economics*, Cambridge: Cambridge University Press.

Lavoie, M. (1992a) *Foundations of Post-Keynesian Economic Analysis*, Aldershot: Edward Elgar.

——(1992b) 'Towards a new research program for post-Keynesianism and new-Ricardianism', *Review of Political Economy*, 4 (1). 37–78.

——(1996) 'Mark-up pricing versus normal cost pricing in post-Keynesian price theory', *Review of Political Economy*, 8 (1): 57–66.

Lawlor, M.S. and Horn, B.L. (1992) 'Notes on the Sraffa–Hayek exchange', *Review of Political Economy*, 4 (3): 317–40.

Lee, F. (1994) 'From post-Keynesian to historical price theory', *Review of Political Economy*, 6: 303–36.

——(1996) 'Pricing, the pricing model and post-Keynesian price theory', *Review of Political Economy*, 8 (1): 87–99.

Littlechild, S.C. and Owen, G. (1980) 'An Austrian model of the entrepreneurial market process', *Journal of Economic Theory*, 23 (3): 361–79.

Loasby, B.J. (1989) *The Mind and Method of the Economist. A Critical Appraisal of Major Economists in the 20th Century*, Aldershot: Edward Elgar.

——(1992), 'Market co-ordination', in B. Caldwell and S. Boehm (eds), 137–56.

Marcuzzo, M.C. (1995) 'Nicholas Kaldor and the real world. Book review', *Review of Political Economy*, 7 (4): 450–4.

McCormick, B.J. (1992) *Hayek and the Keynesian Avalanche*, London: Harvester Wheatsheaf.

Menger, C. (1871) *Grundsätze der Volkswirtschaftslehre*, in F.A. Hayek (ed.) *Carl Menger: Gesammelte Werke*, vol. I, Tübingen: J.C.B. Mohr (1968).

Minsky, H.P. (1982) *Inflation, Recession and Economic Policy*, London: Wheatsheaf Books.

——(1986) *Stabilizing an Unstable Economy*, New Haven, CT: Yale University Press.

Mises, L. von (1949) *Human Action. A Treatise on Economics*, London: William Hodge & Company (3rd edn, 1966).

——(1962) *The Ultimate Foundation of Economic Science. An Essay on Method*, Kansas City, KS: Sheed & Ward (2nd edn, 1978).

Moss, L.S. and Vaughn, K.I. (1986) 'Hayek's Ricardo effect: a second look', *History of Political Economy*, 18: 545–65.

O'Driscoll, G.P. (1977) *Economics as a Coordination Problem*, Kansas City, KS: Sheed Andrews & McMeel.

O'Driscoll, G.P. and Rizzo, M.J. (1985) *The Economics of Time and Ignorance*, Oxford: Basil Blackwell.

——(1986) 'Subjectivism, uncertainty, and rules', in I.M. Kirzner (ed.), 252–67.

Okun, A.M. (1981) *Prices and Quantities. A Macroeconomic Analysis*, Oxford: Basil Blackwell.

Pasinetti, L.L. (1983) *Structural Change and Economic Growth. A Theoretical Essay on the Dynamics of the Wealth of Nations*, Cambridge: Cambridge University Press.

——(1991) 'At the roots of post-Keynesian thought. Keynes's break with tradition', in W.L.M. Adriaansen and J.T.J.M. van der Linden (eds) *Post-Keynesian Thought in Perspective*, Deventer: Wolters-Noordhof, 21–9.

Rizzo, M.J. (1982) 'Mises and Lakatos: a reformulation of Austrian methodology', in I.M. Kirzner (ed.), 53–73.

——(1992) 'Afterword: Austrian economics for the twenty-first century', in B. Caldwell and S. Boehm (eds), 245–55.

Robbins, L. (1971) *Autobiography of an Economist*, London: Macmillan.

Robinson, J. (1975) 'The unimportance of reswitching', *Quarterly Journal of Economics*, 89: 32–9.

——(1978) 'Keynes and Ricardo', *Journal of Post-Keynesian Economics*, 1 (1): 12–18.

Romer, P.M. (1986) 'Increasing returns and long-run growth', *Journal of Political Economy*, 94: 1002–37.

Sawyer, M.C. (1992) 'On the origins of post-Keynesian pricing theory and macroeconomics', in P. Arestis and V. Chick (eds) *Recent Developments in Post-Keynesian Economics*, Aldershot: Edward Elgar, 64–81.

——(1995) *Unemployment, Imperfect Competition and Macroeconomics. Essays in the Post-Keynesian Tradition*, Aldershot: Edward Elgar.

Schumpeter, J.A. (1954) *History of Economic Analysis*, London: Allen & Unwin, 1986.

Shackle, G.L.S. (1966) *The Nature of Economic Thought. Selected Papers 1955–1964*, Cambridge: Cambridge University Press.

——(1967) *The Years of High Theory. Invention and Tradition in Economic Thought 1926–1939*, Cambridge: Cambridge University Press.

——(1972) *Epistemics and Economics*, Cambridge: Cambridge University Press.

——(1983) 'Professor Kirzner on entrepreneurship', *Austrian Economics Newsletter*, 4 (1): 7–8.

Sraffa, P. (1932) 'Dr. Hayek on money and capital', *Economic Journal*, 42: 42–53.

Thomas, B. (1991) 'The London School of Economics and the Stockholm School in the 1930s', in L. Jonung (ed.) *The Stockholm School of Economics Revisited*, Cambridge: Cambridge University Press, 389–90.

White, L.H. (1992) 'Afterword. Appraising Austrian economics: contentions and misdirections', in B. Caldwell and S. Boehm (eds), 257–68.

Wubben, E.F.M. (1995) 'Austrian economics and uncertainty: On a non-deterministic but non-haphazard future', in G. Meÿer (ed.), *New Perspectives on Austrian Economics*, London: Routledge, 106–45.

Wynarczyk, P. (1990) 'Economic crisis and the crisis in economics', unpublished PhD, University of Kent at Canterbury.

——(1992) 'Comparing alleged incommensurables: Institutional and Austrian economics as rivals and possible complements?', *Review of Political Economy*, 4 (1): 18–36.

Zijp, R.W. van (1993) *Austrian and New Classical Business Cycle Theories*, Aldershot: Edward Elgar.

Zuidema, J.R. (1986) 'School of Stijl, een Vraagstuk van Indeling', in J.R. Zuidema (ed.) *Van Alle Markten Thuis*, Rotterdam: Universitaire Pers Rotterdam, 183–201.

10

HAYEK AND RATIONAL EXPECTATIONS[1]

William N. Butos

The relationship between Hayek and new classical economics (NCE) is among the more interesting controversies associated with the re-emergence of Austrian economics during the past 20 years and the nearly simultaneous rise to prominence of NCE. The claim that Hayek and NCE share important similarities with new classical theory was originally mounted by Lucas (1983) and has since become an accepted interpretation among some (but not all) researchers.[2]

Most of the literature addressing this link has used business cycle theory as the context to examine Hayekian and new classical theories of equilibrium. These inquiries examine whether Austrian business cycle theory, especially as presented by Hayek during the 1920s and 1930s, is a precursor to the equilibrium business cycle theories of NCE.[3] Clearly, this literature has helped greatly to clarify many of the issues raised by the controversy, though despite the controversy's widespread attention, the question of compatibility has resisted full resolution. For example, in a recent paper Laidler (1991), an early proponent of the compatibility position (see Laidler 1982), remained unpersuaded that important differences separate Hayek and NCE despite attempts by Hoover (1988) and others to demonstrate otherwise.[4] Although Klausinger (1989: 171) held that 'a majority view' argued in favour of compatibility, recent work emphasizes the importance of differences between Hayek and NCE. Thus, van Zijp (1993: 236) concludes that 'the Austrian School and New Classical Economics study different problems', although he argues that to avoid stagnating, the Austrian school may benefit from 'some cross-fertilization' that includes 'mathematical formalization'.[5]

Relatively little attention, however, has been given to the question of compatibility between Hayek and the rational expectations (RE) hypothesis. Kantor (1979) and Colander and Guthrie (1980) indicated (without detailed argument) that RE resembled an Austrian theory of expectations, while O'Driscoll (1979) and Scheide (1986) claimed that a similarity does exist, provided RE is loosely interpreted to mean that agents simply use the available information in the best way. O'Driscoll and Rizzo (1985: 226) argued that models using RE have 'incorporated essential features of an Austrian-subjectivist theory of the cycle, while at the same time representing an extreme example of anti-subjectivist reasoning'. O'Driscoll and Rizzo attempt to resolve this conundrum by concluding that 'the essential truths of modern macroeconomics can be better presented and defended with a consistently subjectivist monetary theory' (*ibid.*). For them, RE models provide little opportunity to incorporate important elements, such as Cantillon effects, into monetary-macro analysis.[6]

Contemporary Austrians have largely steered clear of carefully examining the alleged compatibility of the expectations theories of Austrian economics and NCE. In part, this may be due to Lachmann's influence in claiming that 'expectations must be regarded as autonomous' and that 'we are unable to postulate any particular mode of change' or 'predict their mode of change as prompted by failure or success' (Lachmann 1976: 129). Certainly, if expectations are truly autonomous, then the attempt to relate them to market processes would be a futile endeavour. Lachmann's position pushes subjectivist economics towards a theory in which, similar to Keynes's long-term expectations, almost 'anything goes' expectationally.[7]

But Austrians should not feel obliged to accept this dour result. To examine why this is so, it is possible to find in the work of Hayek some indications of a theory of expectations. I argue below that in *The Sensory Order* (1952) and other work, Hayek provides a theory of cognitive activity from which it is possible to construct a theory of subjective economic expectations. I find, however, that such Hayekian expectations differ from RE in significant ways. This finding argues for keeping doctrinal lines between NCE and Hayek distinct.

The section 'An overview of Rational Expectations' briefly overviews NCE, especially in regard to RE. My approach here is primarily expository rather than critical. The next section attempts to formulate a Hayekian theory of economic expectations using Hayek's neglected *The Sensory Order*. In the penultimate section I compare Hayek and RE, and my findings are then summarized in the conclusion.

AN OVERVIEW OF RATIONAL EXPECTATIONS

The emergence of rational expectations

Several years after Muth's (1961) treatment of expectations at the individual market level, Lucas (1972, 1975) and others succeeded in applying the rational expectations hypothesis to the system-wide level of analysis. The appropriation of Muth's partial equilibrium analysis of expectations to (Walrasian) general equilibrium models set the stage for significant changes in the way researchers analysed monetary-macroeconomic phenomena. The new classical insistence on constructing models founded on explicit micro-optimizing postulates, and of purging ad hoc Keynesian rules of thumb (Lucas and Sargent 1978: 58), implied changes in the criteria that macro-economic models had to satisfy and in the array of scientifically admissible procedures employed to build and test such models.[8]

NCE formalizes an economy as a sequence of temporary (Walrasian) equilibria. The price-theoretic framework of new classical theory stems from the work of Arrow, Debreu, Hahn and others who demonstrated the mathematical possibility of pre-reconcilable choice in a decentralized exchange system. By invoking the *deus ex machina* of an auctioneer, it was shown that a price vector exists such that if agents pursued their plans in accordance with that vector, the market would generate those same prices. Subsequent developments by Hahn (1971, 1973) indicated that, in the presence of transactions costs, not all forward markets will be operative. As a result, a rationale is provided for reopening markets in the future when commodities can be traded spot. This implies that the treatment of exchange in Arrow–Debreu models as once-for-all is inappropriate. Instead, with positive transactions costs, exchange must be modelled sequentially. Moreover, the notion of equilibrium relevant to such models is no longer static but 'dynamic'.

While early Walrasian models of 'sequence economies' employed perfect foresight, it was clear that the configuration of end-of-period exchanges would depend on agents' expectations of future periods' outcomes. Recognition of this dependency led to the construction of flexible-price general equilibrium models containing an 'expectations function', an exogenously given 'model of the economy' held by transactors. This permitted endogenizing price expectations by specifying a mechanism that manufactured probability distributions of price forecasts from past and current price data.

The development of this line of research, temporary general equilibrium analysis, typically specified adaptive expectations mechanisms (see Grandmont 1977). Although Muth's statement of rational expectations was available, it was not until Lucas's work (1972, 1975) that temporary equilibrium models and RE were fruitfully joined. Muth's critique of the existing treatment of expectations was that too little rationality was assumed in dynamic models. To rectify this deficiency, Muth (1961: 316) suggested 'that expectations, since they are informed predictions of future events, are essentially the same as the predictions of the relevant economic theory'. For Muth, this meant that for a given set of information, the distribution of subjective probability outcomes is the same as that of the objective probability outcomes of the 'true' model. Muth's claim, as Lucas noted later, meant that 'the absence of rents in competitive equilibrium carried the particular implication that these distributions could not differ in a systematic way' (Lucas 1980: 707).

The rational expectations research programme

The application of the optimization calculus to expectations at the theoretical and applied levels stems from a conception of behaviour rooted in 'rationality'. As a postulate, 'rationality' is widely accepted as the claim that individuals purposively act in their own self-interest. Yet, it is also clear that in conjunction with the investigator's aims, a variety of subsidiary assumptions is necessary to render the analysis 'operational' and empirically useful. What makes models hypothesizing RE distinctive is the set of auxiliary assumptions invoked and the special aims to which the analysis is geared. Jointly, these two considerations shape the limits and possibilities of the RE research programme.

According to Lucas (1980: 666) the objective of 'theoretical economics is to provide fully articulated, artificial economic systems that can serve as laboratories in which policies . . . can be tested'. This echoes the statement by Lucas and Sargent (1978: 59) that the aim of new classical economics is to 'discover a particular, econometrically testable equilibrium theory of the business cycle, one that can serve as the foundation for quantitative analysis of macroeconomic policy'. In linking the aims of economics with the construction of macroeconometric models, new classical economists compress theory to explicit modelling *procedures*. Hence, for NCE what passes for good theory is derivative from those techniques that permit translating concepts into formal mathematical structures. This suggests, as Lucas notes (1980: 697), that advances in theoretical understanding are mainly due to 'improvements in mathematical methods and improvements in computational capacity'.

The supporting assumptions in RE models generally refer to the statistical properties of aggregate time series data. Most fundamentally, data are assumed to be random variables so that the parameters of a regression model describe the movement of a process which is stochastic and assumed to be stationary. Deviations around expected values have a mean of zero and are assumed to be normally distributed, a necessary condition for assuming that linear regression techniques will yield rationally expected equilibrium values.

The RE hypothesis enters this framework as the claim that individuals adopt the mean value of the observed distribution as their subjective expectation of future values. This implies that the systematic component of forecast errors equals zero: individuals have been able to identify the parameters of the 'true' model and have thus eliminated all predictable error from expected values. Only random errors remain, but they cannot be serially correlated since autoregressive errors would imply that the model was not 'true'.

These characteristics refer to the formal properties that models employing the RE hypothesis must satisfy. But if such models are to increase our understanding of decision making and how markets work, it is necessary to inquire into the *conception* of expectations embodied in RE models.[9]

In RE models the only kind of expectations that matter are those which correspond to real-valued, explicit data. Such expectations refer to information that is quantitatively specifiable as data (such as prices) and which can be expressed in terms of probability distributions.[10] Even if such information exists in the form, for example, of a monetary policy rule, agents are presumed to expectationally operationalize that rule in terms of the quantitative effects it will have on economic values. In forming rational forecasts, agents are not assumed to acquire all relevant information but only the optimal quantity, a quantity apparently determined by a kind of 'second level' optimal search algorithm. Since agents are postulated to use the 'true' model of the economy in RE models, they are able to identify in principle which (quantitative) information to acquire from the welter of data produced by a complex environment. Agents, in short, know what and how much information to acquire, although they may face in practice a problem extracting locally relevant information (Lucas 1972).[11]

The information that agents acquire, together with the model of the economy which transactors hold as part of their endowment, assumes the character of knowledge upon which transactors generate forecasts and act. In short, the deliverance of data is a sufficient condition for agents to acquire knowledge of the real world. In this way, RE views agents as pure empiricists, since all that can be known is constrained by the amount of information acquired by agents in the form of explicit, quantitative data. This empiricist view of knowledge is also evidenced by those RE models where the 'model of the economy' is not assumed to be given but may be learned by agents. Even if agents do not know a priori the 'true' model, they may learn its structural parameters 'through efficient use of historical information' (Timmermann 1994: 777). During the learning process, however, agents are using the 'wrong' model to manufacture forecasts, so that convergence to an RE equilibrium (should that occur[12]) requires that agents acquire data to inductively learn the 'true' model and its structural parameters. Thus, in RE models forecasts depend on the theory (the model of the economy) that agents use, which in turn depends on an inductive theory of knowledge.[13]

The rendering of information into rationally expected forecasts involves a particular transformation procedure, since non-rational expectations are ruled out by assumption. This follows because, as noted earlier, the subjective probability distributions of transactors must match the objective probability distributions of the relevant economic model. As a result, the assumption of rationally formed expectations identifies the mental processes of agents with statistical algorithms. Accordingly, only those theories of the real world held by transactors that satisfy such algorithms enter as relevant determinants of behaviour in RE models. For this reason it may be useful to describe RE as (well-behaved) 'statistical expectations' rather than cognitively based expectations.[14] While the term 'statistical expectations' may involve a loss in mathematical precision, it nevertheless draws attention to the question of whether expectations ultimately refer to action stemming from complex mental processes or from mathematically specifiable algorithms.

Rational expectationists, however, may not be inconsistent in treating expectations in this fashion. It is important to note in this connection that the principal objective of RE models is not to describe the process of expectations formation. In a sense, the issue of statistical versus cognitive expectations does not arise for RE because only the empirical consequences of (rational) expectations matter. In this way, the rationale for RE is linked to the ability of models to generate good predictions of future outcomes and thus essentially subsumes a theory of expectations to the instrumental value of various hypotheses.[15] Theories in this view are tools which enable better prediction. As such, the conceptual legitimacy or coherence of the tested hypotheses would seem to be of secondary importance.

HAYEK'S COGNITIVE THEORY

The sensory order

Notwithstanding Hayek's contributions to our understanding of the 'knowledge problem', surprisingly little is found in his economic writings that deals explicitly with expectations.[16] The familiar themes of the division of knowledge, the role of the price system in coordinating individuals' activity, and the economy of knowledge necessary for the market's operation might seem to suggest an underlying theory of expectations. However, expectations usually enter Hayek's technical economics only in the context of the conditions necessary for equilibrium to arise (the compatibility of plans) and to persist (correct foresight of external data and others' plans).[17]

This assessment of Hayek's work, however, may be overly restrictive. In his 1937 paper on 'Economics and knowledge', Hayek explicitly connects the empirical tendency of 'the knowledge and intentions of the different members of society to come more and more into agreement' with 'the nature of the *process* by which individual knowledge is changed' (Hayek 1948: 45). Hayek admits that this is something 'we are still pretty much in the dark about' (*ibid.*); yet he speculates that if 'we want to explain social processes' it is necessary to introduce hypotheses about 'the extent and how knowledge corresponds to the external facts' and 'how experience creates knowledge' (*ibid.*: 47). Hayek's resolution of this issue in his 'knowledge papers' of 1937 and 1945 emphasizes the role of the price system in the production and distribution of knowledge. However, his resolution does not specifically offer a theory of learning that explains how an individual acquires such knowledge.[18] Nonetheless, it may be possible to look beyond Hayek's technical economics to find such a theory. In particular, I suggest that Hayek does provide a coherent account of cognitive activity and learning in *The Sensory Order* (1952) and that his account can provide the basis for a theory of economic expectations. My aim here is to highlight the central elements of Hayek's cognitive theory and then in the subsection on 'Hayekian expectations' below to use that theory to adumbrate a theory of Hayekian expectations.[19]

In *The Sensory Order* Hayek provides an explanation of how an individual interprets reality and makes inferences about it. This explanation helps to establish, therefore, the relationship between two orders: the subjective order concerning what the individual believes and the objective order external to the individual. The central problem addressed by *The Sensory Order* is the way cognitive mechanisms allow the individual to adjust his actions to deal more effectively with external reality. For Hayek, this adaptation occurs within a context of constraint regarding inherent cognitive limitations on what an individual can know about the external world.

Hayek's cognitive theory deals with the transformation of sensory inputs into a mental interpretation of reality. This occurs through a process of classification of those sensory qualities by which the mind constructs a particular mental picture of the external reality. For Hayek, classification is the primary activity of the mind. But the qualities so classified, according to Hayek, do not refer to the intrinsic properties of experienced phenomena; rather, these qualities are constructed by the mind. Thus, what we take as a property of things is actually something that is happening to the mind. The 'qualitative differences between experiences' refer to 'mental and not physical events' and what 'we believe we know about the external world is, in fact, knowledge about ourselves' (Hayek 1952: 6–7). Similarly, in 'The primacy of the abstract', Hayek argues that the 'formation of abstractions . . . as something which happens to the mind' (Hayek 1978: 43). In Hayek's theory, what happens to the mind is the construction of structural relations by which sensory data are classified (and reclassified). The arrangement of such sensory data within that structure is based on perceived 'equivalences or differences' (*ibid.*: 41) in the qualities attributed to experienced objects that enables 'the placing of something into one or several classes of objects' (Hayek 1952: 142).[20]

According to Hayek, our perception of external events is a result of the mind's classificatory activity. But how does the mind do this? Hayek claims that the mind's taxonomic activity is rule governed and that these rules are hierarchically ordered according to the level of abstraction at which they operate. If our perceptions are, as Hayek claims, descriptions 'in terms of the relation of the quality in question to other sensory qualities' (1952: 31), then the mind is able to establish those relations because it uses rules to discriminate between experienced objects. 'The mind', Hayek holds, 'must be capable of performing abstract operations . . . to perceive particulars' (1978: 37). Such abstract operations govern the classificatory activity of the mind so that 'all the "knowledge" . . . an organism possesses consists in the action patterns which the stimuli tend to evoke, or . . . what we call knowledge is primarily a system of rules of action' (*ibid.*: 41). Aside from holding important insights for a Hayekian theory of expectations (see below), relating knowledge to a system of abstract rules of action also suggests that these rules must be prior to experience, since without them classification (and hence perception) could not occur. Thus Hayek argues that 'the richness of the sensory world in which we live is not the starting point from which the mind derives abstractions, but the product . . . of abstractions which the mind must possess' to experience that richness (*ibid.*: 44).[21]

The account thus far of cognitive activity as a rule governed and classificatory activity has not dealt specifically with the theory of learning. For Hayek, as noted earlier, learning is the process by which an individual's actions are brought into closer conformity with reality; it is the way the 'rules of action' construct new concepts and theories that allows the individual to make better inferences about the environment. Thus, learning for Hayek is not the accumulation of data points, but the process which enables the individual to generate and interpret an unlimited domain of such facts.

The concepts used by Hayek to explain learning are the 'map' and 'model'. The map is a semi-permanent (or slowly but continuously changing) network which represents the way information has been organized in the past (and found useful to the individual) and the channels that new sensory impulses are likely to follow within the central nervous system. It is the structure that has been built gradually by links representing 'a very imperfect' or 'even a definitely erroneous reproduction of the relations which exist between the corresponding physical stimuli' (Hayek 1952: 108).[22] Mapping, which is analogous to classification, produces a network of relationships that Hayek likens to 'schematic railway maps' in which the structures (maps) comprising this classificatory apparatus 'occur on many successive levels . . . consisting of many vertically superimposed sub-systems which in some respects operate independently of each other' but which serve as 'filters or preselectors for impulses sent on to the higher centres' (*ibid.*: 110, 111). The map, which exists independently of any particular current impulses, represents 'the kind of world in which' the individual 'has existed in the past, or the different *kinds* of stimuli which have acquired significance for it' during its whole past (*ibid.*: 115). But the map is *ex post* and, as such, is unable to directly provide information about the immediate environment that the individual confronts or is likely to encounter. To address this kind of learning, Hayek invokes the concept of the model.

Within the hierarchical structure of the maps, Hayek claims that the flow of impulses will trace a further pattern of relationships (or model) of the particular environment in which the individual finds him- or herself at the moment. The model therefore represents the current interpretation of the environment. It functions, Hayek claims, 'as an apparatus of orientation by representing both the actual state of the environment and the changes to be expected in that environment' (*ibid.*: 118). The model operates as a negative feedback system since its anticipatory activity is checked and corrected, Hayek notes, by perceived changes in the environment as recorded by newly arriving sensory signals.[23] While the model is more dynamic, fluid, conjectural and situationally contingent than the map, Hayek emphasizes that the map itself is not immune to the impulses proceeding through it and may change as a consequence of those impulses.

It is appropriate to consider the central nervous system as a Hayekian self-regulating phenomenon with a complex organization. As Hayek points out (*ibid.*: 122–7), by virtue of its own rule-governed operations the central nervous system is able to continuously change its own structure and, through experience, to alter the range of tasks it is capable of performing. Hayek holds that it will rarely respond in exactly the same way to the same external conditions; its responses are necessarily adaptive and purposive in terms of achieving a better fit with the environment.

Hayekian expectations

It is possible to formulate a general theory of economic expectations based on Hayek's cognitive theory, though as noted earlier Hayek did not undertake that formulation himself. Expectations for Hayek are principally dispositions to act, rather than beliefs, and generally refer to 'knowing what to do' instead of 'knowing that'.[24] The main outlines of such a theory suggest Hayekian expectations to be coherent, competitive and endogenous to the market process.[25]

The coherence of Hayekian expectations derives from the 'constrained creativity' suggested by Hayek's cognitive theory. As indicated above, the mechanisms which Hayek invokes to explain learning – the map and the model – change when sensory impulses are reclassified by the central nervous system into different patterns. In effect, new rules governing cognitive functions replace old rules, but for Hayek, these changes in what an individual knows are constrained by two considerations. First, the relatively fixed framework of the map suggests that changes in knowledge can occur only slowly and in piecemeal fashion; radical and fundamental changes are not likely against the backdrop of 'the events which the organism has met during its whole past' (Hayek 1952: 115). Second, Hayek points out that the rules of action that govern higher cognitive activity operate at a supraconscious (tacit) level.[26] At successively higher (or deeper) levels of cognitive activity, such rules become less conscious. If so, there is only limited opportunity to actually alter the rules by which sensory data are interpreted and transformed into knowledge, and such opportunities diminish as those rules become more deep seated.

At the same time, it was seen in the previous section that the mind in Hayek's theory has the ability to induce changes in it own structure and to perform entirely new functions. A useful way to see this is to remember that the (finite) abstract rules governing cognitive activity are generative in terms of concept and theory construction. This cognitive creativity – the ability to produce a different picture of the world – in conjunction with the impetus of the individual to adapt to the environment, is modified by mechanisms that constrain such creativity. Thus, Hayek's theory reflects a subtle tension of forces inducing novelty and those restraining novelty. On this account, Hayekian economic expectations cannot be described either as 'fixed' or as 'volatile'. However, as a general proposition we can say that they are rule bound or coherent. Hayek's cognitive theory sees mind and the knowledge it produces as rule governed. But to what end is such activity directed?

Cognitive activity for Hayek seeks to increase or improve the individual's fit with the external world. As Hayek observes in 'The primacy of the abstract': 'an abstraction is primarily such a *disposition* towards certain ranges of *actions*' (Hayek 1978: 40, emphasis added). Hayek's thesis that concepts and knowledge reflect dispositions to act means that a change in knowledge produces a change in actions. As discussed earlier, modelling operates as a cybernetic mechanism between the mind and the environment by which the individual's changing knowledge of the environment induces adaptive modifications in behaviour. Whereas this knowledge is anticipatory, the individual's expectations may involve inappropriate actions given the environment. Such falsified expectations, which may derive from inherent cognitive limits on knowledge and from changes in the environment, induce the mind to undertake error-correction measures in the way it perceives and understands reality. In this way, within (and between) individuals, a positive value exists for better expectations because they are likely to be more successful in helping individuals achieve a better fit with the environment. Expectations that are less successful will tend to be weeded out. In a catallactic context, this suggests that Hayekian expectations should be considered competitive and endogenous to the market process.

To summarize my treatment of Hayekian expectations, I have argued that individuals construct a coherent interpretation of reality which is a by-product of abstract (and tacit) rules governing the mind's operation. However, this interpretation of reality is necessarily selective (incomplete) and thus entails inherent epistemological ignorance.[27] Moreover, as Hayek's cognitive theory and other of his writings indicate, our ignorance of the external world often refers to particular events and our knowledge to certain general relationships or patterns. Despite such constraints we have seen that the individual employs coherent rules of action via feedback mechanisms that improve his fit with reality. To the extent that the social milieu satisfies certain conditions (see Butos and Koppl 1993), we would have no particular reason to assume that Hayekian expectations per se would not exhibit tendencies towards coherence and overall coordination.

RATIONAL EXPECTATIONS AND HAYEKIAN EXPECTATIONS: SOME COMPARISONS

The discussion above suggests that important differences exist between RE and Hayek's cognitive theory and Hayekian economic expectations. Hayek proceeds at the foundational level of knowledge while new classical economists, the statistical expectationists, take a neoclassical conception of rationality and attempt to apply it empirically. To compare Hayekian and RE, I focus in summary form on five categories given below.

Data and knowledge

In models employing RE, statistical data are treated as knowledge. Such knowledge is acquired inductively (at positive cost) and pigeonholed into given probability distributions. RE treats this quantitative data as an input that (given the actor's model of the economy) generates an output of quantitative forecasts. The singular problem for the actor is the generation of optimal forecasts under such circumstances.

A Hayekian perspective, in contrast, claims that sensory data is not knowledge until and unless it goes through the process of classification of the central nervous system. Moreover, classification occurs according to qualitative differences in sensory data (not in regard to their statistical properties), so that our knowledge of particular events in the external world is chiefly based on the mind's ability to discriminate between *kinds* or *classes* of phenomena. For Hayek, whatever quantitative attributes of real world phenomena the mind may construct, such attributes are posterior to knowledge about their qualitative attributes. 'Facts' for Hayek are theoretically determined and have no existence apart from the mental process classifying them.[28] The cognitive problem for Hayek is precisely: what are the facts?

According to Hayek, knowledge consists in the 'rules of action' governing the operation of cognitive activity and in 'knowing what to do' in a particular situation rather than 'knowing that'. Thus, there is no requirement that Hayekian expectations require the individual to make (if only in principle) quantitative forecasts. To the extent that Hayekian forecasts in part take on a quantitative dimension, it would be based on the particular and revisable model that the individual employed for the problem at hand.

230

What we can say is that Hayekian expectations, whatever particular form they assume, are likely to be coherent in terms of assisting the individual achieve a better fit with the environment.

Homogeneity versus heterogeneity

RE models in macroeconomics typically assume that the same data evoke the same response across individuals and that each individual employs the 'relevant' (same) model of the economy. As noted earlier (see n. 11 above), this usually shows up in macro models as 'representative agent' models in which all agents are assumed to be identical. Attempts to lessen the strictures of representative agent models are found in RE models which assume agents with asymmetric information. Grossman (1989), for example, models agents with diverse information and rational expectations. Since each agent's information set is different, there is a sense in which it is possible to view such models as containing heterogeneous agents. Consequently, when heterogeneity is defined in terms of agents' information sets, the homogeneity feature of RE models speaks primarily to specific models in which expectational hypotheses are embedded, rather than to the RE concept per se. Of course, if agents use different models, they will have different rational expectations whether each agent's information is symmetric or not.[29]

Instead, Hayek's approach maintains that each individual is intrinsically and necessarily distinct in important ways. In addition to an individual's specific and local knowledge of 'particular time and circumstance' (Hayek 1945: 521), *The Sensory Order* tells us that each individual's interpretation of data, no less than the model of the economy used, depends upon the prior experience and history of the individual as well as the specific environment in which the individual functions. The various theories and concepts an individual holds depend on the mapping and modelling processes unique to that individual.[30] This suggests that Hayekian expectations must differ across individuals.

Models of the economy

RE models assume that agents know the stochastic processes of the relevant model of the economy. This kind of structural knowledge allows them to generate unbiased forecasts of the model's parameters. According to Hayek, however, detailed knowledge of the economy faces abstract constraints that permit only 'pattern prediction' of complexly organized phenomena. Hayek's cognitive theory argues that we can, at best, achieve explanation of the abstract principles according to which systems such as the brain, market systems or social structures operate.

Hayek's economic theory also places considerable emphasis on the importance of decentralized information relating to particular circumstances for successful entrepreneurial activity on the market; Hayekian economic actors do not rely on knowledge about the overall economy's structure. Hayek's cognitive theory tells us that detailed structural knowledge of the economy is effectively impossible to acquire and that whatever model an individual does use, it will be used to improve the individual's fit with the environment in which the individual functions.

In contrast to most RE models, the Hayekian perspective does not treat the individual's theories of the economy as an endowment. Instead, theories evolve for the individual via the effects that experience has on the map and model. As noted earlier, such experience in Hayek's theory will lead to falsified expectations that alter via feedback mechanisms the individual's theories and responses. In a Hayekian approach, an individual's model of the economy would be a set of contingent and conjectural relationships referring to ranges of possible outcomes of significance to the individual.

Explicit versus tacit knowledge

The kind of knowledge relevant to RE models is explicit, fully articulated and quantifiable knowledge. For Hayek, knowledge is embodied in the 'rules of action' involved in classification. This process, Hayek tells us, allows us to form concepts and theories about relationships between sensory data that have been classified as belonging to a certain class (or classes) of phenomena but not others. In his discussion of these processes, Hayek does not define the mental realm as one of consciousness. Instead, this realm is seen as a structure of rules which functions in a tacit fashion. Thus, for Hayek, the essential characteristic of knowledge is not that it must be explicit and articulable, but that it is a by-product of abstract rules whose operation we often are unaware of.

If correct, Hayek's theory would suggest that expectations and the behaviours they induce may not submit so easily to formulations that treat such questions as (quantitative) informational input–output relationships. As a consequence, the attempt to relate information and expectations by quantitative algorithms seems to impose a simple (though, perhaps, tractable) solution on substantially more complex relationships. Hayek's claim of the importance of tacit knowledge and the corresponding limitations it suggests for modelling expectations, provide points of contention between a Hayekian approach to expectations and RE.

Maximizing versus adapting

Agents in RE models are optimizers in their acquisition and use of (statistical) data in the context of their model of the economy. No explanation is given as to how (or why) individuals settle on that particular model. Instead, the model is exogenously given and hence not subject to falsification or rejection by individuals. What they learn are new data points that are fitted into existing probability distributions. The problem facing them is to maximize utility; and this will be achieved whenever the acquisition of additional data suggests the net benefit of so doing.

Under Hayekian expectations, adaptation to the environment provides the motivation for action. As discussed earlier, the rationale for the individual's mapping and modelling activities is to generate more useful interpretations of the external world. The criterion of success for such activities is the closeness of fit that the individual achieves with the environment. Attaining some maximum outcome, though surely the object of the individual's purposeful action, is not what defines the principal issue for expectations theory from a Hayekian perspective. The essential feature of Hayekian expectations is that they are self-correcting by virtue of a learning process. Hayekian expectations are not correct (nor can they be, according to Hayek, given the inherent constraints on knowledge), but they are corrigible. One of the distinctive aspects of Hayekian expectations is that its underlying cognitive theory articulates a well-developed theory of learning.

CONCLUSION

The point of this chapter has been to suggest that Hayek's cognitive theory provides an account of expectations which is markedly different from RE. This suggests that attempts to forge substantive links between new classical economics and Hayek should be approached sceptically.[31] I have tried to show that Hayekian expectations are coherent, competitive and endogenous to the market process. The differences between RE and Hayekian expectations are explained by the supporting cognitive theory provided by Hayek and by the special scientific aims which appear to drive RE. The methodology of NCE imposes requirements on RE which do not apply and cannot be applied to Hayekian expectations. The new classical excision of cognitive dimensions from economic agents has the peculiar consequence that its economic theories which purport to study dynamics encounter difficulties in accounting for how agents learn.

Hayekian expectations, it is true, may fail to satisfy either the quantitative requirements of NCE or the indefiniteness of kaleidicists, such as Lachmann and Shackle. Yet Hayek's cognitive psychology assuages the force of such putative shortcomings by offering a kind of middle-ground perspective on expectations. Hayek's cognitive theory demonstrates that we do not need to stipulate a new classical conception of rationality to analyse market order from a consistent subjectivist position. On the other hand, Hayek's cognitive theory also avoids an approach to expectations whereby an 'unknowable, though not unimaginable' future (Lachmann 1994: 236) makes it difficult to generalize about unintended consequences and coordinating properties of market behaviour.

At the same time, it is useful to note the tensions that exist between cognitive theory and economics. Hayek, like Mises (1957: chapter 12), was explicit about the status of psychology in the social sciences. 'It is a mistake,' says Hayek about social scientists, 'to believe that their aim is to *explain* conscious action.' This, Hayek says, 'is the task of psychology' (Hayek 1955: 39). For both Mises and Hayek, economics deals with purposeful action, not with explaining psychological motivations, emotions and valuations that give rise to action.[32] Thus, it might appear incongruous to claim, as I have in this chapter, that Hayek's cognitive theory carries significant insights for economics.[33] Given Hayek's stated position on the relation between economics and psychology, this claim surely warrants separate treatment. Since that cannot be undertaken here, I merely wish to suggest that Hayek's cognitive theory is distinct from the positivistic and behaviouristic psychological theories that he (and Mises) claimed were not germane to economics.[34]

Perhaps for Hayek, then, (non-positivistic) cognitive theories may be used to shed light on certain kinds of questions in our knowledge of economics. It can therefore be claimed that the aim of *The Sensory Order* was to provide a cognitive basis for subjectivism or, in the language of *The Sensory Order*, for why phenomenal 'events, which on the basis of their relations to each other can be arranged in a certain (physical) order, manifest a different order in their effect on our senses' (Hayek 1952: 5).[35] As argued in this chapter, Hayek's resolution of this question provides a theory of rule-governed action and expectations that differs from RE in essential ways. Although RE has been thoroughly integrated into economics, the way Hayekian expectations might serve the purposes of economics is still an open question.[36]

NOTES

1 An earlier version of this chapter was presented at a conference on 'Austrians in Debate', 19–20 January 1995 in Amsterdam. I owe a special debt of gratitude to Rudy van Zijp for helpful comments made during and after the conference – even if I did not consistently follow his thoughtful suggestions – and to Roger Koppl for his perceptive feedback. I also thank Carlo Zappia, Bert Tieben and other participants at the Amsterdam conference, Ivo Sarjanovic, as well as Jim Wible, Mike Goldberg, Dave Draper and other participants of the University of New Hampshire economics seminar for comments on an earlier draft. The usual caveat applies.

2 We should not lose sight of the irony revealed in a recent interview of Lucas by Snowden, Vane and Wynarczyk (1994). The interviewers asked 'To what extent did the work of the Austrians (Hayek, etc.) influence your ideas?' Lucas responded: 'I once thought of myself as a kind of Austrian, but Kevin Hoover's book persuaded me that this was just a result of my misreading of Hayek and others' (*ibid.*: 222). Lucas is referring to Hoover (1988).

3 See, for example, Butos (1985), Garrison (1986), Garrison and Bellante (1988), Klausinger (1990).

4 Rosner (1994: 64) concludes that 'the models of New Classical Macroeconomics can therefore be seen to be in line with basic ideas of Hayek'. Rosner finds that Lucas's 'island parable' paper involves an 'institutional setting' that is 'too simple to provide an answer to all the problems of business cycles'. Yet Lucas's work goes some distance, Rosner claims, in resolving 'two problems of Hayek's economic theory' related to 'the processing of information and its influence on expectations'.

5 Zijp (1993: 237) qualifies his call for more mathematical formalism in Austrian economics by suggesting that doing so 'may take the heart out of "Austrianism"' by losing its 'dynamic subjectivism and entrepreneurship'. Paqué (1985: 426) believes that unless Austrian economics attempts to 'operationalize [its] ideas in a full-scale empirical research project', presumably in the fashion of neoclassical researchers, 'Austrian economics . . . looks very much like a programme without research'. In contrast, Hoover (1988: 237) sees Austrian research motivated by beliefs 'about the purpose and methods of economics' that are different from neoclassicists' while Garretsen (1994) argues that it is neoclassical economics which should take Austrian economics more seriously if it wishes to deal successfully with coordination issues.

6 According to Zijp and Visser (1994), in equilibrium business cycle models the new classical insistence on highly formalistic methods largely precludes a variety of important elements (such as distribution effects).

7 The varieties of subjectivist thought give rise to different theories of expectations. Butos and Koppl (1997) discuss the philosophical positions of Keynes and Hayek that conduce towards distinctive theories of (subjective) expectations. See note 27 below.

8 Lucas and Sargent critique Keynesian macroeconometric models, arguing that their 'difficulties are *fatal*' and 'that modern macroeconomic models are of *no* value in guiding policy' (Lucas and Sargent 1978: 50).

9 Rational expectationists are notably silent on this matter. My discussion is an attempt to reconstruct such a conception.

10 See, for example, Begg (1982: chapter 4) and Pesaran (1989: appendix A).

11 Rational expectations models typically postulate that all agents use the same probability distribution and model of the economy to manufacture forecasts. Such 'representative agent' models, however, ignore the implications of divergent expectations (Runde and Torr 1985). Haltiwanger and Waldman (1989) show that divergent expectations may not cancel out in the aggregate; this means that the equilibrium generated under these circumstances will systematically differ from that generated by representative agent models. Models of rational expectations with asymmetric information are discussed briefly in note 29 below.

12 Convergence to an RE equilibrium requires that learning occurs 'faster than the model changes' (Visser 1991: 52). Heap (1989) argues that 'subjective beliefs about probability distributions affect outcomes because action is informed by expectations'. This, Heap observes, 'introduces elements of non-stationarity when there is learning' (*ibid*.: 58–9). Consequently, when the 'objective' changes as a result of individuals' learning, there is no guarantee that agents will be able to actually learn the 'true' RE equilibrium. A similar point was made some years ago by Rosenstein-Rodan (1934). Frydman (1982, 1983) argues that convergence to an RE equilibrium may not be possible unless the relevant constraints implied by Hayek's division of knowledge are assumed away. In Frydman's (1982) treatment, agents in decentralized markets are unable to learn the 'true' model because (as in Keynes's beauty contest example) they have no method to learn the probability distribution of 'the

average of forecasts . . . formed by other agents ("the average opinion")' (*ibid.*: 654). Such problems are further complicated if agents pursue strategies knowing that their behaviour can affect each other. In these 'Holmes–Moriarty' situations, a paradox exists because a perfect foresight equilibrium does not exist. See Frydman *et al.* (1982) for a discussion of the policy implications stemming from this paradox. See also Kim (1988).

13 Boland (1986) argues that the implicit theory of knowledge underpinning RE is inductivist. He maintains that 'the problem with the Rational Expectations Hypothesis is not that it lacks a theory of learning, but that it relies on a false theory of learning' (*ibid.*: 122). Interestingly, Boland (1978: 251) claims that Hayek's theory of knowledge is also inductivist. Although questions pertaining to inductivist epistemology fall outside the scope of this chapter, my discussion below in the section on 'Hayek's cognitive theory' indirectly challenges Boland's argument concerning Hayek. On this, see also 'The primacy of the abstract' (Hayek 1978) and especially Nishiyama (1984: xlvi–l).

14 By calling rational expectations 'statistical expectations', I simply wish to distinguish the concept from other conceptions, such as subjective expectations, that do not equate knowledge with the quantitative attributes of data. Zijp (1993) correctly refers to rational expectations as 'model consistent expectations', a designation clearly compatible with Muth's (1961) statement of the hypothesis and Lucas's characterizing it as a 'consistency axiom for economics'. According to Lucas, the hypothesis 'can be given precise meaning only in the context of specific models'. Defining rational expectations in model-free ways 'come out either vacuous . . . or silly' (Lucas 1987: 13, n. 4). If our concern, however, is with theories of expectations as such, it seems desirable to distance ourselves from exclusively adopting Lucas's strictures. Following Lucas's approach tends to focus attention on the models per se (or in empirical work, on the joint testing of a particular model and expectations function) and away from the question of expectations per se. For a recent attempt to grapple with expectations per se, see the interesting paper by Goldberg and Frydman (1996) who, in acknowledging the weak empirical results of RE models, have proposed a framework of forward-looking 'theories consistent expectations' to study exchange rate movements. In their treatment, since agents do not know the 'true' model, they make forecasts by selecting from any number of existing models (theories) and stick with one, even if it is the wrong model, provided it predicts correctly the direction of change in the exchange rate.

15 See Caldwell (1980) for a critique of instrumentalism.

16 It is curious that Hayek did not develop a theory of economic expectations, given that such questions were very much in the air during the interwar years. Hayek's work during the 1920s and 1930s in monetary theory and the trade cycle employed an analytical apparatus he had developed in his earlier intertemporal equilibrium model of 1928 (Hayek 1984). He resolved the intertemporal pricing problem of that model by assuming perfect foresight, an assumption some modern Austrians have found unsatisfactory (see O'Driscoll and Rizzo 1985). It is tempting to suggest that Hayek was positioned during his early career to provide a somewhat more expansive treatment of expectations from a cognitive perspective, given that the basic argument of *The Sensory Order* was 'on paper, though in a very amateurish fashion, by 1920' (Hayek 1982: 288). However, as I have suggested elsewhere (Butos 1985), it must be remembered that during the 1930s Hayek was eager to establish his credentials as an economic theorist. Given the prevailing milieu, this meant stating his case in a theoretically acceptable manner and avoiding explanations

which might have been branded psychologistic. In any case, there is little question that Hayek viewed his work in cognitive psychology and the social sciences as mutually reinforcing. See Hayek (1979: 200, n. 26) and note 35 below.

17 See, for example, Hayek (1941: chapter II; 1975: 138–41).

18 Desai (1994) argues that Hayek actually reverted to the pure logic of choice in 'The use of knowledge in society' (1945), when he claimed the centrality of the price system's informational role. But see Thomsen (1992) for a contrary assessment.

19 Hayek's theory of cognition has not received widespread attention by economists, despite the epistemological flavour of his 'knowledge papers'. A significant exception is Streit (1993). See also Butos and Koppl (1993), from which the discussion in the text substantially draws, and Fleetwood (1995). Aspects of Hayek's cognitive theory from outside economics is found in Nishiyama (1984), de Vries (1994), Smith (1996), and Agonito (1975), though Weimer's (1982) essay, which must be credited with rehabilitating *The Sensory Order*, remains the single best available treatment.

20 The relational aspect of sensory data is evident in the following: 'If sensory perception must be regarded as an act of classification, what we perceive can never be unique properties of individual objects but always only properties which the objects have in common with other objects' (Hayek 1952: 142).

21 As Hayek notes (1978: 43), this position argues against inductivism.

22 These links ('impressions' or 'stampings') are erroneous because 'the signals reaching the higher and more comprehensive centres [of neural activity] will often not represent individual stimuli, but may stand for classes or groups of such stimuli'. Thus, the map will imperfectly represent 'the relationships between the network of connexions' of the central nervous system and 'the structure of external events which it can be said to reproduce' (Hayek 1952: 109). According to Hayek, then, facts are never 'given', but are constructions (or theories) of the external world.

23 The model is anticipatory because incoming sensory data evoke whole ranges of responses geared to possible consequences. Hayek's concept of 'multiple classification' is integral to the dynamic and anticipatory nature of the model. The concept holds that sensory data are classified as belonging to any number of classes or groups, with each group containing sensory data similar in certain ways and different in others (see Hayek 1952: 48–50, 70). Multiple classification means that particular incoming stimuli are not joined to a particular response but may elicit a response that is better able to 'account for the significance which the stimulus has in the context of other (external and internal) stimuli' (*ibid*.: 45). Hayek observes: 'We must therefore conceive of the model as constantly trying out possible developments and determining action in light of the consequences which from the representation of such actions would appear to follow from it' (*ibid*.: 121). Using trial and error to determine 'the effects to be expected from alternative courses of action' means that we 'live as much in the world of expectation as in a world of "fact"' (*ibid*.).

24 See 'The primacy of the abstract' in Hayek (1978), especially pp. 38–42.

25 My discussion follows the more thorough treatment in Butos and Koppl (1993). Unlike that paper, my discussion here does not analyse the implications for market processes under Hayekian expectations when markets are subject to different rules and constraints. The question of whether expectations work to coordinate market activity cannot be separated from the institutional context. Thus, the 'optimality' of expectations can never be deduced from the

rationality postulate alone if constitutional constraints matter. See, for example, Vanberg (1993).

26 Typically, rationality is understood as explicitly and consciously specifiable. However, Hayek (1952: 138–9) holds that 'conscious experience thus rests on a much more extensive basis of less fully conscious or subconscious images of the rest of the surroundings, which . . . give to the conscious representations their place and value' and that 'consciously experienced qualities' share 'relationships which determine these qualities' which 'are not in turn themselves conscious' (*ibid.*: 142). In 'The primacy of the abstract' Hayek notes 'the increasing awareness that all of our actions must be conceived of as being guided by rules of which we are not conscious but which in their joint influence enable us to exercise extremely complicated skills' (Hayek 1978: 38). See also Agonito (1975) and Weimer (1982).

27 It is not difficult to assume in economics 'inherent ignorance' or 'fundamental uncertainty' once historical (real) time is introduced in a serious way. Invoking 'uncertainty of the future', as Lachmann, Shackle and Keynes do, speaks to a different source of ignorance than analysed by Hayek's cognitive theory. Subjective knowledge and expectations matter when the future is uncertain. However, not all theories of subjectivism are alike, but such inquiries fall outside the scope of this chapter.

28 Hayek's cognitive theory claims that we do not learn facts, but concepts and theories which allow us to generate facts.

29 Following Lucas (1972), NCE modelling strategies also use the 'islands approach' whereby the 'representative agent' is replaced by several such agents who differ only in regard to their local information. All agents in each local market are identical. In connection with such approaches, Zijp (1993: 166) observes that 'the claim that the NCE has provided macroeconomics' with a sound methodological individualistic basis 'must therefore be regarded with considerable scepticism'. As noted in the text, Grossman (1989) drops the 'representative agent' approach by considering an RE model of agents with asymmetric information. Here, the allocative equilibrium outcome is the same as would be generated by Walrasian general equilibrium. Provided information is costless to acquire (and certain other conditions are satisfied, including, for example, the existence of a complete set of futures markets), Grossman finds that the 'R.E. price is . . . a sufficient *statistic* for *all* the economy's information' (*ibid.*: 33, emphasis added). It is useful to note that heterogeneous knowledge is situational in Grossman's treatment but constitutive in Hayek's. Zappia (1995) argues that Grossman's general equilibrium model considers only asymmetries in information which arise from exogenous events, such as future states of nature, whereas Hayek's conception of such asymmetries also refers to differences in agents' 'personal' (tacit) knowledge. This kind of knowledge, Zappia holds, is important for understanding the market as a discovery process of unexploited opportunities, something which 'cannot find adequate treatment in Grossman's general equilibrium model' (*ibid.*: 5). See also Thomsen (1992: chapter 3).

30 See Hayek (1952, especially sections 5.20, 5.27–8, 5.66).

31 I do not address here the issue of compatibility between Hayek and the Austrian praxeologists (Mises, Rothbard) and other variants in the recent Austrian revival, including the Lachmann/Shackle radical subjectivists and hermeneuticians. While Austrian economists share interest in common themes and claim a common ancestry, substantive epistemological and methodological differences have become increasingly evident. See, for example, Boehm (1989) and Salerno (1990). Many of these issues are discussed by Vaughn (1994),

though exclusively from the perspective of Austrianism in America. There are legitimate doubts if it is useful to speak of a single Austrian theory of expectations. Sorting out such differences, as well as identifying points of intersection, is a matter for future research.

32 Mises (1966: 11–12) argues that the 'field of [economics] is human action, not the psychological events which result in action . . . The theme of psychology is the internal events that result or can result in definite action. The theme of praxeology is action as such.' For Mises, the theorems of economics are independent of psychology assumptions. See also *ibid.*: 123–7.

33 Despite an otherwise useful overview of the status of psychology in Austrian economics, Runde surprisingly places a synopsis of *The Sensory Order* in an appendix on the grounds that 'Hayek's psychological treatise . . . has little to do with economics' (Runde 1988: 107). However, he insightfully notes that Mises' and Hayek's hostility to psychology is largely directed at behaviouristic psychology.

34 See Weimer (1982). See also Runde (1988: 108) who observes that 'the statements of Hayek, Mises and Robbins on pure psychology in general only become truly hostile when they discuss behaviorism'.

35 In Chapter III of *The Counter-Revolution of Science* (1955), entitled 'The subjective character of the data of the social sciences', Hayek's discussion is unmistakably similar to the argument of *The Sensory Order*. As Hayek indicates: 'My colleagues in the social sciences generally find my study on *The Sensory Order* . . . uninteresting or indigestible. But the work on it has helped me greatly to clear my mind on much that is relevant for social theory. My conception of evolution, of a spontaneous order and of the methods and limits of our endeavors to explain complex phenomena have been largely formed in the course of the work on that book' (Hayek 1979: 199, n. 26).

36 But see Birner (1994), Horwitz (1994), and especially Vanberg (1993, 1994).

REFERENCES

Agonito, R. (1975) 'Hayek revisited: mind as the process of classification', *Behaviourism*, 3 (2): 162–71.

Begg, D. (1982) *The Rational Expectations Revolution in Macroeconomics*, Baltimore, MD: Johns Hopkins University Press.

Birner, J. (1994) 'Introduction: Hayek's grand research programme', in J. Birner and R. van Zijp (eds) *Hayek, Co-Ordination and Evolution*, New York: Routledge, 1–25.

Boehm, S. (1989) 'Hayek on knowledge, equilibrium, and prices: context and impact', *Wirtschaftspolitische Blatter*, 36 (2): 201–13.

Boland, L. (1978) 'Time in economics vs economics in time: the "Hayek problem"', *Canadian Journal of Economics*, 11 (2): 240–62.

——(1986) *Methodology for a New Microeconomics*, Boston, MA: Allen & Unwin.

Butos, W.N. (1985) 'Hayek and general equilibrium analysis', *Southern Economic Journal*, 52 (2): 332–43.

Butos, W.N. and Koppl, R.G. (1993) 'Hayekian expectations: theory and empirical applications', *Constitutional Political Economy*, 4 (3): 303–29.

——(1997) 'The varieties of subjectivism: Keynes and Hayek on expectations', *History of Political Economy*, 29 (2): 327–59.

Caldwell, B. (1980) 'A critique of Friedman's methodological instrumentalism', *Southern Economic Journal*, 47 (2): 366–74.

Colander, D. and Guthrie, R. (1980) 'Great expectations: what the Dickens do rational expectations mean?', *Journal of Post-Keynesian Economics*, 3 (2): 219–34.

Desai, M. (1994) 'Equilibrium, expectations and knowledge', in J. Birner and R. van Zijp (eds) *Hayek, Co-Ordination and Evolution*, New York: Routledge, 25–50.

Fleetwood, S. (1995) *Hayek's Political Economy*, London: Routledge.

Frydman, R. (1982) 'Toward an understanding of market processes', *American Economic Review*, 72 (4): 652–68.

——(1983) 'Individual rationality, decentralization, and the rational expectations hypothesis', in R. Frydman and E.S. Phelps (eds) *Individual Forecasting and Aggregate Outcomes*, New York: Cambridge University Press, 97–122.

Frydman, R., O'Driscoll, G.P. and Schotter, A. (1982) 'Rational expectations of government policy: an application of Newcomb's Problem', *Southern Economic Journal*, 49 (2): 311–19.

Garretsen, H. (1994) 'The relevance of Hayek for mainstream economics', in J. Birner and R. van Zijp (eds) *Hayek, Co-Ordination and Evolution*, New York: Routledge, 94–108.

Garrison, R. (1986) 'Hayekian trade cycle theory: a reappraisal', *CATO Journal*, 6 (2): 437–53.

Garrison, R. and Bellante, D. (1988) 'Phillips curves and Hayekian triangles: two perspectives on monetary dynamics', *History of Political Economy*, 20 (2): 207–34.

Goldberg, M.D. and Frydman, R. (1996) 'Imperfect knowledge and behavior in the Foreign Exchange Market', *Economic Journal*, 106 (437): 869–93.

Grandmont, J.M. (1977) 'Temporary general equilibrium theory', *Econometrica*, 45 (3): 535–72.

Grossman, S.J. (1989) 'An introduction to the theory of rational expectations under asymmetric information', *The Informational Role of Prices*, Cambridge, MA: MIT Press, 11–39.

Hahn, F.H. (1971) 'Equilibrium with transactions costs', *Econometrica*, 39 (3): 417–39.

——(1973) 'On transactions costs, inessential sequence economies and money', *Review of Economic Studies*, 40 (4): 449–61.

Haltiwanger, J.C. and Waldman, M. (1989) 'Rational expectations in the aggregate', *Economic Inquiry*, 27 (4): 619–36.

Hayek, F.A. (1941) *The Pure Theory of Capital*, Chicago, IL: University of Chicago Press.

——(1945) 'The use of knowledge in society', *American Economic Review*, 35 (4): 519–30.

——(1948) *Individualism and Economic Order*, Chicago, IL: University of Chicago Press.

——(1952) *The Sensory Order*, Chicago, IL: University of Chicago Press.

——(1955) *The Counter-Revolution of Science*, New York: The Free Press.

——(1975) *Profits, Interest and Investment*, Clifton, NJ: A.M. Kelley.

——(1978) *New Studies in Philosophy, Politics, Economics and the History of Ideas*, Chicago, IL: University of Chicago Press.

——(1979) *Law, Legislation and Liberty*, vol. 3: *The Political Order of a Free People*, Chicago, IL: University of Chicago Press.

——(1982) 'The Sensory Order after 25 years', in W.B. Weimer and D. Palermo (eds) *Cognition and the Symbolic Processes*, vol. II, Hillsdale, NJ: Lawrence Erlbaum, 287–93.

——(1984) 'Intertemporal price equilibrium and movements in the value of money', in Roy McCloughry (ed.) *Money, Capital, and Fluctuations: Early Essays*, Chicago, IL: University of Chicago Press, 71–117.

Heap, S.H. (1989) *Rationality in Economics*, New York: Basil Blackwell.

Hoover, K.D. (1988) *The New Classical Macroeconomics*, Cambridge: Basil Blackwell.

Horwitz, S. (1994) 'From *The Sensory Order* to the liberal order: mind, economy, and state in the thought of F.A. Hayek', paper presented at the Mont Pelerin Society, Cannes, France.

Kantor, B. (1979) 'Rational expectations and economic thought', *Journal of Economic Literature*, 17 (4): 1422–41.

Kim, K. (1988) *Equilibrium Business Cycle Theory in Historical Perspective*, New York: Cambridge University Press.

Klausinger, H. (1989) 'Hayek and new classical economics on equilibrium analysis', *Jahrbuch fuer Sozialwissenschaft*, 40: 171–86.

——(1990) 'Equilibrium methodology as seen from a Hayekian perspective', *Journal of the History of Economic Thought*, 12 (1): 61–75.

Kuhn, T.S. (1970) *The Structure of Scientific Revolutions*, Chicago, IL: University of Chicago Press.

Lachmann, L.M. (1976) 'On the central concept of Austrian economics: market process', in E.G. Dolan (ed.) *The Foundations of Modern Austrian Economics*, Kansas City, KS: Sheed & Ward, 126–32.

——(1994) *Expectations and the Meaning of Institutions*, D. Lavoie (ed.), London and New York: Routledge.

Laidler, D. (1982) *Monetarist Perspectives*, Cambridge, MA: Harvard University Press.

——(1991) 'The Austrians and the Stockholm School: two failures in the development of modern macroeconomics?', in L. Jonung (ed.) *The Stockholm School of Economics Revisited*, New York: Cambridge University Press, 295–327.

Lucas, R.E. (1972) 'Expectations and the neutrality of money', *Journal of Economic Theory*, 4 (2): 103–24.

——(1975) 'An equilibrium model of the business cycle', *Journal of Political Economy*, 83 (6): 1113–44.

——(1980) 'Methods and problems in business cycle theory', *Journal of Money, Credit and Banking*, 12 (4, part 2): 696–715.

——(1983) 'Understanding business cycles', *Studies in Business Cycle Theory*, Cambridge, MA: MIT Press, 215–39.

——(1987) *Models of Business Cycles*, Oxford: Blackwell.

Lucas, R.E. and Sargent, T. (1978) 'After Keynesian macroeconomics', in *After the Phillips Curve: Persistence of High Inflation and High Unemployment*, Boston, MA: Federal Reserve Bank of Boston, 49–72.

Mises, L. von (1957) *Theory and History*, New Haven, CT: Yale University Press.

——(1966) *Human Action*, 3rd edn, New York: Henry Regnery.

Muth, J. (1961) 'Rational expectations and the theory of price movements', *Econometrica*, 29 (3): 315–35.

Nishiyama, C. (1984) 'Introduction', in C. Nishiyama and K. Leube (eds) *The Essence of Hayek*, Stanford, CA: Hoover Institution Press, xxxvii–lxviii.

O'Driscoll, G.P. (1979) 'Rational expectations, politics, and stagflation', in M.J. Rizzo (ed.) *Time, Uncertainty, and Disequilibrium*, Lexington, MA: D.C. Heath, 153–76.

O'Driscoll, G.P. and Rizzo, M.J. (1985) *The Economics of Time and Ignorance*, Oxford: Basil Blackwell.

Paqué, K.-H. (1985) 'How far is Vienna from Chicago?', *Kyklos*, 38 (3): 412–34.

Pesaran, M.H. (1989) *The Limits to Rational Expectations*, New York: Basil Blackwell.

Rosenstein-Rodan, P.N. (1934) 'The role of time in economic theory', *Economica*, 1 (February): 77–97.

Rosner, P. (1994) 'Is Hayek's theory of business cycles an Austrian theory?', in J. Birner and R. van Zijp (eds) *Hayek, Co-Ordination and Evolution*, New York: Routledge, 51–66.

Runde, J. (1988) 'Subjectivism, psychology, and the modern Austrians', in P.E. Earl (ed.) *Psychological Economics*, Boston, MA: Kluwer, 101–20.

Runde, J. and Torr, C. (1985) 'Divergent expectations and rational expectations', *South African Journal of Economics*, 53 (3): 217–25.

Salerno, J. (1990) 'Ludwig von Mises as social rationalist', *Review of Austrian Economics*, 4: 26–54.

Scheide, J. (1986) 'New classical and Austrian business cycle theory: is there a difference?', *Weltwirtschaftliches Archiv*, 122 (3): 575–98.

Smith, B. (1996) 'The connectionist mind: a study of Hayekian psychology', in S. Frowen (ed.) *Hayek, the Economist and Social Philosopher*, New York: St Martin's.

Snowden, B., Vane, H. and Wynarczyk, P. (1994) *A Modern Guide to Macroeconomics*, Aldershot: Edward Elgar.

Streit, M. (1993) 'Cognition, competition, and catallaxy: in memory of F.A. v. Hayek', *Constitutional Political Economy*, 4 (2): 223–62.

Thomsen, E.F. (1992) *Prices and Knowledge*, New York: Routledge.

Timmermann, A. (1994) 'Can agents learn to form rational expectations? Some results on convergence and stability of learning in the UK stock market', *Economic Journal*, 104 (July): 777–97.

Vanberg, V.J. (1993) 'Rational choice, rule-following and institutions', in U. Mäki, B. Gustafsson and C. Knudsen (eds) *Rationality, Institutions and Economic Methodology*, London: Routledge, 171–200.

——(1994) *Rules and Choice in Economics*, London: Routledge.

Vaughn, K.I. (1994) *Austrian Economics in America: The Migration of a Tradition*, Cambridge: Cambridge University Press.

Visser, H. (1991) *Modern Monetary Theory*, Aldershot: Edward Elgar.

Vries, R.P. de (1994) 'The place of Hayek's theory of mind and perception in the history of philosophy and psychology', in J. Birner and R. van Zijp (eds) *Hayek, Co-Ordination and Evolution*, New York: Routledge, 311–22.

Weimer, W.B. (1982) 'Hayek's approach to the problems of complex phenomena: an introduction to the theoretical psychology of *The Sensory Order*', in W.B. Weimer and D. Palermo (eds) *Cognition and the Symbolic Processes*, vol. II, Hillsdale, NJ: Lawrence Erlbaum, 241–85.

Zappia, C. (1995) 'Private information, contractual arrangements and Hayek's knowledge problem', paper presented at the conference on 'Austrians in Debate', Amsterdam.

Zijp, R. van (1993) *Austrian and New Classical Business Cycle Theories*, Brookfield, VT: Edward Elgar.

Zijp, R. van and Visser, H. (1994) 'Mathematical formalization and the domain of economics: the case of Hayek and new classical economics', in J. Birner and R. van Zijp (eds) *Hayek, Co-Ordination and Evolution*, New York: Routledge, 67–93.

11

ON AUSTRIAN AND NEO-INSTITUTIONALIST ECONOMICS

Nicolai J. Foss

ON THE DISTINCTIVENESS OF AUSTRIAN ECONOMICS

There seem to be two dominant interpretations of the distinctiveness of the Austrian school of economics. One of them is what may be called 'the mainstream interpretation'. Roughly, it is as follows. The distinctiveness of the Austrian school was more a matter of a methodological stance than it was a matter of substantive theorizing. Moreover, the sound Austrian variations on the overall neoclassical theme (such as opportunity costs and intertemporal equilibrium) were gradually incorporated in mainstream economics. What was not incorporated in the mainstream was the distinctive anti-historical and aprioristic methodological stance, shared by Austrians as diverse in many respects as Menger and Mises.

In this reading, the Austrians were primarily distinctive because they saw economics as a matter of spinning out long chains of deduction from a few incontestable axioms (whether given as a matter of introspective certainty or as a matter of incontestable empirical generalizations). Such aloof apriorism naturally excluded a serious concern with empirical reality; in fact, the blindness of Austrian theorists to the realities of the Depression in the 1930s was one of many factors that caused the extinction of the school.

Though not doubting that the Austrians were different in a basic methodological sense, proponents of the second dominant interpretation prefer to highlight an overriding concern with *subjectivism* as the *differentia specifica* of the Austrian school.[1] This interpretation is most notably represented by the modern heirs to older Austrian thought. For example, Israel Kirzner argues that Menger 'glimpsed a radically subjectivist way of understanding the determination of economic phenomena' (Kirzner 1994: xii). However, this 'way of understanding' was not fully understood by the Austrians *themselves* until the advent of the socialist calculation debate made the Austrians aware of their essential distinctiveness (see also Kirzner 1988).

In this chapter, I introduce a third possible understanding of the Austrian school's distinctiveness. It is an attempt that differs both from the modern Austrian emphasis on subjectivism and the mainstream focus on methodology and, though I do not wish to reject these two dominant interpretations per se, they have their weak points. For example, the modern Austrian interpretation of the thematic unity of the Austrian school as a consistent subjectivist, disequilibrium view of economic activities is very much a matter of rational reconstruction. It has its clear problems in connection with Wieser's work or Hayek's early work. On the other hand, the mainstream interpretation (really, caricature) of the Austrians as aloof a priorists simply does not stand up to scrutiny. This is perhaps best argued by presenting the broad outlines of an alternative reading of the Austrian school.

In my reading, the distinctiveness of the Austrians is just as much a matter of a fundamental concern with institutions. As I see it, the Austrians wanted not only an economics *with* institutions, but also an economics *of* institutions. Thus, they wished to make institutions an *explanandum* to economic analysis, rather than at most a part of the explanatory apparatus. In this aim, they clearly anticipate modern *neo-institutionalist economics*. In other words, one way to approach the distinctiveness of the Austrian school is to argue that in some important dimensions, and in contrast to the other marginalist schools, it anticipated some central concerns of contemporary neo-institutionalism; concerns that for a long time made the Austrian school very distinctive indeed. I defend this theme in this chapter, but also argue that modern neo-institutionalists may still have something to learn from the Austrians.

My suggestion that there are important links between an interest in institutions and Austrian economics is not an entirely new one. Almost two decades ago, William Jaffé referred to Menger's economics as 'in a broad sense institutional economics' (Jaffé 1976: 520). Moreover, there is considerable assent today that the theme of institutions was never absent from Austrian theorizing, in marked contrast to mainstream economics (Schotter 1981; Prisching 1987; Hodgson 1993; Langlois 1992). However, these suggestions remain rather underdeveloped in the literature. To present a fuller picture is one of the chief aims of this chapter. But I shall do more than that.

First, I shall concentrate on the role of the socialist calculation debate – and therefore on the role of Mises and Hayek – in the evolution of Austrian economics. Arguably, it was during this debate that the Austrians realized that their attempt to come to grips with real-world institutions ran counter to the market socialists' starting point in the abstract Walrasian model. Second, I also briefly discuss the much more speculative issue of what we may call the opportunity costs of theory choice: what would have happened to economic theory if the Austrian school had not been virtually crushed in the 1930s? To provide some background for the discussion, I begin by very broadly discussing modern neo-institutionalist economics.

NEO-INSTITUTIONALISM

Strictly speaking, all kinds of economics proceed with reference to some institutions and/or organizations even though, in some cases, that reference may be to a highly stylized vision of the exogenously defined market institution, with firms conceptualized as production functions. What is essential is whether institutions are somehow made endogenous. A pertinent distinction is the one between *institutions* and *organizations*. Following Hayek (1973), I here think of institutions as spontaneously emerged regularities in behaviour that are shared among and agreed upon by members of a society (for instance, moral rules). Organizations, on the other hand, are entities that are planned – in principle – by identifiable persons for an explicit purpose (for instance, firms or socialist economies). After a slow beginning from several postwar influences,[2] the economics *of* institutions and organizations has been very rapidly expanding since the mid-1970s. Very broadly speaking, this neo-institutionalism may be thought of as the body of economic thought in which the emergence and existence of institutions and organizations are approached with economic tools.

This broad definition should not suppress the fact that neo-institutionalism is characterized by strong diversity. Thus, it includes transaction cost economics (Coase 1937; Williamson 1991), agency theory (Pratt and Zeckhauser 1985), property rights theory (Coase 1960; Alchian 1965), law and economics, and the game-theoretic approach to institutions (Schotter 1981; Sugden 1986). As well as the attempt to endogenize institutions, these diverse streams are united by methodological individualism and an efficiency orientation. This sets neo-institutionalism apart from the 'old' institutionalism of Veblen, Commons and Ayres (Hodgson 1993).

Several surveys of neo-institutionalism now exist (for instance, Hodgson 1993; Knudsen 1993), but it is clear from a comparison of these that there is little agreement about what precisely neo-institutionalism entails. To Thráinn Eggertson (1990) neo-institutionalism is generalized neoclassical economics in the Coase, Alchian, Demsetz property-rights tradition. For Richard Langlois (1986b), on the other hand, one of the primary conditions for earning the title seems to be whether the relevant theory is *sceptical* towards neoclassical theory. These are extreme examples, but it is not completely off the mark to say that neo-institutionalism is better characterized by its explanandum, namely institutions and organizations, than by the character of its explanatory apparatus.

However, there is at least one convenient way of putting in perspective all neo-institutionalist theories – namely, to say that they all represent *some* break with the classical general equilibrium model. As is well known, the general equilibrium model in its classical formulation operates with only the market institution, has no room for transaction costs and collapses all intertemporal economic activity into the present through the contingent contract construction (Debreu 1959). One way to use this model is simply to say that it describes a setting in which the concerns of neo-institutionalists are largely irrelevant. If we wish to introduce institutions other than the market institution, we have to bring the model closer to reality in some way.

One such way is to introduce transaction costs, that is, the costs of defining, enforcing and exchanging property rights. Among other things, this implies that with a positive rate of discount some contingencies will be left out of contracts. Another, and more radical, way to approach reality is to introduce bounded rationality. This implies that agents simply will not have the wits to optimally enter into all the potentially very complicated, long and interlocking contracts. As a result, they have to rely on other institutions. The third, and most radical, possibility is to introduce 'genuine' uncertainty in the sense of uncompleteable lists of contingencies. This has the same consequence as in the case of bounded rationality: under uncertainty, flexibility is needed, and some institutions may be responses to this demand.

All these possibilities imply some 'market failure' relative to the full general equilibrium model, but they also point to different degrees of the radicality of the break with the formal core of neoclassical economics. In the following two sections, I briefly discuss what may be called the neoclassical version of neo-institutionalism, namely the property rights approach, and then turn to a brief discussion of more heterodox varieties of neo-institutionalism. As I shall later argue, the Austrians anticipated aspects of both of these two strands of neo-institutionalism.

NEOCLASSICAL NEO-INSTITUTIONALISM: THE PROPERTY RIGHTS APPROACH

To the basic neoclassical setting, property rights economics adds the concept after which it is named. Property rights are the agents' rights to the use of resources, as regulated by the laws, norms and mores of society. The system of existing property rights determines how the costs and benefits of actions are allocated among agents (Coase 1960). In a stationary world there are no transaction and information costs, and solving 'the economic problem of society' (Hayek 1945) is only a matter of computation. Agents know all the relevant 'data' confronting them, and the rules of the game as given by the structure of property rights are enforceable at no cost. In the context of the property rights approach, there is a genuine economic problem, precisely because agents do not have immediate and full knowledge of changing economic circumstances, and because it is costly to define, enforce and exchange property rights, including searching for contract partners, negotiating contracts and enforcing them.

Transaction and information costs introduce new constraints. They produce non-price rationing of resources and prevent the full definition and enforcement of property rights. However, agents' maximizing responses to these constraints produce efficient outcomes at an individual level as well as at a systemic level. Opportunities for gain exist for agents who adopt institutions that economize with the costs of information and transacting. Markets are low-cost institutions for handling the information and transaction costs implied by the division of labour; firms are special forms of market arrangements – namely contractual coalitions between input owners which arise to minimize the incentive problems associated with team production (Alchian and Demsetz 1972).

In its property rights manifestation neo-institutional economics is a generalization of neoclassical economics, and more so in a substantial than in a methodical sense. Substantially, it is more general, since standard neoclassical economics may be argued to be a special case of the property rights approach. For example, the model described in Debreu (1959) is valid in a property rights setting under standard assumptions on convexity, *plus* the assumptions that property rights are costlessly defined, enforced and exchanged. It is therefore not generally permissible to use the Debreu model as a normative standard; this implies the fallacy of comparing real-world arrangements with unattainable 'Nirvanas' (Demsetz 1969). Methodologically, however, the property rights approach is distinctly neoclassical in focusing only on efficient outcomes – in terms of individual decisions, contracts and aggregate outcomes.

This implies that the property rights approach does not examine:

- how agents are able to adopt decision rules that produce maximizing decisions
- how consistency arises between decisions that are taken independently
- how property rights (institutions) are defined and changed under the impact of changes (that is to say institutional change is not directly addressed – institutional change merely enters in the guise of comparative institutionalism, so that different institutions are compared in terms of efficiency for different parameters)
- how changes arise and which agents are instrumental in carrying out changes, including institutional innovations (that is to say, the drivers behind institutional change – such as changing technology and entrepreneurship – are not investigated).

In other words, processes of change on all relevant levels are present in an implicit way at most. Changes are taken as given, and the adjustment processes induced by change are forced into a comparative institutional, functionalist mode of explanation (see Demsetz 1967). Changes in parameters are directly associated with corresponding (timeless) changes in property rights/institutions, no interest being paid to adjustment processes between these structures/institutions. This neoclassical mode of explanation is not only characteristic of the property rights approach, it may also be found in agency theory and – though less unambiguously – in Williamson's brand of transaction cost economics.

HETERODOX NEO-INSTITUTIONALISM

The more heterodox strands of neo-institutionalism – such as the game-theory approach of Schotter and Sugden – are set apart from more orthodox strands by their position on the process issue. According to Langlois' (1986b) heterodox reading of neo-institutionalism, an attempt to model economic phenomena in terms of process, rather than solely in terms of equilibrium, is one of the three defining characteristics of neo-institutionalism.[3]

The wish to study process per se can be rationalized in a number of ways. First, a process story provides one part of an invisible-hand explanation (Ullmann-Margalit 1978; Koppl 1992); it is a theory of how the explanandum phenomenon (an institution, a constellation of prices and quantities) arose in a way that was largely unintended by individual actors. The game-theoretic approach to institutions (Schotter 1981; Sugden 1986) typically relies on process stories that are cast within an invisible-hand explanatory mould. Second, process theories capture what really happens 'out there'; they are better able than neoclassical economics to theoretically approach the dynamic adjustment process, processes of technological change and, not the least important, to explain institutional change (North 1990). Third, process theories may provide a more general framework within which neoclassical economics may be obtained as a special case. In fact, this has been convincingly argued by the evolutionary theorists Richard Nelson and Sidney Winter (1982). Inspired by them, many heterodox neo-institutionalists have chosen to focus their process reasoning in terms of the evolutionary metaphor (for instance, North 1990).

Closely related to the process issue, and perhaps even more fundamental, is the issue of behavioural assumptions. The defining characteristic of heterodox neo-institutionalism may be taken to be that it breaks with the neoclassical maximizing assumption. In its place is put Herbert Simon's concept of bounded rationality or rule following (Sugden 1986). This implies that institutions are more than simply side constraints on utility-maximizing individuals; institutions are also the shared behavioural rules and heuristics that agents consciously or unconsciously follow.[4] The basic logic is that uncertainty and bounded rationality produce rule following, and various critical mass and selection effects operate to make some rules general and shared among agents.

AUSTRIAN INSTITUTIONALISM

Not so very long ago, the prevailing wisdom was that American institutionalists and German historicists were practically the sole economists to pay much attention to real world institutions. However, the prevailing wisdom was wrong, primarily because it neglected the existence of a distinct Austrian institutionalism, which clearly implied that institutions should be approached using economic tools. In this respect, the older Austrian institutionalism was a precursor of modern neo-institutionalism. To be sure, there are other precursors to modern neo-institutionalism. For example, the philosophers of the Scottish Enlightenment, particularly David Hume, are often invoked as the patron saints of neo-institutionalism (Sugden 1986). However, I assert that the Austrians were by far the most important precursors.

Arguably, some of the Austrian anticipations of neo-institutionalist insights may be traced back to the older Austrians, primarily to Carl Menger and Eugen von Böhm-Bawerk. The process approach to market activities, a part of heterodox neo-institutionalism and normally thought of as pioneered by Hayek and Mises (Kirzner 1973, 1979), can certainly be seen as having its roots in Menger's work (Streissler 1972). Hayek's approach to cultural evolution, which has strongly influenced Schotter and Sugden, is in important respects anticipated by Menger's thoughts on the same subject. Menger's discussion of marketability and the bid-ask spread in *Grundsätze* (Menger 1871: chapter 7) implicitly introduced transaction costs. In the methodological dimension he elaborated the Scottish distinction between 'organic' (spontaneously emerged) and 'pragmatic' (designed) institutions, which have been strongly emphasized in recent neo-institutionalist work (Schotter 1981; Williamson 1991). Böhm-Bawerk was probably the first economist ever to argue that what was exchanged on the market was not physical goods per se, but property rights (Böhm-Bawerk 1881). Both he and Menger recognized that property rights change predictably under the impact of changing scarcities, thus anticipating the perhaps central conclusion of modern property rights economics (Menger 1871: chapter 2; Böhm-Bawerk 1881).

However, in spite of the fact that much of Hayek's and Mises' work may be traced to their forebears, theirs are in many respects the most complete Austrian anticipations of modern neo-institutionalism. To substantiate this claim, I will discuss the socialist calculation debate. This debate is brought into the discussion for a number of reasons. First, it was preeminently a debate about the essentially neo-institutional theme of the efficiency of alternative ways of organizing economic activities. Second, it is during the debate that the Austrians are seen most visibly in their role as precursors to neo-institutionalism, and third, the debate was instrumental in making the Austrians aware of their own distinctiveness. Specifically, the Austrian process approach matured during the debate (Lavoie 1985), but it also made the Austrians aware that their research style and the economic phenomena they wished to conceptualize differed significantly from those of their Walrasian opponents.

THE SOCIALIST CALCULATION DEBATE

Some neo-institutionalists have recently noted the affinities of Austrian insights in the calculation debates to modern theory (for instance, Milgrom and Roberts 1992: 51), but I shall be more explicit about where the points of similarity lie. Specifically, the relevant Austrian insights can be summarized in the following closely connected points:

- the insight that welfare assessments of institutions and outcomes should not be based on a 'Nirvana approach', but should be 'comparative institutional' (Demsetz 1969)
- the importance of change for understanding institutions and organizations
- an understanding of the principal–agent relation and the importance of property rights, morally hazardous behaviour and incentives more generally.

Comparative institutionalism

To start with the general methodical point, it is apparent from Mises' (1920) opening salvo in the debate, and also in later Austrian contributions such as Hayek (1945) and Mises' restatement of his position in *Human Action* (1949), that what really annoyed the Austrians was their socialist opponents' use of unrealistic and unattainable social ideals – Nirvanas – as standards of comparison. Naturally, on such standards, capitalism would appear inefficient and wasteful: 'The "anarchy" of production appears wasteful when contrasted with the planning of the *omniscient* state' (Mises 1949: 692).

Being the first to insist that socialist economic organization should also be approached with the tools of economic analysis, and that idealized, institutionless models should be banned as standards of comparison, the Austrians were the first economists to consistently pursue a programme of comparative institutionalism. For example, the Austrians implicitly criticized models such as Oskar Lange's version of market socialism for not conforming to the stipulations of a method of comparative institutionalism (Lange 1936/7). This is because the socialist economists (a) neglected the role of incentives (Mises 1936; Hayek 1940), (b) made unrealistic assumptions about the amounts of knowledge that agents can possess (particularly the plan authorities), and (c) formulated their reasoning within static models that obscured all significant economic problems. Or, in a more compact formulation, by basing theory on the economics of the stationary state, market socialists such as Oskar Lange could suppress the knowledge and incentive problems of real economies.

Economic change and institutions

Mises, on the other hand, insisted that 'the problem of economic calculation is of economic dynamics; it is no problem of economic statics' (Mises 1936: 121). Hayek later expressed essentially the same point when he argued that 'economic problems arise always and only in consequence of change' (Hayek 1945: 82). As Mises (1936, 1949) recognized, in a changeless stationary state, the political authorities could implement the existing allocation as its plan and everything would continue the way it was before.

The lesson to be drawn from this Misesian insight is the general one that it is only when economic change is introduced that economic organization is determinate. In the absence of change, it is not possible to discriminate on grounds of efficiency. The overall Austrian conclusion that emerged from this insight was that, in the presence of economic change, economic organization on the basis of private property and a price system was strictly superior to central planning. In general, different types of economic organization arose – found their rationale – because of their ability to adapt efficiently to (unanticipated) change. This Austrian insight into the relation between change and economic organization is of a wider applicability and can be given various interpretations.

One of these is the modern Austrian interpretation that we need the entrepreneurial market process to cope with the knowledge problems introduced by economic change (Kirzner 1973, 1979), and that market process performs most efficiently when fuelled by well-defined and protected private property rights which provide appropriate incentives for entrepreneurial alertness (Kirzner 1973, 1979; Mises 1949). Another and perhaps more pertinent interpretation is to understand the Austrian insight as anticipating the point that, without change, there would be no transaction and information costs.[5] That is, in the absence of the knowledge problems introduced by a changing economic reality there would be no costs of discovering contractual partners, drafting and executing contracts, monitoring production, constructing contractual safeguards or judging quality. In the absence of transaction cost, the choice between price-mediated market transactions and firm hierarchies would be indeterminate. As the Austrians recognized, in real world economies, institutions like markets and hierarchies perform the function of economizing on bounded rationality and dispersed information, precisely the factors that ultimately underlie transaction and information costs.

In a doctrinal perspective, this indicates a link between the Austrian insights in the calculation debate and the Coasian insights in economic organization, though it is not a link that was recognized either by the

Austrians or Coase, probably because they had focused on different institutions. Where Hayek (1945) praised 'the marvel' of the price system, Coase established (eight years earlier) that the reason firms existed was because the 'telecommunications system' of prices did not perform costlessly. This may lead one to view the analysis of Coase and that of Hayek as strongly opposed, but they are not. It is only in the kind of dynamic economic reality visualized by the Austrians that Coase's argument acquires its full force.

Property rights, moral hazard, incentives and agency theory

Although anticipations of modern property rights economics may be found in the works of Menger and Böhm-Bawerk, it is particularly in Mises' works that we find the most complete Austrian theory on the subject. For example, in *Human Action* there is a very clear statement of 'tragedy of the commons'-type problems, and the claim that more precise definitions of property rights – 'rescinding the institutional barriers preventing the full operation of private ownership' – will eliminate such problems (Mises 1949: 652). However, Mises also understood that property rights are composite rights. As he noted, rights to appropriate the rents and profits of assets are crucial to the efficient working of the economy (see, for instance, Mises 1936: 182). One of the reasons why 'the artificial market' of market socialists will not work is precisely because the transfer of goods between socialist managers is not equivalent to the transfer of goods in a capitalist economy. Under socialism it is not full property rights that are transferred; prices and incentives are accordingly perverse. On property rights grounds, it is inherently wrong to believe that 'the controllers of the different industrial units' in a socialist economy can be instructed 'to act *as if* they were entrepreneurs in a capitalistic state' (Mises 1936: 120; see also 1949: 702–5).

Mises most explicitly anticipates modern developments – specifically the modern agency theory of how financial markets (admittedly imperfectly) monitor management – when he points out that for the efficient functioning of the economy, capital markets are absolutely crucial. They alone ensure that the calculation problems in a dynamic economy can be solved through 'dissolving, extending, transforming, and limiting existing undertakings, and establishing new undertakings' (Mises 1936: 215). Only unhampered capital markets and markets for corporate control can perform the two crucial tasks of monitoring management – a principal–agent problem – and pricing assets correctly (*ibid.*: 122). This is to be contrasted with Lange's assertion about 'private corporation executives, who practically are responsible to nobody' (Lange 1936/7: 110). Although modern theory does not imply that markets can solve the agency problem perfectly, it would be more on Mises' side than on Lange's.

One of the modern ramifications of the property rights approach is agency theory. In the course of the calculation debate, the Austrians anticipated several insights from this theory. As a general matter, they insisted that it did *not* follow that, under socialism, individual managers (agents) would act in the interest of the principals, that is the planning authorities (see, for instance, Hayek 1940). They identified the problem of risk allocation between principals and agents: under socialism, managers would be either inefficiently risk averse or risk loving in the face of career concerns and/or the presence of an institution (the planning authorities) which could act as an insurance institution and take over the moral hazard of individual managers (Mises 1936: 122; Hayek 1940: 199).

In contrast, the market socialists had no grasp of the principal–agent problem or, if they did, they effectively assumed it away. As has often been pointed out, Lange (1936/7) implicitly assumed continuous incentive compatibility between the individual managers and the planning authorities. As Mises saw it, one of the primary virtues of the market system organized on the basis of private ownership was precisely that it strongly mitigated potential agency problems. In sum, Mises and Hayek anticipated a number of themes that are perhaps closest associated with neoclassical neo-institutionalism, themes that are particularly visible in the context of the socialist calculation debate. However, they also anticipated the more heterodox varieties of modern neo-institutionalism.

PROCESS, ORGANIZATIONS AND INSTITUTIONS

Although it is usually Mises and Hayek's later (post-calculation debate) contributions that are invoked in discussions of the distinct Austrian process approach (for example, Kirzner 1973, 1979), Mises paid much attention to process issues in his earlier work. His property rights arguments are all formulated in the context of a process view of the market which has a distinctly evolutionary character. This is illustrated by the emphasis that Mises puts on change and differential firm growth.[6] Furthermore, although Mises clearly anticipated a number of insights from agency theory, he did *not* say that managers only differ in terms of how efficiently they pursue their principals' interests, as is customary in modern agency theory. Entrepreneurs' and managers' talents differ; there is an asymmetrical distribution of entrepreneurial competence (see Pelikan 1988). It is the market which selects among entrepreneurial ventures:

> The more successfully [an entrepreneur] speculates, the more means of production are at his disposal, the greater becomes his influence on the business of society. The less successfully he speculates, the smaller becomes his property, the less becomes his influence in business. If he

loses everything by speculation he disappears from the ranks of those who are called to the direction of economic affairs.

(Mises 1936: 182)

This is clearly a kind of selection argument formulated in terms of differential growth rates of firms. As in evolutionary theory in general, it is the rationality of the system as a whole that is important, rather than the rationality of individual market participants (see Alchian 1950). As Mises puts it, entrepreneurs 'earn profit not because they are clever in performing their tasks, but because they are more clever or less clumsy than other people are. They are not infallible and often blunder' (Mises 1974: 114). That is to say 'Even in a world of stupid men there would still be profits' (Alchian 1950: 20).

The process theme begins to figure in Hayek's work from his famous essay on 'Economics and knowledge' (1937). It continues with his later theory of cultural evolution, which is essentially an evolutionary theory of institutional change (Hayek 1973). As Hayek argued, the theory of equilibrium is an exercise in means–ends logic (Hayek 1937), and this logic does not incorporate any causal 'statements about how knowledge is acquired and communicated' (ibid.: 53). It is therefore insufficient for understanding processes of change. In particular, economics is unable to rationalize how equilibrium emerges. In other words, because of its overly narrow behavioural focus, economists are unable to address processes of change. Modern heterodox neo-institutionalists fully concur with these propositions (Langlois 1986b; North 1990; Knudsen 1993).

However, in the essay Hayek identifies rationality with means–ends logic, which means that learning (including the set-up of *new* means–ends structures) cannot be a rational activity. That may be one reason why he turns away later in the same essay from his suggestion that economists pay more attention to learning processes. As Kirzner has pointed out, this creates a problem because if we abstract from learning processes, there is 'nothing in the logic governing the set of choices made by market participants at one date to account for the set of choices they make at future dates' (Kirzner 1979: 27). If we only look at Hayek's work in technical economics, we must conclude that he leaves the problem unresolved. However, extending the focus to his later interdisciplinary work in political philosophy and jurisprudence allows us to construct an argument that Hayek in fact has a sort of theory that unites allocation and learning.

An organizing theme in Hayek's extensive postwar work is his opposition to what he identifies as an essentially Cartesian conception of rationality, that is the conception of rationality as solely a matter of a logical deduction from explicit and given premises. In contrast, Hayek identifies – and endorses – a long philosophical tradition, primarily associated with Scottish Enlightenment philosophers such as David Hume, Adam Ferguson and

Adam Smith, in which rationality meant 'the capacity to recognize truth when one meets it, rather than a capacity of deductive reasoning from explicit premises' (Hayek 1967: 84). In other words, rationality should be identified with learning as well as with rule-following behaviour. What this amounts to is a rejection of the conception of rationality represented by the strict situational logic of 'the pure logic of choice' in which the individual is merely a 'zero' (in Popper's terminology), and adoption of a much more historical view of the individual agent. It is very much the same conceptualization that appears in the work of recent heterodox neo-institutionalists (for example, Sugden 1986).

Although action in such a conception is no longer purely a matter of an individual 'zero' being subsumed under 'the logic of the situation', external influences are still important; action may be constrained and partly determined by norms and institutions. Furthermore, much behaviour may be governed by largely *tacit* rules. However, such social formations as rules, norms and institutions can be explained historically – but informed by economic theory – in terms of the earlier actions of other agents, coupled with various evolutionary and invisible-hand explanations (Ullmann-Margalit 1978). Such 'institutional individualism' is one way in which the demands placed on individual agents' epistemic powers can be relaxed and made more realistic – rules, norms and institutions bring stability and foresight into the social landscape (Langlois 1986b).[7]

IS THERE STILL ANYTHING TO BE LEARNED?

I have suggested that, in several dimensions, the Austrians were precursors to modern institutionalism. Does this mean that all of the sound Austrian thinking on institutions has been incorporated into modern neo-institutionalist thought (whether orthodox or heterodox)? In other words, is there still anything to be learned from the work of Hayek and Mises?

Modern (neo-)Austrian economists (Kirzner 1973, 1979; Lavoie 1985) have argued that the real distinctiveness of Mises and Hayek lies in their pioneering a process approach to market activity. But this is not the whole of the story. Another source of distinctiveness is their *linking* a process view to an economic approach to institutions. In effect, they argued that when looking for the rationales of institutions, a process view of market activity contains a number of pertinent insights. For example, in the context of the calculation debate, Mises argued that under stationary conditions, it is not possible to discriminate among institutions and organizations on the grounds of efficiency. This explicit weaving together of the themes of process and institutions is something that modern neo-institutionalist and evolutionary thought still has to achieve,[8] and it is perhaps here that modern theorists may gain particular inspiration from Mises' and Hayek's theories. I briefly expand on this conjecture in the following.

At the centre of Mises' and Hayek's thinking is the ubiquity of change in the social domain and, when discussing change, they have in mind *unanticipated* change (see Hayek 1945). Anticipated change may, of course, influence economic outcomes – for example, an anticipated change in the relative price of some raw material will surely induce the usual substitution effects in consumption and production – but anticipated changes will not normally make a difference for economic organization and institutions – for example, anticipated change may be incorporated in contracting. Intuitively, the implication is that various kinds of organization and institution derive their efficiency attributes from their ability to handle unanticipated change, that is from their flexibility in this respect.

The economic problem for society is, therefore, not one of static optimal allocation within *given* means–ends structures, as it is in Lange's stationary state *and* in much recent neo-institutional economics, particularly of the neoclassical variety. The economic problem in a neo-institutionalist context is not necessarily finding that institutional or organizational form which minimizes the transaction costs of organizing given inputs to produce given outputs at a given point of time. Rather, it may be a matter of finding the form which maximizes adaptive efficiency, particularly the ability to adapt flexibly to unanticipated change, and this adaptive efficiency may sacrifice present static transaction costs. What this points to is the potential for a productive liaison between evolutionary economics and neo-institutional economics of the transaction cost variety. Such a liaison would mean a revival for the Austrian idea of placing economic organization in a dynamic setting. In other words, contemporary theorists may still find inspiration in the writings of Mises and Hayek. Given the fertility of their ideas and their closeness to modern theory, why was the Austrian school effectively eliminated as an independent theoretical force in the end of the 1930s?

FORMALISM AND INSTITUTIONS

After some initial successes at the beginning of the 1930s (for example, the success of Hayek's business cycle theory), the Austrian school was virtually extinct by the end of the decade, after a number of confrontations with Knight, Keynes, Sraffa and the market socialists. The impression easily conveyed by these episodes is that the Austrian school succumbed to the forces of the cumulative development of better theories. This view is decidedly too naïve; many economists would now recognize the essential soundness of the Austrian arguments in the calculation debate. Forces other than the search for more verisimilar theories were at work; forces that may be most easily identified by taking one more look at the socialist calculation debate.

The rise of formalism and Lange's socialism

Before Mises wrote his famous 1920 article, economic approaches to the economics of socialism were largely institutionalist and historicist, in the sense that the universality of basic economic categories (rationality, incentives – even scarcity) was denied (Lavoie 1986). Although Mises' point about the necessity of pricing could be seen as simply an application of basic microeconomic theory, at a different level it can be seen as emerging from that position which Menger had defended during the *Methodenstreit*: that the universal fact of rational action under scarcity implies necessary and systematic relations, which are invariant relative to spatio-temporal characteristics, and which therefore must also hold under socialism.

In such an interpretation, there is no sharp distinction between Mises-as-methodologist and Mises-as-theorist. However, a division between these two roles was exactly what Oskar Lange tried to impute to Mises, when he argued that according to Mises

> the economic principles of choice between different alternatives are applicable only to a special institutional set-up, i.e., to a society which recognizes private ownership of the means of production. It has been maintained . . . that all economic laws have only historico-relative validity. But it is most surprising to find this institutionalist view supported by a prominent member of the Austrian school, which did so much to emphasize the universal validity of the fundamental principles of economic theory.
>
> (Lange 1936/7: 62)

That would be 'most surprising' indeed, if it were true. However, it is not. Mises consistently argued throughout his career that choice-theoretical principles can be applied to any society.

Lange's misrepresentations were perhaps not as much an attempt to tease Mises as they were a clear expression of the rise of formalism. The drivers behind this are many: the growing role of quantitative economics and the emergence of econometrics with its institutional manifestation in the Econometric Society, the general spread of Walrasianism, and the attempt to place the theory of firms and industries under a more 'rigorous' footing than Marshall had been able to (Loasby 1994). As Koopmans (1957) and Nelson (1981) observed, the socialist calculation debate also played an important role in the rise of formalism, particularly with regard to welfare economics.

Assuredly, there is much to be said in favour of formalization, but it is rather hard to deny that an initial side effect of the rise of formalism was that economists were increasingly directed away from gaining a realistic understanding of real institutions. A transformation of how economists viewed their science accompanied the rise of formalism: neoclassical economists increasingly began to let their conceptualizations be wholly limited by whatever analytical armoury was present. In the context of economic policy, such an attitude easily leads to what Schumpeter called 'the Ricardian vice'; the tendency to jump directly from very abstract models to policy implications.

Clearly, Lange is a practitioner of this vice. He does not hesitate to jump from abstract propositions about a model without, for example, transaction costs, uncertainty and intertemporal trade, to claiming this model of direct applicability. By contrast, the Austrian conceptualization of problems indicated gaps to be filled in existing theory, for example it was conceptualizations of the actual market process as a process of learning that led Hayek (1937) to doubt the validity of the equilibrium approach.

In his famous essay, Lange defines his task in the following way:

> It is . . . the purpose of the present essay to elucidate the way in which the allocation of resources is effected by trial and error on a competitive market, and to find out whether a similar trial and error procedure is not possible in a socialist economy.
>
> (Lange 1936/7: 65)

Lange then 'elucidates' this way; or rather, he undertakes an exercise in Walrasian price adjustment, essentially making use of the purely imaginary construction of the auctioneer (transformed into the planning authorities, of course). The use of this mind construct is legitimate, provided its imaginary character is kept in mind. However, the dominating impression conveyed by Lange's discussion is that Walrasian *tâtonnement* very closely mimics – 'something similar' to – what takes place on real markets (*ibid.*: section 2).

With such a formalist understanding of price formation, it is surely not surprising that Lange could answer his query of 'whether a similar trial and error procedure is not possible in a socialist economy' in the affirmative. Mises may have been too general when he argued that mathematical economists 'deal with equilibrium as if it were a real entity and not a limiting notion, a mere mental tool' (Mises 1949: 251), but such a remark is quite understandable in the light of Lange's formalist discussion. It is also quite understandable that Mises noticed that 'it is hardly possible to construe the market process in a more erroneous way' (*ibid.*: 354) than done by the market socialists.

Austrian institutionalism

A few years before Lange accused Mises of institutionalism, Hayek was criticized by Piero Sraffa (1932) for wholly neglecting the role of institutions in his theorizing and for having theorized on an excessively abstract level. So, in the middle of the 1930s, the Austrians were in the strange position of being simultaneously accused of being atheoretical institutionalist and being excessively abstract. In fact, they were neither. Since Menger, one of the prime motivations for the Austrian developments in value theory had been to understand real institutions, their *raison d'être* and functioning. However, it has become customary to think of the Austrians as aloof a priorists almost solely engaged in spinning out the logical and rather trivial implications of a few self-evident propositions – not as economists with real interest in institutions.

This means that the Austrian-ness of the Mengerian emphasis on the importance of real institutions and the need to explain them, of Mises' work on particularly monetary and credit institutions, and of Hayek's very encompassing theory of cultural evolution has been largely forgotten. The Austrians were never 'against' historical and institutional research per se. As already mentioned, Menger's 1871 contribution contains a largely historical chapter on the evolution of a monetary medium. Mises himself started out as an economic historian and his main treatise on socialism is packed with historical detail (Mises 1936). Furthermore, he was instrumental in setting up the first Austrian institute of empirical business cycle research, with Hayek serving as its first director. The Austrians argued the position that institutional and historical analysis should not – and for basic epistemological reasons could not – stand alone, but should be conducted with the use of theoretical concepts. It is a completely uncontroversial position today.

This is the historical and methodical light in which Austrian arguments in the calculation debate (on the specific level) and the extinction of the Austrian school (on the general level) should be seen. For instance, the formalist socialists misconstrued the Austrian complex property rights-based argument as atheoretical institutionalism because they had little understanding of the role that investigation of institutions played for the Austrians. In some important dimensions, the real clash in the calculation debate was between basic outlooks on the scope and method of economics. To use terminology from the evolutionary theorists, Richard Nelson and Sidney Winter (1982), the Austrians did not only conduct 'formal' theory – common opinion notwithstanding. Their theorizing was also 'appreciative', that is to say a matter of letting real institutions and processes significantly influence theorizing. It is essentially the conviction that this is a desirable and worthwhile task that today informs modern neo-institutional economics.

CONCLUDING COUNTERFACTUAL REFLECTIONS

I have argued that Mises and Hayek in a number of dimensions anticipated modern neo-institutionalism, both in its orthodox and in its heterodox guise. They basically saw institutions and organizations as something which could be approached and explained with economic tools. They marshalled a comparative institutionalism, formulated the arguably first process view of the market, linked this view to institutional and organizational change and anticipated modern neo-institutionalism in specific dimensions (for example, the principal–agent problem). Given the level of the Austrians' 'analytical technology', their small number and the fact that much of their research efforts were put into battling Keynes, Knight, Sraffa and the (market or non-market) socialists, this was a major accomplishment on their part.

The reading of Mises and Hayek presented here may lead to speculations along counterfactual lines (see Loasby 1994). For example, what were the opportunity costs of the economic profession to use an essentially static and institutionless Walrasianism as the analytical core? What would have happened to economics if Keynes, Sraffa and Knight had not virtually eliminated the Austrian school in the 1930s, if Walrasianism had not spread to the extent it did, or if Keynes had not written *The General Theory*? The 'ifs' are almost too many and the abstractions too severe to make much sense of such a *Gedanken*-experiment, but we may nevertheless venture a few guesses.

Abstracting from Walras and his followers, the two remaining marginalist traditions of importance at the turn of the century would be the English (Marshallian) and the Austrian traditions, both of which were occupied with understanding economic change, process and institutions (though in other respects they were very far apart indeed). In both these two traditions the primary motive for developing the abstract categories of economic analysis was the comprehension of reality, and they both emphasized the need for letting reality influence theorizing to a significant degree. What they would *not* have developed into, then, was the kind of institution and processless formalism that long dominated the mainstream of economics. Without assuming that economists would actually have arrived at the very same insights and analytical techniques invented and used by later neo-institutionalists, economics would nevertheless have developed along modern neo-institutionalist lines rather than the course it actually took between the wars and, say, in 1980.

In our brief counterfactual history, it would have been economists' top priority to understand the workings of real institutions with the use of economic theory. For example, the economics of socialism would not have been couched in the terms of Oskar Lange's Walrasian market socialism, but rather in terms of Mises' property rights approach and the Mises/Hayek emphasis on institutions as devices for adapting to change. Competition would not have been (mis)represented as a matter of logical consistency between a set of relations, but would have been seen in terms of active rivalry. Welfare economics would not have been plagued by the economics of Nirvana. In short, we would, on this extremely speculative reading, not have to wait until the mid-1970s or later to arrive at a realistic economic theory of institutions. We would have had something like them much earlier.

NOTES

1 Though sometimes conflated with it, this is different from the methodological issue, since subjectivism is a property of theories, not of the procedures used to generate and evaluate scientific knowledge.
2 Such as the economics of information (Stigler, Arrow), property rights economics (Alchian, Coase, Demsetz), the literature on mechanism design, behavioural research on Carnegie-Mellon University (Simon, Cyert, March), work in the 1960s on the managerial theory of the firm (Penrose, Marris, Baumol) and the early law and economics work done at the University of Chicago (Director, Coase). It should come as no big surprise that what resulted from all these influences was not a coherent set of theories.
3 The other two characteristics are a wish to work with broader conceptions of rationality than maximization and a wish to endogenize institutions.
4 Of course, there need not be any conflict between the rule conception and the side-constraint conception of institutions; traffic rules may provide an example in which the two are clearly interlocking.
5 Of course, the Austrians did not use this terminology. However, the fact that economic change is needed to rationalize transaction and information costs was recognized by Coase (1937), since it is clear from the context in which he discusses 'the costs of using the price mechanism' that these costs are knowledge costs arising from a non-stationary economic reality.
6 Interestingly, Mises' early process view differs rather significantly from the modern Austrian process view of, most prominently, Israel Kirzner (1973, 1979). Kirzner's view is not evolutionary in the sense of placing emphasis on differential adaptation.
7 This indicates that Hayek's (postwar) interest in social institutions as well as his theory of cultural evolution (institutional change) may be seen as attempts to provide an institutionally oriented answer to the coordination problem he highlighted in 1937 (Caldwell 1988; Foss 1995). According to Hayek the institutional setup of society assists the formation of coordinated states (spontaneous orders). In fact, he saw the change in this setup as an evolutionary process in which competing institutions are selected according to their ability to improve this process of coordination (Hayek 1973). Much of the intuition behind Hayek's ideas of cultural evolution and the formation of spontaneous orders has been formalized in modern game-theoretic neo-institutionalism (such as Sugden 1986).
8 Although the recent work of Douglass North (1990) may represent a beginning. For a general discussion of why transaction cost economics needs evolutionary economics, see Foss (1994).

REFERENCES

Alchian, A.A. (1950) 'Uncertainty, evolution and economic theory', in Alchian (1977).
——(1965) 'Some economics of property rights', in Alchian (1977).
——(1977) *Economic Forces at Work*, Indianapolis: Liberty Press.
Alchian, A.A. and Demsetz, H (1972) 'Production, information costs, and economic organization', in Demsetz (1988).
Böhm-Bawerk, E. von (1881) 'Whether legal rights and relationships are economic goods', in H. Sennholz (ed.) (1962) *Shorter Classics of Böhm-Bawerk*, South-Holland: Libertarian Press.

Caldwell, B.J. (1988) 'Hayek's Transformation', *History of Political Economy*, 20: 513–42.

Caldwell, B.J. and Böhm, S. (eds) (1992) *Austrian Economics: Tensions and New Directions*, Boston: Kluwer.

Coase, R. (1937) 'The nature of the firm', *Economica*, 4: 386–405.

——(1960) 'The problem of social cost', *Journal of Law and Economics*, 3: 1–44.

Debreu, G. (1959) *Theory of Value*, New York: Wiley.

Demsetz, H. (1967) 'Toward a theory of property rights', in Demsetz (1988).

——(1969) 'Information and efficiency: another viewpoint', *Journal of Law and Economics*, 10: 1–22.

——(1988) *Ownership, Control and the Firm*, Oxford: Basil Blackwell.

Eggertson, T. (1990) *Economic Behavior and Institutions*, Cambridge: Cambridge University Press.

Foss, N.J. (1994) 'Why transaction cost economics needs evolutionary economics', *Revue d'Economie Industrielle*, 68: 7–26.

——(1995) 'More on "Hayek's Transformation"', *History of Political Economy*, 27: 345–62.

Hayek, F.A. von (1937) 'Economics and knowledge', in Hayek (1948).

——(1940) 'The competitive "solution"', in Hayek (1948).

——(1945) 'The use of knowledge in society', in Hayek (1948).

——(1948) *Individualism and Economic Order*, Chicago: University of Chicago Press.

——(1967) *Studies in Philosophy, Politics and Economics*, London: Routledge & Kegan Paul.

——(1973) *Law, Legislation and Liberty*, vol. 1: *Rules and Order*, Chicago: University of Chicago Press.

Hodgson, G. (1993) 'Institutional economics: surveying the "old" and the "new"', *Metroeconomica*, 44: 1–28.

Jaffé, W. (1976) 'Menger, Jevons, and Walras de-homogenized', *Economic Inquiry*, 14: 511–24.

Kirzner, I.M. (1973) *Competition and Entrepreneurship*, Chicago: University of Chicago Press.

——(1979) *Perception, Opportunity, and Profit*, Chicago: University of Chicago Press.

——(1988) 'The economic calculation debate: lessons for Austrians', *Review of Austrian Economics*, 2: 1–18.

——(1994) *Classics in Austrian Economics: A Sampling in the History of a Tradition*, vols I–III, London: William Pickering.

Knudsen, C. (1993) 'Modelling rationality, institutions, and processes in economic theory', in U. Mäki, B. Gustafsson and C. Knudsen (eds) (1993) *Rationality, Institutions, and Economic Methodology*, London: Routledge.

Koopmans, T.C. (1957) *Three Essays on the State of Economic Science*, New York: McGraw-Hill.

Koppl, R. (1992) 'Invisible-hand explanations and neoclassical economics: towards a post-marginalist economics', *Journal of Institutional and Theoretical Economics*, 148: 292–313.

Lange, O. (1936/7) 'On the economic theory of socialism', in B.E. Lippincott (ed.) (1938) *On the Economic Theory of Socialism*, New York: McGraw-Hill, 1964.

Langlois, R.N. (ed.) (1986a) *Economics as a Process: Essays in the New Institutional Economics*, Cambridge: Cambridge University Press.

——(1986b) 'The new institutional economics: an introductory essay', in Langlois (1986a).

——(1992) 'Orders and organizations', in B. Caldwell and S. Böhm (1992).

Lavoie, D. (1985) *Rivalry and Central Planning: The Socialist Calculation Debate in Perspective*, Cambridge: Cambridge University Press.

——(1986) 'Between institutionalism and formalism: the rise and fall of the Austrian school's calculation argument: 1920–1950', working paper, Center for the Study of Market Processes, George Mason University.

Loasby, B.J. (1994) 'Missed connections and opportunities forgone: a counterfactual history of twentieth century economics', unpublished ms, University of Stirling.

Menger, C. (1871) *Principles of Economics*, New York: New York University Press, 1976.

Milgrom, P. and Roberts, J. (1992) *Economics, Organization, and Management*, Englewood Cliffs: Prentice-Hall.

Mises, L. von ([1920], 1990) *Economic Calculation in the Socialist Commonwealth*, Auburn: Ludwig von Mises Institute.

——([1936], 1981) *Socialism: An Economic and Sociological Analysis*, Indianapolis: Liberty Press.

——(1949) *Human Action*, New Haven: Yale University Press.

——(1974) *Planning for Freedom*, Illinois: Libertarian Press.

Nelson, R.R. (1981) 'Assessing private enterprise: an exegesis of tangled doctrine', *Bell Journal of Economics*, 12: 93–111.

Nelson, R.R. and Winter, S. (1982) *An Evolutionary Theory of Economic Change*, Cambridge, MA: Harvard University Press.

North, D.C. (1990) *Institutions, Institutional Change, and Economic Performance*, Cambridge: Cambridge University Press.

Pelikan, P. (1988) 'Can the imperfect innovation system of capitalism be outperformed?', in G. Dosi *et al.* (eds) *Technical Change and Economic Theory*, London: Pinter.

Pratt, J.W. and Zeckhauser, R.J. (1985) *Principals and Agents*, Boston: Boston Business School Press.

Prisching, M. (1987) 'Evolution and design of social institutions in Austrian theory', *Journal of Economic Studies*, 16: 47–62.

Schotter, A. (1981) *The Economic Theory of Social Institutions*, Cambridge: Cambridge University Press.

Sraffa, P. (1932) 'Dr. Hayek on money and capital', *Economic Journal*, 42: 42–53.

Streissler, E. (1972) 'To what extent was the Austrian school marginalist?', *History of Political Economy*, 4: 426–41.

Sugden, R. (1986) *The Economics of Rights, Cooperation and Welfare*, Oxford: Basil Blackwell.

Ullmann-Margalit, E. (1978) 'Invisible hand explanations', *Synthèse*, 39: 282–96.

Williamson, O.E. (1991) 'Economic institutions: spontaneous and intentional governance', *Journal of Law, Economics, and Organization*, 7: 159–87.

12

PRIVATE INFORMATION, CONTRACTUAL ARRANGEMENTS AND HAYEK'S KNOWLEDGE PROBLEM[1]

Carlo Zappia

The increasing interest in Hayek's theory of knowledge centres mainly on his analysis of the competitive market as a mechanism for the discovery and conveyance of privately known economic facts. The most prominent instance of this is the neo-Austrian literature, which has emphasized the dynamic aspect of market coordination through prices as the major contribution to economic theory by Hayek (see Kirzner 1992).

The purpose of this chapter is to review Hayek's notion of knowledge in order to verify whether it might be useful for a different aim, that is for the analysis of the competitive market as an institution. It is now taken for granted that asymmetries of information are at the basis of every coherent analysis of economic institutions. There is also general agreement that the endogenous enforcement of contracts is a major problem in the description of how markets work, and that rational behaviour does not exclude the emergence of conventional behaviour in the aggregate (for example, see Kreps 1990: 723–4; Milgrom and Roberts 1990). In this chapter I will discuss the relevance of Hayek's analysis of coordination of differently informed agents for the theory of competitive markets as seen from this broader perspective.

There is a considerable degree of consensus in neo-Austrian literature as to the way this issue matters in Hayek's analysis. In fact, the issue has been dealt with mostly in relation to Hayek's contribution to the debate on socialist calculation. For instance, some critics have shown that one aspect of Hayek's analysis which has not been adequately appreciated is precisely the fact that his study of the market process is founded on his peculiar notion of knowledge. Since this knowledge is practical and mostly inarticulate – in other words, difficult, if not impossible, to communicate – the competitive market must be considered a better mechanism of resource allocation than those which can drive centralized economies (Lavoie 1985).

However, little attention has been paid to the question of whether Hayek considers competitive markets as an institution performing just an allocative function. Recent developments in microeconomic theory have shown that a comparative analysis of feasible alternative institutions cannot be confined to the comparison between market and planned economies – not only because of the existence of firms, as claimed by scholars studying the theory of organizations, but also because when information is dispersed, markets may perform a number of different functions (for instance, a disciplinary function as in Bowles and Gintis 1993). In my view, it might be useful to compare some perceptive insights by Hayek on this subject with recent developments in the theory of contracts and incentives. For Hayek's notion of knowledge in fact emphasizes certain aspects of informational asymmetries in decentralized systems that constitute the subject for analysis of current microeconomic theory.

This chapter is structured as follows. The next section reviews the unifying role performed by personal knowledge in Hayek's long-standing contribution to both economic theory and social philosophy, and briefly compares the notions of private information and personal knowledge. The second section examines the perspective offered by some authors in the Austrian tradition, with specific reference to their interpretation of Hayek's so-called knowledge problem. The third section deals with the relevance of Hayek's notion of knowledge for a more thorough understanding of the functions performed by competitive markets. I will contend that, in the light of his peculiar notion of knowledge, Hayek's viewpoint can usefully be compared with current developments in microeconomic theory. Finally, in the conclusion, there is an outline of the implications of the analysis put forward.

THE ROLE OF THE NOTION OF KNOWLEDGE IN HAYEK'S THEORY

There is increasing consensus, in the literature on Hayek's contribution to economic theory and social philosophy, about the central role performed by his notion of knowledge. It is generally maintained that this issue was first addressed by Hayek in his 1937 essay on 'Economics and knowledge', which led some critics to argue that from then on Hayek assumed a sharply critical attitude, not only towards pure economic theory, but also towards his own previous position on the usefulness of Walrasian equilibrium. Without getting involved in the dispute about the actual significance of Hayek's change of position (on which see Caldwell 1988), it is worth mentioning a few points which show that his concern about the problem of the diffusion of knowledge in economic systems was in fact stated well before 1937.

First, Hayek's theory of the business cycle can be reinterpreted as an analysis of intertemporal discoordination between investments and savings, when the investment sector does not share information on technology with the credit sector (as emphasized by Hayek himself in Hayek 1935a, and reassessed by O'Driscoll 1977). Second, Hayek's critical remarks on the view held by the supporters of planned economies show that he was aware of the shortcomings implicit in Walrasian equilibrium analysis of 'objective data' right from the start of the debate on socialist calculation, in contrast to the widespread view that he dealt with this problem only in the second phase of the debate (see, in particular, Hayek 1935b: 154–5).[2] Third, Hayek's first methodological essay pointed to 'the incomplete nature of our knowledge' as one of the reasons for 'a presumption against interference' with the working of a decentralized economy, in what may be considered a preliminary version of his fierce opposition to rationalism and economic planning (Hayek 1933: 34).

Of course, something crucial to Hayek's fundamental purpose of assessing the way in which economics explains coordination between individual agents is missing in these early contributions. To be exact, it was only when he took into consideration 'the knowledge of the basic fact of how the different commodities can be obtained and used' and 'the knowledge of the particular circumstances of time and place' (Hayek 1937: 51; 1945: 80), that it became unquestionable, in his view, that competitive markets guarantee a more efficient use of dispersed information than planned economies – a fact which he stated explicitly only in 'Economics and knowledge' and later. Furthermore, Hayek's late awareness that intertemporal equilibrium was both impossible to achieve and devoid of any Pareto-optimal property is analytically grounded in his particular notion of knowledge. In fact, since he was interested in knowledge, which is not only dispersed but also mainly fragmented and inarticulate, mutual compatibility of decentralized individual plans could only be a qualitative reference point for analysis, contrary to what he might have thought in the early 1930s (Hayek 1937: 53; 1948: 94). Finally, Hayek's construct of spontaneous order replaced strict equilibrium as a significant theoretical object only when he became interested in explaining the proper institutional context of a decentralized economy with differently informed agents (Hayek 1967: chapters 4, 6; 1973: chapter 2).

However, if one wants to hold the view of a substantial continuity in Hayek's thought through his whole intellectual life – which I find more appropriate than distinguishing two, or more, distinct phases (see Zappia 1993) – what must be emphasized is the unifying function performed in his long-standing contribution to social sciences by the consideration of privately known economic facts.[3] In what follows, I will use the term *personal* knowledge to denote Hayek's notion of knowledge.

Against this background, it may be interesting to analyse what kind of link can be established between the notions of private information that are used in current economic theory and the notion of personal knowledge used by Hayek. On the one hand, some of Hayek's views can be examined in the light of the main results that emerge from the economics of information. For example, it is well known that Hayek's thesis about the role performed by the price system in a decentralized economy has been widely commented on in recent years (see, in particular, Grossman 1989). I will make a comparison with certain aspects of contract theory. On the other hand, as I intend to show in what follows, some of the results achieved in the economics of information are challenged by Hayek's explanation of how the market economy actually works.

Let me make a preliminary point. In the economics of information there is a crucial distinction between private information about events which do not depend on the actions of economic agents – in other words exogenous events or moves by nature – and private information about events whose realization may depend on them. This distinction must be taken into consideration whenever results of informational efficiency in decentralized markets are shown to hold, as in asset market models or in general equilibrium models with rational expectations (for example, see Grossman 1981; Bray 1989). In particular, since Hayek is given the credit for arguing against the supporters of planned economies that competitive markets are more efficient than any other mechanism in the use of existing knowledge – sometimes even that competitive markets make the best possible use of it (for a recent example, see Eatwell and Milgate 1994) – this point is of great relevance for our study. It must be emphasized, then, that even in a perfectly competitive context, where agents are described by 'well-behaved' functions and have rational expectations on future events, the properties of informational efficiency that may characterize market equilibria – such as the fact that equilibrium prices reveal the whole information to everybody in the system – depend strictly on the assumption that *ex ante* informational asymmetries refer to exogenous events only. Accordingly, the subject of these studies is restricted to situations where all that matters is differences of information on future states of nature. Such phenomena as moral hazard and adverse selection must be assumed away from this kind of general equilibrium analysis (Radner 1982).

The significance of this distinction, not only as regards Hayek's theory but also for economic theory in general, can be seen by examining the way in which contracts are designed in the two different cases. When informational asymmetries concern only exogenous events, individual agents make transactions by signing contracts which specify an action to be undertaken in every possible future contingency. This means that the parties to the transaction must be able to observe *ex post* the characteristics of the event on which they do not share information – or that a third party can verify them. This is the rationale under the contingent contract used in Arrow–Debreu general equilibrium models. On the other hand, when informational asymmetries concern aspects of economic activity which are not publicly observable *ex post*, the contingent implementation of contracts is no longer possible. In this case, incomplete contracts must be drawn because it turns out to be impossible to specify what actions are to be taken in all possible future contingencies.

What we have here is information which individual agents have private knowledge of, and which affects how contracts are characterized – such as the intrinsic skill of a worker which is studied in adverse selection models, or the effort of a worker in moral hazard models.[4] When incomplete contracts have to be designed, the need for self-selection and incentive constraints generally bring about second-best outcomes. More generally, transactions among individual agents are now informationally complex transactions, since they may involve both monitoring costs about performances and sanctioning costs whenever performances do not conform to the contract (Milgrom and Roberts 1990: 60). Moreover, the properties of general equilibrium are now difficult to define and Pareto optimality is no longer a possible outcome. As a consequence, the entire neoclassical explanation of how competitive markets work is called into question (Bowles and Gintis 1993).[5]

Two important general points can now be made. First, the claim that Hayekian concern about the role of prices as transmitters and conveyors of information in a general equilibrium setting has been superseded – a claim made by scholars studying the informative properties of equilibria (see in particular Grossman 1989: 1–2) – turns out to be ill founded. In fact, as is well known, Hayek's idea of personal knowledge refers to individual skills, techniques of thought and alertness to unexploited opportunities, all of which are aspects of knowledge which both explain informational asymmetries among agents and affect economic activity endogenously. As we have just noted, these aspects cannot find adequate treatment in Grossman's general equilibrium model.[6] Therefore, if some similarities between Hayek's notion of knowledge and modern notions of private information can be found, these must apply to those notions which deal with uncertainty on 'endogenous' events. I will come back to this issue in the third section.

Second, the results on informationally efficient equilibria are not useful for establishing the superiority of the market over forms of deliberate organization of exchange. In general equilibrium models with asymmetric information, a planner who is endowed with all the information dispersed throughout the economy can implement allocations which mimic the competitive allocations, even if he cannot implement allocations which Pareto-dominate them. Therefore, the rationale for Hayek's main argument against planned economies – that it is theoretically impossible for planned economies to deal with the diffusion of knowledge efficiently – must be looked for elsewhere.[7]

The rest of this chapter examines two different ways of interpreting Hayek's theory of knowledge. The next section reviews the neo-Austrian treatment of the market process. It will be argued that the division of Hayek's knowledge problem into two components has restricted the interest of neo-Austrian literature to market process in disequilibrium, while Hayek's concern for the institutional context of interaction among individual agents has been substantially disregarded. The section after that presents a tentative analysis of how Hayek's notion of personal knowledge can be used to explain why markets perform functions different from the allocative one which seems to preoccupy the neo-Austrians.

HAYEK'S KNOWLEDGE PROBLEM AS SEEN FROM A NEO-AUSTRIAN PERSPECTIVE

According to the neo-Austrian approach, Hayek's theory of the diffusion of knowledge in a market economy is clearly stated in his essays on competition. The genuine interpretation of the issues raised in his first essays on knowledge is given by Hayek himself in 'The meaning of competition' (1948), and reassessed in 'Competition as a discovery procedure' (1976b).

Seen from this perspective, the market process is the necessary mechanism through which two fundamental allocation functions are accomplished in decentralized economies. First, during the market process the existing knowledge, which is dispersed throughout the economy, is used by individual agents who privately possess bits of it to get a return on it. In this case, the market process refers to how (potentially incorrectly) perceived profit opportunities by individuals can be exploited, and mutual consistency of individual plans achieved. Second, during the market process new economic facts are discovered by individual agents. In this case, the market process shows how those agents who are more alert than others can exploit previously unperceived profit opportunities. These two functions constitute the essence of the market process. They represent the way in which competitive markets solve Hayek's so-called knowledge problem, that is 'how to secure the best use of resources known to any of the members of society, for ends whose relative importance only these individuals know' (Hayek 1945: 78; for the definition of the knowledge problem, Kirzner 1984b: 153).

The fact that the allocative function performed by market process is divided into two distinct components might be interpreted simply as a matter of better representation of the question at issue. Indeed, since much of the knowledge dispersed throughout the economy is in a constant state of flux – the relevant knowledge being 'the knowledge which he [an individual agent] is bound to acquire in view of the position in which he originally is, and the plan he then makes' (Hayek 1937: 53) – the market process is a disequilibrium process which cannot be understood if one looks only at the properties of attainable equilibria. It has recently been restated that 'the defining characteristic of equilibrium is the absence of the knowledge problem' (Thomsen 1992: 7). Furthermore, Hayek's viewpoint can be made clearer by looking at the role performed by the price system. Since the coordination of individual actions which is achieved through the competitive mechanism refers mainly to the disequilibrium process rather than to the attainable equilibrium position of the economy, the role of market prices is not so much that of communicating to individual agents the information dispersed in the system as that of indicating possible opportunities which have not yet been exploited. In other words, market prices are discovery devices, more than informational signals. In following this perspective, Kirzner (1984a) explicitly regards as quite misleading Hayek's 1945 emphasis on market prices as conveyors of knowledge. In Kirzner's view, the 1945 essay did not adequately distinguish between the respective role of equilibrium and disequilibrium prices, in contrast with the much clearer explanation of the function that prices perform during competition he gave later, for example in 'The meaning of competition'.

The direct consequence that stems from this way of assessing Hayek's contribution is still controversial, even among neo-Austrian theorists (for a recent example, see Vaughn 1994). Indeed, the first function of the market process resembles something close to the adjustment process that can be assumed as implicit in the standard neoclassical approach to equilibrium. When information is dispersed throughout the economy, individual plans may turn out to be inconsistent in the aggregate; in particular, since some opportunities may be perceived incorrectly, agents' expectations concerning the actions of others may be disappointed. As a consequence, it is maintained that in competitive economies the mutual consistency of individual plans can be guaranteed only by the market process. In following this line of argument, current analyses of adjustment processes to equilibrium seem well suited to address Hayek's concern about the diffusion of *existing* knowledge – when it is clearly emphasized that, while equilibration forces are at work constantly, this does not entail that equilibrium will be achieved, since *new* relevant information will be discovered in the meantime. Indeed, the knowledge problem has been divided into two potentially separate problems, as Kirzner (1990) has recently recognized. Accordingly, the solution to the first knowledge problem – or knowledge problem A, as Kirzner calls it – can be found by following mainstream economic theory, while the core of Hayek's argument is his proposed solution to the second knowledge problem – or knowledge problem B – which cannot find adequate treatment within mainstream economic theory.

The significance of focusing on the second component of Hayek's knowledge problem seems to be that, even in the light of the results offered by the economics of information in dealing with the problem of existing differences in information, the superiority of the market over centralized economies can be demonstrated only if the dynamic content of Hayek's knowledge problem is stressed. A clear attitude of this kind is shown by Kirzner himself:

It has been pointed out that emphasis on fragmented knowledge is not quite enough to dislodge mainstream welfare concepts. 'Coordination' (in the sense of a *state* of coordination), while it may refer to coordination of decentralized decisions made in the light of dispersed knowledge, still turns out to involve standard Paretian norms. It is only 'coordination' in the sense of the process of coordinating hitherto *un*coordinated activity that draws attention to the discovery norm identified through Hayek's insights.

(Kirzner 1984a: 114–15)

And, as far as the literature on the transmission of information by prices is concerned:

the importance of prices for coping with the Hayekian knowledge problem does not lie in the accuracy of the information which equilibrium prices convey ... rather ... in the ability of disequilibrium prices to offer pure profit opportunities that can attract the notice of alert, profit-seeking entrepreneurs.

(Kirzner 1984b: 160)

The puzzling element which is inherent in this perspective on Hayek's theory is that it is based on a representation of the developments of the economics of information which is questionable. Let us see, for example, how Hurwicz reacted to Kirzner's representation of Hayek's knowledge problem. Hurwicz's attitude towards the knowledge problem is that of a welfare economist well aware of the need for an 'informational perspective' (Hurwicz 1984: 419). In Hurwicz's view, the claim made for the efficiency of competitive markets is not reinforced by assuming an informational perspective. On the contrary, he emphasizes that efficiency theorems are not robust in relation to the assumptions on the informational structure of the economy. Moreover, the tendency to competitive equilibrium is shown not to be general even in perfectly competitive markets. And when he mentions his own results, which show that the market mechanism minimizes the dimension of message space needed for transmitting information, he still makes it clear that they hold only if they are based on the usual assumptions about perfectly competitive markets. The rationale of Hurwicz's remarks then appears to be the following. If Hayek's knowledge problem is examined from an equilibrium perspective, it is difficult to ascertain the superiority of the market over centralized economies, because efficiency standards lose their precise meaning in an informational setting. Moreover, if it is examined from a disequilibrium perspective, the previous argument can only become more compelling, since the stability of competitive equilibrium has not yet been proven to hold in general.[8]

So, a more accurate analysis of the 'informational perspective' inherent in many current developments of microeconomic theory would have unearthed a different point, which is relevant for Hayek's theory as well. The fact that the knowledge problem cannot be addressed properly in an equilibrium perspective is definitely true if we study the coordination of economic activities in the standard Walrasian equilibrium framework. But when the influence of private information on transaction activities is dealt with in detail, Walrasian equilibrium no longer constitutes a reference point for analysis. Informative equilibria are substantially different from standard Walrasian equilibria (Stiglitz 1987). To be specific, markets may not clear in equilibrium and coordination of decentralized decisions does not still involve standard Paretian norms, as contended in most neo-Austrian literature.[9] Moreover, the emergence of conventional behaviour and norms is now compatible with equilibria.

In so far as my assessment of the neo-Austrian viewpoint is correct, the complexity of the coordination process has been restricted to a specific component of the market process. This is, no doubt, a major component: markets are a relatively more efficient mechanism of resources allocation not because they can guarantee certain efficiency standards, but because they can better diffuse and discover the concrete knowledge dispersed in the system by letting individual agents use it directly – while these agents themselves may be unable to explain how they actually use it. However, the basic element which could show the superiority of the market mechanism is not so much its capacity to deal with the phenomena that explain the dynamics of economic systems, as its ability to deal with personal knowledge. I intend to show that, in considering the two elements jointly, the neo-Austrian perspective is taking a questionable step: the dynamic implications of Hayek's theory are fully drawn, while the influence on economic activities of certain important aspects of the knowledge component has not been deepened.

It is worth emphasizing the following point. If, when dealing with the informational content of Hayek's market theory, it is the aspects of discovery rather than those of communication that are stressed, then one might be led to maintain that the impossibility of reaching Pareto-efficient allocations is caused solely by earning opportunities which have not been exploited by economic agents. This appears more compelling if the problem is enlarged from incorrectly perceived opportunities to unperceived opportunities, as contended by those scholars studying the market process. If this were Hayek's contribution to the analysis of the market process, one could assert that a refinement of the notion of rationality among agents, or a more thorough analysis of cognitive processes, could overcome Hayek's criticism of pure equilibrium analysis – which is the kind of objection made in the neoclassical field to all the analyses based on disequilibrium. However, what I will emphasize in the following section is that the meaning of Hayek's criticism can already be understood in the more limited context of equilibrium coordination, once this context is adequately redefined to account for the Hayekian notion of personal knowledge. To be specific, this criticism is grounded in an analysis of the means through which the communication of private information takes place in decentralized economies which is peculiar to Hayek.

It should also be emphasized that the fact that I will not focus on the dynamic aspects of market coordination does not imply a denial of their importance in Hayek's theory, in so far as I view the analysis of the properties implicit in Hayek's notion of knowledge both preliminary to and compatible with the market process interpretation stressed by the neo-Austrians.[10]

PERSONAL KNOWLEDGE AND PRIVATE INFORMATION

As we briefly noticed in the previous section, the main theoretical argument used by Hayek against centralized economies is that knowledge is not only dispersed, but also specialized and inarticulate, that is mostly difficult to communicate. This characteristic of the kind of knowledge which is relevant for economic activity shows why, in his view, the competitive mechanism is more efficient than other possible procedures of exchange. Indeed, even if it is possible to design appropriate incentives for individual agents to reveal which knowledge they privately possess, important aspects of personal knowledge will not be transferable to a central operator. In fact, these bits of knowledge could only be used by the individual agents themselves. Hayek himself referred to Michael Polanyi in maintaining that the 'knowledge how' to do something refers mainly to skills and can be considered tacit (Polanyi 1958; Hayek 1967: 43–5).

That personal knowledge is tacit, or inarticulate, can be interpreted in two different ways. First, tacit may mean simply that it is unreportable to others, since it is difficult, or impossible, to represent it by following formal rules. Second, tacit may mean also that the knowledge is actually unknown to its owner, and that she gains awareness of her previous ignorance only during the market process.[11] To distinguish between these two interpretations of tacit knowledge I will refer to unreportable knowledge and to unconsciously possessed knowledge respectively.

In their analysis of the market process, the neo-Austrians stressed mainly the second interpretation of tacit knowledge. The reason for considering knowledge as if it was mainly unconsciously possessed may be found in the argument discussed in the previous section, that is in the neo-Austrian emphasis on the dynamics of the market process as the main subject for analysis. But Hayek's emphasis on the tacit nature of knowledge is mainly intended to deny the possibility of treating market knowledge as given to an outside observer or to a planner. The first interpretation catches precisely this question. Let us then concentrate on the first interpretation and ask how an individual agent can get a return on unreportable knowledge. Of course, he can use his informational advantage in the competitive process by bidding up the price of certain resources he knows he can use more profitably than they are currently used. On the other hand, this kind of knowledge is essential also as regards the way transactions are designed. If it is taken into account that informationally complex transactions cannot be based on the usual Arrow–Debreu contingent contracts, then individual agents can profit from this kind of knowledge only when markets spontaneously give birth to reliable institutions, such as contracts and customary business procedures.

This problem was considered by Hayek on many occasions. As Moss has recently remarked, in Hayek's 1940 essay on socialist calculation, he maintained that 'without the threat of job loss and reorganization such as provided by "take-over" mechanism in the market for corporate control', it is not clear how 'organizational structures and incentive systems that encourage loyalty and hard work' could be implemented (Hayek 1940: 199–203; Moss 1994: 104).[12] Moreover, in the 1948 essay on competition, where the main concern was the analysis of competition as a dynamic process, Hayek criticized the 'explicit and complete exclusion from the theory of perfect competition of all personal relationships existing between the parties' to a transaction, as the most remarkable example of the lack of interest of contemporary mainstream economics towards 'what institutional arrangements are necessary in order that the unknown persons who have knowledge specially suited to a particular task are most likely to be attracted to that task' (Hayek 1948: 96–7). Other references to the question can be found in his analysis of the rules of orders and organizations (Hayek 1973: chapter 2; 1976b: chapter 10).

In my view there are at least two general points which emerge from this analysis, and which are fundamental to Hayek's peculiar conception of how the market system works. First, Hayek is well aware that the institutional context within which transactions take place matters. This is a truly Hayekian statement, or more generally, an Austrian one. Needless to say, a great number of studies on Hayek's analysis of economic and social institutions have pointed to this issue (see, in particular, Vanberg 1986; Caldwell 1988; Vaughn 1990). In spite of this, Hayek's quest for a more thorough understanding of the function performed by competitive markets has been substantially interpreted as a secondary component of the much broader problem of the development of institutions. But, following our line of argument instead, Hayek's point emerges as a consequence of his awareness that the achievement of state coordination does not merely require an effective price system. To deal with informationally complex transactions, customary rules of behaviour are also necessary.[13]

Second, in Hayek's theory the fact that the transactions which take place in competitive markets are complex is the direct consequence of taking into account a specific kind of knowledge. Accordingly, the idea that the market

274

mechanism can cope with the problem of complex transactions more efficiently than other mechanisms does not simply rely on the effectiveness of the price mechanism, it relies on the mechanism's ability to spontaneously generate the appropriate incentives within contractual relationships. In this respect, it is worth remembering that, in examining how competitive systems could deal with personal knowledge, Hayek (1945: 87) realized that even competitive prices could not completely aggregate the knowledge dispersed throughout the system. His appreciation of the market order then shifted from the precise notion of equilibrium – which no longer implies Pareto-optimality, or informational efficiency – to the more qualitative construct of spontaneous order (Hayek 1973: chapter 2; 1978).

We are now led to the following interpretation of Hayek's theory. Hayek's analysis of how coordination can be achieved through the market mechanism cannot be appreciated completely by emphasizing only its dynamic component. To understand his viewpoint the analysis of the *process* of coordination does not suffice. It is also necessary to study the institutional framework in which a *state* of coordination can be achieved. In fact, this second aspect cannot be addressed within the limits imposed by a Walrasian perspective, essentially because the market mechanism is not an impersonal mechanism driven only by market prices.

The aspect just mentioned has much in common with the clearest general suggestion that emerges from recent developments in microeconomic theory. The problem of finding optimal incentives under conditions of asymmetric information, which current literature generally refers to as the endogenous enforcement problem, is inherent to an economy in which exchanges are based on such informational asymmetries. Indeed, the study of market institutions concerns not only the way in which the price system operates and the limits to the dimensions of deliberate organizations – as has long been taken for granted – but also the structure of contractual arrangements by means of which the actions of individual agents can be implemented in competitive markets (in particular, see Bowles and Gintis 1993: 86–9).[14]

My interpretation so far has pointed out that Hayek's consideration of the rules through which market exchange actually takes place has not been addressed consistently by the literature which was inspired by him. No doubt this may depend on the fact that Hayek himself showed more concern for other aspects of his theory of the market, but many insights on the necessity of a more thorough analysis of contractual relationships in market have not been deepened as they deserve. The relevance of this question is increased by the fact that post-Walrasian developments have stressed the importance of those contractual structures apt to enforce market claims. The question addressed by post-Walrasian developments then shares some elements with Hayek's contention about the knowledge problem. Moreover the comparison between these two perspectives on the problem of knowledge diffusion in competitive markets is, in my view, useful not only because it may help in clarifying Hayek's role in the improvement on the Walrasian approach as seen from the post-Walrasian perspective, but also because some shortcomings of these developments can be pointed out. To introduce this last question, let us examine in more depth the features of Hayek's notion of knowledge.

The widespread view on this issue is that Hayek's notion of 'knowledge' cannot be subsumed under the notion of 'information' because of the way information is dealt with in modern microeconomic literature. To be exact, it has been argued that Hayek's notion of knowledge is not to be regarded as an economic commodity which could be acquired at a given cost, and therefore cannot be subject to negotiation – unlike the commodities studied in equilibrium theory to which it is usually compared in the literature (Boehm 1994). This interpretation refers specifically to those practical and concrete aspects of knowledge which are relevant for production processes, rather than to technological knowledge. It therefore refers to a representation of knowledge which does not differ from that considered in the previous sections. However, my point is that some aspects of personal knowledge can be approximated to the notion of private information used in modern contract theory; to be more specific, they can be subject to negotiation and therefore a formal analysis of their influence on the structure of contracts can be pursued.[15]

We saw earlier that Hayek's analysis of market behaviour emphasizes certain characteristics of economic agents, such as specific working skills, techniques of thought and, more generally, entrepreneurial alertness to new investment opportunities. It has been contended by neo-Austrians that these characteristics are crucial for the definition of the competitive market mechanism, as regards both agents' search for economic improvement and reaction to exogenous changes in the data. However, to study the influence of these elements on competitive dynamics, and on the equilibria which the economy may achieve, it is also necessary to define appropriate contractual forms through which market exchanges can take place. In other words, it remains to be explained in what way exchange between agents can be affected, for example by the specific working skills of individuals.[16]

Although we do not yet have a general theory of contracts in situations of informational asymmetry, a number of specific situations have been studied where it is profitable to design a contract in which it is possible to check some of the information possessed by the agent with an informational advantage. This can occur only if the agent who possesses certain information finds it worthwhile, in the contractual relationship, to implicitly communicate the private information available to her. In the majority of cases, this private information bears a direct relation either to the agent's skills, or to her specific role within the production process. Furthermore, this type of information is costless for the agent who possesses it, but it contributes to defining the reward scheme, thereby proving to be subject to monetary evaluation in the drawing up of the contract. It is also worth stressing that it is not necessary to impose the condition that the agent with the informational advantage must be able to explain how she managed to do something. She only has to agree to do it within the contractual agreement; her skill will be valued on the basis of the outcomes in an uncertain environment.

Hayek's notion of personal knowledge shares all these features with the notion of private information used in modern microeconomic theory. Indeed, it remains true that some aspects of personal knowledge cannot be 'reduced' to private information, specifically because it is difficult to imagine personal knowledge as if it was given completely *ex ante*. This fact is strengthened by the neo-Austrian interpretation of the tacit nature of knowledge. Being knowledge mostly unconsciously possessed, the neo-Austrians contend, it is difficult to imagine how a contractual agreement can be reached by following the approach of modern contract theory.

But my first goal here is to examine if our assessment so far needs to be emended when only unreportable knowledge is taken into account. Indeed, by following our perspective, the critical point is that the analysis developed in the study of incentive contracts still assumes that every possible contingency on which the drawing up of the contract is based can be imagined *ex ante*. As we have already noticed, the Arrow–Debreu contingent contract cannot be used in this case, but the typical incentive contract which emerges, for example in the principal–agent literature, is still to be considered a kind of complete contract because there is no possible disagreement on which payments have to be done *ex post*, given the actions of the agents and the realization of the exogenous events (as clarified by Hart and Holmstrom 1987).[17] If this is the case, the implicit assumption is that the principal knows in advance the entire set of actions the agent may undertake, or the entire set of skills she may possess. Hence the assumed informational asymmetry concerns only the specific action that the agent will undertake (or the specific skill with which she is endowed). Then contract theory is implicitly assuming that the principal knows in advance what may happen, and designs a contract which gives the appropriate incentives for the agent to undertake the action he, the principal, finds it worthwhile to be undertaken (for a similar viewpoint, see Minkler 1993).

This analytical procedure seems to be well suited for answering the question of informational asymmetries, when all the agents involved know what may happen in the contractual relationships. But it does not capture a crucial aspect of Hayek's notion of knowledge; that only the 'man on the spot' knows how to do something and that he cannot report (or he prefers not to report) on his personal knowledge. Hence, new developments in microeconomics still fail to give adequate explanation to this kind of structural uncertainty. In my view, however, this does not mean that we should consider the Hayekian analysis as incompatible with these developments in economic theory.[18] On the contrary, Hayek's insights indicate a fruitful direction for further research. The most prominent example of this is the possible permanence of rents in equilibrium stressed by post-Walrasian developments, but which seems to be more plausible when personal knowledge is taken into account.

To sum up on this point, in discussing Hayek's notion of knowledge, I find it more convenient to start with assuming that Hayek's perspective is similar to that taken by new developments in the theory of contracts, and then pointing at those aspects which differentiate the two theories. On the one hand, to assume a similar perspective helps in better identifying Hayek's role as a contributor to the improvement over the Walrasian approach. Among a number of contemporary scholars interested in the questions of uncertainty, expectation and information in the 1930s, Hayek was more explicit than others in stressing the question of knowledge in his critical remarks towards Walrasian economics. On the other hand, current attempts to give a formal representation to the use of private information still fail to give appropriate consideration to Hayek's emphasis on personal knowledge as the cause for rents which cannot be cleared by the market exchange.

CONCLUSION

This chapter tries to evaluate the importance of assuming a non-Walrasian equilibrium perspective in the analysis of Hayek's theory of coordination in decentralized systems. By assessing Hayek's theory of knowledge in the light of new developments in microeconomic theory, I have argued that many aspects of Hayek's viewpoint about the way competitive markets work can be understood even without making direct reference to the dynamics of the market process. In fact, Hayek's notion of personal knowledge calls for a more thorough understanding of the contractual arrangements which competitive markets require – a line of argument which is once again the focus of interest in pure economic theory.

The chapter draws on a tradition of thought which contends that Hayek never abandoned his interest in the coordinative features of the price system and that his analysis was based not only on rational behaviour by individual agents, but also on rules, routines, habits and those social institutions which emerge at the aggregate level and carry out the task of holding the system together. Accordingly, Hayek's view of coordination in competitive markets cannot be limited to a strictly Walrasian equilibrium perspective.[19]

Against this background, the first step towards establishing the current relevance of Hayek's theory of knowledge in a more general equilibrium perspective appears to acknowledge the following point. Recognizing that Hayek has in mind a type of information which cannot be utilized, other than by directly involving the agent who possesses it, does not necessarily entail referring to knowledge which cannot be represented formally as private information, and so cannot be contracted upon. In fact, from an economic point of view, the critical point is how to verify *ex post* the actions undertaken on the basis of *ex ante* informational differences. At the same time, since the aim is to assess the influence of private information on market exchange, it becomes necessary to analyse allocation mechanisms which are alternatives to impersonal allocation through the market. To do this, it is first of all necessary to analyse the methods of contractual agreements which provide an alternative to the contingent contract. It is essential, therefore, to determine to what degree the *ex ante* informational differences are reduced – or disappear – *ex post* in a more complex, but probably more interesting context than the Walrasian one. This involves regarding the market no longer solely as an allocative mechanism, but as an institution in which exchange of both goods and information takes place through several contractual forms.

This outline of the interpretation of how the competitive market works may be considered an elaboration of the Hayekian view of the market as an institutional mechanism through which actions undertaken in a decentral-ized system are coordinated. For Hayek, the coordination of economic actions depends not only on the impersonal working of the prices system, but also on alternative exchange activities whose emergence may bring about conventional behaviour, and whose aggregate outcomes cannot be considered as the intended result of the actions undertaken by individuals alone. In his attempt to return to the original meaning of the market mechanism – the meaning introduced by Smith and obscured by Walrasian developments – Hayek emphasizes the role of the price system as the most effective means of conveying dispersed information. He also stresses the impossibility of interpreting the general equilibrium of the economy simply as the sum of individual behaviour. In his view, the exchange of information is achieved through a process which is far more complex than that which is usually considered. In this process, forces which are different from those of Walrasian competition come into play: imitative behaviour, rules and traditions. It is the complexity of these economic activities which led Hayek to believe that equilibrium theory was not capable of providing a convincing formal representation of the competitive market mechanism.

As I have tried to show in this chapter, it is mainly for this reason that, in his criticism of 'pure economic theory' from the point of view of the philosophy of the social sciences, Hayek came to assert that coordination through the market could give rise to states of 'spontaneous order' in the economy, rather than to actual general equilibria. If seen from this perspective, the approach followed by certain developments in the economics of information is probably the first partial attempt by 'pure economic theory' to address Hayek's contention on this point.

NOTES

1 A previous draft of this chapter was presented at the Annual Meetings of the History of Economics Society (10–13 June 1994, Babson College, Babson Park, MA). I wish to thank Young Back Choi, Larry Moss, Ugo Pagano and Bert Tieben for their comments. Financial assistance from MURST (60 per cent funds), the Italian Ministry for the University and Scientific Research, is gratefully acknowledged.

2 The most widespread interpretation of the socialist controversy until the 1980s is that, after acknowledging the logical possibility of Lange's market socialism, Hayek mainly concentrated on demonstrating its practical impossibility. In his first assessment of 'the state of the debate', Hayek used the argument of the practical impossibility of finding a solution for a system of simultaneous equations by a possible planner if one accepts 'the usual theoretical abstractions used in the explanation of equilibrium in a competitive system [which] include the assumption that a certain range of technical knowledge is "given"' (Hayek 1935b: 154). If these abstractions are not used, one is led to 'another problem of even greater importance', the problem which, after the 1937 article, is identified as Hayek's knowledge problem. In fact, Hayek asserts at the outset of the debate on socialist calculation, 'much of the knowledge that is actually utilized is by no means "in existence" in this ready-made form' (*ibid.*: 155). On this point see Lavoie (1986). Vaughn (1990: 391) contends that Hayek himself did not sufficiently stress this point at first.

3 It has been convincingly maintained by critics that even Hayek's works in psychology (such as *The Sensory Order*) and in political philosophy (such as *The Constitution of Liberty*) are originated by his interest in different perspectives on the problem of the diffusion of knowledge (see, for example, Moss 1994, and Vaughn 1994: 121ff.).

4 To clarify the issue, let us consider an example from the literature on incentive contracts in which information on exogenous and endogenous events may interact (Arrow 1986). In the overly simple fire insurance example, an Arrow–Debreu contingent contract would pay the insured conditional on the occurrence of those natural events that can cause fire, whereas actual real world contracts make it dependent upon the occurrence of fire itself. This depends on the fact that it can be difficult to infer whether the fire is due to an unusual exogenous event, or to a more usual exogenous event coupled with insufficient care by the insured (hidden action) or with unfavourable privately known characteristics of the insured himself (hidden knowledge).

5 On this point see also the comments by Arrow (1987) and Hahn (1990).

6 For a more detailed account, see Zappia (1996). Interestingly, while the neo-Austrian literature has paid much attention to Grossman's results, it did not raise this point. In particular, see the comments by Kirzner (1984a: 112–15), O'Driscoll and Rizzo (1985: 102–3) and Thomsen (1992: chapter 3).

7 As we shall see in what follows, the argument that an equilibrium perspective is inadequate for claiming the superiority of the market mechanism over centralized mechanisms of allocation is crucial for the neo-Austrian interpretation of the socialist calculation debate.

8 It is worth noting that even some critics who follow the Austrian approach are sceptical about the possibility of actually proving that the tendency towards intertemporal coordination is a direct consequence of successful dissemination of knowledge by means of prices (see for example Langlois 1985).

9 It has been recently noted from the neo-Austrian side that there seems to be no real difference between this view and that held by those scholars studying the

problem of information transmission by prices in general equilibrium models with rational expectations, to which we made reference in the previous section (Thomsen 1992: 29–37). It has been contended that both of them try to address Hayek's concern about the diffusion of knowledge by choosing an equilibrium perspective. Accordingly, Hurwicz and Grossman have missed the crucial point stressed by Hayek. It is worth noting that while this interpretation catches a very important point, it fails to understand the differences as regards the welfare implications of the two analyses. Indeed, Grossman's result can be interpreted as an extension of the standard general equilibrium efficiency properties to informational efficiency, while the economics of information mainly stresses inefficiency results.

10 In arguing about the logical priority in Hayek's theory between the two elements of personal knowledge and the dynamics of the system, one should note that, although Walrasian economics could still deal with the dynamics of the system in the case of the absence of personal knowledge, it is not suited to deal with the knowledge problem even if no dynamic element is taken into account.

11 I will not consider the possibility that tacit knowledge refers to knowledge which is not consciously possessed even by those individual agents who make use of it, which I find more difficult to accept.

12 Hayek's references to incentives in competitive markets have been commented on many times, especially after the reassessments of the socialist calculation debate by Vaughn (1980). For a recent analysis, see Streissler (1994).

13 In a remarkably modern comment, Hayek (1948: 97) argues that 'competition for reputation or good will' is one of the most important facts which enables agents with 'inadequate knowledge' to undertake market exchanges.

14 Bowles and Gintis contend that Hayek did not realize that the endogenous evolution of institutions does not only concern changes in preferences and norms, but also rules for endogenous enforcement (Bowles and Gintis 1993: 98–9). An accurate analysis of their position would require more space, but in so far as my viewpoint is correct, Hayek's interest in this subject seems difficult to deny (on this point see Zappia 1995).

15 As I have remarked above, the kind of private information which is analysed in contract theory should be considered qualitatively different from that used in the studies on general equilibrium. Accordingly, the Walrasian representation of the contract as a contract contingent upon the realization of exogenous events cannot be considered satisfactory. This crucial distinction is not dealt with by Boehm, who uses the definition of 'information as a commodity' given by Allen (1990). On the contrary, Allen's analysis applies only to differences of information on exogenous events, and thus follows the line of research opened by Grossman we referred to above (Allen 1990: 268).

16 Moreover, if the conclusion that Hayekian equilibrium does not entail the full exploitation of the opportunities offered by informational differences is well founded (in particular, see O'Driscoll and Rizzo 1985: 102–9), then it is necessary to examine alternative mechanisms through which agents with an informational advantage, or more simply with personal knowledge, can get a return on it. On this point see Dardi (1990: 62–4).

17 Even if the contingencies are now defined in a way which differs from that of the Arrow–Debreu model, since they may depend on the action of the agents themselves, the contract unambiguously specifies each party's obligations in each conceivable contingency. However, in following a Hayekian perspective, the alternative of considering incomplete contracts of the type described by

Hart and Holmstrom does not seem to be fruitful, since in this case the informational asymmetries between the parties to the exchange do not reveal.

18 For instance, in the literature on decision theory one can find an increasing number of attempts to give a formal representation of 'unforeseen contingencies', even if they are limited to individual choice (in particular, see Loomes and Sugden 1986; Kreps 1992; Modica and Rustichini 1994).

19 This viewpoint has been held by Klausinger (1990) and Moss (1994), among others.

REFERENCES

Allen, B. (1990) 'Information as a commodity', *American Economic Review*, 80: 268–73.

Arrow, K.J. (1986) 'Agency and the market', in K.J. Arrow and M.D. Intriligator (eds) *Handbook of Mathematical Economics*, vol. III, Amsterdam: North-Holland.

——(1987) 'Rationality of self and others in an economic system', in R.M. Hogarth and M.W. Reder (eds) *Rational Choice*, Chicago, IL: University of Chicago Press.

Boehm, S. (1994) 'Hayek on knowledge: a critical assessment', in M. Colonna, H. Hagemann and O. Hamouda (eds) *Capitalism, Socialism and Knowledge*, Aldershot: Edward Elgar.

Bowles, S. and Gintis, H. (1993) 'The revenge of homo economicus: contested exchange and the revival of political economy', *Journal of Economic Perspectives*, 7: 83–102.

Bray, M. (1989) 'Rational expectations, information and asset markets', in F. Hahn (ed.) *The Economics of Missing Markets, Information and Games*, Oxford: Oxford University Press.

Caldwell, B. (1988) 'Hayek's transformation', *History of Political Economy*, 20: 513–42.

Dardi, M. (1990) 'Il mercato nell'analisi economica contemporanea', in G. Becattini (ed.) *Il pensiero economico. Temi, problemi e scuole*, Torino: UTET.

Eatwell, J. and Milgate, M. (1994) 'The problem of price determination and Hayek's theory of competition', in M. Colonna, H. Hagemann and O. Hamouda (eds) *Capitalism, Socialism and Knowledge*, Aldershot: Edward Elgar.

Grossman, S. (1981) 'An introduction to the theory of rational expectations under asymmetric information', in Grossman (1989).

——(1989) *The Informational Role of Prices*, Cambridge, MA: MIT Press.

Hahn, F.H. (1990) 'Expectations', in J. Hey and D. Winch (eds) *A Century of Economics*, Oxford: Basil Blackwell.

Hart, O. and Holmstrom, B. (1987) 'The theory of contracts', in T. Bewley (ed.) *Advances in Economic Theory*, Cambridge: Cambridge University Press.

Hayek, F.A. (1933) 'The trend of economic thinking', *Economica*, 13: 121–37.

——(1935a) 'Price expectations, monetary disturbances and malinvestment', in *Profit, Interest and Investment*, London: Routledge.

——(1935b) 'Socialist calculation II: the state of the debate', in Hayek (1976a).

——(1937) 'Economics and knowledge', in Hayek (1976a).

——(1940) 'Socialist calculation III: the competitive "Solution"', in Hayek (1976a).

——(1945) 'The use of knowledge in society', in Hayek (1976a).

——(1948) 'The meaning of competition', in Hayek (1976a).

——(1967) *Studies in Philosophy, Politics and Economics*, Chicago, IL: University of Chicago Press.

——(1973) *Law, Legislation and Liberty*, vol. I, Chicago, IL: University of Chicago Press.

——((1976a) [1948]) *Individualism and Economic Order*, London: Routledge & Kegan Paul.

——(1976b) *Law, Legislation and Liberty*, vol. II, Chicago, IL: University of Chicago Press.

——((1978) [1968]) 'Competition as a discovery procedure', in *New Studies in Philosophy, Politics and Economics*, Chicago, IL: University of Chicago Press.

Hurwicz, L. (1984) 'Economic planning and the knowledge problem: a comment', *Cato Journal of Economics*, 2: 419–25.

Kirzner, I.M. (1984a) 'Prices, the communication of knowledge, and the discovery process', in Kirzner (1992).

——(1984b) 'Economic planning and the knowledge problem', in Kirzner (1992).

——(1990) 'Knowledge problems and their solutions: some relevant distinctions', in Kirzner (1992).

——(1992) *The Meaning of Market Process. Essays in the Development of Modern Austrian Economics*, London: Routledge.

Klausinger, H. (1990) 'Equilibrium methodology as seen from an Hayekian perspective', *Journal of the History of Economic Thought*, 12: 61–75.

Kreps, D.M. (1990) *A Course in Microeconomic Theory*, London: Harvester Wheatsheaf.

——(1992) 'Static choice in the presence of unforeseen contingencies', in P. Dasgupta, D. Gale, O. Hart and E. Maskin (eds) *Economic Analysis of Markets and Games, Essays in Honour of Frank Hahn*, Cambridge, MA: MIT Press.

Langlois, R.N. (1985) 'Knowledge and rationality in the Austrian school: an analytical survey', *Eastern Economic Journal*, 9: 309–30.

Lavoie, D. (1985) *Rivalry and Central Planning. The Socialist Calculation Debate Reconsidered*, Cambridge: Cambridge University Press.

——(1986) 'The market as a procedure for discovery and conveyance of inarticulate knowledge', *Comparative Economic Studies*, 28: 1–19.

Loomes, G. and Sugden, R. (1986) 'Disappointment and dynamic consistency in choice under uncertainty', *Review of Economic Studies*, 53: 271–82.

Milgrom, P. and Roberts, J. (1990) 'Bargaining costs, influence costs and the organization of economic activity', in J.E. Alt and K.A. Shepsle (eds) *Perspectives on Positive Political Economy*, Cambridge: Cambridge University Press.

Minkler, A.P. (1993) 'Knowledge and internal organizations', *Journal of Economic Behaviour and Organization*, 21: 17–30.

Modica, S. and Rustichini, A. (1994) 'Unawareness: a formal theory of unforeseen contingencies', *CORE Discussion Papers*.

Moss, L.S. (1994) 'Hayek and the several faces of socialism', in M. Colonna, H. Hagemann and O. Hamouda (eds) *Capitalism, Socialism and Knowledge*, Aldershot: Edward Elgar.

Moss, L.S. and Vaughn, K.I. (1986) 'Hayek's Ricardo effect: a second look', *History of Political Economy*, 18: 545–65.

O'Driscoll, G.P. (1977) *Economics as a Coordination Problem*, Kansas City, KS: Sheed & Ward.

O'Driscoll, G.P. and Rizzo, M.J. (1985) *The Economics of Time and Ignorance*, Oxford: Basil Blackwell.

Polanyi, M. (1958) *Personal Knowledge: Towards a Post-Critical Philosophy*, Chicago, IL: University of Chicago Press.

Radner, R. (1982) 'The role of private information in markets and other organizations', in W. Hildenbrand (ed.) *Advances in Economic Theory*, Cambridge: Cambridge University Press.

Stiglitz, J.E. (1987) 'The causes and the consequences of the dependence of quality on prices', *Journal of Economic Literature*, 25: 1–48.

Streissler, E.W. (1994) 'Hayek on information and socialism', in M. Colonna, H. Hagemann and O. Hamouda (eds) *Capitalism, Socialism and Knowledge*, Aldershot: Edward Elgar.

Thomsen, E. (1992) *Prices and Knowledge. A Market-Process Perspective*, London: Routledge.

Vanberg, V. (1986) 'Spontaneous market order and social rules: a critical examination of F.A. Hayek's theory of cultural evolution', *Economics and Philosophy*, 2: 75–100.

Vaughn, K. (1980) 'Economic calculation under socialism: the Austrian contribution', *Economic Inquiry*, 18: 535–54.

——(1990) 'The Mengerian roots of the Austrian revival', in B. Caldwell (ed.) *Carl Menger and His Legacy in Economics*, Durham, NC: Duke University Press.

——(1994) *Austrian Economics in America. The Migration of a Tradition*, New York: Cambridge University Press.

Zappia, C. (1993) 'The economics of Hayek: a comment', *History of Economic Ideas*, 1: 193–205.

——(1995) 'The informational efficiency of economic systems and Hayek's paradox', *Quaderni del Dipartimento di Economia Politica*, Università di Siena, n. 181.

——(1996) 'The notion of private information in a modern perspective: a re-appraisal of Hayek's contribution', *European Journal of the History of Economic Thought*, 3 (1): 107–31.

INDEX

action: defined 67; human 65, 172,
174–7, 205, 211; planned 186; social
67, 130–1; and time 65–6
actual domain 129–30, 140
adverse selection 267, 268
agency theory 245, 252–3
agents: coordination 63; expectation
136; Hayek 133, 135, 253;
information 266–7, 268, 269;
knowledge 133, 136, 246; optimizers
232–3; and principals 80, 253, 277;
profit maximizing 247; rational
expectations 224; rules 248; and
structures 130–1
aggregate concepts 22, 37, 55, 96
Alchian, A. A. 245, 247
alertness, entrepreneurial 180–2, 183–4,
189 (n29), 261, 268, 276–7
Alter, M. 9
American Economic Review 113
Andvig, J. C. 111, 113
appraisement 175, 188 (n14)
Arestis, Philip 192, 195, 208
Arrow, K. J. 222
Arrow–Debreu: contingent contracts
277; general equilibrium models
267–8
auctioneer *see* Walras
Austrian school: conjectural history
165–7; coordination 8, 23, 203;
eclipse/resurgence 11–13; and
empiricist methodology 2, 3, 4;
future 14–17; human action 65, 172,
174–7, 205, 211; institutions 210–
12, 244, 249–50, 255–6, 258–9;
knowledge 202–3; mathematical
formalism 235 (n5); methodology 3,
4, 164, 212–13; money neutrality 99,
207; and neoclassical school 8–11;

origins 5–7; process approach 29–30,
253, 254–5; reasoning style 194–5;
reputation 3–5, 243–4; and Swedish
economists 42–3, 45–7, 51–9, 64;
thought experiments 151, 152–9,
163–4; time element 33–6; US
monetary policy 39; value 259; *see also*
neo-Austrian school

banking system: business cycle 101,
102–3; credit 208; Hayek 108–9;
money supply 108–9;
uncertainty/surveillance 211
Barens, I. 12
Barone, E. 10, 77, 78, 81, 82
Barro, Robert 23
barter 45, 60, 99
Bator, Francis 159
Bellinger, W. K. 16
benevolent dictator model 152–8, 168
(n3)
Bergsten, G. S. 16
Bhaskar, R. 128, 130, 131–2
*Biographical Dictionary of Dissenting
Economists* (Arestis and Sawyer) 192
Birner, J. 95
Blaug, M. 12, 154, 165, 193
Boehm, S. 78, 202, 213, 276
Boettke, P. J. 14, 15, 16, 151, 167,
192, 212
Böhm-Bawerk, Eugen von 194; capital
42, 44–5, 198; institutions 249;
interest rates 5, 90; investment 68
(n2); Marx's labour theory of value 6;
and Menger 165; *Positive Theory of
Capital* 154–5; socialism 168–9 (n6,
n7); and Wicksell 42, 43–7
Boland, L. A. 203
Bostaph, S. 4

285

Richter, R. 81, 87
Rizzo, M. J. 9, 14, 201–2, 205,
   214, 220
Robbins, Lionel 11, 12, 83, 111,
   194, 199
Robbins–Keynes debate 200
Roberts, J. 250, 264, 268
Robertson, D. H. 107–8, 117
Robinson, Joan 195, 196
Romer, Christina and David 31
Romer, P. M. 197
Romer, R. 23
Rosches, Wilhelm 3
Rosenstein-Rodan, P. 194
Rothbard, M. N. 29, 61, 79, 85, 159,
   161, 162, 190 (n30), 195
Rubin, I. 140

Samuels, J. W. 78
Samuels, Warren 152–3, 168 (n4)
Samuelson, P. A. 9, 78, 92–3 (n10), 89
Sargent, Thomas 23, 222, 223
savings: entrepreneurial 62; forced 117;
   investment 34, 44–5, 53–4, 85, 97,
   107–8; and money capital 62;
   socialist 85
Sawyer, M. C. 192, 209, 210
Sayer, D. 145
Say's Law 25
Scheide, J. 220
Scherer, F. M. 79, 88, 89, 91
Schmoller, G. 4, 5, 6
Schneider, E. 87, 88
Schönfeld-Illy, L. 194
Schotter, A. 244, 245, 248, 249
Schumpeter, Joseph: and Böhm-Bawerk
   5, 154; *Capitalism, Socialism and
   Democracy* 75, 77–8, 79–84, 89, 90–
   1; dynamics 84–5, 91;
   entrepreneurship 172, 178–9; general
   equilibrium analysis 88–9; on Hayek
   82–3; Hayek on 77, 78; *History of
   Economic Analysis* 76, 82, 83, 87;
   interest rates 92–3 (n10); *In
   Memoriam* for Walras 87, 88;
   methodological individualism 164;
   Mises on 78; as non-Austrian school
   78–80; schools of economics 193;
   socialist calculation debate 76–87;
   Theory of Economic Development 85;
   uncertainty 85–6; Walrasian general
   equilibrium model 82, 86, 87–8, 89–
   91; writing style 88–9

Schutz, Alfred 67–8, 194
Scottish Enlightenment 166, 249,
   254–5
Seidl, C. 80, 89, 90
sequence economies 222
Shackle, G. L. S. 104, 196, 197, 204,
   207, 212, 213, 233
shareholders, rentier 80
shocks 23, 100–1, 102, 109
Simon, H. 248
Simpson, D. 79
Skidelsky, R. 114
Skouras, T. 195
Smith, Adam 255
social action 67, 130–1
social institutions 151
social production 141
social rules 134–5, 136–7
social theory 130–1, 134, 147 (n13)
socialism: Böhm-Bawerk 168–9 (n6,
   n7); bureaucracy 86–7; Lange 257–8;
   market 10, 77, 250, 252, 256;
   neoclassical 77; production 154–5;
   progress 85; saving/investment 85
socialist calculation debate 250–3;
   formalism 257; Hayek 10, 24, 244,
   264, 274, 280 (n2); Mises 4, 10, 24,
   155–6, 244, 250, 259; Schumpeter
   75, 76–87
socialist economics 250–1
socio-economic process 139, 141, 145
South Royalton conference (1974) 13
Sraffa, Piero 195, 196, 198, 206, 258–9
Sraffa–Hayek debate 198–9, 206
statistical expectations 225, 236 (n14)
Steele, G. R. 95
Stigler, G. 154, 165
Stiglitz, J. 209, 272
Stockman, A. C. 23
Stolper, W. F. 88
Streissler, E. 1, 5–6, 249
Strongin, S. 23
subjectivism 243, 261 (n1); creativity
   203–4; economic good 5–6;
   entrepreneurial 173–8, 179; human
   action 65–8; marginalist 1; Menger
   174; Mises 65–8; new 173–8, 187;
   post World War II 201; price 9;
   radical 212–13; value 1, 9
Sugden, R. 245, 248, 249, 255
supply, and demand 32, 60–1
Swedish economists 42–3, 45–7, 51–
   9, 64

For Product Safety Concerns and Information please contact our EU
representative GPSR@taylorandfrancis.com
Taylor & Francis Verlag GmbH, Kaufingerstraße 24, 80331 München, Germany